Adolphus Washington Greely

Three Years of Arctic Service

An account of the Lady Franklin bay expedition of 1881-84, and the attainment of

the farthest north. Vol. 1

Adolphus Washington Greely

Three Years of Arctic Service
An account of the Lady Franklin bay expedition of 1881-84, and the attainment of the farthest north. Vol. 1

ISBN/EAN: 9783337322755

Printed in Europe, USA, Canada, Australia, Japan

Cover: Foto ©Andreas Hilbeck / pixelio.de

More available books at **www.hansebooks.com**

Three Years of Arctic Service

AN ACCOUNT OF THE

LADY FRANKLIN BAY EXPEDITION

OF 1881-84

AND THE ATTAINMENT OF THE

FARTHEST NORTH

BY

ADOLPHUS W. GREELY

LIEUTENANT U. S. ARMY, COMMANDING THE EXPEDITION

WITH OVER ONE HUNDRED ILLUSTRATIONS MADE FROM PHOTOGRAPHS
TAKEN BY THE PARTY, AND ORIGINAL DRAWINGS, AND
WITH THE OFFICIAL MAPS AND CHARTS

VOL. I.

NEW YORK
CHARLES SCRIBNER'S SONS
1886

COPYRIGHT, 1885, BY
CHARLES SCRIBNER'S SONS

TROW'S
PRINTING AND BOOKBINDING COMPANY,
NEW YORK.

To the
LADY FRANKLIN BAY EXPEDITION
THESE VOLUMES ARE DEDICATED:
TO ITS DEAD WHO SUFFERED MUCH—TO
ITS LIVING WHO SUFFERED MORE.
THEIR ENERGY ACCOMPLISHED THE FARTHEST NORTH;
THEIR FIDELITY WROUGHT OUT SUCCESS;
THEIR COURAGE FACED DEATH UNDAUNTEDLY;
THEIR LOYALTY AND DISCIPLINE IN ALL THE
DARK DAYS ENSURED THAT THIS RECORD
OF THEIR SERVICES SHOULD BE GIVEN TO
THE WORLD

PREFACE.

THESE volumes appear in response to the demands of the general public for a popular account of the Lady Franklin Bay Expedition; and in their preparation I have spared neither health nor strength since the rendition of my official narrative to the War Department has left me free. The Secretary of War kindly granted me authority to incorporate in this work such official journals, maps, etc., as I might desire.

This narrative, however, is based on my diary, though I have drawn freely, always with credit, from the official field reports, and also from the very complete journals of Lieutenant Lockwood and Sergeant Brainard, the only regular diaries, with my own, kept during the retreat and our subsequent life at Camp Clay.

Fearing exaggeration, I have occasionally modified statements and opinions entered in my original journal, believing it better to underrate than enlarge the wonders of the Arctic regions, which have been too often questioned.

I have profited largely by the acute criticism of my

wife, who, stimulated into intense activity by the critical situation of the expedition during its last year of service, acquired a more than cursory knowledge of Arctic work. During the doubtful time she noted with keen perception the vital importance of the rejected bounty scheme and urged it through sympathizing friends to final passage.

The engravings are faithful reproductions of an unequalled series of Arctic views, the work of Sergeant Rice, the photographer, except field sketches—always noted—and original drawings made under my supervision, for the correctness of which I personally vouch.

No pen could ever convey to the world an adequate idea of the abject misery and extreme wretchedness to which we were reduced at Cape Sabine. Insufficiently clothed, for months without drinking water, destitute of warmth, our sleeping-bags frozen to the ground, our walls, roof, and floor covered with frost and ice, subsisting on *one-fifth* of an Arctic ration—almost without clothing, light, heat, or food, yet we were never without courage, faith, and hope. The extraordinary spirit of loyalty, patience, charity, and self-denial,—daily and almost universally exhibited by our famished and nearly maddened party,—must be read between the lines in the account of our daily life penned under such desperate and untoward circumstances. Such words, written at such a time, I have not the heart to enlarge on.

The tragic experiences of the party excited such a

public interest, further intensified by exaggerated and unfounded statements on many points, that I have felt obliged to touch briefly upon all disagreeable questions. In so doing I have adhered to the stern facts, while I have modified the acerbity of my judgments, remembering always that I speak of the dead, and being able in comfort and plenty to judge more leniently than when slowly perishing from cold, disease, and starvation.

For a quarter of a century a public servant, in war and in peace, my faults are known. Cruelty and injustice, however, are foreign to my nature; and I rejoice that during the nine months I commanded a party of suffering, starving, and dying comrades, I never treated any man other than he justly merited.

In this spirit I submit these unvarnished records of Arctic service to the public.

A. W. GREELY.

WASHINGTON, January 5, 1886.

ORDERS AND INSTRUCTIONS GOVERNING THE ORGANIZATION AND MANAGEMENT OF THE LADY FRANKLIN BAY EXPEDITION.

SPECIAL ORDERS, No. 57.	HEADQUARTERS OF THE ARMY, ADJUTANT-GENERAL'S OFFICE, WASHINGTON, March 11, 1881.

(Extract.)

* * * * * * * *

2. By direction of the President, First Lieutenant *A. W. Greely*, Fifth Cavalry, acting signal officer, is hereby assigned to the command of the expeditionary force now organizing under the provisions of the acts of Congress approved May 1, 1880, and March 3, 1881, to establish a station north of the eighty-first degree of north latitude, at or near Lady Franklin Bay, for the purposes of scientific observation, etc., as set forth in said acts.

During his absence on this duty Lieutenant *Greely* will retain station at Washington, District of Columbia.

* * * * * * * *

BY COMMAND OF GENERAL SHERMAN:

R. C. DRUM,
Adjutant-General.

GENERAL ORDERS, No. 35.	HEADQUARTERS OF THE ARMY, ADJUTANT-GENERAL'S OFFICE, WASHINGTON, April 12, 1881.

The following order, received from the War Department, is published for the information of the Army:

In order to carry into execution the act approved May 1, 1880, and so much of the act approved March 3, 1881, entitled "An act making appropriations for sundry civil expenses of the Government for the fiscal year ending June 30, 1882, and for other purposes," as provides for "observation and exploration in the Arctic seas; for continuing the work of scientific observation and exploration on or near the shores of Lady Franklin Bay, and for transportation of men and supplies to said location and return, twenty-five thousand dollars," it is ordered:

1. First Lieutenant *A. W. Greely*, Fifth U. S. Cavalry, acting signal officer, having volunteered for the expedition, shall take command of the expeditionary force now organizing under said act to establish a station north of the eighty-first degree of north latitude, at or near Lady Franklin Bay, for the purpose of scientific observation.

2. Lieutenant *Greely* shall have authority to contract for and purchase, within the limits of the appropriation, the supplies and transportation deemed needful for the expedition; and the appropriation for this purpose, made by the act approved March 3, 1881, shall be drawn from the Treasury and disbursed, upon proper vouchers, by the regular disbursing officer of the Signal Service, under the direction of the Chief Signal Officer.

3. The force to be employed in the expedition shall consist of two other officers, who may volunteer their services; twenty-one enlisted men, who may volunteer from the Army or be specially enlisted for the purpose; and one contract surgeon. The latter to be contracted with at such time as he may be able to join the party.

4. The commander of the expedition is authorized to hire a steam sealer, or whaler, to transport the party from St. John to Lady Franklin Bay, for a fixed sum per month, under a formal contract that shall release the United States from any and all responsibility, or claim for damages, in case the steamer is injured, lost, or destroyed. The said contract shall include the services and subsistence of the crew of the vessel, and shall require that the said crew shall consist of one captain, two mates, one steward, two engineers, two firemen, and seven seamen —not less than fifteen in all. Such steam sealer, or whaler, shall not be hired until it has been inspected by an officer to be detailed by the Secretary of the Navy for that purpose, and found by him fit for the intended service.

5. The expeditionary force shall be assembled at Washington, District of Columbia, not later than May 15, and at St. John not later than June 15, 1881.

6. During their absence on this duty Lieutenant *Greely*, and the other officers of the Army accompanying the expedition, will retain station at Washington, District of Columbia. The enlisted men, who may volunteer or be specially enlisted for this duty, shall receive the pay and commutation allowances (except commutation for quarters and fuel) that accrue to men detached for duty in Washington, District of Columbia.

7. The several bureaus of the War Department will furnish, on requisitions approved by the Secretary of War, the necessary subsistence, clothing, camp and garrison equipage, transportation to St. John, Newfoundland, and return, medicines, books, instruments, hospital stores, arms, and ammunition. The subsistence stores to be furnished as above directed are for sale, not for issue, to the officers and men of the expeditionary force.

By command of General Sherman:

R. C. DRUM,
Adjutant-General.

War Department,
Special Orders, Office of the Chief Signal Officer,
No. 9. Washington, D. C., June 17, 1881.

1. By direction of the Secretary of War, the following-named officers and enlisted men are assigned to duty as the expeditionary force to Lady Franklin Bay:

First Lieutenant A. W. Greely, Fifth Cavalry, Acting Signal Officer;
Second Lieutenant Frederick F. Kislingbury, Eleventh Infantry, Acting Signal Officer;
Second Lieutenant James B. Lockwood, Twenty-third Infantry, Acting Signal Officer;
Sergeant Edward Israel, Signal Corps, U. S. Army;
Sergeant Winfield S. Jewell, Signal Corps, U. S. Army;
Sergeant George W. Rice, Signal Corps, U. S. Army;
Sergeant David C. Ralston, Signal Corps, U. S. Army;
Sergeant Hampden S. Gardiner, Signal Corps, U. S. Army;
Sergeant William H. Cross, General Service, U. S. Army;
Sergeant David L. Brainard, Company L, Second Cavalry;
Sergeant David Lynn, Company C, Second Cavalry;
Corporal Daniel C. Starr, Company F, Second Cavalry;
Corporal Paul Grimm,* Company H, Eleventh Infantry;
Corporal Nicholas Salor, Company H, Second Cavalry;
Corporal Joseph Elison, Company E, Tenth Infantry;
Private Charles B. Henry, Company E, Fifth Cavalry;
Private Maurice Connell, Company B, Third Cavalry;
Private Jacob Bender, Company F, Ninth Infantry;

---

* Grimm having deserted, he was replaced by Private Roderick R. Schneider, First Artillery.

Private Francis Long, Company F, Ninth Infantry;
Private William Whisler, Company F, Ninth Infantry;
Private Henry Bierderbick, Company G, Seventeenth Infantry;
Private Julius Frederick, Company L, Second Cavalry;
Private James Ryan, Company H, Second Cavalry;
Private William A. Ellis, Company C, Second Cavalry.

2. First Lieutenant A. W. Greely, Fifth Cavalry, Acting Signal Officer and Assistant to the Chief Signal Officer, is hereby assigned to the command of the expedition, and is charged with the execution of the orders and instructions given below. He will forward all reports and observations to the Chief Signal Officer, who is charged with the control and supervision of the expedition.

W. B. HAZEN,
Brigadier and Brevet Major General,
Chief Signal Officer, U. S. A.

Instructions, }   War Department,
No. 72.   Office of the Chief Signal Officer,
                         Washington, D. C., June 17, 1881.

The following general instructions will govern in the establishment and management of the expedition organized under Special Orders, No. 97, War Department, office of the Chief Signal Officer, Washington, D. C., dated June 17, 1881:

The *permanent* station will be established at the most suitable point north of the eighty-first parallel, and contiguous to the coal seam discovered near Lady Franklin Bay by the English expedition of 1875.

After leaving St. John, Newfoundland, except to obtain Esquimaux hunters, dogs, clothing, etc., at Disco or Upernivik, only such stops will be made as the condition of the ice necessitates, or as are essential in order to determine the exact location and condition of the stores cached on the east coast of Grinnell Land by the English expedition of 1875. During any enforced delays along that coast it would be well to supplement the English depots by such small caches from the steamer's stores of provisions as would be valuable to a party retreating southward by boats from Robeson Channel. At each point where an old depot is examined or a new one established, three brief notices will be left of the visit—one to be deposited in the cairn built or found standing; one to be placed on the north side of it; and one to be buried twenty feet north (magnetic) of the cairn. Notices discovered in cairns will be brought away, replacing them, however, by copies.

The steamer should, on arrival at the *permanent* station, discharge her cargo with the utmost despatch and be ordered to return to St

John, Newfoundland. After a careful examination of the seam of coal at that point has been made by the party, to determine whether an ample supply is easily procurable, a report in writing on this subject will be sent by the returning vessel. In case of doubt, an ample supply must be retained from the steamer's stores.

By the returning steamer will be sent a brief report of proceedings, and as full a transcript as possible of all meteorological and other observations made during the voyage.

After the departure of the vessel the energies of the party should first be devoted to the erection of the dwelling-house and observatories, after which a sledge party will be sent, according to the proposal made to the Navy Department, to the high land near Cape Joseph Henry.

The sledging parties will generally work in the interests of exploration and discovery. The work to be done by them should be marked by all possible care and fidelity. The outlines of coasts entered on charts will be such only as have actually been seen by the party. Every favorable opportunity will be improved by the sledging parties to determine accurately the geographical position of all their camps, and to obtain the bearing therefrom of all distant cliffs, mountains, islands, etc.

Careful attention will be given to the collection of specimens of the animal, mineral, and vegetable kingdoms. Such collections will be made as complete as possible, will be considered the property of the Government of the United States, and are to be at its disposal.

Special instructions regarding the meteorological, magnetic, tidal, pendulum, and other observations, as recommended by the Hamburg International Polar Conference, are transmitted herewith.

It is contemplated that the *permanent* station shall be visited in 1882 and in 1883 by a steam, sailing, or other vessel, by which supplies for and such additions to the present party as are deemed needful will be sent.

In case the vessel is unable to reach there in 1882, she will cache a portion of her supplies and all of her letters and despatches at the most northerly point she attains on the *east coast of Grinnell Land*, and establish a small depot at Littleton Island. Notices of the locality of such depots will be left at one or all of the following places, viz., Cape Hawks, Cape Sabine, and Cape Isabella.

In case no vessel reaches the *permanent* station in 1882, the vessel sent in 1883 will remain in Smith Sound until there is danger of its closing by ice, and, on leaving, will land all her supplies and a party at Littleton Island, which party will be prepared for a winter's stay, and will be instructed to send sledge parties up the *east side of Grinnell Land* to meet this party. If not visited in 1882, Lieutenant Greely will abandon his station not later than September 1, 1883, and will retreat southward by boat, following closely the *east* coast of *Grinnell Land* until the relieving vessel is met or Littleton Island is reached.

In view of the familiarity of Lieutenant Greely with the methods pursued by previous expeditions, and of the confidence reposed in his judgment and discretion, it is not thought necessary to furnish him with more definite instructions than those contained in the following pages. While he is left at full liberty to vary the details according to circumstances, yet the main points here given should be held in view as of predominant importance.

W. B. HAZEN,
Brigadier and Brevet Major General,
Chief Signal Officer, U. S. A.

TECHNICAL TERMS USED IN THESE VOLUMES.

BORING is the operation of forcing a ship through crowded ice by steam or sail.

WARPING is moving a vessel ahead by means of ropes fastened to some distant fixed object.

A FIELD consists of pieces of closely aggregated ice covering an extensive area.

BAY-ICE or HARBOR-ICE is that annually formed in closed bays or seas.

PANCAKE is a piece of bay-ice of considerable size and thickness.

FLOE is a large piece of bay-ice (or palæocrystic ice), sometimes miles in extent.

BESET.—The situation of a vessel when closely surrounded by ice through which it can move with difficulty or not at all.

ICE-BLINK, or ICE-SKY.—A brightness in the sky caused by large bodies of ice in that quarter.

HUMMOCKS.—Uneven, irregular parts of floes which rise above the level, as hills above the plain.

LAND-ICE, or FAST-ICE.—Ice attached to land either in floes or in heavy grounded masses.

LANE, or LEAD.—A narrow channel between masses of ice, through which a vessel may pass.

NIPPED.—The situation of a ship when forcibly pressed or jammed by ice.

PACK.—Large masses of ice in close proximity covering considerable area. When the pieces are densely crowded it is a *close* pack, when water-spaces and lanes are frequent it is an *open* pack.

SAILING-ICE.—A pack sufficiently *open* to allow a sailing-ship to pass through.

STREAMS.—Long, narrow collections of broken ice.

WATER-SKY.—A dark-looking sky, indicating open water in that direction.

RUBBLE.—Small, sharp, irregular pieces of ice, many of which are loose. Formed generally from *young ice*, which has been broken or ground up by action or pressure of heavy floes.

TIDAL CRACK.—Cracks formed by the action of tides—generally a break between the main body of ice and that which remains fast to the land. Through this, during heavy, rising tides, water flows, which is called *tidal overflow*.

PALÆOCRYSTIC ICE is that of such character and great thickness as must have required many years' time for its formation. Its general shape is in floes, with undulating surfaces, like hills and valleys of a rolling country.

FLOEBERG.—A palæocrystic iceberg differing from common icebergs in its regularly cubical shape, level top and bottom, strictly perpendicular sides, regular lines of cleavage, and apparent stratified structure.

ICE-FOOT.—Sea-ice which forming against the land remains attached to it unmoved by action of tides. It is separated from the main, movable ice by a tidal crack.

YOUNG ICE.—Ice recently formed, in contradistinction to old ice which is at least of previous winter's formation.

CONTENTS.—VOLUME I.

CHAPTER I.
PAGE
THE PIONEERS OF SMITH SOUND, ... 1

CHAPTER II.
INTERNATIONAL CIRCUMPOLAR STATIONS, ... 19

CHAPTER III.
GREENLAND, ... 25

CHAPTER IV.
ORGANIZATION AND EQUIPMENT, ... 36

CHAPTER V.
THE VOYAGE TO UPERNIVIK, ... 41

CHAPTER VI.
MELVILLE BAY TO FORT CONGER, ... 56

CHAPTER VII.
THE RETURN OF THE PROTEUS, ... 80

CHAPTER VIII.
FORT CONGER, ... 87

CHAPTER IX.
AUTUMN SLEDGING, ... 95

CHAPTER X.
SUNLIGHT TO DARKNESS, ... 115

CHAPTER XI.
OUR SCIENTIFIC OBSERVATIONS, ... 124

CHAPTER XII.
HYGIENE AND ROUTINE, ... 134

CHAPTER XIII.
SLEDGING IN THE ARCTIC TWILIGHT, ... 147

CHAPTER XIV.
OUR FIRST DARK DAYS, ... 154

CHAPTER XV.
CHRISTMAS AND THE NEW YEAR, ... 171

CHAPTER XVI.
WINTER EVENTS, ... 179

CHAPTER XVII
PREPARATIONS FOR SLEDGING, ... 196

CHAPTER XVIII
THANK GOD HARBOR AND HALL'S GRAVE, ... 213

CHAPTER XIX
ESTABLISHING DEPOTS, ... 227

CHAPTER XX
NORTHWARD OVER THE FROZEN SEA, ... 238

CHAPTER XXI
CHANDLER FIORD, ... 258

CHAPTER XXII
LAKE HAZEN, ... 272

CHAPTER XXIII
THE FARTHEST NORTH.—CONGER TO CAPE BRYANT, . 295

CHAPTER XXIV
THE FARTHEST NORTH.—CAPE BRYANT TO CAPE WASHINGTON, ... 320

CHAPTER XXV
LOCKWOOD ISLAND AND RETURN, ... 336

CHAPTER XXVI.

SPRINGTIME AND SUMMER, ... 351

CHAPTER XXVII.

SUMMER EXPLORATIONS, ... 366

CHAPTER XXVIII.

SUMMER EXPLORATIONS (*Concluded*), . . . 391

CHAPTER XXIX.

LAUNCH TRIPS, ... 417

LIST OF ILLUSTRATIONS.

VOLUME I.

PORTRAIT OF LIEUTENANT A. W. GREELY, U.S.A......*Frontispiece.*
    ENGRAVED ON STEEL BY CHARLES SCHLECHT.

FULL-PAGE ILLUSTRATIONS.

Engraved, without drawings, from photographs by Sergeant George W. Rice, Photographer of the Expedition.

	Face Page.
ESKIMO KAYAKERS OFF THE COAST OF DISCO........................	1
GENERAL VIEW OF GODHAVN, GREENLAND, FROM ADJACENT CLIFFS..	29
MEMBERS OF LADY FRANKLIN BAY EXPEDITION, 1881–84.............	40
ICEBERGS IN DISCO BAY...	50
MUSK-OX KILLED NEAR FORT CONGER..............................	104
LAKE ALEXANDRA, NEAR DISCOVERY HARBOR, LOOKING WEST.......	122
GAME-STAND AT CONGER, WITH BELLOT ISLAND IN BACKGROUND......	138
MAKING READY FOR A SLEDGE JOURNEY FROM FORT CONGER........	152
ICE-FOOT AND PRESSED-UP ICE, CAPE MURCHISON, ROBESON CHANNEL.	168
LIEUTENANT GREELY'S CORNER, AT FORT CONGER..................	180
ARCTIC CLOUDS OVER BELLOT ISLAND.............................	195
"THE ARCTIC HIGHWAY"—RUBBLE AND HUMMOCK ICE..............	225

LIST OF ILLUSTRATIONS.

Face Page.

LIEUTENANT GREELY AND PARTY STARTING FOR EXPLORATION OF GRINNELL LAND, APRIL, 1882.................................. 260

PORTRAIT OF LIEUTENANT JAMES B. LOCKWOOD, U.S.A.............. 295

LIEUTENANT LOCKWOOD, BRAINARD, AND CHRISTIANSEN RETURNING FROM 83° 24' N... 347

ESKIMO RELICS FOUND AT JUNCTION OF RUGGLES RIVER AND LAKE HAZEN, JULY, 1882.. 406

ILLUSTRATIONS IN THE TEXT.

(From photographs by Sergeant George W. Rice.)

Page

SANDERSON'S HOPE... 1
(The farthest of John Davis, 1587.)

CRYSTAL PALACE CLIFFS FROM LITTLETON ISLAND, WITH CAPE ALEXANDER AT THE RIGHT.. 5
(Discovered by Admiral Inglefield, R.N., 1852.)

SITE OF POLARIS HOUSE.. 12
(Built at Life-Boat Cove by Polaris Crew, Winter 1872-73.)

GODTHAAB, GREENLAND, INTERNATIONAL STATION, 1882-83.......... 19
(Furthest point reached by Davis, 1585.)

GREENLAND COAST.. 25
(View near Godhavn.)

ARCTIC BELLES.. 32

UPERNIVIK.. 34
(The most northerly civilized settlement in the world.)

ENGLISH CAIRN, S. E. CARY ISLAND, 1875....................... 36
(Baffin discovered this island, 1616.)

LIST OF ILLUSTRATIONS.

	Page
NATURAL MONUMENT NEAR GODHAVN	42
SERGEANT RICE AND GREENLAND ESKIMO	53
TASIUSAK	54

(The most northerly settlement of Danish Eskimo.)

UPERNIVIK AT MIDNIGHT	56
CAPE YORK	58
"AN ILAND WE CALLED HAKLUIT'S ILE."	62

(Baffin's Farthest Land, July 4, 1616.)

PORT FOULKE	66

(Winter-quarters of Dr. Hayes, 1860–61.)

WASHINGTON IRVING ISLAND	70

(Opposite Cape Hawks.)

NARWHAL SKULL	76

(Showing abnormal developments of tooth in left side, upper jaw.)

ESKIMO BOYS FISHING	79
THE PROTEUS IN DISCOVERY HARBOR	80
PROTEUS FIRST STOPPED BY ICE	83
PLAN OF HOUSE AT FORT CONGER	90
AN ARCTIC BROOK	92
ENTRANCE TO BELLOWS VALLEY, OCTOBER, 1881	107

(Northeastern side, near Bleak Cape.)

SUNLIGHT TO DARKNESS	115
OBSERVER MAKING TEMPERATURE OBSERVATIONS AT FORT CONGER	126
THE FROG	133

(A floeberg in Robeson Channel, May, 1882.)

LIST OF ILLUSTRATIONS.

	Page
Lunar Halo at Fort Conger, February 1, 1882	187
Hudson Bay Sledge Pattern	196

(From a photograph by Relief Expedition, 1884.)

Hunt's St. Michael Sledge	199

(From a photograph by Relief Expedition, 1884.)

Greenland Dog Sledge	200
Ancient Eskimo Sledge—Found at Cape Baird, 81° 30′ N.	201
Three-man Buffalo Sleeping-bag	212
Greenland Coast from Cape Beechy	216
Devil's Head (The Bellows Valley), June, 1882	237
Dr. Pavy's Party Starting North, March 19, 1882	240
Dr. Pavy and Jens Skinning Seal at Conger	256
Chandler Fiord Looking East from Camp 3	265
Henrietta Nesmith Glacier	284

(Showing eastern edge crowding against the mountains.)

Icebergs	294
An Arctic Wolf Killed near Fort Conger	303
Stephenson Island from Cape Britannia	323

(From sketch by Lieutenant Lockwood.)

Beaumont Island from Cape Britannia	327

(From sketch by Lieutenant Lockwood.)

Looking into Chipp Inlet	330

(From sketch by Lieutenant Lockwood.)

Cape Alexander Ramsay	338

(From sketch by Lieutenant Lockwood.)

LIST OF ILLUSTRATIONS.   XXV

	Page
ELISON ISLAND	340

(*From sketch by Lieutenant Lockwood.*)

FACSIMILE OF LIEUTENANT BEAUMONT'S RECORD	345
LONG AND WHISLER RETURNING FROM ARCHER FIORD, MAY, 1882	354
COAL SEAM SHOWING ABOVE WATERCOURSE CREEK	357
DECORATION DAY AT CONGER, 1882	359
MUSK CALVES AT CONGER, FOUR MONTHS OLD	363
BIFURCATION CAPE, SEPARATING BELLOWS AND BLACK ROCK VALLEYS	368
PLAN OF ANCIENT ESKIMO HOUSE	381
ESKIMO STONE LAMP, FOUND NEAR CAPE BAIRD, 81° 30' N	420
CHANDLER FIORD LOOKING WESTWARD, IDA BAY TO EXTREME LEFT	424

LIST OF MAPS.

	Face Page.
ARCTIC REGIONS, SHOWING LOCATION OF CIRCUMPOLAR STATIONS, 1881-83	23
FORT CONGER AND VICINITY	87
EXPLORATIONS BY LIEUTENANT J. B. LOCKWOOD, U.S.A., 1882	304
DISCOVERIES MADE IN NORTH GREENLAND BY LIEUTENANT J. B. LOCKWOOD, U.S.A	325
DISCOVERIES IN GRINNELL LAND MADE BY LIEUTENANT A. W. GREELY, U.S.A	391

ESKIMO KAYAKERS OFF THE COAST OF DISCO.
(From a photograph.)

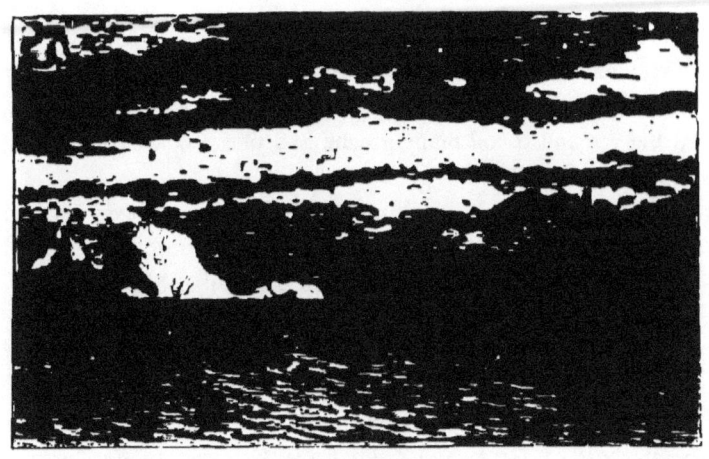

Sanderson's Hope.
[*The farthest of John Davis*, 1587.]

CHAPTER I.

THE PIONEERS OF SMITH SOUND.

JUST three centuries ago, on a fair day of June, 1585, two tiny craft sailed from Dartmouth in quest of the Northwest Passage. They were commanded by a brave man, a daring explorer and skilful seaman, John Davis, of Sandridge.

This venturesome voyage of one of England's most distinguished seamen resulted in the rediscovery of Greenland, and may be said to have opened the Smith Sound route to the Pole.

Davis sighted Greenland July 20th. He well describes it as a "land being very high and full of mightie mountaines all covered with snowe, no viewe of wood, grasse or earth to be scene, and the shore two leagues off into the sea full of yce. The lothsome view of the shore, and irksome noyse of the yce was such that it bred strange conceites among us." On July 29th he was off the west coast, near Godthaab, having "past al the yce and found many greene and pleasant Isles bordering upon the shore."

Crossing the strait which now bears his name, Davis reached Cape Dyer, and later sailed nearly to the head of Cumberland Sound. He returned to Dartmouth September 30th.

In 1586 and 1587 he visited Davis Strait, and in the latter year reached, on the western coast of Greenland, latitude 72° 41′ N., about fifty miles south of Upernivik.

Davis' discoveries were remarkable. They covered the west coast of Greenland from Cape Farewell to Sanderson's Hope, and, on the American side, from Cape Dyer, Cumberland Island, to Southern Labrador.

His descriptions of the Greenlanders are quaint, curious, and instructive, showing them to have been, three centuries ago, the same "tractable people void of craft or double dealing" as we know them to be at the present time.

Davis was followed by another able seaman and great discoverer, William Baffin, who, in the Discovery, a craft of only fifty-five tons, sailed, March 26, 1616, from Gravesend. He sighted Greenland, May 14th, and on the 30th of that month had reached Davis' farthest point, Sanderson's Hope, in 72° 41′ N. June 9th he was stopped by ice at Baffin Islands, 73° 54′ N. Leaving his anchorage, June 18th, he took what is known as the "Middle Passage" across Melville Bay, and reached, July 1st, an open sea—the "North Water" of the whalers of to-day. Passing Capes York, Atholl, and Parry, he yet pushed northward, and on July 5th attained his farthest point, within sight of Cape Alexander. His latitude, about 77° 45′ N., remained unequalled in that sea for 236 years. Baffin, in quaint language, says he was forced by ice "to stand backe some eight leagues to an iland we called Hakluits Ile—it lyeth betweene two great Sounds, the one Whale Sound, and the other Sir Thomas Smith's Sound; this last runneth to the north of 78°, and is admirable in one respect, because in it is the greatest variation of the compasse of any part of the world known; for by divers good observations I found it to be above five points, or 56 degrees varied to the westward."

A few days later Baffin turned southward, having in this wonderful voyage sailed over three hundred miles farther north than his predecessor, Davis. He thus added to geographical knowledge Ellesmere and Prudhoe Lands, and Baffin Bay, with its outlying sounds of Smith, Jones, and Lancaster.

Sixteen hundred and sixteen was evidently a good year for ice-navigation, as Baffin's time to Cape York, in his tiny sailing craft, has not been greatly surpassed by the powerful steamers of to-day. In 1871, Captain William Adams, the veteran whaler, reached the "North Water" June 3d, and rounded Cary Islands to the north on the 7th. The Arctic, under Captain Adams, reached Cape York June 9, 1873, and in 1883 several whalers were off that point by June 3d. In 1884 the Relief Squadron and three whalers entered the "North Water" June 18th. They had been stopped by ice on the 4th, near the same point where Baffin had been similarly delayed, June 9, 1616, in the Discovery.

For two centuries the waters first navigated by Baffin remained unvexed by any keel, and the very credit of his discoveries passed away. In 1818 Barrington, in "Possibility of Approaching the North Pole Asserted," put forth a chart with the legend, "Baffin's Bay, according to the relation of W. Baffin, in 1616, but not now believed." Sir John Barrow, in his "Chronological History of the Voyages into the Arctic Regions," 1818, omitted Baffin Bay from his circumpolar chart.

The same year in which these maps appeared (1818), Captain John Ross, commanding, in the Isabella, with Lieutenant (since Admiral) William Parry, in the Alexander, sailed from Lerwick, May 3d.

They were stopped by ice June 17th, just north of Disco Island. The vessels crossed Melville Bay with some difficulty, and remained moored to the land-ice near Bushnan Island, off Cape York, for about a week. On August 9th they first met the natives of that region, to whom Ross gave the name of Arctic Highlanders.

From the account of Ross we learn that the natives at that time had sledges, dogs, knives, spears, and lances suited for the chase of land or sea game. Their iron for knife-blades and other purposes was obtained from meteoric blocks near Cape York. They apparently had no idea of other people living to the south. Ross pushing on, at midnight August 19th the Isabella was in latitude 76° 54′ N., the Cary Islands bearing S.E. This was the most northerly point reached. He considered the sound to the northward a closed bay, and says: "Smith Sound, discovered by Baffin, was distinctly seen, and the capes forming each side of it were named after the two ships, Isabella and Alexander: I considered the bottom of this sound to be about eighteen leagues distant." It is evident that the points seen were not Capes Isabella and Alexander of to-day, as they are from eighty to ninety miles distant from Ross' position. More probably he sighted Capes Faraday and Robertson, which correspond better to the estimated distances. Ross in like manner reported Jones and Lancaster Sounds, which he cursorily examined later, to be closed bays. He returned to England in October, having, with his well-found ships, accomplished results far less striking and important than those wrought by Baffin with his frail shallop.

It is to Admiral Inglefield, R.N., that the credit belongs of first determining the extent of Smith Sound.

Captain Inglefield left the Thames, July 5, 1852, in the screw-schooner Isabel, one hundred and forty-nine tons, with the intention of searching the deep inlets of Baffin Bay for Sir John Franklin's party, and with the hope of setting at rest the question of an entrance into the great polar basin through Smith Sound. Cape Farewell was sighted on the 30th, and

Crystal Palace Cliffs from Littleton Island, with Cape Alexander at the right.
[*Discovered by Admiral Inglefield, R.N., 1852.*]

Upernivik reached August 15th. On August 21st the Isabel was off Cape York, and the following day Captain Inglefield communicated with Eskimo, near Petowik glacier. He was convinced that they had never before seen Europeans. They were clad in bear, fox, reindeer, and seal skins. No European wares were found, nor were any kayaks seen.

At North Omenak caches of meat and winter clothing were found. In summer the natives occupy seal-skin tents, and in winter an underground burrow. In Bardin Bay an Eskimo village was found, where there were many dogs and sledges, but no kayaks.

At 12 P.M. of the 26th, Cape Alexander, the farthest point seen by Baffin, was passed, and Inglefield says: "Then I beheld the open sea stretching through seven points of the compass . . . bounded on the east and west by distant headlands" (Cape Albert to the west). On the 27th, at midday, he reached 78° 21' N.; placing the Isabel "about one hundred and forty miles farther than had been reached by any previous navigator, of whom we have any record."

A strong northerly gale with low temperature obliged Inglefield to return southward. Thence he ran into Jones Sound, where, on September 1st, he reached 84° 10' W., 76° 11' N. He later visited Sir Edward Belcher's squadron, at Beechy Island, and turning homeward remained within the Arctic circle *until October* 12*th*. He reached Stornness November 4th.

Sir Francis Beaufort well called this voyage one of the most remarkable on record. Inglefield laid down nearly six hundred miles of new coast, corrected many errors of position, outlined Smith and penetrated far into Jones Sound, and brought back valuable meteorological and other scientific data.

An American, Elisha Kent Kane, first passed the northern portal of Smith Sound, and entered the sea which bears his name. Kane's vessel, the Advance, was fitted out at the expense of Henry Grinnell and George Peabody. She left New York May 30, 1853. Fiskernaes was visited, and Hans Hendrik, then a youth, engaged as hunter and dog-driver. Furs, skins, and dogs were gathered up at various points, and Upernivik was reached July 17th. They passed Cape York August 4th, and were off Littleton Island on the 7th. Life-boat Cove, to the eastward of the island, received its name from the cache of life-boat and provisions there made.

Kane attempted to push northward along the Greenland coast, but strong gales and the heavy floes, with new ice already forming, drove him, August 24th, to the nearest shelter, Van Rensselaer Harbor, in 78° 37′ N., 70° 40′ W. During the autumn several caches were established for spring travelling. Nearly all the dogs died during the winter. Scurvy attacked the party, but fortunately no death occurred among them. An unfortunate sledge-journey, in March, 1854, however, resulted in the death of two men, and the maiming by frost of two others. A journey to the northeast, made by Kane in April, had no result. Dr. Hayes, leaving on May 20th, succeeded, in twelve days' absence, in crossing Kane Basin, and reached 79° 43′ N., in the vicinity of Cape Frazer. Hayes was the first explorer to put foot on Grinnell Land. Morton, on the Greenland coast, succeeded, June 24th, in scaling the south side of Cape Constitution, about 80° 35′ N. From an elevation of five hundred feet, he saw open water as far north as eye could reach, probably to Cape Lieber, 81° 32′ N. In other words, he found Kennedy Channel open, a condition which doubtless occurs nine years out of ten.

In July, 1854, the ice not having broken up in Van Rensselaer Harbor, Kane realized his dangerous position and attempted to reach Beechy Island, some four hundred miles distant, by boat. He hoped to find there an English vessel, and to obtain assistance. He was forced to return, having been unable even to reach Cape Parry. On August 28th, Hayes with eight others, leaving Kane, started south with the object of reaching Upernivik, preferring the dangers of such a trip to a second winter in the ice. After great suffering they returned in December to the Advance, in a state bordering on starvation. Kane received them kindly, though Hayes's departure bore to many the stamp of desertion. The second winter brought renewed and increased scurvy, which left the party in a deplorable condition as the spring of 1855 approached. The only recourse then was the abandonment of the brig, and a boat journey to Upernivik. The vessel was formally abandoned May 20th, and on June 17th Kane launched his boats in open water near Cape Alexander. By indefatigable efforts the party, with its invalids, records, and most important instruments, had been moved over the intervening eighty miles of rough, difficult ice. One man, Ohlsen, died en route, from an internal strain, and was buried on Littleton Island in sight of the cape which bears his name. Hans Hendrik, deserting, remained with the Etah Eskimo. Cape York was doubled by the party July 21st, and, following the fast ice of Melville Bay, on August 6th they reached Upernivik.

Kane's search for Franklin was fruitless, but he increased largely our knowledge of Arctic lands. His physical observations were more valuable and complete than those of any preceding expedition. He added to geography new lands, the most northern of his day, and made known to the world the life and customs of the Etah Eskimo. His heroic steadfastness, restless energy, and manly fortitude did honor to America, and his stirring narrative, unfortunately marred by exaggerations, gave a new impetus to Arctic work, and doubtless excited in many a youth his first longings for exploration and adventure.

Dr. I. I. Hayes, Kane's surgeon, next attempted the Smith Sound route, to complete its surveys and reach the "open Polar Sea." He left Boston in the schooner United States, July 7, 1860, and on August 12th reached Upernivik, where he added six to his crew, making its total complement twenty-one. On August 25th the vessel was off Cape York, and there Hayes communicated with the Etah Eskimo. Hans Hendrik, who five years previous had deserted Kane on his retreat, was here added to the party, with his Etah wife and babe. Meeting near Cape Alexander a succession of furious northerly gales which injured his vessel and retarded his progress, Hayes was obliged to winter south of Littleton Island, in Foulke Fiord, 78° 18′ N., 73° W.

During the winter Hayes lost his astronomer, Sonntag, who perished on a sledge trip with Hans Hendrik in an attempt to communicate with the Eskimo in Whale Sound. One of the Eskimo, Peter, deserted his party and also perished. In March, 1861, Hayes, with dog-sledges, made a preliminary journey northward. His slow progress from rough ice caused him to abandon his idea of exploring the Greenland coast, and to decide on crossing Kane Basin and following its western shores to the north. Hayes started on his final journey with two dog-sledges, April 3d. A third sledge, hauled by men, carried a boat which was abandoned at Cairn Point. The man-sledge was sent back to the ship April 28th, from the middle of Kane Basin. On May 11th, Hayes with the dog-sledges reached Cape Hawks, about seventy miles from his ship. Thirty-eight days had been occupied in making that distance, yet he claims to have reached Cape Lieber, about *one hundred and seventy miles* beyond Hawks, *six* days later.

It is a thankless and ungracious task to criticise our predecessors in exploration. They are men who have struggled and suffered under the same trying and adverse circumstances as ourselves, and we appreciate their labors and dangers accurately. But at times adverse criticism is necessary in the interests of truth and history. Unfortunately no experienced, nay inexperienced critic, who has compared his narrative with his astronomical and meteorological records, can so reconcile them as to substantiate Hayes's claim to have reached, with Knorr, Cape

Lieber, May 18th, 19th, 1861. The topography of Lieber is incorrect, its latitude two and a half miles in error, and its longitude *six degrees* to the westward of the true position. No cairn exists at Lieber, and Hayes's picture of that headland bears a striking resemblance to a sketch of Cape Joseph Goode, made by Sergeant Gardiner of my party.

Sir George Nares has pointed out that Cape Frazer is placed ten miles too far north by Hayes, and that the latitude of other places are similarly erroneous.

Hayes's ship broke out of Foulke Fiord July 10th, and the solid ice of Kane Basin barring his progress northward, he crossed Smith Sound and examined its west coast from Cape Sabine southward to Isabella.

It was thus his good fortune to have been the first known civilized man * to tread the new lands of Ellesmere and Grinnell. Turning southward, he reached Boston that autumn and supplemented his Arctic career as an explorer by good service as a surgeon during the late civil war.

The next expedition to enter Smith Sound was commanded by Charles F. Hall, in the Polaris. She left New York June 29, 1871, with a complement of twenty-three souls, which was subsequently increased in Greenland to thirty-three. The object of the expedition was to reach the North Pole. The United States Steamship Congress was sent as far as Godhavn as a supply-vessel. The Polaris left Godhavn, August 17th, and Tasiusak the 24th. Melville Bay was crossed in thirty-four hours, and the Polaris was first stopped by ice off Hakluyt Island. Smith Sound was found open, and the voyage northward was delayed only by occasional detours westward to avoid the main pack. Kennedy Channel was navigated

---

* Baffin landed in 1616 at Jones Sound, but it is uncertain whether on North Devon, Coburg Island, or Ellesmere Land.

without trouble, except from fog. The Polar Ocean was reached on the morning of August 31st; latitude 82° 11' to the northwestward of Repulse Harbor.

Returning southward the Polaris anchored in Thank God Harbor, where she wintered. Hall with two dog-sledges reached Cape Brevoort in October, but died of apoplexy shortly after his return, on November 8th. Hall's death proved fatal to further advance. The winter was passed without disease or serious discomfort. Robeson Channel remained open throughout the winter. In the spring of 1872 Dr. Bessels and Mr. Bryan partly explored Petermann's Fiord and surveyed the coast as far south as Cape Bryan. Chester and Tyson, in June, attempted boat journeys northward, but reached only as far as Cape Sumner; from which point Sergeant Meyer, of the Signal Service, visited Repulse Harbor, reaching 82° 9', the highest latitude to that time attained on land. Captain Budington decided to return home, but the Polaris was unfortunately beset at the mouth of Kennedy Channel, about latitude 80°, August 14th. The vessel drifted steadily south in the pack despite all efforts to release her, and on October 12th was in 78° 28' N., not far from Littleton Island. On October 15th, in sight of Northumberland Island, during a violent gale, the Polaris was nearly destroyed.

While the crew were landing stores upon the floe the vessel broke away, leaving nineteen persons on the ice. The floe party, among whom were Captain Tyson and Sergeant Meyer, drifted southward that winter and were picked up off the coast of Labrador by the sealer Tigress, April 30, 1872. For one hundred and ninety-six days, eighty-three of which were without the sun, they had lived on ice-floes, subject to great privations and dangers. They had drifted in the meantime over fifteen hundred miles, and their escape from death was almost miraculous.

Captain Budington, who remained on the Polaris, succeeded in beaching her in Life Boat Cove. The party wintered there, constructing a house from the disabled vessel. They passed the winter in health, and much to his credit, Dr. Bessels, assisted by Mr. Bryan, not only managed to keep up the regular scientific observations, but also attempted surveys northward.

Under Mr. Chester's direction two boats were built, and on

Site of Polaris House.
[Built at Life Boat Cove by Polaris Crew, Winter, 1872-73.]

June 3, 1873, the party left Life Boat Cove for Upernivik. Fortunately they were met and rescued by the whaler Ravenscraig, June 23d, off Cape York.

The voyage of the Polaris was most fruitful in geographical results. The extension of Greenland and Grinnell Land northward over a degree and a half of latitude, the charting of Hall Basin and Robeson Channel, and the discovery of the extensive frozen sea to the northward, were all substantial and most important contributions to Arctic geography.

The meteorological observations were complete, and the tidal observations established the important fact that the Atlantic tides, flowing to the north and south around Greenland, meet near Cape Frazer. The value of these observations has been greatly impaired by the publication of erroneous means, resulting from the employment of an unreliable computer. Observations made with such care and under such difficulties deserve a better fate. They should be computed and discussed anew.

On May 29, 1875, the Alert and Discovery left Portsmouth, England, under command of Captain George Nares. His orders indicated that "their scope and primary object should be to attain the highest northern latitude, and, if possible, to reach the North Pole, and from winter quarters to explore the adjacent coast." The complement of the squadron was one hundred and twenty officers and men, supplemented by three dog-drivers obtained in Greenland. The Valorous accompanied the expedition as a tender as far as Ritenbenk.

On July 22d the vessels left Upernivik, and, taking the "middle passage" across Melville Bay, Cape York was reached three days later. A depot of thirty-six hundred rations with a whale-boat was left on the southeast island of the Cary group. Detained three days in Payer Harbor, a depot of two hundred and forty rations was cached for a possible sledge party. Cape Sabine was rounded August 4th, and ten days later, after constant battle with heavy ice, the vessels reached Dobbin Bay. Thirty-six hundred rations were there cached, just north of Cape Hawks.

The journey northward was a constant struggle with immense floes, but by improving every chance afforded by wind or tide, the two ships finally reached Discovery Harbor August 25th. In that harbor the reserve ship, Discovery, under Captain Stephenson, R. N., wintered within two hundred yards of the subsequent site of Ft. Conger.

The Alert pushing northward was moored August 31st near Cape Sheridan at Floeberg Beach, 82° 25' N., 61° 30' W., in the highest latitude which has ever been reached by any vessel. Here, on the exposed shores of the Polar Ocean, the Alert wintered. On the northward journey one thousand rations had been cached in Lincoln Bay.

Several sledging parties were sent out by Captain Nares during the autumn to establish other depots to the northward. Eight men of the parties were badly frost-bitten, three of whom suffered amputation. Lieutenant Aldrich, on September 27th, reached latitude 82° 48' N., and saw land reaching to Cape Columbia, 83° 7' N. Aldrich thus surpassed the heretofore unexcelled latitude of Parry, attained in 1827, north of Spitzbergen, by boat and sledge.

The winter was passed in health and comfort by the crews of both vessels, despite the longest Arctic night and severest prolonged cold ever experienced by man.

Communication was had between the Alert and Discovery in early spring, but at the expense of the life of Christian Petersen, who died from severe frost-bites, notwithstanding the heroic and unselfish exertions of Lieutenants Rawson and Edgerton with whom he was making the journey.

On April 3d, seven sledges manned by fifty three men and officers left the Alert for northern exploration. One party, under Commander Markham, was to push northward from Cape Joseph Henry over the Frozen Sea, and the second, under Lieutenant Aldrich, was ordered to explore the north Coast of Grinnell Land.

Markham, equipped with two boats, was early obliged to

abandon one, and after indescribable exertions succeeded, by indomitable energy, in reaching on the frozen ocean May 12, 1876, the highest latitude to that time attained. That point was 83° 20′ 26″ N., 63° 5′ W. The sea was found to be seventy-two fathoms deep, with clay bottom; surface temperature, 28.5°; bottom temperature, 28.8°. At that time five of Markham's seventeen men were on the sledges disabled by scurvy. His outward journey entailed two hundred and seventy-six miles of travel, although his farthest point was but seventy-three miles distant from the ship. On the return journey his men grew steadily worse, and although the second boat was abandoned May 27th, yet on June 7th it was evident the party would perish without help. Lieutenant Parr in this emergency made alone a forced march of twenty-four hours, and reaching the Alert, obtained assistance. One of the party died, however, and eleven others of the original seventeen were carried to the ship on relief-sledges.

Lieutenant Aldrich's journey along the north coast of Grinnell Land was a most remarkable one, and in my opinion has never been duly appreciated by the general public. He reached, May 18th, Point Alert, near Cape Alfred Ernest, 82° 16′ N., 85° 33′ W.; whence, he says, "the trend was gradually southward and westward." He had surveyed two hundred and twenty miles of new coast. His party, also attacked by scurvy, would not have reached the ship without the assistance which came to them through Lieutenant May. Only Lieutenant Aldrich and one man out of the eight were able to haul, when met by the dog-sledge.

During this time, Captain Stephenson of the Discovery had parties in the field. Lieutenant Archer, ordered to explore Lady Franklin Sound, succeeded in defining its limit, and reached the head of the Fiord, which now bears his name.

Lieutenant L. A. Beaumont was detailed to explore the north coast of Greenland. He left the Discovery with two eight-man sledges, April 6, 1876, and first visiting the Alert, afterward crossed Robeson Channel to Repulse Harbor. His supporting sledge under Dr. Coppinger turned back May 4th.

Beaumont reached Cape Bryant May 11th, and, pushing on, succeeded with one man in reaching, May 20th, the eastern coast of Sherard Osborn Fiord, 82° 20′ N., 50° 45′ W. Scurvy had already attacked the party, and their return-trip was made under most distressing circumstances. To save their strength Lieutenant Beaumont made a depot at Cape Bryant of extra rations.

Repulse Harbor was reached June 10th, by which time the party was in desperate straits, only Lieutenant Beaumont and Gray being able to work. Abandoning everything not absolutely indispensable, Lieutenant Beaumont had to decide whether to cross Robeson Channel to the Alert, or proceed forty miles to Thank God Harbor. He soon found that rotten ice and frequent water-pools forbade his crossing Robeson Channel, and with but little hope he turned his face southward. Struggling on with failing strength, his party was saved by the advent of Lieutenant Rawson and Dr. Coppinger, June 24th, who assisted them to Thank God Harbor, which was reached July 1st. Two men, Paul and Hand, died and were buried near Captain Hall. Lieutenant Beaumont after the recuperation of his party, crossed Robeson Channel by boat and sledge with great difficulty, reaching Cape Baird August 12th.

In the meantime, Captain Nares had decided in July to return to England, mainly on account of scurvy, of which thirty-six cases had occurred on the Alert alone. In addition to the break-down of his sledge-parties from this disease, he was convinced of the impracticability of successful navigation in the Polar Sea, and, from the lack of land to the northward, equally doubtful of sledge-journeys over the frozen sea toward the Pole. The Alert left Floeberg Beach July 31, 1876, and through daring seamanship succeeded in retracing her course down Robeson Channel, without receiving serious injury.

Both ships rounded Cape Lieber August 20th, and ten days later were in Dobbin Bay. In their passage southward the sledging depots at Joe Island, Capes Collinson and Sabine, as well as the larger depots at Lincoln Bay and S.E. Cary Island were left untouched. A large portion of the Cape Hawks depot was re-embarked during an enforced delay. The voyage from Kennedy Channel southward was difficult, tedious, and dangerous, but finally on September 9th both vessels reached the open sea, off Bache Island, and recrossed the Arctic circle October 4th.

This expedition, costing three-quarters of a million, commanded by an officer of Arctic experience,—one of the finest seamen in her Majesty's service,—composed of picked officers and men from the English Navy, fitted out under the advice of Arctic veterans, thoroughly and efficiently equipped, withstood the experiences and privations incident to Arctic life and explorations but a single year.

They had, however, explored Archer's Fiord, outlined the entire northern coast of Grinnell Land, added nearly a hundred miles to the Greenland coast, pushed an English vessel into the highest known latitude, and planted the Union Jack both on land and sea nearer the Pole than ever before. They brought back an elaborate set of tidal, magnetic, and meteorological observations, which are valuable contributions to the physical sciences. They charted Greenland and Grinnell Land with remarkable exactitude, and depicted the circumstances of their sufferings and experiences in narratives which are notable both for their modesty and accuracy.

My own experiences regarding Arctic service somewhat resemble those of Payer. He relates: "In the year 1868, while employed on the survey of the Orteler Alps, a newspaper with an account of Koldewey's first expedition one day found its way into my tent on the mountainside. In the evening I held forth on the North Pole to the herdsmen and *Jägers* of my party as we sat around the fire, no one filled with more astonishment than myself, that there should be men endued with such capacity to endure cold and darkness. No presentiment had I then that the very next year I should myself have joined an expedition to the North Pole; and as little could Haller, one of my *Jägers* at that time, foresee that he would accompany me on my third expedition."

Surprised, as all the world, at their return, I read one day in London that the Arctic squadron had reached the Irish coast, and with all England I was absorbed in the story they had to tell. It had then for me a deep, although impersonal, interest, but never in my wildest fancies did I picture myself as one of the *next* expedition which should sail northward between the "Pillars of Hercules" into the "Unknown Regions."

Godthaab, Greenland. International Station, 1882-83.
[*Farthest point reached by Davis*, 1585.]

CHAPTER II.

INTERNATIONAL CIRCUMPOLAR STATIONS.

THE establishment of the International Circumpolar Stations was due to the exertions of Lieutenant Charles Weyprecht, Austrian Navy. Weyprecht was born in Hesse-Darmstadt in 1838. Entering the Austrian Navy at eighteen, he was decorated and promoted for gallantry in the naval action of Lissa, July, 1866. Prevented by ill-health from serving in the German Polar Expedition of 1868, he began his Arctic career with Payer in 1871. That year, in the Isjbörn, he opened up Barentz Sea to future explorers, reaching, in his small sailing vessel, latitude 78° 45′ N., longitude 41° E., a point two and one-half degrees north of Nova Zembla.

In 1872, with Payer again as an associate, Weyprecht entered the Arctic circle in command of the Tegetthoff, which had been fitted out by the Austro-Hungarian Government, and Count Wilczek, for the purpose of Arctic exploration in the direction of the northeast passage. Beset the first day after leaving Nova Zembla in 76° 22′ N., the vessel drifted the ensuing year over three degrees northward to the southern shore of a new land. This new Arctic domain, Franz Josef Land, was partly explored by Lieutenant Julius Payer and found to extend at least from 80° to 83° N. and from 50° to 63° W.

Despairing of release from the pack, Weyprecht, after a second winter's imprisonment, abandoned the Tegetthoff, May 20, 1874, and conducted his party safely by sledge and boat to the west coast of Nova Zembla, where he fell in with Russian fishing-vessels. They reached Vardo September 3, 1874.

Undismayed by his hardships, but profiting by his experiences, Weyprecht, at the meeting of the German Scientific and Medical Association, at Gratz, in September, 1875, presented a plea for systematic polar exploration and research. He proposed that scientific investigations, heretofore subordinated to geographical discovery, be now made the primary object.

Insisting on the great importance of Arctic exploration to a better knowledge of the laws of nature, he pointed out that minute topography was comparatively unimportant, and that geographical discoveries were of marked value only when they extended the fields for scientific inquiry. Observation stations, he said, should be chosen, particularly with reference to the subject to be investigated, and the series of observations should be continuous and unbroken.

A Commission, comprising some of Germany's most eminent scientific men, was appointed by Prince Bismarck to consider the question. The Commission strongly commended the plan to the Bundesrath and to all interested nations. It expressed its convictions as to the great value of the work, and its opinion that the united action of several countries was essential to a complete solution of the problems involved.

In May, 1877, Count Wilczek and Weyprecht drew up a plan for the work, but the Turko-Russian war prevented the meeting of the International Meteorological Congress to which it was to be presented. The Congress finally met at Rome, April 22, 1879.

The Conference was of the "opinion that these observations will be of the highest importance in developing meteorology and in extending our knowledge of terrestrial magnetism." It recommended general participation, and called an International Polar Conference, which met at Hamburg, October 1, 1879. Eight countries sent delegates and three sent communications favoring the project. Dr. Neumayer was elected President. Twelve stations (four in the Antarctic regions) were agreed on, one of which was to be in the Archipelago of North America. Rules for obligatory and optional observations were formulated. An agreement was made that no nation should be bound until eight stations should be guaranteed.

The second Conference met at Berne, August 7, 1880, and Professor Wild was elected President, *vice* Neumayer resigned. Nine nations, Austria–Hungary, Denmark, France, Germany, Italy, Netherlands, Norway, Russia, and Sweden, sent delegates. The Conference adhered to its previous decision regarding the general principles and details of the plan. Sufficient progress had been made to justify the expectation of enough nations participating to ultimately make the scheme successful. Its execution, however, was deferred until 1882–83.

In the meantime, Captain Howgate, United States Army, had especially interested himself in Arctic matters, and in 1877 sent to Cumberland Gulf the schooner Florence with the view of collecting dogs, skin-clothing, etc., for a projected colony at

Lady Franklin Bay. Failing in his direct plan for a polar colony, Captain Howgate succeeded in having Lady Franklin Bay designated as the point in the Archipelago of North America which was to be occupied by the United States Signal Service as a polar station.

The importance of Lady Franklin Bay as a station was undeniable, as comparable observations in meteorology and magnetism would thus be obtained. Captain Howgate's indefatigable exertions finally resulted in the Act of Congress, approved May 1, 1880, which authorized the establishment of a temporary station at Lady Franklin Bay for scientific observation, etc., and provided for the acceptance and fitting out for such work of the steamship Gulnare, which he had purchased.

Lieutenants Greely, Doane, and Lowe, United States Army, were detailed for duty in this service, and Dr. Octave Pavy employed as surgeon. The expedition was to carry out the programme outlined by the Hamburg Polar Conference. The refusal of the Navy Department to accept the Gulnare for the work caused Lieutenant Greely to decline the command of the expedition, but the others proceeded to Disco, whence the Gulnare returned disabled leaving Dr. Pavy in Greenland.

Dr. Wild, President of the International Polar Commission, in September, 1880, informed the Chief Signal Officer that two stations were yet lacking—Point Barrow and "some point in the Archipelago of North America." The Sundry Civil Bill of March 3, 1881, appropriated $25,000 for the station at Lady Franklin Bay, already authorized by Congress. General W. B. Hazen had in the meantime become Chief Signal Officer, and, impressed with the scientific importance of the work and the propriety of the United States doing its part, not only took a personal and active interest in the international station of Lady

Arctic Regions, Showing Location of Circumpolar Stations, 1881-83.

INTERNATIONAL CIRCUMPOLAR STATIONS. 23

Franklin Bay, but also established independently the second station, in a much lower latitude, at Point Barrow.

Eventually fourteen stations were established as follows:

Government.	Station.	Latitude.	Longitude.	Chief.
Austria—Hungary	Jan Mayen,	70° 59' N.	8° 28' W.	Lieut. Emil von Wohlgemuth.
Denmark	Godthaab,	61° 11' N.	51° 40' W.	Asst. A. F. W. Paulsen.
Finland	Sodankyla,	67° 24' N.	26° 36' E.	Asst. E. Biese.
France	Orange Bay, Cape Horn,	55° 31' S.	70° 21' W.	Lieut. Courcelle-Seneuil.
Germany	Kingawa Fiord, Cumberland Sound,	66° 36' N.	67° 14' W.	Dr. W. Giese.
Germany	Royal Bay, S. Georgian Islands,	53° 31' S.	36° 5' W.	Dr. C. Schrader.
Great Britain and Canada	Ft. Rae,	62° 39' N.	115° 44' W.	Capt. H. P. Dawson, R.A.
Holland	Dicksonhaven,	73° 30' N.	81° E.	Dr. M. Snellen.
Norway	Bossekop,	69° 56' N.	23° E.	Asst. A. S. Steen.
Russia	Sagastyr Id., Lena R.,	73° 23' N.	126° 35' E.	Lieut. Jürgens.
Russia	Nova Zembla, Little Karmakuli,	*72° 30' N.	53° E.	Lieut. Andrejew.
Sweden	Spitzbergen,	78° 28' N.	15° 45' E.	Candidate N. Ekholm.
United States	Point Barrow,	71° 18' N.	156° 24' W.	Lieut. P. H. Ray, 8th Inf.
United States	Lady Franklin Bay,	81° 44' N.	64° 45' W.	Lieut. A. W. Greely, 5th Cav.

* Estimated.

To these stations should be added the Danish exploring steamer Dijmphna, Lieutenant A. P. Hovgaard, which, beset by the pack, wintered in the Kara Sea about 71° N., 64° E.

Many great observatories in lower latitudes co-operated with the Polar stations, and other important points were occupied, which raised the number of stations observing in concert to over forty. Among the auxiliary stations may be mentioned Pola, Munich, Utrecht, Moncalieri, Velletri, Peking, Tiflis, Pavlosk (St. Petersburg), Zi-ka-Wei (Shanghai), Taskend, Nertschinsk, Moscow, Coimbra, Los Angeles, Stonyhurst, Naples, Rio Janeiro, Bombay, and Upsala.

In the establishment and relief of these stations some seven hundred men incurred dangers incident to all Arctic service, but such has been the improvement in Arctic equipment that save in the case of the Lady Franklin Bay expedition no man perished.

The scientific work of each expedition was to a greater or lesser extent successful. Weyprecht died, but the work he planned was carried on and is finished. Progress in the development of physical sciences and the discovery of new laws largely proceeds from tentative efforts. The scientific work of these stations must be justly measured by the final result. Geodesy, meteorology, and magnetism may, or may not, profit as fully as sanguine advocates anticipated. Be that as it may the work of the International Polar Commission will live in history as a great one, if only as an epoch in modern civilization marked by the union of eleven great nations in planning and executing for strictly scientific purposes so extensive and dangerous a work.

Greenland Coast.
[*View near Godhavn.*]

CHAPTER III.

GREENLAND.

AN account of explorations in Smith Sound would be incomplete without a brief description of Greenland. Vague and indefinite ideas regarding that country prevail, even among intelligent classes, and many know it only as depicted in Heber's celebrated hymn.

The materials of this account have been drawn partly from the standard works of Crantz and Rink, although other authorities have been freely consulted.

The contour of Greenland is that of an irregular lozenge, over fourteen hundred miles long and some nine hundred miles wide. Its greatest width closely coincides with the 78th parallel, from Cape Bismarck, of Koldewey, westward to Cape Alexander. Cape Farewell at its southern extremity, seven degrees south of the Arctic circle, is nearly on the same meridian as Cape Washington, six degrees south of the Pole.

Greenland might well be called the glacial continent, as fully three-fourths of its known area are covered by an eternal ice-cap, known as the inland ice.

Much discussion has been had as to the real extent of this ice and the exact conditions of the interior of Greenland. Repeated attempts have been made to penetrate its frozen waste, none of which were very successful until 1883. Keilson in 1830 reached a point eighty miles from Holstenborg. Baron Nordenskiold, the most famous Arctic explorer of the age, in 1870, reached a point about twenty-two hundred feet above the sea, about 68° 22′ N., 49° W. "The inland ice continued to rise toward the interior," he says, "so that the horizon to the east, north, and south was terminated by an ice-border almost as smooth as that of the ocean." In 1883 Nordenskiold himself succeeded in reaching a point eighty miles from the edge of the ice, and his Lapps pushed on one hundred and thirty miles beyond, their farthest being about 69° 30′ N., 40° W. The ice, then over six thousand feet above the sea, still arose gradually toward the east, but no peaks were visible. The continent had been crossed more than half way to the east coast without any change in the ice-cap being noted, or its summit attained. The inland ice is of an unknown thickness, but Dr. Brown says from one thousand to three thousand feet is not uncommon.

The east coast swept by the Spitzbergen ice-stream is but little known, despite the fact that for over two centuries the sea that washes its shores was annually visited by adventurous whalers.* Steadily and continually an arctic current sets this

---

* Scoresby points out that Holland in one hundred and seven years fitted out over fourteen thousand ships for the Greenland whale fisheries, only four per centum of which were lost, and took from these seas oil and bone to the value of fifty-five million dollars. The same nation in sixty years drew from

ice-stream southward from the Polar Sea into the North Atlantic. In winter it is a solid pack covering the sea from Spitzbergen and Iceland to the Greenland coast. In summer, however, southerly winds, high temperatures, and the warm current to the north (discovered by Nordenskiold's expedition of 1883, to exist fifty miles off shore), loosens and disintegrates the pack, leaving along the shore an ice-belt varying from twenty to a hundred miles in width.

From the 70th parallel successive explorers have indeed outlined the coast as far northward as Cape Bismarck, latitude 77°, but to the southward it is a blank for over three hundred miles, until from Cape Dan we sight Graah's Islands, reached from the south by that energetic Dane on his fruitless search for the lost colonies.

This land is freer from the inland ice than the western coast, and its shores less frequently broken by intersecting inlets. It presents several remarkable fiords, one of which, Kaiser Franz Josef, vividly described by Payer, is among the grandest and most beautiful in the world. To the westward of this fiord Petermann's Peak, perhaps the only true mountain of Greenland, raises its head some eleven thousand feet toward the heavens.

Sixty years ago a few scattered Eskimo lived near the 75th parallel, but in 1870 Dr. Pansch found the huts desolate, their occupants vanished. Doubtless they had withdrawn toward Cape Farewell, near which, in 1861, Mr. Rosing reported the east coast natives as numbering from eight hundred to a thousand.

Nordenskiold who succeeded, August, 1883, in landing on that

---

the waters of Davis Strait wealth amounting to nearly thirteen million dollars. These incomplete figures may convey to the reader some faint idea of the solid contributions of the Arctic seas to the wealth of the world.

coast, discovered recent traces of Eskimo in King Oscar Harbor, just north of Cape Dan, about 66° N., a fact which shows that occasional parties yet frequent that vicinity, probably in search of game.

Danish Greenland covers the western coast from Cape Farewell nearly a thousand miles northward. Its northern Inspectorate is divided into seven, and the southern into five districts. Each portion is governed by a royal inspector as the representative of the King of Denmark. He has, to a certain extent, supervision of the officials of the Royal Trade, and acts in a magisterial capacity whenever necessary.

The Royal Trade monopoly was originally a private corporation, but was, in 1774, acquired by the Danish Government, of which it forms a special bureau known as the Royal Greenland Board of Trade. The chief stations, or "colonies," are generally in charge of an administrator, a chief trader, who is frequently called Governor by the whalers. The subordinate clerks, known as assistants or volunteers according to their grades, are placed in charge of smaller stations.

In the southern inspectorate the four most important districts, containing over half the population of Greenland, are without the Arctic circle. In these districts are several Moravian missions, established a century and a half ago. They were for a time as important as the missions in our own State of Pennsylvania, which then, strange as it may seem, constituted, with Greenland, a diocese, which was visited by the same bishop.

The face of the earth has changed, and now no Moravian missionary wends his way to Pennsylvania, bearing to its suffering proselytes sympathy and charity from the natives of Greenland. By a curious chance, however, commerce keeps up the connection, and the cryolite of Ivigtut finds its way through Philadelphia to the industries of the world.

The cryolite deposit at Ivigtut was discovered by Giesecké in 1806. A license to work it was granted in 1857, and in eighteen years, says Rink, eighty-four thousand tons were mined, for which Denmark received nearly $300,000 royalty.

Whalebone, oil, feathers, eider-down, skins of the seal, fox, bear, and reindeer, form the greater balance of the exports, aggregating annually, for all Greenland, $33,000 in value.

The coast line free from inland ice in this inspectorate averages perhaps sixty miles in width. Crowberries, bog, and red whortleberries are found in favorable localities. Copses of birches, alders, and willows prevail, the trees attaining occasionally a height of ten or twelve feet.

The chief colony, Godthaab, 62° 11' N., was one of the International Circumpolar Stations. Its population, including the adjacent mission, is nearly three hundred. It is the residence of the Royal Inspector of Southern Greenland; has a brick church, a seminary, and the usual houses for the Danish officials. A view of Godthaab is given on page 19.

New Herrnhut and Lichtenfels, the two Moravian communities, are represented by Rink as contrasting unfavorably with Godthaab. Of their population he says they "numbered 773 in 1855, 711 in 1860, and 538 in 1872. This striking decrease is not owing to any accidental cause, but merely to a prevailing mortality arising from the miserable condition of the natives belonging to these communities as regards their habitations, clothing, and whole mode of life." Rink's figures must be accepted, but his opinions can scarcely be considered conclusive regarding these missions of a religious faith differing from that of the Danish officials.

It is a matter of interest that the estimated population of the ancient Norse settlements — ten thousand souls — coincides closely with the population as given by Crantz a century and a half ago, and as determined by the Danish census of late years.

Numerous traces of the Norsemen are yet visible in this inspectorate in the shape of interesting ruins, eight of which are churches, the most remarkable being the Kakortok Church near Julianehaab.

The northern inspectorate is better known from the annual visits of whalers to Godhavn and Upernivik. At the former station, called Lievely by the English whalers, the Danish inspector resides. An excellent land-locked harbor insures security to visiting ships.

The inland ice, which in the southern part of this inspectorate retreats nearly a hundred miles from the outer shores, almost reaches the sea-coast in the extreme north, and debouches into ice-fiords at Jakobshavn and Upernivik. These remarkable fiords yearly send out hundreds of icebergs, many of which find their way into the Atlantic.

As might be supposed the Eskimo live principally by hunting and fishing. Seals, white whales, birds, and fish afford seven-eighths of their subsistence, the balance being bread, pease, and barley from the Trade.

The natives learn quickly the rudiments of a handicraft, and many find employment in government service. As neither industry nor commerce exists in Greenland, the only outlet for energy and ability, apart from hunting and fishing, is in the Royal Trade. About ten per centum gain a livelihood in government service, fifteen by fishing, and seventy-five by seal-hunting.

The seal, when caught, affords blubber and skin, which is sold to the Trade for the catchers' profit; but the flesh or meat is by force of public opinion almost common property from the obligation of the hunters to share with their neighbors. The money received for skin and blubber goes for coffee, bread, cotton goods, sugar, and tobacco in the order named. Intoxicating drinks are not sold. Although much relishing spirituous liquors the Greenlanders are not given to intoxication.

One-fifth the amount paid for articles sold to the Trade is held as a Poor Fund, which is distributed by a council composed of the missionary, a trade official, and certain elected representatives, only providers being eligible to the position. This council determines to whom and in what way aid shall be given, discriminating between the necessities springing from idleness and those from misfortune. The fund remaining undistributed each spring is divided among hunters and fishers who have not required assistance the previous season.

The naturally amiable qualities of the Eskimo have been fostered by the Christianizing influences of the Danish pastors and the Moravian missionaries. Religious and instructive books have been printed in Eskimo text, and a large portion of the natives read, although but few of them can write. In general they are devout, honest, truthful. Their vices are negative. A gentle folk, violence and theft are rarely known among them, and in twelve years but one murder, and that in passion. The municipal council investigate and punish offences, which are generally trivial, but they have no means of enforcing punishment, which is usually light, such as denial of trade privileges, which entails abstention from bread and coffee. Occasionally temporary expulsion from the settlement is decreed.

Marriages, christenings, and burials conform to Christian usages. Dancing and singing festivals are favorite amusements, and coffee parties are fashionable for birthdays and other anniversaries.

Two-thirds of the houses are miserable, partly underground

hovels, with no means of heating or cooking except the Eskimo lamp.

Men and women are alike clothed with jacket and trousers. The jacket is a hooded jumper with openings only for face and hands. The hood is enlarged when necessary so as to admit of

Arctic Belles.

an infant being carried inside against the woman's back. The women's trousers are very narrow and extend barely from hips to knees, so that a bit of white chemise is sometimes seen at the waist, and a portion of the naked thigh above the knee. Formerly the women's jumper had two flaps, and reached far below the hips, but fashion has changed all that. The outer clothing was once entirely of sealskin, but now the jumper is frequently of cotton cloth. The women's boots, of variegated white, red, and purple leather, are elaborately ornamented with fancy seams. Boots, trousers, and jumpers are sometimes trimmed with fancy fur.

The Eskimo boot is of smooth, well-tanned sealskin, which resists occasional immersion in water. The soles projecting at heel and toe are skilfully curved up and united to the uppers, in such a manner that no seam is found on a bearing surface.

The women gather their hair in tufts on the very top of the head, the central tuft rising an inch or two above the outer circlet. The size of the tuft is a matter of pride, and in tying the hair up gay ribbons are much in vogue, which by their color of red, yellow, or green betoken the woman's condition as maid, wife, or widow.

Although hard working and industrious on occasion, yet there is an almost universal spirit of improvidence. The paternal care of the Danish Government is the only thing which stands between the Eskimo and ultimate extinction. The Royal Trade indeed forbids free traffic, and purchases the result of the hunt at a nominal price, but when bad seasons come and starvation impends, the natives are fed at its expense. The charity of the officials, however, is not always effective in warding off starvation.

A famine in 1856–57, in Southern Greenland, caused by the failure of the seal catch, resulted in the death of a hundred and forty persons, owing to the impracticability of communicating with the supply stations.

The mean annual temperature of Southern Greenland (33°) is about the same as that of the Red River Valley in Dakota, but correspondingly low temperatures are not known, as $-50°$ has never been noted at any Greenland settlement. The climate resembles much that of Northern Norway.

The mean temperature at the northern stations rapidly decreases after crossing the Arctic circle, and at Upernivik is 13° for the year and −10.3° for February. The coldest month ever noted was −20.6° at Upernivik, January, 1874. The highest single temperature recorded was 68° and the lowest −47°. At Upernivik the extremes in the past ten years have been +59.7° and −39.6°.*

Upernivik.
[*The most northerly civilized settlement in the whole world.*]

It is not generally known that two ice-streams exist in Davis Strait, with a belt of open water between, the greater part of the year. The one on the American side carries the Baffin Bay ice steadily southward. That on the Greenland side is a narrow offshoot of the Spitzbergen ice-stream, which, rounding

---

* All temperatures given are in degrees Fahrenheit, except such as are marked C. for Centigrade.

Cape Farewell from the east coast, extends northward to the neighborhood of Godthaab. Ports to the southward of that place are reached only by passing to the northward of this stream. It is only after the Arctic circle is crossed that the open sea of Davis Strait is liable to be frozen over, and even then it is not a solid covering, but rather a cemented drifting pack which moves steadily southward, as shown by the drift of the Advance, the Fox, and the Polaris party.

Greenland, from Cape York northward, is treated of in other portions of this work, but to that point from the last Danish settlement, latitude 73° 24′, extends three hundred miles of unknown coast, probably covered by the inland ice to its very shore. This desolate region has, as far as we know, never been trodden by the foot of man, and its very outlines will doubtless remain unknown until among the Danes another adventurous Graah shall rise up, to search out and tell us the mysteries of that vacant land.

English Cairn, S. E. Cary Island, 1875.
[*Baffin discovered this island,* 1616.]

CHAPTER IV.

ORGANIZATION AND EQUIPMENT.

THE organization and equipment of the Lady Franklin Bay Expedition were accomplished under great disadvantages, arising not only from inadequate means, but from the avowed hostility to the work of the Cabinet chief, under whose charge it necessarily was. No friendly board of Arctic experts, with lavish funds at its command, assisted by its counsel and advice, but the preparation in this case devolved entirely on the commanding officer of the expedition. The detailed requisitions for food, clothing, and other supplies were prepared in seventy-two hours, and under stress of knowledge that the question of sending the expedition depended very largely on the character and quantity of supplies asked for. Although assigned to com-

ORGANIZATION AND EQUIPMENT. 37

mand March 11th, the whole matter was later held in abeyance by Mr. Lincoln, then Secretary of War, and until April 1st, despite the personal efforts of Senator Conger and the persistent labors of General Hazen, it was undecided if the expedition should go. The formal approval (General Order 35, War Department) was not issued until April 12th, barely two months prior to the departure of the main party.

The detailed orders as to the organization and duties of the Lady Franklin Bay Expedition appear elsewhere.

The plan contemplated the transportation of the expedition in a chartered vessel from St. John's, Newfoundland, to Lady Franklin Bay, where the party was to establish their quarters, the ship returning. A steamer was to visit the station annually with supplies and recruits. Several designated vessels were carefully inspected under directions from the Secretary of the Navy, and from those reported to be fit for the service the steamer Proteus was selected. She was a new (7 years old) barkentine-rigged steamer of oak, with two compound engines; 110 horsepower; 467 tons register; had an iron armed prow, and was sheathed with ironwood from above the water-line to below the turn of the bilge. She had been built for the sealing business under personal supervision of her owners, and conformed in all respects to the most approved methods of construction for use in heavy Arctic ice. Her screw was self-lifting, she had spare rudder and propeller, and was in every respect suitable for the projected work. Her master, Richard Pike, had for many years been engaged in the dangerous seal-fishery of the Labrador ice, and was one of the most experienced captains and ice-navigators of Newfoundland. His crew were selected men from the hardy fishermen of that island. The charter of this vessel consumed over three-fourths of the appropriation, leaving less than six thousand dollars for the special outfit of the party.

This small sum was economically spent for our supply of coal, scientific instruments, boats, dogs, dog-food, special woollen and fur clothing, pemmican, lime-juice, spirits, special articles of diet, natural history supplies, table and household equipage, etc. Nothing was purchased except after most careful consideration as to its necessity and cost. In consequence many very desirable articles were omitted, and in all cases the supply reduced to a minimum. The War Department declined to facilitate or make special the requisition for the appropriation, which was not available, in any event, until July 1st. In consequence, rather than abandon the undertaking, it became necessary at the last moment to guarantee many bills for special articles purchased. For friendly services in this as in other important respects, both the expedition and myself were under special obligations to Major Charles Appleby, of New York.

The various bureaus of the War Department furnished excellent arms and ammunition, clothing, and camp equipage (army pattern only), hospital stores, and the usual field supply of medicines. Ample subsistence stores, of superior quality, were furnished on requisition for sale to officers and men.

Lieutenant Kislingbury and two men left New York, May 31st, to supervise the stowing of cargo. On June 14th the main party, under command of Lieutenant James B. Lockwood, sailed from Baltimore for St. John's on the steamer Nova Scotian.

Professor Daniel C. Gilman, President of Johns Hopkins University, took a decided interest in this scientific work of international importance. His desire to evidence this in some public manner, in conjunction with other prominent Baltimoreans, was thoroughly appreciated. The early hour of sailing, and the limited time the party could remain in Baltimore, were cogent reasons why his kindly thought assumed no tangible form.

MEMBERS OF LADY FRANKLIN BAY EXPEDITION, 1881. (*From a photograph by Rice.*)

Whisler.　Ellis.　Bender.　Cross.　Frederick.　Lynn.　Biederbick.　Henry.　Long.　Ralston.　Salor.　Dr. Pavy.　Gardner.　Ellison.
Connell.　　　Brainard.　　　Lt. Kislingbury.　　　Lt. Greely.　　　Lt. Lockwood.　　　Israel.　　　Jewell.　　　Rice.

I had hoped to sail from St. John's, Newfoundland, July 1st, but the condition of affairs was such on my arrival at that point, on June 27th, as to render it impossible. Certain essential supplies had not arrived, and the stores on board the Proteus were in endless confusion. The Secretary of the Navy had kindly furnished a small steam-launch, but its boiler proved entirely unsuitable for salt-water, and had to be replaced at St. John's. Such results necessarily flowed from a policy which rendered it obligatory to perfect in two months and a half the outfitting of a party destined for over two years' separation from the rest of the world. Though succeeding experiences proved that no article really essential to health or success was wanting, yet other results might have easily followed, and certain deficiences did occur which, in longer time, could have been remedied to our later pleasure and comfort.

As to the members of the expedition, it is hardly necessary to remark that all were highly recommended, passed a strict medical examination, and were volunteers. Lieutenant Kislingbury, in a service of over fifteen years, had a fine reputation for field duty. Lieutenant Lockwood had served eight years, almost always on the frontier, and was highly recommended as an officer of sterling merit and varied attainments.

Edward Israel and George W. Rice, in order to accompany the expedition, cheerfully accepted service as enlisted men. The former, a graduate of Ann Arbor University, went in his chosen profession as astronomer, while the latter, a professional photographer, hoped to add to his reputation in that art by service with the expedition. Sergeants Jewell and Ralston had served long and faithfully as meteorological observers; while Gardiner, though of younger service, was most promising. Long and hazardous duty on the Western frontier had inured the greater part of the men to dangers, hardships, and exposure, and developed in them that quality of helpfulness so essential in Arctic service.

On July 4th, with all on board, the Proteus dropped to anchor off Queen's wharf, awaiting the final supplies. They came on the 7th, and at noon of that day we passed the majestic cliffs which form the narrows of St. John's, and turned our prow toward Greenland with fine weather, blue sky, and favoring wind.

There was a touch of sadness mingled with our exultation; for, while we sped on to the icy north, not only were loving hearts left behind us in the sunny south, but our great nation with bated breath was watching over its dying chief.

CHAPTER V.

THE VOYAGE TO UPERNIVIK.—July, 1881.

BONAVISTA with its shining light was passed the evening of the 7th, from which point we hoped—and not in vain—to be reported. A few scattered icebergs were seen between Funk Island and the straits of Belle Isle, the lingering remnants of the enormous ice-fields which cover the Newfoundland waters during the spring months.

Northwesterly gales and thick weather delayed us, but on the 13th we were in Davis Strait off Frederickshaab, where the first ice was encountered. The pack was a loose one and consisted of two streams of ice from ten to thirty miles wide, which in no way impeded the ship's progress. These floes were offshoots of the great Spitzbergen ice-stream which, drifting down the coast of East Greenland, are set along the west shore by the prevailing northerly current. The greater part of the ice ranged from three to five feet above the water, and almost without exception each piece was deeply grooved at the water's edge, evidently by the action of the waves. Above and below the surface of the sea projected long tongue-like edges. The novel and fascinating scene engaged the attention of all.

The advancing and receding waves along the tongues of ice continually changed their aspect, and gave forth colors which resolved themselves into indescribable hues of great beauty. The most delicate tints of blue mingled quickly and indistinguishably into those of rare light green, to be succeeded later as the water receded from the floe's side, by shades of bluish white. Occasional floes were twelve or fifteen feet high and in these at times the level surfaces gave way to pinnacles or hummocks.

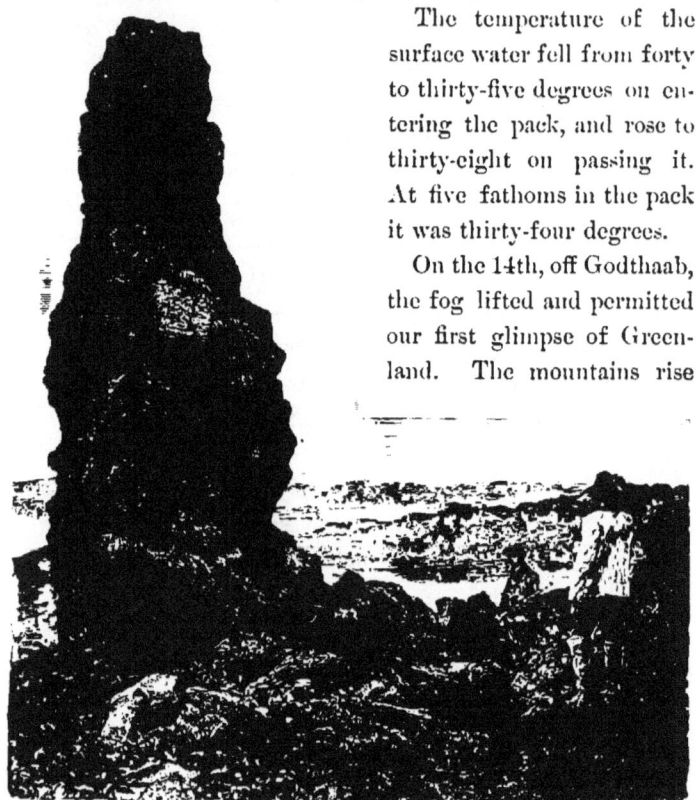

The temperature of the surface water fell from forty to thirty-five degrees on entering the pack, and rose to thirty-eight on passing it. At five fathoms in the pack it was thirty-four degrees.

On the 14th, off Godthaab, the fog lifted and permitted our first glimpse of Greenland. The mountains rise

Natural Monument near Godhavn. (From a Photograph.)

some three thousand feet, displaying their glacial garb as a fitting border to the desolate coast in the foreground.

The northerly gale broke sufficiently on the 14th to afford glimpses of the sun, and our noonday observation—the first of the voyage—placed us within the Arctic circle. The bleak highlands of Disco were hidden by an Arctic fog, and only disclosed themselves, after hours of tedious waiting on the evening of the 15th, when we found ourselves but a few miles from Godhavn. The south coast of Disco Island rises precipitously some twenty-five hundred feet out of the sea, and in some seventy miles it breaks only at Godhavn, to form a secure and land-locked harbor. The entrance is so hidden, however, that in making it one seems to be beaching the vessel, until an abrupt turn leads to the tranquil cove in front of the very settlement.

As we entered, a small gun belched forth a salute, and the Danish flag was displayed from the station's flagstaff. Our vessel was hardly anchored when a kindly gentleman, evidently of Scandinavian origin, boarded it, and in good English bade us welcome to Disco. It was Herr Krarup Smith, the Royal Inspector of North Greenland, an official of unvarying courtesy, whose helpful kindness and advice was always at the command of whaler or explorer. His death in May, 1882, created a void in Northern Greenland which it will be difficult to fill.

Inspector Smith was about leaving for his annual tour of inspection to Upernivik, on the Danish brig which lay in the harbor. He delayed his departure a day that he might extend to the expedition all possible assistance.

The usual visits of ceremony were duly made, and later the officers of the party dined with Mrs. Smith. The dinner was a surprise to us all, as we expected but little variety in that part of the globe. A tiny bouquet of cultivated flowers for each, first greeted our vision. The principal dishes were fresh Greenland salmon of delicate flavor, larded eider-ducks, and tender Arctic ptarmigan; all served with excellent wines.

Regarding vegetables, it should be said that, except radishes, lettuce, etc., they are imported canned, as they will not grow at

Godhavn. There was no fresh meat there except a little which we were able to spare. Reindeer (which formerly roamed over Disco alone of the Greenland islands) is the favorite meat with Europeans, though many relish seal meat. The latter, though tender and juicy, has a slightly sweetish taste, which is as unpalatable to some as its coarse, dark meat is unpleasing to the eye. It can be recommended, however, as very nutritious.

At Godhavn it is a case of the mountain and the sea, for as you turn your back to Disco Bay the cliffs spring over two thousand feet out of the very water. The upper half, a dark beetling precipice, impresses one equally by its grandeur and desolation. The lower half is clothed more or less with vegetation, and at one point a break in the cliff leaves a sloping valley, through which glides a sparkling brook, which from above plunges wildly down its bed of rugged rock. This brook hardly seems an Arctic one, as its banks and borders are covered with a vegetation which would be luxuriant even in lower latitudes. The valley is called the "heath-field," and the visitor well believes the statement that it is the best botanical spot of Greenland, and that over forty varieties of plants can there be gathered.

The surroundings of Godhavn are striking and impressive. The settlement itself is situated on a small syenite island, which is sparsely covered with soil and vegetation. Its highest point is of scarcely a hundred feet elevation, but so numerous were the icebergs on that July day, that from it more than a hundred could be counted at once.

These huge masses of castellated ice broke with their snowy whiteness the monotony of the sea, and as they drifted past, drew after them unceasingly our thoughts and attention. In general, these white-winged ships were silent messengers of peace, but in entering the harbor our gentle swell struck lazily and softly a beautiful berg of lofty arches, slender pinnacles, and stately colonnades, down the sides of which miniature torrents poured. It needed but this slight impulse to destroy its equilibrium, and in an instant it burst into countless fragments which whitened the sea with foam, and rolled huge billows in all directions. The thundering report startled us all, and the resistless force shown by this mountain of ice inspired the least impressive with feelings of awe.

The external aspects of the colony of Godhavn represent well the principal trading stations of Greenland. The few dwelling-houses for the Danish officials are commonly wooden structures with thick walls of rough hewn logs, which insure thorough dryness and sufficient warmth. The dark tarred walls are relieved by white or red window-casings, and generally the roof has a reddish tinge quite in consonance with the predominating color of the adjacent rock-masses. It is perhaps needless to say that the interiors of these houses are Danish homes, and that in some of them one would not know, save from the trim, neatly-dressed Eskimo servants, that it was Greenland and not Denmark. Several of the latest books lay on the table at Inspector Smith's, and we were favored with piano accompaniments for many songs, from The Star Spangled Banner to Denmark's national anthem. A neat church with spire and bell, the indispensable trade storehouses, with workshops and oil manufactory, conclude the list of Government buildings.

The Eskimo houses are, as a rule, very poor, generally stone and turf structures lined with wood, and provided with the usual wooden, raised platform, serving as a bench by day and for a bed at night. The better class of houses replace the flat roof of dirt and turf by a sloping one of wood, and, besides adding a wooden floor, substitute glass for the old membranous panes from the intestines of the seal.

One rarely can stand erect in a house, and the odors peculiar to the universal Eskimo lamp, united to others, are hardly less trying within, than are the strong-smelling heaps of refuse without, the doors. A cursory view of their interiors was enough for me, and it seems strange that the enforced conditions, under which the inmates of these densely-crowded huts pass the long Arctic winter, do not cause greater ravages by disease.

A very short visit to an Eskimo dance, which was given in honor of our arrival, was sufficient to convince me that the natives understand how to enjoy such gatherings, but did not awaken any inclination to participate therein, though others of the expedition thought otherwise. In Greenland as elsewhere, *chacun à son goût.*

On landing you are at once impressed with the number and character of the dogs. The dog is an important animal in Northern Greenland, and he seems to know his vantage. He looks on every stranger as an enemy, who must be watched and harassed. They are annoying only on their own domain, and are experts in those false attacks which are trying to one's temper and dignity.

It is amusing, when not personally interested, to note how suddenly a snarling, yelling pack, snapping at one's heels, will turn and flee when they near the ground of some other king. He is a rare dog, indeed, who dares travel alone through the entire village of Godhavn. A stick or stone generally quiets a pack, but occasionally, when very harshly treated, and when long starved they are dangerous to children, and even, though very rarely, to men.

Our team purchased at Godhavn were stout, surly animals of apparently incurable viciousness, which, as we shall see later, completely vanished under the benign influences of kind treatment and good food.

Twelve dogs with a supply of dog-food were purchased, and the house and pemmican, stored there by the unfortunate Howgate expedition of 1880, were taken on board.

On July 20th Dr. Octave Pavy arrived from Ritenbenk, where he had passed the preceding year as naturalist of the Howgate expedition. He was contracted with as an acting assistant surgeon of the army for duty with the expedition, and took the oath of service that day.

The last hours at Godhavn were given to our mail, as two days later a Danish brig was to sail from Egedesminde, which should convey to our friends by the end of August full news of our safe arrival in Greenland. A few hours' steaming on the morning of July 21st, took us along the bold, high coast of Disco Island to the entrance of Waigat Strait. Along this coast for fifty miles to the eastward no shelter exists for vessels, and for over five miles from Godhavn, the most active mountaineer would search in vain for a foothold to scale its precipitous cliffs.

Our passage was a charming one with frowning barren crags to our left, and to our right the smooth blue sea, dotted with countless bergs of endless variety, bright and beautiful under Arctic sunshine. But "by and by a cloud took all away," for a dense Arctic fog shut quickly down, and made it difficult for our sharp-eyed Innuit pilot to guide the Proteus safely to anchorage in the narrow deep fiord which separates Ritenbenk from Arveprins Island.

The governor bore a name well known in connection with Greenland, Mörch. Half Dane, half Eskimo, a man of refinement and sentiment, he had been educated in the mother country, and had come to do service in his native clime. He made us at home in Ritenbenk, and greeted us with genuine Scandinavian hospitality. The same old Danish brig, Tialfe, which

Hayes found at Upernivik in 1860, was in the harbor, and we dined with the governor and her officers that evening. At the end of the meal the old Scandinavian custom of grace, by universal handshaking and the salutation, "Much good may it do you," first fell under my notice.

A number of dogs, with additional food and other supplies, were obtained at Ritenbenk. The new-comers were not at all welcomed by the old dogs, and a series of battles commenced which never ended to the very day of our retreat.

Mr. Henry Clay joined the expedition at Ritenbenk, as a military employé at a nominal salary. The grandson of Henry Clay the great commoner, a cultivated, refined gentleman, and an ardent sportsman, he had become thoroughly imbued with a longing for Arctic experiences. He had joined the Howgate expedition of 1880, and also obtained authority to accompany the present one, and, to fit himself for some part of the work, he had spent the preceding year with Dr. Pavy in Greenland.

While stores were being purchased, dogs brought on board, and accounts adjusted, and as the fog still held, I sent Lieutenant Lockwood with a boat's crew to the loomery on Arveprins Island for birds. They were only moderately successful, owing to the height of the lower ledges above the sea, and brought back but sixty-five Bruennich's guillemots (*Alca arra*), which were simply drawn, and hung up in the rigging to dry for future food.

The bird cliffs on Arveprins Island deserve a passing notice, not for Arctic travellers, but for the general reader.

For over a thousand feet out of the sea these cliffs rise perpendicularly, broken only by narrow ledges, in general inaccessible to man or other enemy, which afford certain kinds of seafowl secure and convenient breeding-places. On the face of these sea-ledges of Arveprins Island Bruennich's guillemots, or looms, gather in the breeding season, not by thousands, but by tens of thousands. Each lays but a single gray egg, speckled with brown, yet so numerous are the birds, that every available spot is covered with eggs. The surprising part is that each bird knows its own egg, although there is no nest and it rests on the bare rock. Occasional quarrels over an egg generally result in a score of others being rolled into the sea.

The clumsy, short-winged birds fall an easy prey to the sportsman, provided the cliffs are not too high, but many fall on lower inaccessible ledges and so uselessly perish. A single shot brings out thousands on the wing, and the unpleasant cackling, which is continuous when undisturbed, becomes a deafening clamor when they are hunted.

The eggs are very palatable. The flesh is excellent; to my taste, the best flavored of any Arctic sea-fowl, but, to avoid the slightly train-oil taste, it is necessary to keep the bird to ripen, and to carefully skin it before cooking. The looms obtained on Arveprins Island and Sanderson's Hope were a great addition to our table the following spring.

The little auk (*Mergellus alle*) and the dovekie (*Uria grylle*) similarly breed in large numbers farther north, and generally the fulmar (*Procellaria glacialis*) and glaucous gull (*Larus glaucus*) resort for nesting to like cliffs.

If you go to Ritenbenk, you must see the garden, the most famous in Northern Greenland. It is a small plot, scarcely fifty feet by forty, surrounded by a substantial fence to keep out the ubiquitous dog, and on one side has a miniature garden-house with sashed windows, where the governor sits and enjoys the growing vegetables, which comprise lettuce, onions, radishes, parsley, and turnips. The soil was in large part originally brought from Denmark, and has been supplemented by earth from old Greenland houses, and so is rich and strong. This bright spot of green contrasted most delightfully with the bleak, brownish syenite of the otherwise barren island.

It gave me much pleasure, sitting awhile in the summer-house, to listen to the good governor and enjoy the grand scenery, while I heard, in answer to an idle question, that an old Eskimo over the mountain toward Umanak had a dozen hens, which laid eggs a part of the year, and which he traded only for schnapps.

The snowy peaks of Kangek half-veiled in curling clouds the lovely blue of Disco Bay, and the countless icebergs ever drifting southward from the ice-fiords near, pleased the eye, while the torrents of Arveprins Island plunging into the sea made music for the ear. It seems now to me the most idyllic of my Arctic experiences.

Ritenbenk was founded in 1755. It is situated on a small island of the same name, which lies to the eastward of the more important Arveprins Island, from which it is separated by a narrow, deep fiord. The scenery around it was truly grand. In general bordering the shores are steep cliffs, broken by sharp, narrow ravines, all deeply scored by the impetuous Arctic torrents which throughout the short summer rush headlong into the fiord.

Opposite to Ritenbenk the twin peaks of Kangek Mountain raise their heads over two thousand feet above the sea, and afford views of unequalled magnificence.

To the northeastward a clear and beautiful prospect is had of the Torsukatak ice-fiord (one of the five remarkable fiords of Greenland), from which, at a moderate estimate, five million cubic yards of ice is discharged *daily*. High land to the southward prevents a view of the ice-fiord of Jacobshavn (which discharges more than double the amount of Torsukatak), but the entrance to it can be noted. This fiord is interesting, not only

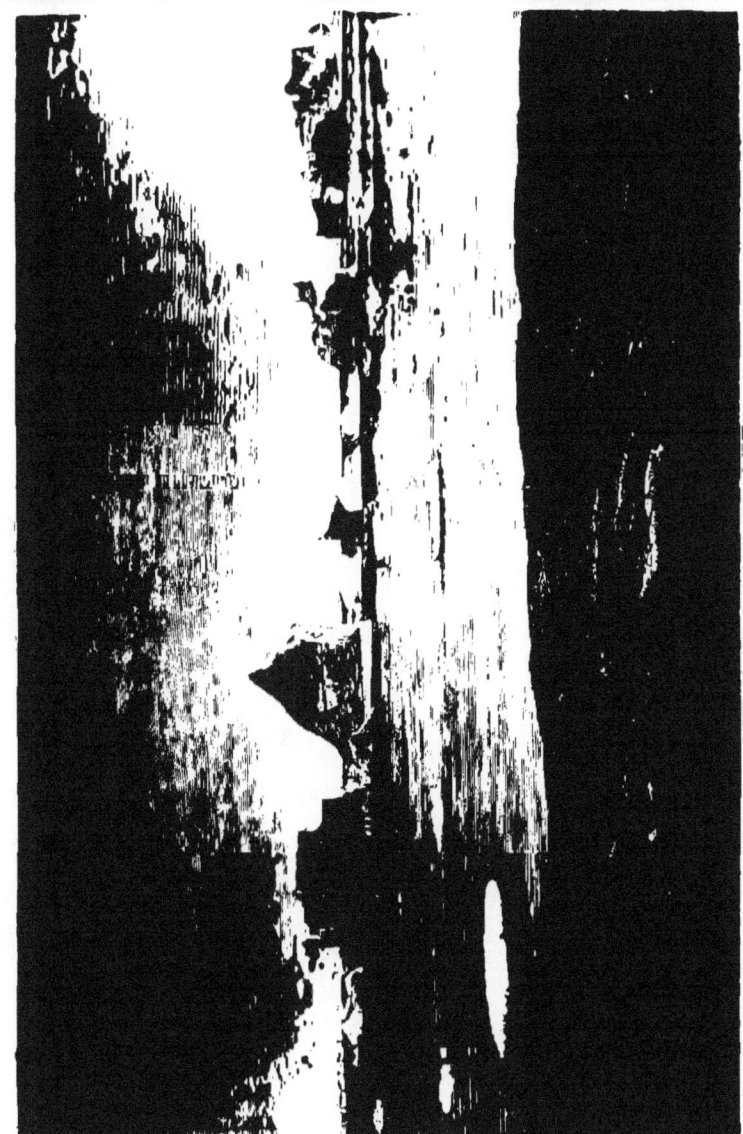

ICEBERGS IN DISCO BAY.
(From a photograph.)

as the most remarkable ice-fiord, with its central glacier point advancing over sixty feet into the sea daily, but as having for many years been thought to be the entrance to a strait, which was believed to extend to the east coast, and to divide Greenland into two parts.

From Ritenbenk we steamed slowly northward through the Waigat Strait, which separates Disco Island from the mainland. Low clouds covered in many places the high land, which on either hand rose from three to four thousand feet in precipitous heights, which generally reached the very sea on the island, but which were abutted on the main-land by frequent, gentle slopes, covered by pleasing verdure. Along the Disco coast are a number of coal-mines, which have been known a century and a half, but which are rarely worked. The coal answers indifferently for steaming purposes, but is excellent fuel for general use; many expeditions have used more or less of it.

The main-land along the Waigat is the Noursuak Peninsula, an extensive land, far from the inland ice, drained by one of the largest rivers in Greenland, and clothed with a vegetation of remarkable luxuriance. Near its extremity is the most northerly remains which are from other than Eskimo hands, a remarkable ruin, usually called the Bear Trap.

We were not ill-pleased to sight Hare Island, and enter the free sea of Baffin Bay, just as strong wind and rain came. The navigation of the Waigat is extremely dangerous in foggy and stormy weather, owing to the thousands of icebergs which are ever present in its waters.

Occasionally the clouds broke, and afforded fine views of the rugged, rock-bound coast, which is of the most precipitous character. Though much pleased with Svarte Huk, yet our interest centred in Sanderson's Hope, that beautiful, commanding headland, which was sighted by John Davis three centuries ago. The capriciousness of an Arctic summer cut off by its fog all view above that point, and we lay many tedious hours off Upernivik until a favoring wind rolled back the curtain, and allowed our native pilot to show us the safe way into the wretched cove which is called a harbor.

Our first experience was a heavy squall, in connection with a touch of the Greenland *Foehn*, which caused the chafing and subsequent breaking of one of the hawsers, and the Proteus drifted against a rock, from which she swung free without damage, through Captain Pike's prompt measures.

The first American soldier enlisted in Greenland was doubtless Private Maurice Connell of the expedition, who was discharged by expiration of term of service, and re-enlisted at Upernivik.

Inspector Smith had arrived before us, and had interested himself in the supplies wanted. It was found that only ten suits of clothing, made to order for the expected Danish international station, could be procured, and that boots, which we much needed, could only be had by a week's delay.

The two Eskimo dog-drivers were lacking, but two men at Proven were highly recommended, and I decided to send for them. As Proven was some fifty miles to the south, it was necessary to put the launch Lady Greely (as Lieutenant Lockwood has christened her) into the water. A severe westerly gale prevented sailing on the 25th, but the next day, before the storm had subsided, Lieutenant Lockwood started, accompanied by Governor Elberg. They took the inside passage, between the islands and main-land, but it was necessary at one point to venture into the open sea. Lieutenant Lockwood returned on the 28th, bringing two Eskimo, Thorlip Frederik Christiansen, aged thirty-five, and Jens Edward, aged thirty-eight. These men were contracted with, and joined the expedition the same day, bringing with them their kayaks and hunting implements. They ever proved themselves faithful, industrious, honest, and truthful, as Inspector Smith pledged they would.

Lieutenant Lockwood obtained a considerable quantity of skin clothing at Proven, and Sergeant Rice made several photographs. On the return trip, a few hours' delay at Sanderson's

Sergeant Rice and Greenland Eskimo. (From a Photograph.)

Hope resulted in the addition of one hundred and twenty-seven birds to our larder; guillemots (Bruennich's) and little auks (*Mergullus alle*). Lieutenant Kislingbury, at the same loomery, had also obtained three hundred and five auks and guillemots. An Eskimo who accompanied Lieutenant Kislingbury's party with his kayak while picking up birds capsized, and not handling his double-ended paddle with sufficient skill to recover himself, would have perished but for assistance from the whale-boat, which was promptly rendered by Sergeants Brainard and Connell.

During these days I had an opportunity of seeing Upernivik and its surroundings. The name in Eskimo means spring; but, although Inspector Smith told me that in fourteen years it had not before been so green, it did not present an attractive appearance. The island, though not very rocky, yet had a barren, desolate look, with but few spots of scanty vege-

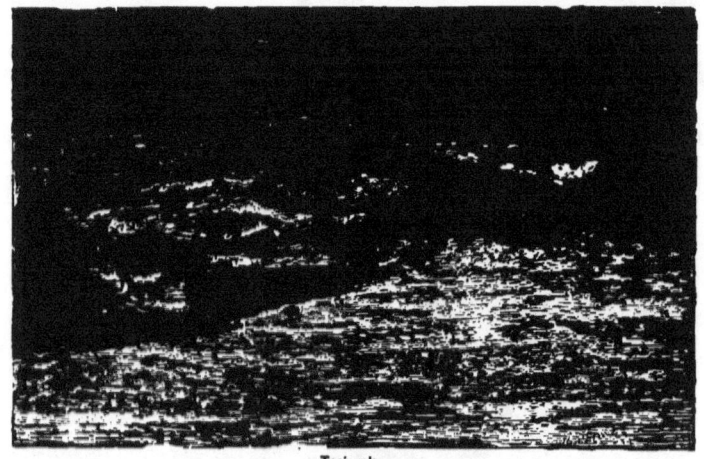

Tasiusak.
[*The most Northerly Settlement of Danish Eskimo.*]

tation. From the highest ground there is a view of Augpadlarsok ice-fiord, which claimed my daily attention. The fiord sends out thousands of icebergs yearly, and its glacier front is a sight to be long remembered.

To the northward the projecting, rugged coast cut off the view of Tasiusak, the most northerly of the settlements of the Danish Eskimo, a dreary spot difficult of access and rarely visited.

Governor Elberg showed much courtesy to the expedition,

but his greed for gain appeared to have overcome that sense of honesty which is so general in Danish Greenland. His prices for supplies were very high, and his sale of infected dogs caused the loss of the greater part of my draught animals, and later seriously affected our geographical success. I suspected disease from a dog hung up by the neck, but its existence was denied by him.

The usual Greenland hospitality was shown us at Upernivik, not only by Inspector Smith and Governor Elberg, but also by the gentle, kindly-hearted Danish priest and his good wife. Greenland hospitality is most frequently shown in what seems to be the only possible way in that remote country—by the proffer of every variety of wine or liquor in the larder, and in urging a most indiscriminate participation of them. It requires much tact, judgment, and discretion to avoid giving offence by refusing, but at the same time, to escape unpleasant consequences, it is sometimes necessary to do so.

At last the unruly dogs were on board, the bewildering accounts with Danish values adjusted and settled, the winding channels to the westward between rocky islets and sunken ledges safely passed, the final farewells and hearty God-speeds uttered, and with high hopes and strong courage we left Upernivik and civilization behind, to adventure the dangers of the high north.

CHAPTER VI.

MELVILLE BAY TO FORT CONGER.

WE ran northward until Berry Islands were sighted, and, noting the entire absence of ice, other than the numerous bergs from Augpadlarsok fiord, I ordered that a direct course be laid for Cape York, believing that the "middle passage" would be both practicable and safe at that late season of the year, especially as the spring and summer had been so unusually warm. The ship was running at full speed in an iceless sea as I went to rest at midnight. It should be remembered that we had long been in the region of perpetual daylight, if not sunlight; for, though the sun sets not in the far north, yet the prevalent Arctic fog hides his face for days at a time.

Our run on July 31st was through an open sea, in which no semblance of a pack was noted until about 5 P.M. It then consisted of small pieces of pancake ice, which would in no way interfere with the progress of any steaming vessel; it was scarcely three miles long, and barely reached a mile or two to the westward.

As we were passing the northern edge of this pack, a Polar bear was descried on a small piece of pan-ice. He was busily engaged in eating a young seal which he had just caught, and apparently did not notice the vessel until it was within a half mile of him. He ran a few yards from the seal, but later returned to it, and, strangely enough, seemed much disinclined to leave the ice for the water, returning to the floe after a temporary plunge. A large number of shots were fired at him from the vessel, one or more of which seemed to strike him. The Proteus was stopped and a boat lowered, in which Lieutenants Kislingbury and Lockwood, with one or two others, effected his capture. He was killed by a bullet, probably from Lieutenant Kislingbury's rifle, but for many days there were long and unsatisfactory discussions as to whom should be awarded the credit for his death.

Our bear was a young one, seven feet six inches long, and probably of some six hundred pounds weight. His flesh was quite palatable, more so, it was generally considered, than that of the cinnamon of our own country. He was photographed by Sergeant Rice, and skinned by the Eskimo.

No further ice was met with, and at 4 P.M. of the 31st the mate and quartermaster, through a break in the light fog, sighted land, which must have been the high cliffs of Cape York. The fog grew denser, instead of breaking as we hoped, and obliged the vessel to run at half speed until 8 A.M., when the speed was reduced to steerage-way, as the dead reckoning put us in the neighborhood of Cape York. Later the fog broke for a few moments, and showed land some five miles to the northward, but closed again before it could be identified. We were obliged to remain under steerage-way during the rest of the day, and scarcely ran more than twenty miles.

The remarkably open condition of Melville Bay had enabled

us to make an unprecedentedly rapid crossing, but thirty-six hours' time being occupied in its passage.

The ice of Melville Bay is justly dreaded, but in latter years, steam, experience and modern equipment have done much to insure the safety of its regular navigators, the hardy whalers, who brave its dangers at the earliest moment, and under the most unfavorable conditions. For years their vessels have been boldly pushed into the ice in May, and at least two sea-

Cape York.

sons have seen them in the "North Water," near Cape York, as early as June 3d.

Discovery- and relief-ships have hazarded nearly sixty times the perils of ice-navigation within its limits, and invariably without loss of life or vessel. This immunity from disaster has arisen from their usual practice of attempting the passage of Melville Bay much later than the whalers,—at a time when navigation is substantially safe,—in July or August. Except the Relief Squadron of 1884, and McClintock in the Fox, I recall no vessels of that class which have entered its ice in June.

During the day and evening the compasses unfortunately gave

us much trouble, being very sluggish, and consequently unreliable.

Several soundings, from six to eight miles west and southwest of Cape York, gave no bottom at one hundred and eighty-five fathoms. A layer of warm water was found between the surface and the greater depth, the temperature of the surface varying from 33.2° to 35°; at five fathoms, 35.7° to 36.7°; and at one hundred and eighty-fathoms, 31.5°.

A young male square-flipper seal (*Phoca barbata*) was killed on a detached ice-floe during the day.

On the morning of August 1st the fog lifted, and the vessel's position was found to be about twenty miles southwest of Petowik glacier, which lies just northward of "The Crimson Cliffs" of Sir John Ross. A sounding thirteen miles west of the glacier gave rocky bottom at one hundred and ten fathoms, and a temperature of 35° at surface and five fathoms, which remained steady as we ran inward and obtained a second sounding, with mud bottom at seventy-two fathoms, two miles off the glacier front. The heavy sea prevented successful photographing of the glacier.

Some patches of snow of a dirty reddish color were observed from the Petowik glacier northward toward Wolstenholme Island, being without doubt drifts of the famous red snow, first discovered by Sir John Ross, in 1818. Though desirous of obtaining specimens of *Protococcus nivalis*, which gives the color to this snow, I was unwilling to land for that purpose alone. The vegetable character of this phenomena has been quite clearly settled by Dr. Robert Brown.

At 10.15 A.M. we were off Wolstenholme Island, and at 1 P.M. left it behind, as we laid our course for the Cary group.

Icebergs, which were rare in the neighborhood of Cape York, were found to be very numerous near the northern end of Wolstenholme Island, and in one of these a large spot of the deepest and most exquisite blue was seen, which contrasted finely with the bluish-white of the main berg, and was sufficiently marked to remain visible for nearly an hour.

The Cary Islands were sighted at 3 P.M., and about two hours later the Proteus stopped at the north end of the southeast island of the group. To the southward of this island, at least thirty large icebergs were seen, evidently grounded, but elsewhere there was scarcely a particle of ice in sight.

Lieutenant Kislingbury and Dr. Pavy examined the cairn erected by Sir George Nares in 1875, and visited by Sir Allen Young in the Pandora (afterward the Jeanette) later that year and again in 1876. The records left by the latter officer were found in good condition, wrapped in a number of the London *Graphic*. A copy of these records was left, and a short note was also deposited, giving a brief account of our visit to the island, for the information of our successors.

The enthusiastic photographer of the expedition, assisted by some of the men, succeeded with great difficulty in transporting his apparatus to the summit of the island, which is some five hundred feet above the sea, and obtained a photograph of the cairn. The island is so rough in general that it is with some trouble that an unencumbered man can ascend the greater part of its cliffs. Vegetation was exceedingly scanty.

The depot of thirty-six hundred rations, left by Sir George Nares in 1875, was found in a small cove at the southern point of the island. The supplies were located on a rocky shoulder, some thirty feet above the sea, which commanded Baffin Bay to the southwestward. The depot was in quite good condition, excepting a certain portion of the bread, which was found to be somewhat mouldy, though still eatable. The bread which was bad was in casks which had been left with the head upward, while that in the barrels, which were on their sides, appeared to be in perfect condition. The cans of Australian beef were laid in rows on the surface of the bare rock, so that they had been alternately exposed to the direct heat of the summer sun and subjected to intense winter cold from radiation. Notwithstanding this severe trial, the cans of meat tested were in good condition—strong proof of their original good quality.

It would seem advisable that caches of such kind should be at least covered, so as to avoid both direct sun and intense cold. Thus protected they would longer remain serviceable.

The whale-boat was carefully examined, and found to be in serviceable condition, despite the long time it had been cached.

Quite a number of pieces of drift-wood were found upon the western shore of the island, among which were a worn but still serviceable oar, and a charred piece of the ornamental work of a ship. I am informed that the whaler Xanthus was burned the previous year just north of Tasiusak. It is probable that the burnt wood was from the Xanthus, as it evidently had not been exposed any very great length of time to the action of the sea. The fragment was in any event of an old vessel, as it had originally been painted red and yellow, and later a coat of white had overlain it.

The presence of this drift-wood is interesting, as showing that a northwest current extends occasionally this far to the northward in Baffin Bay. Inglefield mentions finding near Cape Atholl a portion of a ship's deck, which was evidently part of an American whaler which had been lost in Melville Bay that year. He considered this as giving evidence of the strong northerly current along that coast, especially as the fragment had drifted so far in a few weeks despite the heavy northerly gales.

Sir George Nares, in 1875, experienced a southerly current, which is doubtless the prevailing one.

We left the Cary Islands at 8 P.M., and five hours later were abreast of Hakluyt Island, which is particularly interesting, as being the farthest land touched by William Baffin in 1616, although he sailed some eight leagues to the northward of this point. Inglefield was hardly fair to the old explorer when he claimed Northumberland and the adjacent isles as newly discov-

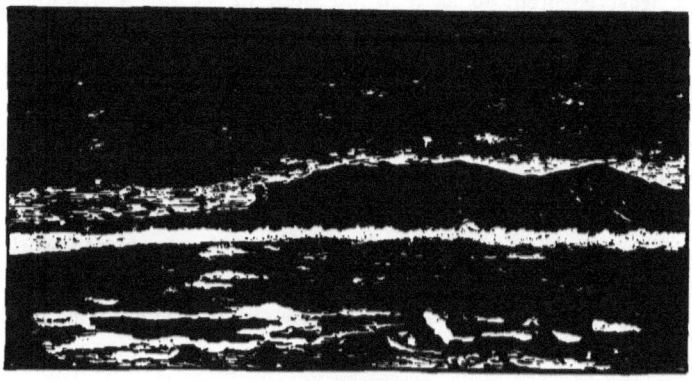

"An Iland we called Hakluit's Ile."
[*Baffin's Farthest Land, July* 4, 1616.]

ered, for it is evident that Baffin must have seen these islands as well as Hakluyt, although the map of his remarkable discoveries of 1616 is lost to the world.

From Cape Chalon northward a close watch was kept upon the main-land, in hopes some Etah natives might be seen and communicated with by us.

The remarkable tabulated masses of land in the neighborhood of Cape Alexander have been made familiar to the world by the vivid descriptions of Kane and Hayes, with whose labors they must ever be associated.

To the southward of that cape the great Mer de Glace is

nearly always in sight from the open sea, and, being a predominating feature in the landscape, naturally conveys a sense of barrenness and desolation; but to the northward the inland ice has retreated far from the sea, leaving the land free from ice or snow, and broken in at many points by fertile valleys, which impress themselves more strongly upon one through their contrast with the shores just passed.

Along the coast only an occasional bit of ice-foot was seen, and in the sea but a single berg and a few pieces of floe-ice to the southward of Littleton Island.

Pandora Harbor was passed at 10 A.M., and at noon the Proteus anchored between Cape Ohlsen and Littleton Island.

Lieutenant Kislingbury, with a party including the Eskimo, was sent to Life-Boat Cove to examine the winter quarters of the crew of the Polaris, and open communication with the Etah Eskimo, if any could be found. They brought back the transit instrument, which was found badly damaged about fifteen feet from the cairn in which it had been originally deposited. Polaris house had entirely disappeared, but its site was marked by a cooking-stove, steam-gauge, and many different pieces of metal, but no wood. A thermometer scale was found which belonged to an instrument manufactured by Tagliabue, scaled from 120° down to minus 100°, and on which the name of Hall had been scratched with some pointed instrument.

Lieutenant Lockwood improved our stay by landing a quantity of coal on the extreme southwestern point of Littleton Island, the only article of our supplies which could well be spared.

While these parties were thus engaged, I thoroughly examined the island for the purpose of finding the mail which had been landed there in 1876, for the Nares expedition, by Sir Allen Young. Some fifty cairns, great and small, were found, none of which contained a record save one, which informed us that the whaler Erik, under Captain Walker, touched at the island June 20, 1876. Six hours' fruitless search on foot had no results; but later, taking a boat, I followed the coast with two men, along the shore from fifty to two hundred yards from the water's edge, so as to cover the entire ground, and eventually succeeded in discovering the mail at the extreme northern end of the west coast, some thirty yards from the water's edge. Four boxes and three casks of mail matter were discovered, marked by a very small cairn, which contained no record.

On the western coast of the island I also found a wet wad of paper, which was carefully dried, and examined a few days later. It seemed to show conclusively that the Nares cairn had been opened, probably by the Eskimo, as the paper proved to be part of the London *Standard*, dated May 17, 1875, in which was contained intact an account of a lecture of Captain Nares on the Arctic expedition, delivered at Winchester Guildhall, April 30, 1875.

While at Littleton Island, walrus were found in considerable numbers. The party which visited Life-Boat Cove encountered a herd near that point. Two of the animals, a female and her calf, were fired at and wounded. The calf sank, and was possibly killed. The female, after one plunge, came again to the surface, and, infuriated by her wounds, rapidly approached the boat, evidently with hostile intentions. The Eskimo, who better than the rest realized the danger, counselled a retreat, but two shots at a few yards caused the walrus to dive again, and she appeared no more. The boat landing coal had similar experiences, except that the entire herd when fired on rapidly approached the boat with threatening actions, but drew off when very near. Their great strength, enormous size, and ferocious appearance are very trying to inexperienced hunters, and these qualities, added to fearlessness and curiosity, make it a dangerous animal to attack in its own element.

The full-grown walrus is from twelve to fifteen feet in length, has a small, short head, with strong bristles about the size of large darning-needles. The broad fore and hind paws are about two feet long, and the tusks of adults generally about a foot and a half, although they have been known to exceed thirty inches, in length. The tusks of the female are much more slender than those of the male. They are very gregarious, and seem to find a certain pleasure in frequent bellowing, by expelling the air through their nostrils.

The northern portion of Littleton Island appeared to be a favorite resort of eider ducks. Hundreds were found nesting, but from the lateness of the season the eggs were unfit for eating. The nests were beds of rich, soft down, which were but partly concealed by adjacent rocks or vegetation. The female birds left their nests with great reluctance, and only when approached within a few yards. Our larder was increased by only eleven ducks, as no time was given to hunting.

Private Henry discovered at a low point on the south side of Littleton Island, opposite Cape Ohlsen, the remains of an Eskimo woman buried in an old Eskimo house. The house was carefully examined by me, and evidently had been at some time a permanent habitation. Not only the house itself, but the external surroundings, and the rank and luxuriant vegetation near, were quite conclusive on that point. From the location of the body, it is possible that this was the last of a family. Inglefield states, that a winter hut at Bardin Bay was found blocked up by a stone, which removed disclosed the dead body of a man within, and he was advised that it was a frequent custom to let the house form the tomb for the last of a family.

An accident had occurred to the wheel just after passing

Cape Alexander, and the stop at Littleton Island was improved by putting it in order, which delayed us until nearly midnight.

I should have been glad to have visited Hayes' old winter-quarters in Port Foulke, a few miles south of Littleton Island, in hopes of seeing some of his old Etah friends, but lack of time forbade.

The view from Littleton Island to the northward some forty miles showed the sea entirely free from ice. Aware of the extreme rapidity with which ice conditions change in that sea, I

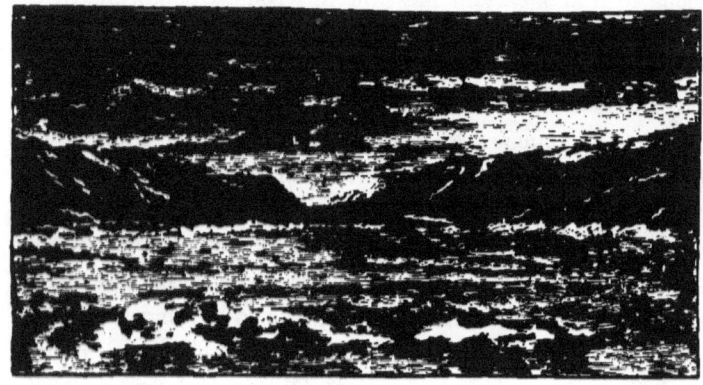

Port Foulke.
[*Winter-quarters of Dr. Hayes,* 1860-61.]

decided not to touch at Cape Sabine to examine the sledging depot at that point, but to shape a direct course for Cape Hawks.

Cape Sabine was passed about 2 A.M., and shortly after small amounts of floe-ice were seen, but not in sufficient quantities to form even an open pack. To the westward, in Buchanan Strait, what appeared to be an ice-foot was seen, but from later experiences I am satisfied that it was a series of low floes, or more probably the unbroken ice of the previous winter.

At 4 A.M. a seemingly close pack was seen to the eastward,

but later it developed into stream-ice of small extent. I came on deck at that time, and found our position to be off Cape Camperdown. The scene then was one of remarkable beauty, and, rather than an Arctic night, seemed to recall a bracing October morning in New England. It was probably about the turn of the tide, as the entire sea was as smooth as a mill-pond. In occasional places during the night, a bare film of new ice had formed which indicated the approach of winter.

At 4.30 A.M. we were opposite the centre of Bache Island, and from its appearance to me at that time, from the bridge of the Proteus, I could readily understand how Hayes mistook the single island for two. A long, broad valley separated Victoria Head from Cape Albert, and its vanishing point was many miles to the westward.

The vessel was stopped a few moments, in order to obtain a photograph of Bache Island and the land to the westward. The landscape at that time was one of unusual interest. The sun appeared especially brilliant, the sky was free from all except a few delicate cirrus-clouds, and the air was in that state of visibility which renders the outlines of distant objects particularly sharp and distinct. The entire coast of Ellesmere and Grinnell Lands was not only visible through the air, but its image was perfectly reflected from the smooth sea. The view of that shore was clear and distinct, from Cape Sabine northward to Cape Napoleon. To the southeastward, near Van Rensselaer Harbor, made immortal by the heroism of Kane, the highlands were plainly visible.

Although the expedition, as a rule, was little given to sentiment or enthusiasm, yet the scene and its conditions caused general excitement and the deepest feeling. But three vessels had ever before attained so high a latitude in those waters, and none with such ease; and the appearance of these Arctic lands, devoid, as a rule, of snow, and glorified by the rays of the autumn sun, presented a prospect which was entirely different in its details from any we had ever anticipated. The stern grandeur and desolation which are marked characteristics of Arctic landscapes were not wanting, but the poetical picturesqueness and delicate beauty of the scene were its predominant features.

The absence of ice was particularly marked. The north end of Bache Island was reached at 5 A.M., and at that time but few pieces of floe- or harbor-ice could be seen in Kane Sea, and but two bergs were sighted from Cape Sabine to Cape Hawks.

To the northward of Bache Island, the ice of the previous winter still remained solid and unbroken in Princess Marie Bay, to the westward of Norman Lockyer Island.

A photographic view of Cape Hawks and the coast to the northward was obtained at a point some eight miles distant from that cape, which, though not valuable as a photograph, was useful for topographical purposes.

Cape Hawks was passed, and the Proteus stopped at 9 A.M. opposite the rocky ledge in Dobbin Bay on which the English depot of 1875 had been cached.

While Sergeant Rice, the photographer, was diligently plying his profession from a large floe of harbor-ice, I visited the depot and carefully examined its contents. At the time of our visit the tide was low, and at the edge of the land we were confronted by a perpendicular ice-wall of eight to ten feet in height, which was scaled with some little difficulty.

Seven casks of bread, aggregating twenty-seven hundred pounds; two casks of stearine, of four hundred pounds; one barrel of preserved potatoes, two hundred and ten pounds; two kegs of pickles, and two partly filled, kegs of rum, composed the remains of the depot. These articles were in good condition, except a portion of the bread, which was mouldy, though generally eatable. The casks had been deposited on a ledge of uneven surface, and the melting snow in summer had gathered in pools around, and later had frozen them from an eighth to one-half deep in solid ice. The casks were all cut out of the ice and placed in such location as would better protect them from the moisture. A half-filled keg of rum, the piccalilli, and sample cases of the preserved potatoes were taken with us, as well as the jolly-boat, which was also cached there. Insufficient means had not allowed the proper equipment of the expedition with boats, or this would have remained undisturbed at Cape Hawks.

The excellent workmanship and fitness of this boat for Arctic service was exemplified by the fact that, despite its six years' exposure to the dry Arctic atmosphere, it was yet in such condition that, though leaking, it was seaworthy at once. It was named the Valorous, from the ship to which it formerly belonged.

The cache at Cape Hawks, deposited by the English in 1875, was one of the two principal depots established under the advice and direction of a board of Arctic experts, who had given the subject of exploration by the Smith Sound route careful and considerate attention. The second depot consisted, equally with that of Cape Hawks, of thirty-six hundred rations, and was the one which had been visited by us August 1st, at Southeast Cary Island. The very small cache established at Payer Harbor, Cape Sabine, was for use, as Sir George Nares said, of any possible sledge party travelling in that direction. It contained only two hundred and fifty sledging rations and a small quantity of dog-food.

It is now evident to the whole world that Cape Sabine is the key of Smith Sound, but such fact was by no means clear to the English Arctic board, while the problem was an unresolved one. If the English expedition of 1875 had lost their ships, the four weeks' provisions at Cape Hawks could never have carried their crews to Southeast Cary Island, except under favorable conditions, which rarely occur in Kane Sea. This statement, showing that the views of the highest and most competent Arctic authorities were followed in our original plan, by

Washington Irving Island.
[*Opposite Cape Hawks.*]

no means precludes the admission that Cape Sabine should have been provisioned at that time.

Five walruses were seen at Cape Hawks, which, in connection with the observations of the English on Norman Lockyer Island, indicate that these animals yearly frequent that part of Kane Sea.

The serial sea temperatures at Cape Hawks showed a fall in the temperature of the water since Cape Sabine had been passed; that of the surface being 32.3°, and at thirty fathoms 30.7°.

The vegetation at Cape Hawks and on Washington Irving Island was scanty and stunted. Three varieties only of plants were found on the main-land and eight on the island.

As the Proteus passed Washington Irving Island, we picked up our photographer, as well as Dr. Pavy and Lieutenant Lockwood, who had been searching the cairn on the island. The latter officer brought back Captain Nares' record of August, 1875, and September, 1876, which gave a brief account of his visit and action. Copies of these papers were left, and a new record added, which gave briefly our experiences to date. The old cairn was carefully rebuilt.

The harbor-ice of Dobbin Bay was solid and unbroken. Its margin reached the north end of Washington Irving Island, so that we were obliged to pass to the southward on leaving Cape Hawks.

At 3 P.M. Cape Frazer was reached, from which Washington Land of Kane was first sighted, the high land to the northward of Cass Bay showing up clearly. This point, Cape Frazer, is a notable one in more than one respect. It was Hayes' farthest thirty years ago, while serving as a surgeon with Kane, and it is in the immediate neighborhood of this cape that the Atlantic tide, surging northward through Davis Strait and Smith Sound, meets its sister tide twelve hours older, which has passed northward by the Spitzbergen Sea, and rounding Cape Washington has flowed southward through the Polar Ocean and Robeson Channel.

In the neighborhood of this point the first palæocrystic floebergs fell under our observation. To the uninitiated, rough and heavy field-ice, which has been increased in thickness by underrunning or doubled up by pressure, may be mistaken for palæocrystic, but the latter ice once seen the mistake never occurs again. Its identity is unmistakable.

Four floe-bergs only were seen, two to the northward and two to the southward of Frazer, and no palæocrystic floe was met until Cape Baird was reached.

At 5 P.M. Cape McClintock was passed and the eightieth parallel crossed. Scoresby Bay was not only full of harbor-ice, evidently unbroken that year, but a delicate fringe of new ice at its margin extended a mile or more into the sea.

Fog and drizzling rain set in shortly after, obliging us to run at half-speed. It was so dense on sighting Cape Collinson, at 5.30, that I did not feel justified in attempting the examination of the small depot there cached, particularly as its exact location was not known, and the search would have necessitated securing the vessel in Richardson Bay. At 10 P.M. the fog was so dense that the vessel was kept merely under steerage-way during the rest of the night.

The fog lifted on the morning of the 4th sufficiently to allow an hour's run, and Franklin Island was passed about noon. We obtained a sounding of one hundred and thirty fathoms with no bottom, at a point some eight miles southwest of that island. To the southeast, a close, hummocky pack was sighted, which was of such limited extent that from the "crow's-nest" open water was visible on both sides.

At noon Kennedy Channel was entirely free from fog, and both coasts showed up plainly, from Cape Constitution to Polaris Promontory to the east, and from Cape Lawrence to Cape Defosse to the west.

I decided to establish a small depot in Carl Ritter Bay, and while the Proteus remained in the extreme northeastern portion, I went on shore with a party and cached two hundred pounds of meat and about two hundred and eighty pounds of bread. The pemmican and hard bread in water-tight casks, were placed on a high bench on the north side of a creek about a half mile southwest of the cape near Mount Ross.

This creek was of moderate size, and drained a valley of considerable extent, which extended to the northwestward. The vegetation seemed more abundant than at Cape Hawks, and eight varieties of flowers were gathered during our brief stay, but the general appearance was of desolation.

Lieutenant Kislingbury travelled up the valley a short distance, and traces of musk-cattle, hare, and fox were found.

A number of delicate star-fish and crustaceans were obtained in a sounding of forty-two fathoms half a mile off the shore.

The designation of the indentation at that point as a bay would seem to be a courtesy on the part of our English cousins toward Dr. Hayes, who located there an inlet some twenty-five miles deep. The actual indentation is so slight, and the curve so great, that it is a bight rather than a bay.

On our passage northward, Richardson and Rawlings Bays were not seen by us, but all indentations sighted were filled with unbroken harbor-ice. Carl Ritter Bay itself was free of such ice, which must originally have formed so intimate a part of the main pack that it must have moved out in the first break up of the year.

From Littleton Island northward the number and variety of birds rapidly decreased, and north of the eightieth parallel only dovekies had been observed until we left Carl Ritter Bay, when a Greenland falcon (*Falco candicans*) was seen.

At 8 P.M. off Cape Lieber, a large number of heavy floes were met with, which pressed against the coast and obliged the Proteus to make a considerable detour to the eastward. In passing the ice near Cape Lieber, for the first time in our voyage.

the "crow's-nest" was of practical benefit to us. At 9 p.m. we entered the extreme southeastern part of Lady Franklin Bay, about two miles southeast of Cape Baird.

On nearing that cape we met a close, heavy pack, and for the first time in our remarkable voyage were stopped by ice. We ran seven or eight miles to the eastward in hopes that a lead to the northward might present itself. The result of our observations showed a dense polar pack of palæocrystic floes, cemented together by thinner ice, which extended in a semicircle from Cape Baird to the Greenland coast above Cape Tyson. These floes ranged from twenty-five to fifty feet in thickness, and proved to be veritable islands of ice—the true palæocrystic floes of Nares.

We returned to the neighborhood of Cape Baird, and tied up to the pack to await future movements of the ice.

On August 5th, with a small party, I visited and examined carefully Cape Lieber, which was about four miles distant. The precipitous cliffs rise some two thousand feet from the sea, and it is possible to scale them only at one point, through a rugged, rocky ravine, which the summer stream in course of ages has worn through the disintegrated rock. The ascent was made only with great difficulty. Lieutenant Lockwood and Dr. Pavy climbed different peaks at the extreme summit, which was entirely barren, save miniature glaciers in two places. No cairn of any kind was in sight, though any present could not have failed to meet the eye, nor were there any other traces of a previous visit. Two small cairns were erected by our party.

The Grinnell Land coast was visible many miles to the northward, a rugged, bold highland, although its mountain masses presented to the eye very gently rounded contours, with no distinctly rising peak in any direction.

Through the pack in Hall Basin there were many lanes of

water visible, and the general movement of the detached pieces showed a southward tendency.

That evening we were able to advance about a mile toward Discovery Harbor, through a large number of floes breaking off and drifting slowly southward.

During the day a number of schools of white whales (*Beluga catadon*) were seen, there being as many as thirty at one time. Mr. Norman, the mate of the Proteus, saw with them their active enemy, a sword-fish (*Orca gladiator, Bonn.*)

On the 6th a number of narwhals (*Monodon monoceros*) were seen, and another school of white whales. The two Eskimo pursued them in their kayaks, and Jens succeeded in striking a narwhal, but after an exciting struggle, during which he came to the surface of the water twice, the animal managed to break the line and carried away the harpoon with him.

The white whale is from twelve to eighteen feet in length, and yields not far from a thousand pounds each of meat and blubber. It is a very beautiful animal, with a smooth, unwrinkled hide, which is of waxy-white color in adults, but of a light grayish brown in the young. They are very active, swim with great rapidity, and usually travel in schools. In Greenland from five to six hundred are caught yearly, almost all by nets. The skin, called "mattak" by the Eskimo, is esteemed a great dainty in Danish Greenland when fresh, and that eaten by me tasted like a superior kind of tripe. It is much valued as an anti-scorbutic, and we obtained a considerable quantity of it dried, in which condition it resembles pieces of inferior glue.

The narwhal, or unicorn, is of a yellowish-white color, mottled with dark grayish spots in the adult. In the young both ground-color and spots are of considerably darker shade than in the full grown. The strikingly characteristic feature in the male is an abnormally long tooth projecting from the *left* side of the upper jaw, its fellow of the right side being almost always undeveloped. In the females both teeth are immature, as a rule. This tusk is sometimes developed to a length of ten feet, and, as the body is not much longer, it gives the animal a most striking appearance.

The tusk points slightly downward, is nearly straight, is spirally striated, tapers to a blunt point, and is of a yellowish-white substance, denser and harder than ivory. The spirals

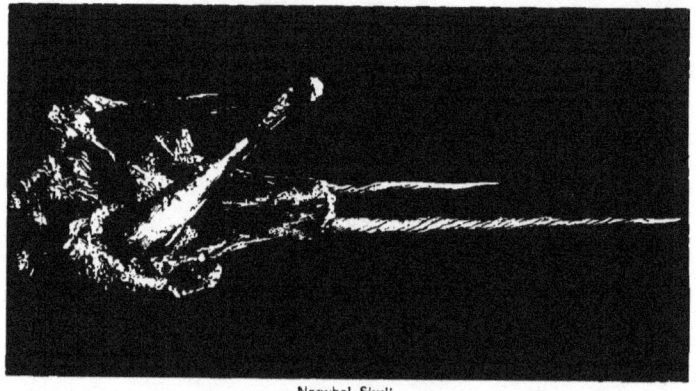

Narwhal Skull.
[*Showing Abnormal Development of Tooth in Left Side, Upper Jaw.*]

terminate some six inches from the point, which is smooth and white as if from constant use. The tusk varies in thickness from two to three inches at the base, and from one-third to one-half inch at the point. Its use is not definitely known, but most probably it serves as a weapon, as but few are obtained in perfect condition. The animals are quick swimmers, active, gregarious, not easily alarmed, and are often found with the white whale, which they follow. The tusks and oil are valuable, and the flesh palatable. They are hunted by the Eskimo from the kayak only.

The sword-fish, or grampus, is a different species from the

common sword-fish of lower latitudes. It is a fierce, voracious fish of the dolphin family, possessing great strength and activity, and pursues whales and seals with ruthless energy. Dr. Eschricht is said to have taken thirteen porpoises and fourteen seals from the stomach of one of these voracious animals, who was choked swallowing yet another seal.

We saw many dovekies, and shot several during the day; they frequent the cliffs of Cape Lieber, and evidently breed there.

An attempt was made in the evening to reach Cape Baird over the floe, but some changes in the ice appearing probable, the party was recalled.

Several brent geese, a boatswain, and a snowy owl visited us during the day.

On the 7th a northeasterly wind prevailed, which sent large quantities of heavy ice down Kennedy Channel, and obliged the Proteus to frequently change her location to avoid besetment, and at 10 P.M. we were tied up to a floe in Kennedy Channel, five miles south of Cape Lieber. Many of the floes which passed south were from one to five miles long, and from ten to fifty feet thick.

In order to be on the safe side, the captain made arrangements during the day for a possible nip, so that the propeller-screw and rudder could be readily hoisted. We were then in a large, open-water space, ten miles long and from one to five miles broad, with the main pack to the northward and the detached floes to the southward.

White whales were again seen, and a number of birds, including the snow bunting, ringed plover, and ivory gull.

During the 8th the pack from the northward filled Hall Basin completely, and Kennedy Channel to the southward of Bessels Bay, while the detached pack to the southward appeared to be caught between Hans Island and the north cape of Carl Ritter Bay. In case of a heavy northerly gale, if the main pack had broken, the only available shelter would have been at Hans Island, which possibly could have been passed to the eastward. The narwhals still remained with us, and several were seen during the day, and a number of seals, one of which was shot.

On the 9th the ice opened considerably, but snowy weather prevented movement in any direction. A square-flipper seal (*Phoca barbata*) was killed; a falcon, tern, and glaucous gull were seen.

We were surprised to see on the 10th a harp seal (*Phoca Groenlandica*), which, as well as dovekies and a number of gulls, visited the vessel. Snow still continued, which obscured the land for the greater part of the day, and with continued inaction was very trying to our spirits.

It was true that the situation remained unchanged, and no ground was lost to the southward, but our position was by no means encouraging. Since the 4th of the month we had lost over forty miles of latitude, and instead of being eight miles from our destination were nearer fifty. It was, therefore, with a peculiar feeling of gratification that we saw the wind, shortly after noon, back from the north to the favorable southwest quarter.

On the morning of the 11th the sky showed signs of clearing, and at 7 A.M., under the influence of a southwesterly gale, the fog lifted to the northward. Very little ice was then in sight, and what there was crowded well to the eastern coast. We were then off Hans Island, from which we started northward at full speed, and on rounding Cape Lieber were delighted to see Lady Franklin Bay equally clear of ice.

The southwest wind continued strong, and at 2 P.M., while we were crossing Archer fiord, attained an hourly velocity of thirty-six miles.

On reaching the entrance of Discovery Harbor, a narrow channel free from ice was found, separating the main ice of Archer fiord from a considerable pack which was visible in Water-Course Bay. Discovery Harbor was in the same condition as the bays to the southward—covered with heavy harbor-ice of the previous year's formation.

Eskimo Boys Fishing.

The Proteus steamed slowly into the curved water-space to the northward of Dutch Island, the powerful engines stopped, an ice-anchor was thrown on the harbor-floe, and our voyage to Lady Franklin Bay was prosperously ended.

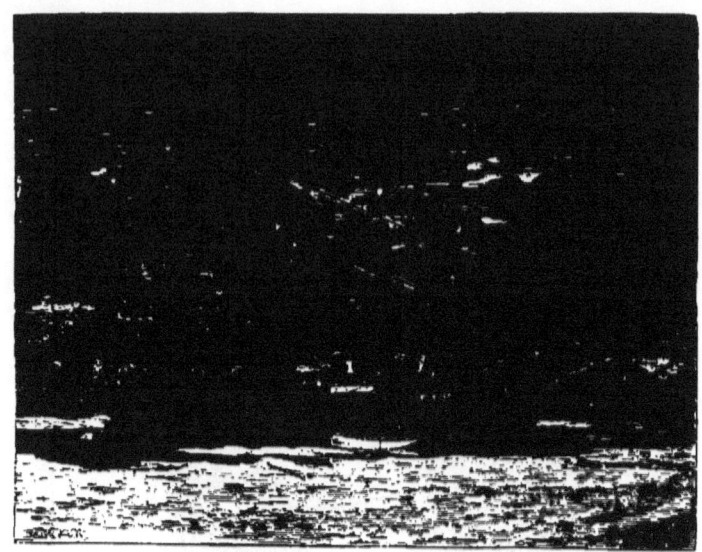

The Proteus in Discovery Harbor.

CHAPTER VII.

THE RETURN OF THE PROTEUS.

AS the Proteus neared the entrance of the harbor, a black speck appeared high up on the steep sides of Cairn Hill, which was soon determined to be a musk-ox. The moment the vessel touched fast-ice five or six eager sportsmen started in pursuit of him. Somewhat to the chagrin of the huntsmen of the expedition, he fell a prize to the boatswain, who being in better condition to climb the steep cliffs, first succeeded in getting within gun-shot. At the first ball the bull appeared to start toward the hunter, but a second shot caused him to stagger and fall for some two hundred feet down the steep cliffs, on the edge of which he was grazing.

While the musk-ox was being secured, I went direct to Discovery winter-quarters, where the post-office cairn of Captain Stephenson was visited. Two copper cases were obtained, labelled "Records and General Information," the latter of which, by coincidence, was dated August 11, 1876, just five years previous to a day.

A Hicks glacial thermometer, set five feet in the ground, recorded a temperature of 26°. As the unfrozen ground attains its maximum temperature not far from that time of the year, this temperature seems reasonably the maximum of the earth at that depth. Later observations and experiences show that the earth thaws only to a depth of twenty-two to twenty-four inches, remaining eternally frozen below that point.

About twenty-five barrels of spoiled pork and beef, left by Captain Stephenson in 1876, were standing near, and numerous empty cans and other débris, such as usually mark old encampments were strewn around.

A large flock of eider-ducks had settled in an open pool near by, and to the northward some three-quarters of a mile ten musk-oxen were quietly grazing. The adjacent brook-slopes and margins were clothed with vegetation, composed of thick beds of *Dryas*, or clusters of *Saxifraga*, varied with sedges, grasses, or the familiar buttercup. Higher up, on glacier-drift of clayey nature, countless Arctic poppies of luxuriant growth dotted with fair yellow the landscape. Surely this presence of bird and flower and beast were kindly greetings on Nature's part to our new home.

But in Arctic life one grows practical, and, in default of gun for duck and rifle for musk-oxen, I started to tell the huntsmen to pursue them, but while I was on the way they were discovered by Lieutenant Lockwood, who with Mr. Clay and Private Ryan, followed them up, and killed all on the south side of Mount Cartmel.

Sergeant Brainard and a party were at once sent out to disembowel and skin the animals, as the musky flavor, which sometimes marks the otherwise excellent meat, is generally attributed to the animals remaining undressed for some time after their slaughter. The indefatigable photographer, Sergeant Rice, accompanied them, and at midnight made a photograph of the animals.

The Captain of the Proteus was desirous of landing the party in Discovery Harbor, but I was unwilling to abandon the contemplated location at Water-course Bay, owing to its proximity to a seam of excellent coal. Lieutenant Lockwood was in consequence sent to examine the existing conditions in Watercourse Bay and to report thereon. He returned at 6 A.M. of the 12th, having killed during his absence three more musk-cattle. He reported the coal seam as of excellent quality and easily accessible, and that the shores of the bay were well adapted for a station. The northern half of the bay was then filled with pressed-up floes from the influence of the southwest gale, which yet continued. He thought it doubtful if a vessel could approach nearer the land than one-eighth of a mile, and further reported that no sheltered anchorage was possible.

In view of these conditions I decided to land at the Discovery winter-quarters, where it also seemed that the observations, strictly comparable with those of the English expedition, would better subserve our scientific objects.

The Captain commenced at once breaking up the harbor-ice, a work which lasted for seven hours continuously until we anchored opposite the post-office cairn, and within a hundred yards of it. It was very troublesome to force a passage, as there was no place for the broken floes to be driven to. The ice averaged sixteen inches in thickness, but in many places it was eight or ten feet. The latter was in moderately rotten condition, or the vessel could never have made its way through it. It was surprising that she did her work so well.

Proteus First Stopped by Ice.

The Proteus would back several hundred yards from the edge of the ice, and then going ahead at full speed would strike the heavy floes squarely with her iron prow. Her impact was such that, surging and rising, she would plunge into the solid ice from half to her whole length. As she moved ahead the entire crew rolled the vessel, so as to give a motion sideways, which tended to further break up the floes and prevent the ship from being caught and wedged.

Great skill is needed for the proper handling of a ship under such conditions, for she must be stopped and backed before she has entirely lost headway, in order to avoid wedging. Despite Captain Pike's great experience, the ship was several times caught, thus entailing loss of time and expenditure of fuel.

A site was immediately chosen for the house, which was arranged to stand north and south. The men were divided into two parties for unloading the vessel. All were engaged in this task except the necessary scientific observers, carpenters, and one or two who were detailed to secure the musk-meat cached near by.

The station was named Conger, after Senator Conger, who had interested himself specially in behalf of the expedition.

Mr. Clay informed me on the 16th of his desire to return to the United States, saying that he thought such a course calculated to promote the harmony and interests of the expedition. Though regretting to lose his society I could not but concur in his opinion, as the surgeon of the expedition had shown a marked disposition to extreme measures if Mr. Clay remained. Our surgeon was indispensable, and all honorable concessions to retain him should be made. Corporal Starr and Private Ryan having developed physical ailments, which unfitted them for prolonged Arctic service, were also ordered to return by the Proteus, much to their regret.

On the 15th the boatswain killed another musk-ox, which went to the crew of the Proteus, but later the Captain forbade any of his crew from hunting more, on my representation that the necessities of our situation, separated as we were from the rest of the world, demanded the conservation of these animals for our future use.

At 6 P.M. of the 18th I finally discharged the Proteus.

At that time, in addition to all our general supplies, one hundred and thirty tons of coal had been landed.

On the 25th Lieutenant Kislingbury spent the day on the Proteus and the next day, dissatisfied with the expeditionary regulations, requested that he be relieved from duty with the expedition. He was relieved and ordered to report to the Chief Signal Officer. Unfortunately the Proteus got under way just as Lieutenant Kislingbury was leaving the station, and he was obliged to return to Conger. He remained consequently at Conger, doing no duty, and with no further requirement than that he should conform to the police regulations of the station. He at no time requested to return to duty as an officer of the expedition. An excellent shot and an assiduous hunter, he contributed by his skill at various times to our stock of game and thus to our health and comfort. He accompanied several short sledge parties, as will be noted hereafter.

These unfortunate episodes emphasize the necessity of selecting for Arctic service only men and officers of thorough military qualities, among which subordination is by no means of secondary importance. If in all military commands that element is of great importance, it is of predominating weight in Arctic work, where isolation and self-dependence impose peculiar and rigid conditions. If subsequently the discipline and subordination of the party insured extraordinary success in field-work and in retreat, it was despite the unfortunate commencement.

The Proteus made an attempt to leave the harbor on the morning of the 19th, but was only able to reach Dutch Island, where the heavy crowded ice in Lady Franklin Bay, driven in by the easterly storm of the 18th, prevented her departure. She returned to the point adjacent, which was named

Proteus Point, where the rest of her stay was occupied in taking on ballast.

Lieutenant Lockwood, with the launch, attempted to follow the Proteus as she left her anchorage on the morning of the 19th, but owing to the extremely heavy ice found it impossible to do so. This was a matter of much regret to us, as, if the launch could have been got into open water near Dutch Island, she would have been of great service during that autumn.

Hourly meteorological observations had been regularly made from August 8th on board ship, and on the morning of the 19th were regularly commenced on shore. Two days later a tide-gauge was up, and tidal observations regularly commenced.

From the 18th the men and officers were quartered camp-fashion in tents, but from fourteen to sixteen hours' work daily did wonders on our house, and on the 21st the cook's range was set up. The very low temperature made us feel the importance of quarters, especially for such articles as would be much damaged by frost. Already from August 18th freezing temperatures occurred daily, and at 3 P.M. of the 29th the temperature fell below the freezing point, there to remain for a period of nine months.

In the meantime the ice remained piled up at the eastern entrance to the harbor, and the Proteus, despite almost daily attempts to leave, was ice-bound in sight. Daily a note was sent to her, that the latest tidings might reach our homes. Finally, on August 26th, she made a desperate attempt, and broke through the dense, narrow strip of packed floes which had cut her off from open water. Archer Fiord was packed with ice, and she was compelled to run northeastward. All followed her movements with lively interest, and about 7 P.M., some miles east of Distant Cape, she passed from our sight, as it proved, forever.

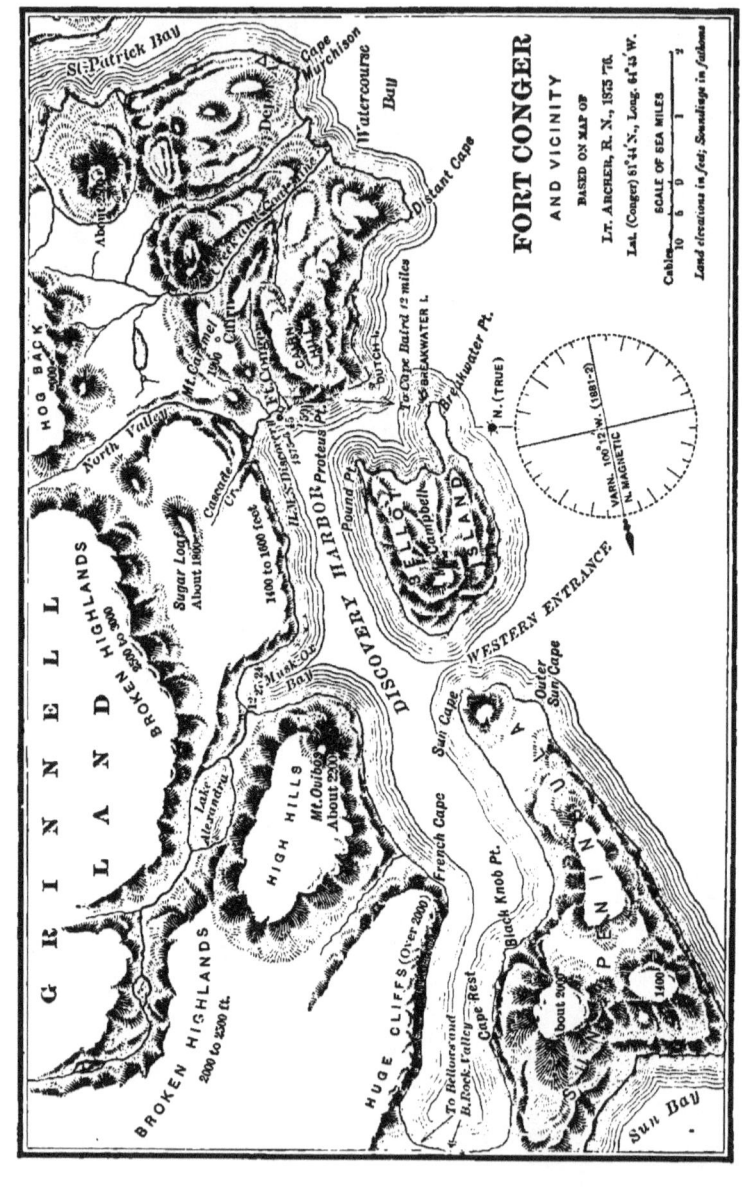

CHAPTER VIII.

FORT CONGER.

IT was but natural that many a longing glance should be sent after the departing ship, but, on the whole, I doubt not there was a certain sense of relief that the ship had actually gone, and that our work had fairly commenced. While the ship remained in the harbor it caused a feeling of restlessness and uneasiness, which quite disappeared as soon as she departed.

The work on the house was pushed with the utmost rapidity, and by August 25th some of the party moved in; there being a roof to cover their heads, although the floor and windows were not yet completed. A portion of the party remained a short time longer in the tents which formed our original quarters, some preferring to wait until everything was in order, and their places finally allotted to them; and others because they realized that the quarters in the house would soon become monotonous, and that it was best to defer their occupation until the last possible moment.

The first Sunday on which I felt justified in resting was August 28th, on which day all unnecessary work was discontinued. At ten o'clock the entire party were assembled, and the programme for future Sundays outlined.

In dealing with the religious affairs of a party of that kind, which included in it members of many varying sects, I felt that any regulations which might be formulated should rest on the broadest and most liberal basis. I said to them that, although separated from all the rest of the world, it was most proper and right that the Sabbath should be observed. In consequence, I announced that games of all kinds should be abstained from on that day. On each Sunday morning there would be read by me a selection from the Psalms, and it was expected that every member of the expedition should be present, unless he had conscientious scruples against listening to the reading of the Bible. After services on each Sunday, any parties desiring to hunt or leave the station should have free and full permission, and such exercise was deemed by me especially suited to our surroundings, as serving to break in on the monotony of our life, and thus be conducive both to mental and physical health. The selection of Psalms for the 28th day of the month was then read. Although, as a rule, during our stay at Conger, I refrained from any comments on what was thus read, I felt obliged that morning to especially invite the attention of the party to that verse which recites how delightful a thing it is for brethren to dwell together in unity. A few words were added upon the depressing effect which an isolated and monotonous life produced upon men experiencing the trials and hardships of a long Arctic winter. I further expressed the hope, that every one would endeavor to conciliate and reconcile those who drifted into any unpleasant controversy instead of exciting them to further feeling.

That the conditions under which we lived and by which we were surrounded may be known, a brief description of our house and the adjacent country is given as follows:

The house was 60 by 17 feet in the clear. Its walls were double, the two coverings of half-inch boards being separated by an air-space of about a foot. Great reliance was placed on the non-conductivity to heat of these air-spaces to contribute to our warmth. The inside lining consisted of well-fitted boards, which were tongued and grooved by our own carpenters, but to insure freedom from draughts a covering of thin tar-paper was nailed upon the rafters before the covering of boards was fastened. A covering of much heavier tar-paper was placed on the outside of the external boards. The external wood was fastened vertically instead of horizontally, and though there was but a single covering, yet we managed by strong battening to securely fasten the tar-paper and prevent serious draughts. The roof was but the thickness of a single board, and, like the sides, was covered by tar-paper secured by battening. The paper used for outside covering was of the heaviest character, and, being black, absorbed during the early spring and summer, when external heat was most desired, the rays of the sun to such an extent as to materially contribute to the warmth of the interior. During the winter the external wall and covering of ice and snow prevented any extreme cold from radiation. The house was ceiled with tongued-and-grooved boards, which not only contributed to our warmth, but added also to our room, by affording above an excellent storage-place for various kinds of articles which would have been materially injured by exposure to the weather.

The interior of the house was divided into three rooms, one 17 by 15 feet for the officers, which was separated from the large room of the men by an intermediate space of 8 by 17 feet, of which 6 by 8 feet served as an entry, and a small space of 11 by 8 feet was allowed the cook as his special domain. At the north and south ends lean-tos of canvas and tar-paper were constructed, which served useful purposes as store-houses, and also afforded intermediate stopping-places between the warm quarters and the wintry air. A similar addition was made in the second year to the west side of the house.

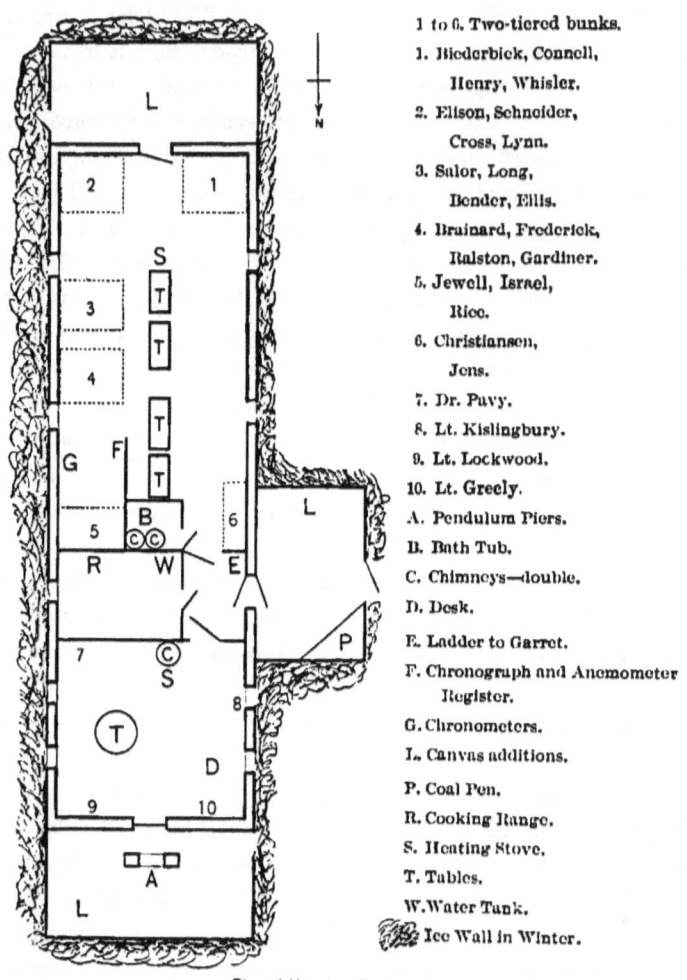

1 to 6. Two-tiered bunks.
1. Biederbick, Connell, Henry, Whisler.
2. Elison, Schneider, Cross, Lynn.
3. Salor, Long, Bender, Ellis.
4. Brainard, Frederick, Ralston, Gardiner.
5. Jewell, Israel, Rice.
6. Christiansen, Jens.
7. Dr. Pavy.
8. Lt. Kislingbury.
9. Lt. Lockwood.
10. Lt. Greely.
A. Pendulum Piers.
B. Bath Tub.
C. Chimneys—double.
D. Desk.
E. Ladder to Garret.
F. Chronograph and Anemometer Register.
G. Chronometers.
L. Canvas additions.
P. Coal Pen.
R. Cooking Range.
S. Heating Stove.
T. Tables.
W. Water Tank.
Ice Wall in Winter.

Plan of House at Fort Conger.
Scale, 10 feet to the inch.

The accompanying plan shows the general arrangement of the house and the location of the party. It will be observed that the bath-room abutted against the chimneys, so that this indispensable adjunct of an Arctic house was always comfortable for persons using it. An excellent bath-tub was made, which was in frequent use; the order requiring complete ablutions weekly being necessary only as a matter of form.

The only comparatively level part of the country was that in the immediate neighborhood of the house. The building was conveniently and pleasantly situated within thirty yards of the water's edge on a small tableland between two brooks, which for a few months in the year ran into the sea.

To the southward, along the steep shore to Dutch Island, which was about two miles distant, and at the very entrance of the harbor, rose up abruptly a high hill, whose elevation was over fifteen hundred feet. It was called Cairn Hill from the cairn established by the English.

To the eastward a comparatively low valley stretched, separating Cairn Hill from Mount Cartmel, which, some two thousand feet high, was to the northwestward of the station. The valley separating Mount Cartmel and Cairn Hill led up to a gentle divide, through which Water-course Creek and the coal mine, some four miles distant, were reached, over a country which, though affording the best travel of the neighborhood, was an exceedingly rough one.

Directly to the northward was a sharp break in the high cliffs, which was known as the north valley. Through that opening rose to view, some five miles distant from the sea, an elevation of nearly three thousand feet, the Hogback. It received its name from the gently curving outlines of its summit, the common form of most hill-tops in Grinnell Land; many of which will be mentioned later under that generic name.

To the northwest, about a mile distant, emptied into the sea a creek from Cascade Ravine. This ravine was so named from its series of beautiful cascades, where the summer torrents

An Arctic Brook.

plunged downward in the distance of a mile over fourteen hundred feet through a bare cleft in the solid rock. This creek drained the upper plateau around the Sugar Loaf, a pointed elevation of eighteen hundred feet.

From Cascade Ravine westward to French Cape, for a distance of ten miles, cliffs from fourteen hundred to two thousand feet rose so nearly perpendicular from the harbor that they were inaccessible, except possibly at one or two places. About five miles west of the station these cliffs turn sharply to the northward, making a large indentation, which is known as Musk-ox Bay, into which drained, through a break in the cliffs, a series of fresh-water lakes, the largest of which was named by the English expedition Alexandra, after the Princess of Wales. On the western entrance of Musk-ox Bay Mount Ovibos raises its snow-capped head over two thousand feet. To the northward of French Cape a narrow ravine breaks into the high cliffs, which there are nearly two thousand feet in height. Beyond that cape a bay three miles long by a mile wide, which was temporarily called Basil Norris Bay, brought one at its western shore to the only extensive lowland in that vicinity. A gentle slope to the south carries you over a bench of low elevation to Sun Bay. To the northward a broad valley about two miles wide, known as the Bellows, gradually narrowing, extends some twenty miles into the interior. Nearly parallel to the Bellows, with a slightly more westerly course, Black Rock vale similarly extends some twenty miles to the westward, until it reaches a narrow "divide," by which it is separated from Lake Hazen.

To the southwest of the station Bellot Island, about three miles long by two wide, separates Discovery Harbor from Archer Fiord, leaving to the westward a broad channel between itself and Sun Peninsula. The island is a beautiful one, rugged and high, with its summit (Mount Campbell) of about twenty-one hundred feet attractively marked with eternal drifts of snow.

It is thus seen that our immediate surroundings were on nature's grandest scale. So perfect was the harmony, and so proportionate the parts, that the grandeur at first, as of Niagara, was hardly appreciated.

The great harbor, with its twenty square miles of immense ice-floes, hemmed in at every point by precipitous walls, which ranged from hundreds to thousands of feet in height, seemed at landing but a small bay surrounded by moderate hills.

But at times our thoughts and eyes turned homeward, and from the station far to the southward the bold capes of Morton and Tyson stood forth on clear days, grim sentinels that overlook the eternal ice-stream which pushes downward from the interior of Greenland into Petermann Fiord.

CHAPTER IX.

AUTUMN SLEDGING.

THE house was scarcely completed before field-work commenced. The difficulties and dangers of such work in autumn are obvious, and have been dwelt on to a marked extent by most Arctic writers. The snow gone from the ground renders land travel by sledges impossible, while along the edge of the sea the ice-foot is similarly impracticable. The sea itself, especially in very high latitudes, is always more or less full of ice, which if not dangerous soon becomes so through being cemented together by young ice, an obstacle the most difficult of all for a boat to pass through.

The sun shines but little and feebly; the nights—the bugbear of all Arctic travellers who have endured them—lengthen with fearful rapidity; the moist, penetrating air readily chills and stupefies, while the cold steadily increases with the growing autumn. The young ice, formed rapidly by low temperatures, is a thick, leathery substance, the surface of which is covered an inch or more with a moist, saline efflorescence, beautiful to the eye, but which binds and impedes the passage of a sledge much the same as wet sand checks the movement of an engine on the rails. This substance congealing only at very low temperatures, melts and saturates the foot-gear of the travellers. In addition, a light coating of snow frequently conceals thin, young ice when the serious danger of its breaking under the sledge, and the consequent immersion of the whole party is encountered. In autumn temperatures the travelling-gear of a man once wet, the chances of dangerous frost-bites and disaster largely increase. It is sound doctrine that autumn sledging should be carefully planned, attempted with great caution, and never pushed to great distances.

On August 29th Lieutenant Lockwood was sent, with two men on foot and with packs, to ascertain the practicability of inland travel to and around St. Patrick Bay. He was gone but two days, during which time he was fortunate enough to kill a musk-ox, and unfortunate enough to freeze one of his feet. The temperature at that time was about 25° ($-3.9°$ C.), but travelling through occasional pools dampened his foot-gear and frosted his foot without his knowledge. St. Patrick Bay was found to be fringed with precipitous cliffs of nearly a thousand feet in elevation, which were broken only by a narrow valley at the very head of the bay itself. Occasionally a narrow ravine worn by the summer streams was found, up or down which an unencumbered traveller could pass with great difficulty.

This result was somewhat of a disappointment to me, as I had at that time a small depot of provisions on a wheeled conveyance, which were to be cached for travelling parties at the most practicable crossing. These articles were left at the head of the bay, and later in the month were removed to Cape Murchison, where they formed Depot "A."

In the early days of October Lieutenant Lockwood made a second journey in the same direction, and spent a few days in exploring the valley which extends northward from the head of St. Patrick Bay. A mile and a half wide at its entrance, it reached some six miles to the northwest, where the lower level of the valley terminated, but a narrow ravine enclosing a river-bed still continued several miles farther toward the north. The valley through its whole extent was hemmed in by precipitous bluffs of great elevation, rarely broken by steep, narrow ravines on either side. To the left a narrow gorge broke into the valley, which subsequent explorations two years later showed conclusively to be the main valley, through which drains the greater part of the water which flows into St. Patrick Bay.

Of the valley proper Lieutenant Lockwood says: "It has two levels, that of the stream, and a second of level mesa-lands from fifty to a hundred feet above the general level. These mesa-levels seem to be washings from the lofty sides of the valley, and project first on one side and then on the other, like the mud flats of a river. A narrow gorge, the river-bed, illustrates glacial action at some past period, the rocky sides being deeply worn and grooved."

In connection with subsequent similar discoveries, I entertain no doubt that within a reasonably remote period this valley was below the level of the sea, and the glacial ice-cap now withdrawn far from the sea discharged by an offshoot into St. Patrick Bay, and during the gradual retreat of the ice alternate beaches naturally formed from deposits of the muddy stream, as in many other rivers.

On August 30th I sent the surgeon, Dr. Octave Pavy, and Sergeant Rice, the photographer of the expedition, on an overland trip northward. Their instructions required them to proceed as far as practicable toward Cape Joseph Henry, searching carefully on the way for traces of the missing steamer Jeannette. In addition, they were to examine the condition of the English depot at Lincoln Bay, and report on the practicability of autumn and spring travelling by sledge along the Grinnell Land coast to the northward. They travelled with packs, carrying a dog-tent, blankets, and sufficient provisions to last them as far as the English depot, where their supplies could be renewed. They struck across the country from Conger nearly in a straight line to the head of St. Patrick Bay, and thence by a direct course to Mount Beaufort, near Cape Beechy, where they saw numerous traces of musk-cattle and foxes.

Their route from Shift-rudder Bay to Wrangel Bay was through inland valleys, which were separated at their head by a narrow water-shed of some fifteen hundred feet in elevation. In these valleys were found a number of small lakes, in one of which Sergeant Rice saw a small fish some six or eight inches long. The depot at Lincoln Bay was missed in going northward.

On September 3d Cape Union was reached, where, at an elevation of one thousand feet, Dr. Pavy found "an horizon as clear as can be possible to find." In Robeson Channel the ice was packed closely to the Greenland coast, while to the north the sea was covered with level ice, broken in occasional places by water-spaces. On the Grinnell Land side a broad channel of open water, two miles wide at Cape Union, stretched as far northward as eye could reach.

Returning southward, Lincoln Bay was reached, and the depot discovered in generally bad order. The packages were strewn around in disorder, and apparently several which could not be found had been blown over the high cliffs by a violent wind. Nearly a thousand rations of Australian beef, curry paste, onion powder, and matches were in perfect condition, as also six hundred rations of stearine. A defective bung had caused the loss of all but a few gallons of the rum. A small quantity of tobacco, chocolate, and sugar were good, the rest having become mouldy; the tea, sugar, and salt had suffered from dampness, while the potatoes and bread were spoiled by mould.

Water-tight cases of very light tin should be used in protecting stores thus cached. Particular attention should be given to the tightness of bungs, and to securing casks containing liquids so that none can be lost. Of five depots examined by my expedition, there was no case where there was not a portion, and generally a very large portion, of the rum and alcohol lost by lack of proper attention in this respect.

Such of the small stores as were serviceable were repacked in one cask, and all of these supplies were of great benefit the succeeding spring, when a party was sent northward over the Polar Sea. At Lincoln Bay a hare was killed by Sergeant Rice, and Dr. Pavy found at the head of the bay coal similar to that of the mine in Water-course Ravine.

Sergeant Rice, who had broken through the young ice and saturated his foot-gear on his way north, was disabled while at Lincoln Bay by an attack of acute rheumatism. His sufferings were intense, and every step caused agonizing pain in his feet, but his indomitable pluck and great enduring powers enabled him, with the judicious aid of Dr. Pavy, to proceed slowly homeward. Arriving at the valley near the head of St. Patrick Bay, he was unable to go farther. Light snow had fallen during the march, and the temperature had fallen to 17° (-8.3° C.). The doctor then erected the tent, and, making him as comfortable as possible, returned to the station for assistance, reaching Conger at 4 A.M. of September 9th.

I immediately sent Sergeant Brainard, with hot coffee and food, a bottle of Sauterne wine, and the needful medicines, to make him comfortable pending relief; three hours later a party of four followed, with sled and an improvised stretcher. The sled could be taken only as far as the top of the precipitous cliffs overlooking St. Patrick Bay, and it was necessary to transport him several miles to reach that point. Later six additional men were sent, as the original party were unable to bring him up the steep cliffs, and with them a buffalo-robe to make a warm and more comfortable stretcher.

While awaiting additional assistance, the first party carefully examined the cliffs for several miles for some ravine of gentle slope, but none could be seen. In the search, however, Private Connell and Frederik found a large coniferous tree on the beach just above extreme high water-mark. It was about thirty inches in circumference, some thirty feet long, and had apparently been carried to that point by a current within a couple of years. A portion of it was cut up for firewood, and for the first time in that valley a bright, cheery camp-fire gave comfort to man. Eventually the party reached Conger shortly after midnight; none too soon, as the temperature had fallen to 8° (−13.3° C.), and a northerly storm followed a few hours later.

Sergeant Rice recovered rapidly, and ten days later was in the field. While suffering from this attack he had travelled fifty-five hours in three days, and when relieved could scarcely move a limb; his suffering was so great during this trip that he lost twenty-four pounds in weight.

It is unnecessary to say that no traces of the Jeannette were found, as that unfortunate ship had sunk three months before. On the very day of Dr. Pavy's return, the gallant De Long was camped on the opposite side of the Arctic Circle on one of the new Siberian Islands, with only a week's provisions, but courageously hoping, "with God's aid, to reach the settlements on the Lena River."

During Dr. Pavy's absence the fortunate opening of the straits had enabled me to establish a large supply-depot near Cape Beechy. On August 30th Robeson Channel had cleared wonderfully of ice, and I decided immediately on sending a boat-party northward. Unfortunately our steam-launch was cut off by heavy ice from the open water, and the use of the whale-boat was necessary.

Sergeant Brainard, my orderly and commissary-sergeant, was

selected for this important work, in consequence of Lieutenant Lockwood's temporary disability from a superficial frost-bite.

Nearly two thousand pounds of provisions, fuel, bedding, and other necessary field-supplies were transported to the whale-boat over the harbor-floe, not without difficulty and danger, owing to the rotten condition of the young ice.

Jewell, Cross, Salor, and Connell were detailed as the crew. They left on the morning of the 31st, and moved northward under great difficulty, consequent on the violent currents in the vicinity of Distant Cape, which frequently threatened to injure the boat through the small floes, and later drove them for a short time to the shore at Cape Murchison for safety. The falling temperature caused new ice to form rapidly in St. Patrick Bay, and it was crossed only with great difficulty.

They succeeded in reaching Cape Beechy on September 1st, but grounded floebergs, with the great height and crowded condition of the ice-foot, rendered a landing at the cape impossible; and, owing to the threatening appearance of the pack, Sergeant Brainard gave way a short distance to the southward. They landed the stores and hauled up the boat through a break in the ice-foot about two miles from the cape, near the base of Mount Beaufort.

A northwest gale setting in filled Robeson Channel with heavy ice from the Polar Ocean, and precluded any immediate chance of returning by boat. In consequence they securely cached the boat, pitched the tent, in which the provisions were stored, and returned overland to Fort Conger, which was reached on the 3d. During their absence the new ice in St. Patrick Bay had increased with such rapidity that it was sufficiently strong to admit of their crossing it. Private Connell killed a fiord-seal at Cape Murchison, which was secured and cached under the boat. Although the temperature only fell to 19.5°

(−7° C.), yet the strong winds with moist air caused the party to suffer much more from cold than they did the following spring when exposed to temperatures in dry calm air much below zero (−18° C.). Sergeant Brainard developed in this trip the qualities of prudence, energy, and sound judgment which ever characterized his service with the expedition.

Sergeant Gardiner and Corporal Salor, a few days later, examined the foot-hills of St. Patrick Bay, to see how far westward from Cape Murchison they would be practicable for loaded sledges. In connection with Sergeant Gardiner's report, which showed the impracticability of loaded sledges following the coast for more than a mile beyond Cape Murchison, I decided to establish a depot at the point where a party travelling northward would leave the coast, and so removed, through Sergeant Lynn and party, a small depot previously located at the head of the bay. The depot thus established near Cape Murchison was known as Depot "A."

During these trips Sergeant Gardiner found on the shore of St. Patrick Bay an eight-man sledge, pickaxe, cooking-lamp, and a twelve-foot cedar boat with paddles. These articles needed only slight repairs to make them immediately and thoroughly serviceable. They had evidently been abandoned by sledging parties from H. M. S. Discovery in 1876.

Sergeant Lynn found on the shore of Water-course Bay a cart, evidently abandoned by the same expedition. Later, these articles, except the boat which was used elsewhere, were all brought to the station, and proved of service to us. The cart, however, was of too heavy a pattern to be of much practical benefit.

This cart, or a part of it, was used by Lieutenant Lewis A. Beaumont, R.N., in his attempt to reach Robeson Channel from Discovery winter-quarters (site of Fort Conger), in

October, 1875. The experiences of that great Arctic traveller, Sir Edward Parry, were sufficiently fortunate to justify the opinion that for overland travel a sledge may well be replaced by a cart. Lieutenant Beaumont in attempting to carry out his opinion, sustained by so sound an authority, was unfortunate in having so heavy a vehicle. I thoroughly concur with him in the opinion that overland travelling, in Grinnell Land at least, can be better done by cart than sledge, and that I so held in 1881 contributed in a marked degree to my successful journey into the interior of that country in the summer of 1882.

On September 7th, the harbor-floe being fit for sledge travel, I decided to visit the entrance to the Bellows, a valley which was situated some fifteen miles southwest of the station at the extreme point of Discovery Harbor, which I temporarily named Basil Norris Bay. The Bellows Valley received its name from the officers of the English expedition of 1875, on account of the high and constant winds which were always experienced in it. It is separated from Black Rock Vale to the westward by a high, peculiarly shaped bluff called Bifurcation Cape. I was accompanied by Lieutenant Kislingbury, and Sergeants Brainard and Ralston, with Eskimo Jens as a dog-driver.

Excellent ice for the sledge was fallen in with, and the trip was made in about three hours, notwithstanding some delay in the centre of Basil Norris Bay, on our discovery of ten eider-ducks in a water-space surrounding a palæocrystic floe. They were evidently two females, with their full-grown broods, which, incautiously delaying their migration to the southward, the sudden advent of winter had caught and detained. The young ones were killed with pikestaff, but the older ones flew away some distance after being driven from the water, and were killed by Lieutenant Kislingbury with his rifle.

On nearing the shore Sergeant Ralston discovered a herd of

fourteen musk-cattle, which were quietly grazing on a low plateau near the entrance to Black Rock Valley, some three miles distant. The party were armed only with one rifle and revolver, so Lieutenant Kislingbury and the sergeants were sent to surround the herd, of which I ordered that eight only should be slaughtered. It seemed then to me, as now, that unless there was immediate necessity for the meat, this interesting species should not be exterminated by indiscriminate slaughter.

The musk-cattle thus killed, with those already obtained in the vicinity of Conger, afforded us a liberal and satisfying diet of fresh meat until the ensuing summer. While the hunters were securing the game, I sent Jens with the sledge to the place selected for the temporary camp, and proceeded myself to Sun Bay, in order to find and examine the depot cached near Stony Cape by Lieutenant Conybeare in 1876.

On my way across the low divide which separated the two bays, I was fortunate enough to find two musk-oxen, and by taking advantage of the ground succeeded in approaching within forty yards of them without attracting their attention. For a quarter of an hour I was able to examine these rare and peculiar animals, who did not notice my presence for a considerable time, and when they did so were not alarmed, as I remained perfectly quiet.

The circumstances were such as afforded me an excellent opportunity of observing the manner in which these animals obtain their food in winter, as they were feeding while the ground was covered with snow sufficiently deep to conceal the scanty vegetation of the valley. Moving from one patch of *Dryas* or *Saxifraga* to another, the animal with its hoof scraped away carefully the snow from the plants, and later supplemented this action by the farther use of horns or proboscis as

MUSK-OX KILLED NEAR FORT CONGER.
(*From a photograph.*)

circumstances required or convenience dictated. In no case did either animal fail to first remove the bulk of the snow with its hoof.

Their food at that time was almost entirely *Dryas octopetala* and *Saxifraga oppositifolia*; the grasses and lichens were almost entirely lacking, and in no case did I ever note the musk-ox feeding on the latter vegetation, although in many places near Conger the ground was covered with scanty, minute lichens for acres in extent. The animals, although active, agile climbers, displayed on this and other occasions, when feeding, an awkwardness of gait and movement which was particularly striking.

A long and tedious search for the depot had but scanty results. In a thorough search over acres of pointed rocks overlain by a thin covering of snow, I found nothing but two six-quart cans full of rum and alcohol. I was finally forced to the conclusion that the provisions must have been cached in bags, and eaten by wild animals, as the remains of bags were found near the alcohol cans, and the lair of a wolf was situated near by.

While hunting for the depot I unfortunately fell in a mass of loose, pointed rocks, and seriously injured my right knee. During the search I went along the new ice which had formed in Sun Bay to within one hundred and fifty yards of Stony Cape. The ice thence southward of Archer Fiord was entirely new, and in perfect condition for travelling.

On returning to the party I learned that nine musk-oxen had been killed. Camp was moved to the foot of the steep cliffs where the cattle had been killed, in order that the process of skinning and dressing might be the easier accomplished. Early the following morning Lieutenant Kislingbury killed another musk-ox, which had been wounded the night before.

The morning proved snowy and stormy, with low temperature, 15° F. or −9.4° C. I decided in consequence to return to the station with as much of the meat as could be sledded to the harbor-ice over the partially snow-covered ground. We were three hours in reaching the ice, although the distance was only two miles and our load but six hundred pounds. By that time we were exhausted by our labors, and the steel runners were worn through by rocks protruding from the snow.

At the water's edge a large number of pieces of drift-wood were found near or slightly above the high-water mark. Some of the pieces were six or seven feet long, and from four to eight inches in diameter. Nearly all were coniferous woods.

We cached a portion of our provisions for the use of future parties, and struck out across the harbor-floe, which we were able to reach over the ice-foot only with difficulty, owing to the high stage of the tide and consequent pools of water along the tidal crack.

On September 11th, Lieutenant Lockwood's frosted foot being well, accompanied by Christiansen and Sergeant Gardiner, he was sent with dog-sledge to explore the Bellows, and was to bring back as much of the musk-meat as could be hauled to the water's edge. He returned on the 13th, having gone about twelve miles beyond the point reached by Lieutenant Archer, R.N., and, like that officer, he saw in advance a narrow ravine, which was then thought to be a termination of the valley, but a year later it was found to extend somewhat farther.

From Bleak Cape, he says, the Bellows appears to be "A broad valley, probably two or three miles wide and quite level, walled in by high and steep cliffs and mountains. Its *apparent* termination is probably seventeen miles distant, and bears N. 34° W." From the *apparent* end the valley was followed some six miles, turning first north and then about northwest, and rapidly narrowing from a mile to a few hundred yards in width. "Through the gap at the end of the valley," says Lieutenant Lockwood, "I could see one high peak covered with snow."

He had the same difficult experience with the sledge, while travelling up the valley, as had been encountered by our English predecessors. The level ground was but scantily covered with snow, and the sharp, flinty stones and hard substances which formed the bed of the valley rendered travelling exceedingly

Entrance to Bellows Valley, October, 1881.
[*Northeastern Side, near Bleak Cape.*]

difficult, and quite wore out the steel shoes of the runners. The last portion of his outward trip was necessarily made on foot. He found between Black Cape and Devil's Back a considerable quantity of lignite coal in small pieces, but was unable to discover the seam from which it came. It is evident that this coal was likewise seen by Lieutenant Archer, R.N., who "found the valley to consist of . . . shingle, . . . mixed with some substance very much like charcoal." The coal in every way resembled that which came from the ravine near Watercourse Bay.

One of the interesting results of this trip was the discovery of a large piece of knotty pine, three feet long and eight inches in diameter, frozen in the earth in the bed of the valley, two miles or more from Black Cape, at an elevation above the sea of nearly one hundred and fifty feet. Two musk-cattle were seen by Lieutenant Lockwood near the head of the valley, but, in accordance with his orders, they were not killed. Vegetation, though scanty in many places, was yet sufficient in the whole valley for large herds of musk-oxen.

The highest point of the valley-bed above the sea was about six hundred feet. The temperature was low during the whole trip, sinking to 1° (–17.2° C.) on September 13th, and, with the constant wind, which gave the Bellows its name, made the trip a trying one.

On September 15th I concluded that the new ice in Archer Fiord must be sufficiently strong for travelling, and with its excellent condition as seen by me a few days before I hoped that a party could reach Beatrix Bay in a couple of days' travel, and thus make an attempt to cross the Grinnell Land coast to the westward, or at any rate establish, for the use of a future party, a cache at the farthest point reached. Dr. Pavy being very desirous of making the trip, he was sent with Private Whisler, Eskimo Jens, and two sledges. He returned the following day, with the information that the late storm had broken up the new ice in Archer Fiord, and that it had been impossible for him to pass around Rocky Cape. He cached his provisions on the shore of Sun Bay, and, visiting the slaughtered musk-cattle, brought to the station about five hundred pounds of meat.

September 16th, with Sergeant Brainard and Private Bender, I started on a three days' inland journey toward the northwest, in the hope of learning something of the physical conditions of the interior of Grinnell Land. My knee, injured the week before, was not sufficiently recovered to enable me to make the journey, and I was obliged to send in my place Private Connell who had accompanied us a few miles. The party succeeded in penetrating some twenty-five miles to the northwest, where they reached a high "divide," from which they had reason to believe water drained to the westward. A heavy snow-storm springing up prevented any views to the westward, and obliged them to return to the station. This journey was made on foot, the sleeping-bag, food, and cooking apparatus being carried in packs.

Although the ice of Discovery Harbor, composed of old floes cemented by young ice, was practicable for sledging early in September, it was not until the end of the month that the sea around Distant Cape was sufficiently frozen to be passable for sledges. The heavy tides and strong currents which prevailed off that point caused ice to form late in the autumn, and to break up at an equally early date in the spring. This proved unfortunate for us, as I had hoped to obtain for use at the station an additional supply of coal from the mine in Water-course Ravine, which, difficult of access overland, could be reached by sledges over an easy route around Dutch Island and Distant Cape. On September 20th I examined the ice around that cape, and found that by crossing the extreme point overland, and by using the axe freely, a sledge could be got by the open water at the point of the Cape. The following day I sent Dr. Pavy and Jens with sledge and seven hundred pounds of provisions to be taken to Cape Murchison. He returned, unable to pass Distant Cape, but later in the day, with Sergeants Brainard and Rice, I got the sled around the Cape; a runner breaking in Watercourse

Bay, the supplies were not moved to the north side of St. Patrick Bay until the next day, by Sergeant Brainard.

Lieutenant Lockwood, with five men, started, September 24th, to add stores to Depot "B" (Cape Beechy). The eight-man sledge was used, and the party, hauling about one hundred and fifty pounds to the man, made the outward journey, some twenty-eight miles, in two days. Sergeant Rice followed them with a dog-sledge with additional supplies. Lieutenant Lockwood's trip resulted most satisfactorily, in adding important supplies to Depot "B," and in giving him valuable experience in sledging work. During the absence of the party the average temperature was $-2°$ ($-19°$ C.), and one observation was as low as $-10.9°$ ($-23.8°$ C.). Despite the severe spell of autumn cold, the work was done without disaster or material suffering.

Lieutenant Lockwood, in returning from Depot "B," brought from near the head of St. Patrick Bay a section of a large coniferous tree, probably pine. This section, from the centre, was nine and one-half inches in diameter. The tree as found was a smooth, perfect bole, unworked and but little worn by tidal action. It was in the same position, just above tide-water, as when first seen by Connell and Christiansen, September 9th.

Dr. Pavy believing sledge travelling practicable along the Grinnell Land coast, and expressing his confidence of reaching the vicinity of Cape Joseph Henry, I determined to send him again northward. On this occasion he was to be accompanied by Private Whisler, and use the two dog-teams of the expedition, driving one himself, while the other was to be under the skilful management of Eskimo Jens.

His orders required them to leave September 30th, but, much to Dr. Pavy's disappointment, I postponed his departure, not deeming it prudent to send a party into the field in the face of a driving snow-storm at a temperature of zero, Fahrenheit.

He left October 2d, with instructions to proceed to Cape Joseph Henry, searching *en route* for drift-wood or other traces of the Jeannette. In addition to this work, he was also directed to lay out along the Grinnell Land coast such depots of provisions as would facilitate spring travel in that direction. He took certain supplies from the home station, and was authorized to add the balance from Depot " B."

To the northward of Cape Beechy the party found a narrow, broken ice-foot, which was covered in many places by floebergs and heavy pack-ice forced up by the violence of late storms. Farther north the ice-foot was found to have been broken up by the sea in some places, and, becoming worse and worse, finally failed altogether, as it had not yet formed for the winter. It was consequently necessary to turn back at the southern termination of the Black Cliffs, to the south of Wrangel Bay. The ice to the eastward, in Robeson Channel, was reported by Dr. Pavy to consist of quantities of rubble cemented by new ice, and occasionally broken in by small lanes of water, the presence of which rendered a passage around Black Cliffs over the sea-ice utterly impossible. Dr. Pavy then returned to Depot " B," and attempted an inland passage to the westward of Mount Beaufort. He eventually found connecting valleys, which enabled him with difficulty, owing to the scanty amount of snow on the ground, to reach Wrangel Bay, by passing over the low " divide " which separated the valleys at an altitude of about seventeen hundred feet above the sea.

While crossing the " divide " into the bay, two ptarmigan were seen, one of which Eskimo Jens killed with his revolver. Although these birds are without doubt permanent habitants of Grinnell Land, and traces were seen later in the season, yet but one other covey of them was seen until spring. The natural coloring, which has been vouchsafed in such a remarkable degree to the rock-ptarmigan, renders it nearly impossible to see them, except by acute observation and in very close proximity.

Dr. Pavy pushed northward through Wrangel Bay, finding the narrow ice-foot of the same broken and difficult character as that below. He eventually reached with his man a point near Mount Parry, where he cached a hundred and fifty pounds of pemmican and fifty pounds of bread. Lack of ice-foot farther and the open condition of the floe-ice in Robeson Channel prevented advance beyond that place. They were obliged to spend one night on an insecure ice-foot but a few yards in width, in constant danger on one side by falling stones from the high, precipitous cliffs, and on the other from the effect of the heavy gale, which, forcing huge palæocrystic floebergs against the unsheltered ice-foot, was liable at any moment to topple large overhanging ice-blocks upon the camping party.

Some alarm, which turned into amusement, arose from Whisler being attacked by "nightmare," which caused him to believe that the ice-foot, with tent, was being carried into the straits, and to rush with fright from his sleeping-bag and the tent, awakening and alarming his comrades.

Dr. Pavy reached Conger October 9th, convinced, from his experiences, that travelling northward along the Grinnell Land coast was rarely practicable in autumn.

Having made autumn trips and explorations in all other quarters, our attention was turned toward Cape Lieber, with the intention later of exploring the interior of Judge Daly Peninsula. Near the end of September Sergeants Brainard and Jewell made an attempt to reach Cape Baird, which proved unsuccessful, owing to the unsafe condition of the ice in Lady Franklin Bay. The character of the ice in that direction was exceedingly rough. It was evident that the old floe had not been firmly united by young ice, but was yet liable to separate during heavy tides or strong winds.

Lieutenant Lockwood tried the ice again unsuccessfully October 7th, but, finding conditions more favorable on October 10th, established a small depot near Cape Baird for hunting or exploring parties. Sergeants Brainard and Rice were at the same time engaged in obtaining photographs of the country adjoining the Bellows, and in bringing in the musk-cattle killed and cached near the entrance to that valley. In both these trips the Hudson Bay sledge, constructed by our carpenters, Elison and Cross, did excellent service. Lieutenant Lockwood reported the sledge as satisfactory, and Sergeant Rice said that the work devolving on his party could have been done by no other sledge.

These trips closed what I have considered as autumn sledging, and others later are treated as winter work.

Autumn went and winter came with the departure, for four and a half months, of the sun. The beginning of the long Arctic night found the party in excellent health and spirits, and with firm faith and confidence in their ability to meet the hardships of the next season, and to improve in the coming spring on the quantity and quality of their sledging work.

Our autumn labors, as regarded the Grinnell Land coast, had been successful beyond my anticipations. Four depots had been established to the northward, the condition of the stores at Lincoln Bay ascertained, points previously unknown reached toward the interior, over three tons of fresh meat obtained by the hunt, and much valuable and practical information gained as to the physical character of the country, and as to other conditions bearing on field-work in that region.

In acquiring a practical knowledge of sledging in such high latitudes, and under trying conditions common to all autumn work, it was gratifying that no accident or disaster had occurred. Not the least benefit resulting from this experience was the development of minor, but none the less important, defects in our sledging-gear and the manner in which the work was conducted. Nowhere more than in Arctic sledging do widely varying and quickly changing conditions demand greater shifts and expedients to insure moderate or complete success.

CHAPTER X.

SUNLIGHT TO DARKNESS.

OUR life at the station during this time was by no means devoid of interest. The completion of the house, the placing of our scientific instruments, the construction of meteorological, astronomical, and magnetic observatories had kept our carpenter force busy for many weeks, and until the middle of September no one had scarce a breathing spell.

The birds had generally disappeared before the Proteus departed, and such game as was in our immediate neighborhood had been secured. Twenty-six musk-oxen, ten ducks, a hare, two seal, and a ptarmigan rewarded our hunter's efforts during September and October, which afforded about six thousand pounds of fresh meat for the party, and nearly an equal amount of offal for our dogs.

Lieutenant Kislingbury hunted assiduously in the immediate

neighborhood from the end of August, but no game was to be found. The only visible life noted by him at that time were spiders, mosquitoes, flies, caterpillars, moths, and "daddy longlegs" on the hills, and a few chubs and minnow in Lake Alexandra. The mosquitoes, numerous and troublesome at the Greenland ports, were fortunately few.

The severe temperatures in August (as low as 15.6° or –9.1° C. was noted) covered the sea with ice, dried up our running brooks, drove southward the migratory birds, and played sad havoc with the vegetation. The gay, yellow poppies were cut down, but other hardy flowers, purple and snowy saxifrages and the white daisy, flourished during the early days of September. The summer birds had gone the middle of August—an unusually early date, as Lieutenant Aldrich on September 10, 1875, saw a flock of turnstone on this coast nearly seventy miles to the northward. The fabled instinct of the feathery tribe to foretell a severe season was not needed to explain their departure, which resulted from the frost cutting off their supply of food.

I was somewhat surprised to learn, on September 3d, that the shallow ponds, to which the dried-up creeks drove us for water, were full of animalculæ of considerable size. The water was strained for a few days, but as otherwise inexplicable headaches and nausea occurred among some of the men, I had recourse for cooking- and drinking-water to ice obtained from the palæocrystic floes in the harbor.

The first signs of the coming polar night were noted on the evening of September 9th, when a grateful change to the eyes came, with a bright moon and the sight of a star of the first magnitude. While the mental irritation and depression consequent on the Arctic night are not experienced during the polar day, yet the latter has disadvantages. In some a marked tendency to sleeplessness developed, and even the most methodical fell into irregular hours and habits, unless routine was imposed on them.

September 6th was marked by Jens killing a fiord seal (*Phoca hispida*), and by Lieutenant Lockwood making a trip over the harbor-floe to Bellot Island, the ice being strong and firm the whole distance.

Although we had passed far beyond the confines of civilization, yet the same official routine was necessary in many respects as in lower latitudes. On the 10th of the month Private Julius Frederick was formally discharged from service for expiration of term of enlistment and as formally re-enlisted on the following day. Sergeant Brainard's discharge and re-enlistment followed in a like manner a few days later.

On September 10th a heavy northerly gale occurred, which, in conjunction with the position of the moon, caused an unusually high tide. Advantage was taken of these circumstances to cut the launch Lady Greely out of the ice, and haul her up inside of the ice-foot. With the whole force we finally succeeded in getting her to a point where, at the extreme high tide, there was less than a foot of water under her keel. She remained in that condition, undisturbed by the winter gales or the moving ice-foot, until launched again the ensuing summer.

Our usual psalms on the 11th were supplemented by prayer for those who travel, a practice regularly followed whenever sledge parties were in the field.

Much surprise and excitement was caused, September 13th, by the appearance of a large band of wolves upon the harbor-floe near the house. Their gaunt, slight forms showed up in a remarkable manner as the light fog, which at that time covered the country to the westward, magnified greatly their size, and some of them appeared to be as large as yearling steers.*

Thirteen to eighteen were counted in the pack. While they showed no signs of timidity, yet they were very careful to keep a proper and discreet distance, and none of our hunters were able to get within gun-shot. This caution, while in keeping with the general habits of the Arctic wolf, which has been rarely killed by hunters, seems surprising, when we reflect that these animals could never have been hunted, and doubtless had never seen anything but a bear which could injure them.

The tenacity with which Arctic animals hold to life was frequently instanced in our experiences, and it occurred to me whether it did not arise from the survival of the strongest and hardiest in a clime where nature ever seems at strife with nature's life. A few days later Lieutenant Kislingbury and Private Henry while hunting ran across a small pack of wolves, of which they shot two, but both escaped. The ball from Henry's rifle went completely through the body of one of the animals, which bled profusely. The wolf was closely followed by its bloody trail for several hours, but could not be caught.

September 26th a wolf came within a hundred yards of the house, and in the early twilight was for a time mistaken for one of the dogs. He was eventually pursued by Lieutenant Kislingbury and several men, and was shot through the body by that officer. The wolf, knocked down by the ball, lost at least a cupful of blood, and afterward continued to lose it steadily. He

---

* This exaggeration of size by a fog is well illustrated by an incident in Franklin's second journey. His men, by great patience and caution, had succeeded in stealing upon some deer, and were congratulating themselves on their good fortune in getting within gunshot, when to their amazement and annoyance, the animals took to wing, and by cackle and scream left no further doubt as to their identity as geese.

was chased for some time without any one getting again within gun-shot. He was let alone for a time in the hope that he would die, and pursued by the hunters later, travelled on, leaving drops of blood on the snow, until he fell down dead, with his body substantially bloodless.

Disturbed by the proximity of such a pack, and fearing for the safety of our dogs, which showed terror and dismay at the approach of the wolves, I decided to destroy them by poison. They showed, with the foxes, much craft and caution in approaching the poisoned meat, and would touch none, though several poisons were tried, until good was mixed with the poisonous meat. Even then they avoided it at times. Lieutenant Kislingbury reported that on one occasion the meat was visited by foxes, who ate all the good meat and left untouched that which contained poison. Eventually four wolves and a fox were poisoned, and the rest disappeared for that season at least.

Lamps were first lighted for general use on September 16th, and the next day our bath-room, a warm, well-arranged place, was completed.

The first birthday at Conger occurred on September 17th, that of Private Whisler, who completed his twenty-fourth year. The occasion was taken to inaugurate a practice, which was invariably followed during our service at Conger, of exempting the man from duty and of allowing him to select the dinner from our entire list of dainties and provisions. In addition, a quart of rum was given him for such disposition as he thought fit to make of it. The equitable disposition of it by Whisler among the party established a precedent which was regularly followed.

The temperature fell below zero on the 20th, reaching $-6.9°$ ($-21.6°$ C.) during the day. This was probably the earliest autumn date on which zero, Fahrenheit (−17.8° C.), had been recorded, the earliest approximate date being that of Parry at Melville Island, 1819, −1.1° (−18.3° C.), September 26th.

Occasional solar haloes were seen during the month, some of which were of very great beauty. That on the 21st was a brilliant display, which lasted for five hours. These were parts of two concentric rings, distant 23° and 46° respectively from the sun, which were marked by five mock suns, where the rainbow tints were most clearly displayed. This was followed the same evening by our first auroral display—delicate, convoluted ribbons of colorless light of varying intensity, which glowed and burned a short hour south of the zenith till the gathering clouds obscured it.*

The halo of the 24th was one of the most beautiful I have ever seen. It was a double halo, there being two perfect concentric half-circles, distant 23° and 46° from the sun, each half-circle having a contact arch of marked clearness. Six mock suns, two on either hand and two above the real sun, appeared during a part of the day, the prismatic colors in each case being as vivid and clear as in any rainbow. For the greater part of the forenoon the heavens were filled with such glory and wealth of color as surpassed any powers of description. Similar magnificent phenomena were observed by Lieutenant Lockwood and his party from Depot "B."

The comparatively short distance between the observer and the phenomena is shown by various observations. At one time a considerable part of the circle of 23° with its mock sun was

---

* This ribbon-like form to the aurora appears to be an arctic characteristic. As far as I know, it was first noted by Whymper during his Alaskan experiences, and later by Nares. It was the most general form of all during our many auroral displays.

most distinctly and clearly outlined against Cairn Hill, the background of the halo not exceeding three-fourths of a mile in distance from the station. Captain Nares at Floeberg Beach, noted a mock moon but two hundred and fifty yards distant. Later our astronomer, Sergeant Israel, a very reliable observer, observed a mock sun against our meteorological observatory, at a distance of less than thirty yards.

Our first fire occurred on the 22d—a large hospital tent, pitched near the house and used as a carpenter's shop. Despite prompt efforts, the use of fire extinguishers, and plenty of water, the tent and its contents were a total loss. Fortunately we had duplicates of most of the tools elsewhere. I had made it a point to scatter and divide our stores, and, though an inconvenient arrangement at times, it afforded security against irreparable disaster from fire. Carelessness, as usual, caused the conflagration. Early in the month a fire-hole six feet square had been opened in the harbor-floe, so water was at hand. Later a fire organization was planned, and one or two false alarms made all familiar with their places and duties.

Although the straits were jammed with ice, yet considerable open water remained in the neighborhood of Distant Cape, and on September 28th Private Connell shot a fiord seal (*Phoca hispida*), which he was unable to obtain on account of the ice.

September closed with the entire party in excellent health. In addition to considerable meat eaten in the field, nearly four hundred pounds of birds and fresh musk-meat was consumed during the month. Our stoves proved unsuitable for the inferior quality of coal, and, worse than that, burned five tons of coal monthly, nearly double the proper amount.

The mean temperature for September was 10.92° (—11.71° C.), the lowest on record, except that of Kane at Van Rensselaer Harbor, 1854, which was 9.81° (—12.33° C.). The minimum,

−11.9° (−24.4° C.), is the lowest on record as far as my knowledge goes. Through the effects of this remarkable cold the new harbor-floe increased during the month from four and three-eighths to fifteen inches in thickness.

The last few days of sunlight were filled in with hunting trips and short excursions in the neighborhood of the station. The fishermen then failed in Lake Alexandra as the hunters by land, but game and fish were to be had, for fish had been seen and glimpses of game obtained. Lieutenant Kislingbury saw seven ptarmigan (*Lagopus rupestris*) on October 2d, which had replaced their summer plumage of black and brown by a perfect coat of spotless white. These birds beyond doubt are winter habitants of Grinnell Land, but these were the last specimens seen that autumn. During the Arctic twilight they could be seen only by accident, for their plumage so resembles the color of new-fallen snow that only a keen eye can distinguish their outlines. A prowling wolf visited our meat-caches, and a cunning fox was seen near, only a few days before the sun left us for the winter.

Sergeants Brainard and Rice succeeded in reaching the summit of Mount Ovibos, but to do so they were obliged to make a long detour to the westward by way of Lake Alexandra. The lake was two hundred and sixty feet and the summit of Mount Ovibos twenty-two hundred and forty-four feet above the sea. Their labors were rewarded by the sight of a few snow-covered hogback mountains, far to the northwest.

The extremely rapid approach of darkness is a marked characteristic of all very high latitudes. It will be remembered that the first star at midnight was not seen by us until September 9th, and yet on October 8th the use of lamps became necessary within doors, except for an hour at midday.

Our last day of possible sunlight came—October 15th. All

LAKE ALEXANDRA, NEAR DISCOVERY HARBOR, LOOKING WEST.
(*From a photograph.*)

had an uneasy, restless feeling while watching and waiting for the sun's appearance, the clouds in the south rendering it uncertain if we should be favored with its rays at the station. I visited high ground some distance to the northward for a better standpoint. Just after midday, my journal says, "A few rays breaking through the clouds gilded to the north the rounded, snowy summit of the Hogback (two thousand and nine hundred feet in elevation), while dense water-clouds, which rose from Kennedy Channel to serve as a beautiful background to the mountains of Daly Promontory, cut off all direct rays from lower ground. From time to time the brightly illumined clouds would drift slowly to the south, and as the delicate shades of pearly gray gave way to gorgeous coloring of mellow orange and fiery red, from moment to moment I hoped the curtain would roll back and the sun shine forth. Once for a few moments the red rays of refracted light lighted up the inner harbor and outer bay. This magic touch of color, blending with the snowy covering, gave a new glory to our Arctic scenery, which was further intensified and idealized by the rosy, curling columns of vapor rising in the dense, cold air from the few water-spaces." The reds faded into yellow, the pearly grays were rapidly replaced by the dull leaden hue, which told that sunshine had passed and the polar day had given way to the long reign of twilight and Arctic darkness.

CHAPTER XI.

OUR SCIENTIFIC OBSERVATIONS.

THE primary object of the Lady Franklin Bay Expedition being to carry out the scientific programme of the Hamburg Polar Conference, the utmost care was given to physical observations. The series commenced on July 1, 1881, at St. Johns, Newfoundland, and terminated June 21, 1884, forty hours before the rescue of the survivors.

Summaries of these, and such other observations as are of general interest, will be found in the appendices of this work. To avoid tediousness and repetition, allusions are made in the body of the narrative only to such as are of special interest or importance.

The observations as to the pressure of the atmosphere, temperature and dew-point of the air, direction and force of the wind, quantity, kind and movement of clouds, the aurora and the state of the weather, were made hourly after the vicinity of Fort Conger was reached.

On the upward journey by vessel the temperature of the sea-water at the surface and when practicable at ten metres (32.8 feet), was noted first every four hours, and later hourly. On occasion these observations were supplemented by soundings, with serial deep-sea temperatures by means of the Negretti-Zambra thermometer. After our arrival at Conger, serial sea-temperatures were recorded on the 1st, 11th, and 21st of each month, at which time the thickness of the sea-floe was also noted. Surface sea-temperatures were observed the second year at every high and low water.

Our observations were always made by Washington mean time, and reference to that time is invariably meant when only the hour and minute are given. To reduce to Conger mean time, it is necessary to add forty-nine minutes.

The temperatures given in this narrative are corrected from tests with frozen mercury, that metal being assumed to solidify at a temperature of $-37.9°$ F. ($-38.8°$ C.). Thermometers having but very small errors at high temperatures required large corrections at $-40°$ ($-40°$ C.), reading from two to five degrees too low. Some of our alcohol thermometers were so unreliable that they were never used. I could have sent these costly spirit thermometers into the field, from which actual though erroneous readings of $-80°$ ($-62.2°$ C.) to $-90°$ ($-67.8°$ C.) could have been obtained. Extremely low temperature readings, made in connection with Arctic explorations or otherwise, must be received with caution, unless the history and accuracy of the thermometer can be vouched for. Honest but inexperienced observers, in ignorance of the true facts, have frequently misled themselves and others.

Some excellent standard thermometers, of bisulphide of carbon, pure spirits of wine, and ether, were made for the expedition, under the careful supervision of Professor Waldo of Yale College Observatory. They were graduated in millimetres arbitrarily, and so served as an excellent check on other instruments. Their errors at freezing mercury proved to be inconsiderable, less than a degree Fahrenheit.

Our thermometers were exposed in a large wooden shelter of Louvre pattern, four feet square and seven high, which was situated about forty yards northeast of the house. The instruments were fastened to a sheet-iron drum, so made as to revolve, which was shielded by another small shelter, made after the Louvre pattern, of galvanized iron.

The anemometer and wind-vane were placed on the ridge-pole of the main building, where the exposure was excellent.

Observer making Temperature Observations at Fort Conger.

In order to secure most reliable barometric readings, the observer, before making the current observation, verified each hour the vernier reading of the preceding hour, and in case a change greater than .03 inch in the hour had occurred the observer reported it to me, whether day or night.

The solar and terrestrial radiation thermometers furnished the expedition had such limited range to their scales, that the observations were necessarily discontinued at the most important seasons, *i.e.*, from the middle of October to March 1st.

The magnetic observatory was situated about two hundred yards northeast of the main building. It was a wooden structure, about eight by fourteen feet in size, which was secured and fastened by wooden pegs in default of copper nails. A heavy bank of earth and sod to its eaves, supplemented by snow and ice during the winter, somewhat ameliorated its Arctic temperature, but it still remained an uncomfortable building the first year. During the term-days of the second year, when the observers remained in it the entire day, it was made comfortable by the construction of a small fireplace and chimney.

The magnetometer was mounted on a stout tripod, its solidity being ensured by freezing the legs of the stand into the earth. Of this instrument ten readings were made hourly, except on the 1st and 15th of each month, which were known as term-days. On term-day two readings were made every five minutes, except during one hour, when two readings were made every twenty seconds.

For the uninitiated it should be said, that the object of these readings was to note the declination of the magnetic needle.

In the greater part of the world the compass does not point to the geographical pole, and the saying, "true as the needle to the pole," is only an inaccurate simile. The magnetic declination of any place is the difference between the geographical pole and the quarter to which the needle actually points, and is measured in degrees to the east or west. For instance, where the needle points to the true west, the declination is said to be

90° W., and when pointing to the southwest, to be 135° W. At Fort Conger, in 1882, the magnetic needle pointed between the west and southwest, the declination being 100° 13′ W.

In the magnetometer a small magnet, freely suspended by a single fibre of untwisted silk, swings readily in any horizontal direction. This magnet, at Conger, was never quiet, not even on what are technically known as *calm* days, but swung to and fro in a restless, uneasy way, which at various times impressed me with an uncanny feeling quite foreign to my nature. As it swung to right and left, its movement was clearly outlined on a fixed, illumined, glass scale, which served as a background, and the extreme oscillations, seen through a small telescope by the observer, were recorded.

In the other end of the building was placed, on a stable pier, a dip-circle, from which the inclination or dip of the magnetic needle was hourly determined. A magnetic needle, nicely and delicately balanced, in the middle latitudes assumes a nearly level position. At Conger, however, the needle, adjusted so that it can move freely in a vertical plane, shows a strong tendency to assume an upright position. At a dip of 90° the needle would be erect, while at Conger the inclination was about 85°.

In speaking of this instrument, it is necessary to say that a dip-circle was especially made for the Lady Franklin Bay Expedition, but it was by error shipped to the United States Coast Survey. On calling for it, when the duplicate instrument ordered could not be had in time, the late Mr. Carlisle Patterson, then Superintendent, promptly promised that it should be sent to me at New York. On the day of my sailing, a dip-circle, carefully boxed, was received; but on opening it, at St. Johns, an old, rusty, unreliable instrument was found in the place of the new circle. This resulted in unsatisfactory and incomplete observations at Conger, for the old circle having upright standards instead of transverse ones, as in the new, but one end of the needle could be read. It must always be a matter of regret that this unwarrantable and unauthorized substitution by some person was made, which materially impaired, if not effectually destroyed, the value of our two years' dip-observations.

Accurate tidal observations in high latitudes have always been difficult to obtain. As far as I know, the two years' observations obtained by the expedition formed the first unbroken series of any length ever made from a fixed gauge in a very high latitude. For the greater part of the time, the gauges in use were iron rods, forced as far as possible into the stiff clayey bottom. To keep open the tide-hole required the constant labor of two men, and occasionally other assistance was given when the gradual, steady movement off shore of the main-floe required a corresponding extension of the tide-hole. The main floe moved in one winter nearly twenty-five feet *off shore*. To prevent the rapid formation of ice in the tide-hole, a large snow-house was built over it. Additions were made to the original house from time to time as the floe moved. Despite this protection, the ice in the tide-house formed to a thickness of eight feet, partly from tidal overflows. The tidal observations of Conger were supplemented by observations on fixed gauges at Black Horn Cliffs and Repulse Harbor on the North Greenland coast, at Capes Sumner, Baird, Beechy, Cracroft, and Distant Cape, which, being simultaneous with those at Conger, can readily be reduced. These readings have been submitted to the Superintendent of the United States Coast Survey, and, united to those of the British expedition at Floeberg Beach and Discovery Harbor, in 1875, and by Bessels at Thank God Harbor, in 1871, will probably enable that tidal-expert, Assistant Charles Schott, to determine satisfactorily the co-tidal curves of Robeson and Kennedy Channels and the entrance to the Polar Sea.

Our time observations were made from a transit kindly loaned the expedition by the superintendent of the Coast Survey, which was in moderately serviceable condition. The chronograph, however, which was furnished for the especial purpose of registering the star observations for time in connection with the pendulum observations, was an incomplete, broken-down affair. It certainly was sent by a careless or incompetent person, whose action came near frustrating the plans of his department for a valuable and unparalleled series of observations. Fortunately, Sergeant Gardiner, of the Signal Corps, was an instrument-maker, and while he with other aid rebuilt the chronograph, I reconstructed the electrical portion of it.

The pendulum observations were due to the intelligent and liberal action of the Superintendent of the United States Coast Survey. Under the instructions and supervision of Assistant Charles S. Pierce, of that bureau, a beautiful pendulum was especially made for this work. In default of a break-circuit chronometer, for use with the chronograph in time observations, Professor Pierce kindly loaned his own chronometer, which was used in the pendulum work. As a recognition of this action, I felt it incumbent on me to see that the instrument was returned, and so, in all the dark days of our retreat, that chronometer was carefully looked after, and has since been delivered to Professor Pierce.

My astronomer, Sergeant Edward Israel, had received from Professor Pierce careful and detailed instructions concerning the pendulum work. Professor Pierce had pointed out to me the importance not only of uniformity of temperature, but of determining accurately the temperature of the pendulum. The problem was not an easy one, from the stubborn way in which heated air rises and cold air falls. The necessity of piers with great stability was obvious, but the conditions at Conger required the construction of such piers on frozen ground and at temperatures below zero Fahrenheit.

Sergeant Gardiner and Private Connell, under my directions, succeeded in building strong, stable piers. Brick and Portland cement had been purchased for the purpose at St. John's. The site selected was in a lean-to built on the north side of the officers' room. Holes three feet square were dug to a depth of about twenty-seven inches, the ground being found frozen at a depth varying from twenty-two to twenty-four inches. Over these holes a tent was pitched, and alcohol lamps lighted within it to raise the temperature. On the bottom of the holes dry, hot ashes were spread, and then two courses of bricks were laid. As the bricks had been previously heated to a temperature of 150°, the cement formed before the temperature fell to the freezing-point. In this manner the piers were finally built in a solid, substantial manner. Around the piers a house was erected of ice-slabs, which maintained an almost constant and exceedingly uniform temperature. French plate-glass being set in the front of the ice-house, and in the door leading into the officers' room, the observer was able to remain comfortably in the latter room, and by a set of reflectors throwing light on the pendulum to read its oscillations through a telescope.

Several sets of maximum and minimum thermometers were so disposed as to show the ranges of temperature at the head, the centre, and the bottom of the pendulum, and one thermometer was so placed that it could be read at any time by the telescope from the officers' room. These arrangements were so successful that the range of temperature rarely exceeded five degrees Fahrenheit, during an entire set of observations. Forty-eight swings of the pendulum with corresponding time observations were successfully made, and it is probable that these observations, under Professor Pierce's skilful discussion, will prove of marked value to geodesy.

Near the end of November, 1881, the observers began to obtain samples of the air, according to instructions furnished by Professor Edward Morley. The samples were to have been analyzed by that gentleman in connection with his investigation as to the variations of oxygen in the atmosphere. Unfortunately for his researches, the samples were necessarily abandoned, with other bulky and weighty collections, on the occasion of our retreat.

An excellent series of observations as to the velocity of sound at low temperatures was obtained, which generally confirm the theoretical law as to the effect of temperature on its velocity in air, as deduced from observations at higher temperatures. These experiments are dwelt on elsewhere more in detail.

Experiments were made with a view of comparing the actual with the theoretical dew-point; and also many other special and comparative observations were made which need not be here referred to at length.

The number of observations made and recorded each day were as follows: Meteorological, 234; tidal, 28; magnetical, 264—aggregating 526 daily. On term-days the number of magnetical observations were increased to over twelve hundred, so that the observers were always busy.

Sergeant Israel had all the astronomical work, and the observations of magnetic intensity to attend to, and was also in general charge of the magnetic work. Lieutenant Lockwood and I did duty as observers on term-days. Sergeants Gardiner, Jewell, and Ralston were particularly charged with meteorological and tidal work, being occasionally assisted by Sergeant

OUR SCIENTIFIC OBSERVATIONS. 133

Israel and Private Henry. Sergeant Rice, the second year, noted the high and low tides and sea-temperatures, being at times relieved by Private Long. Private Connell likewise assisted at times in making meteorological observations, and during all pendulum, time, and sound, experiments was in charge of the chronograph.

The Frog.
[*A Floeberg in Robeson Channel, May,* 1882.]

Fortunately systematic preparation and wise prevision secured the safe return to this country of the observations made at the cost of so much labor and care, though the bulky original records were necessarily stored at Fort Conger.

CHAPTER XII.

HYGIENE AND ROUTINE.

THE question of the health of any Arctic expedition cannot fail to interest most deeply the commander, and requires at all times the utmost care and attention on his part. As touching the health, but two complaints pertain especially to Arctic service—scurvy and frost-bite; in both of which "an ounce of prevention is worth a pound of cure."

As regards the question of scurvy, it would seem useless for a layman to dwell on a subject concerning which the doctors so decidedly disagree. The ground taken by the faculty in general, that it is owing to mal-nutrition, is probably correct, but when they go farther, and attribute it to "a deficient supply of fresh vegetable food," I think this opinion should be received with caution, especially as the exact substances deficient are undetermined, and no positive preventive against the disease has been offered by any expert. As against the fresh vegetable theory may be advanced the Danish Eskimo, ten thousand in number, who eat no pound of vegetable and not a dozen pounds of bread annually. They are substantially exempt from the disease, as are their brethren of Cape York, and the thousands who occupy the shores of the polar basin from Cumberland Gulf to Point Barrow and the Alaskan Archipelago. Bread, vegetables, and scurvy are equally wanting among them. The exemption of the Hudson Bay and the North American Indian tribes, similarly non-bread and non-vegetable eaters, is equally marked. Ignorant of the subject of medicines and diseases, it seems rash for me to advance a theory, or even a suggestion. But is not the disease owing to previous as well as continued mal-nutrition, in connection with which the abnormal conditions, checked in the patients by certain substances of their normal diet, develop into scurvy when the deteriorated physical condition is aggravated by adopting a diet affording less than usual nutrition? Is not the acknowledged fact, that men who have been immoderately addicted to the use of alcohol first succumb, a significant one? Its prevalence among men from nations which are accustomed to daily and systematic use of alcoholic drinks may be only a coincidence. In any event, an observer cannot but be struck by the freedom of American expeditions from this disease—De Long's, Hall's, Hayes', De Haven's (I believe), and my own. Despite the scorbutic symptoms in Kane's ill-fed party, no man died of it.

Nordenskiold, speaking of Maosoe (near North Cape, in about 71° N.) as having a raw, moist air, says: "Scurvy, especially in humid winters, attacks the population, educated and uneducated, rich and poor, old and young." The remedy mentioned by Nordenskiold caused me to add cloudberries (*Rubus chamæmorus*, L.) to my dietary, but they were not obtained in time. The freedom of Nordenskiold's crew from sickness on the Vega expedition, though he wintered on the Arctic Circle, and I a thousand miles north of it, had an influence on my dietary; the exemption in his voyage seeming to me in a measure due to variety, quantity, and quality of food.

My dietary list was shaped on the assumption that scurvy is a disease resulting from mal-nutrition, which would be fostered by dampness, uncleanliness, mental ennui, too strict discipline, excessive exercise or labor, and by *regular* and *systematic* use of alcoholic beverages. I by no means assume that our exemption from this disease resulted from my dietary list and hygienic rules, but let who will pass on the vexed question. I believe, however, that our large supply of fresh meat played a most important rôle in our freedom from scurvy.

From the commencement I considered it of primary importance, that the food-supply should be of excellent quality, liberal amount, and of a diversified character. The British Arctic expedition of 1875-1876 were fortunate in having such men as Admirals Richards, Sir L. McClintock, and Sherard Osborn as an Advisory Committee, to arrange the details as to stores and provisions to be required, and as to the sanitary arrangements to be followed. A large and intelligent medical staff was also at hand to suggest and to remedy any oversights which might occur in the requisitions.

The experiences of that expedition had shown, however, that in regard to this great Arctic disease the surgeons had been unable to recommend such diet as would infallibly guard against its occurrence. Over forty-eight per cent. of the entire complement of the British expedition suffered from scurvy, and, excluding those who did no field service, the percentage probably reached as high as seventy.

My surgeon was in Greenland at the time of outfitting, and it fell to me in three days' time to complete my list of stores, which lack of funds prevented my properly supplementing later. I had, indeed, given much attention to the question of equipment and food-supply, but my knowledge was entirely theoretical. It is proper that I should acknowledge my indebtedness to that most celebrated Arctic explorer, Professor A. E. Nordenskiold, for the benefits derived from his varied experience as given to the world. In selecting articles of food I profited largely from the judicious advice and opinions of his surgeons and himself. Advantage was also taken of recom-

HYGIENE AND ROUTINE.

mendations made by Sir George Nares in his published comments on the articles provided for his expedition. It is natural that one should have ideas and theories peculiarly their own, and such gave direction to certain features of my supply table.

Condensed milk, butter, and oatmeal were taken in quantities from a ton to a ton and a half each, so that the habit of daily use of these articles in middle latitudes should not be discontinued in the high north. Cheese, maccaroni, condensed eggs —all considered important—were in liberal quantities. The supply of fruits, canned in as nearly a natural state as possible, was very large, consisting of apples, peaches, pears, grapes, quinces, etc., supplemented by rhubarb, gooseberries, etc. Of vegetables there were canned onions, potatoes, tomatoes, beets, carrots, squash, okra, asparagus, corn, beans, peas, etc., of which I considered the first three the most important. In dried fruits were apples, peaches (unpeeled), dates, figs, prunes, raisins, etc. Preserves were in quantities, as also pickles, condiments, etc. The amount of food per man each day actually eaten in our two years at Fort Conger was as follows:

	Ounces.		Ounces.
Fresh musk-meat	16.0	Flour	5.5
Fresh birds and hare	0.8	Oatmeal and cornmeal	2.3
Canned meats, soups, etc.	1.6	Hard bread	3.2
Canned fish	0.5	Maccaroni	0.4
Pemmican	0.4	Farina, corn-starch, etc.	0.3
Pork, bacon, and salt beef	2.6	Rice and hominy	1.5
Butter	2.3	Beans and pease	0.4
Lard	0.6		
Ham	0.6	Total—farinaceous	13.6
Milk	1.6		
Condensed eggs	0.4		
Cheese	0.4	Canned apples	1.2
		Other canned fruits	1.5
Total—meat, etc.	27.8	Cranberry sauce and rhubarb	2.0
Canned vegetables	10.0	Total—fresh fruits	4.7
Sugar (white)	3.5	Dried fruits	0.8
Syrup	1.8	Preserves (including fruit-butters)	1.0
Total—saccharine	5.3	Pickles	1.1

This aggregrate of 64.3 ounces would doubtless be increased by coffee, chocolate, tea, spices, condiments, etc., to nearly 70 ounces. This amount may reasonably be assumed as the quantity of food necessary for the maintenance of a man's health in a latitude such as Conger, where the annual mean temperature is $-4°$ F. ($-20°$ C.). The above food was eaten, not wasted. The garbage from the cook-house was but trifling, this resulting from the plan followed—the men receiving a certain amount per day, from which they paid for their food. The quantity and quality of food depending solely on my judgment, which guarded on one side against the temptation to save, as the other plan did against waste. My avoidance of larger quantities of canned meats resulted from my opinion that their nutritive qualities are materially impaired by their tastelessness, and I quite concur with the opinion put forward by Dr. Envall, of Nordenskiold's expedition, 1872-73, who, speaking of the tasteless condition of certain of their meat supplies, says: "One gets disgusted with it, and this effect on the taste probably has an influence on the nutrition, and thereby indirectly on the nutritive value of the food."

It is needless to say that the above list of supplies varies somewhat from that which I would now make. This result is in accordance with the invariable experience of Arctic commanders. Even in as carefully a considered undertaking as the British Arctic expedition of 1875, common salt, by an oversight, was omitted in the Alert's supply. In a list of twenty articles of food, Sir George Nares comments on fully one-quarter as being, in his opinion, insufficient as an allowance for Arctic service. There have been few expeditions which have not found similar deficiencies in quantity, variety, and quality of their provisions.

The most material changes toward an improvement of my

GAME STAND AT CONGER, WITH BELLOT ISLAND IN BACKGROUND.
(From a photograph.)

own list would consist in the increase of vegetables to 12½ ounces, of flour to 9 ounces, and a more diversified selection of canned meats. Tomatoes were found to be our best vegetable, our experience being that the last cans were as good as the first, and no large eater of them was otherwise than in health. Apples and peaches were our best fruits. Of beverages, coffee, tea, and chocolate were in ample quantity. Enough good cider (not yet hard) was taken to insure a half pint once a week for the first year. Apart from the regular medical supplies of brandy and whiskey, I took one hundred gallons of New England rum, which was a modest allowance of one and a half gills *weekly*. The amount, owing to a number being non-drinking men, was about two gills weekly for each man. One gill was issued as a rule each Sunday, and the other on birthdays and festivals. The influence of the liquor was undoubtedly beneficial, as it invariably tended to enliven the spirits and increase the cheerfulness of the men. In addition to an equal or slightly larger amount, I would recommend to future expeditions that it be supplemented by half a pint of light wine weekly. In no instance was rum served *regularly* as a ration, either in quarters or on sledge journeys. Dr. Envall expresses my opinion, when he says: "I believe spirituous liquors to be of great use in small and moderate quantities, but exceedingly mischievous and pernicious in case of the least excess." I took personally twenty-five gallons of wine, but the officers, deciding at St. John not to follow my example, carried no supply of liquor, a course they especially regretted afterward.

Except for a few weeks, and during my absence in the field, I made the dietary my personal care. No one knew a day beforehand (except in special cases) what the dinner would be. Every attempt was made to prevent the men from tiring of any food, and a general liking for any article caused it to be served sparingly. The cooks, as a rule, were changed monthly, which gave variety to the style of cooking, and rarely resulted in cause for complaint. Soup was served daily, and on alternate week-days the dessert was a made one or consisted of canned fruits, while on Sunday it included both classes. Oatmeal or cracked wheat was served every morning, in addition to meat of some kind. Fresh baked bread under Long's skilful manufacture was always light and sweet, and was served for one meal daily, except during three days in the week of the last year, when it was necessarily replaced by fresh corn-bread. Both coffee and tea were regularly served, and chocolate once or twice a week.

In addition to breakfast at 7.30 A.M. and dinner at 4 P.M., two lunches were provided, which consisted of hard bread, butter, tea, and coffee in unlimited quantities.

The following bills-of-fare for four successive days are taken at random from my journal, and give an idea of our table. To avoid repetition, tea, coffee, butter, milk, etc., are omitted, as they were always served:

SUNDAY.

Breakfast.—Musk-beef hash, oat-meal, fresh bread, chocolate.

Dinner.—Pea-soup, roast musk-beef, baked maccaroni with cheese, rice pudding, fresh peaches.

MONDAY.

Breakfast.—Corned-beef, oat-meal, fresh bread.

Dinner.—Vegetable soup, baked pork and beans, corn-bread, stewed peaches.

TUESDAY.

Breakfast.—Musk-beef hash, oat-meal, fresh bread.

Dinner.—Bean soup, roast musk-beef, tomatoes, fresh apples.

WEDNESDAY.

Breakfast.—Musk-beef hash, baked pork and beans, fresh bread.

Dinner.—Vegetable soup, boiled codfish, hominy, and cake.

The table of the officers was supplied from the same dishes as that of the men, and the only difference consisted in the occasional addition of peaches, pineapples, marmalade, etc., or a can of shrimps, crabs, or some other delicacy. I had selected a quantity of these stores for the use of the officers, but later decided it was best to throw them into the general mess. There was no article which was not shared to a greater or less extent among the entire expedition. This course, while not perhaps practicable in larger expeditions, should be followed as far as is possible in all. The officers' meals were served by the cook, while the second cook, who was changed each week, waited on the table of the men.

Every attempt was made to insure careful serving of food, and to this end regular crockery (with soup-tureens, soup-plates, etc., complete), silver-plated spoons and forks, and several table-cloths were purchased for the men's use. The table-linen, changed twice a week, was kept neat and clean, and the table always presented a tidy, creditable appearance. The room-orderly, detailed daily, assisted the undercook in setting the table and in removing and washing the dishes. The midday and evening lunches were not served, but simply set out on a side-table, where each man took what he pleased during a half hour's time. The night observer was allowed a midnight lunch.

The party was particularly free from prejudices as to the various articles which made up our diet, antipathy to tea and chocolate being the most marked. The former was fortunately, on the part of men who did little field service, a place where the use of this indispensable and favorite Arctic beverage was obligatory.

The experiences of all Arctic expeditions point to a well-planned routine and proper discipline as of the greatest importance in the maintenance of health. At first I was not disposed to insist on fixed hours for retiring, and none were ever obligatory on the officers. The hopes that the novelty of continual day would wear off, and regular hours follow, proved fruitless, and an order was issued requiring the men to retire at 11 P.M., Washington mean time, which corresponded to 11.49 P.M. local time. Breakfast was at 7 or 7.30 A.M., at which hour all were required to be present, except observers who had night duty.

It was strange that the same disinclination to retire or to rise was noticeable during the long Arctic night, as is so common in parts of the world where day and night are more equally divided. During the second winter the inclination to sleep was so marked that an order was issued forbidding the general party from occupying their beds between 8 A.M. and 3 P.M., except on Sundays. For ten consecutive days during that winter my officers, by observation, slept from fourteen to sixteen hours daily, and it was only by effort that I reduced my own sleeping-hours to nine daily.

I think it admits of no doubt, that cleanliness and the use of the bath tend greatly to promote and conserve healthy physical conditions. The pores of the skin, freed from perspiration and foreign substance, and stimulated to activity by the bath, must better perform their important functions. Most expeditions, housed in vessels, have been obliged, owing to the trouble from moisture engendered by the bath, to discontinue the practice entirely or in part. With us a well-warmed bath-room, a large, convenient tub, with a plentiful supply of water at any desired temperature, made the bath a matter of pleasure and luxury rather than duty and penance. The obligatory rule of a bath weekly needed no enforcement, for many bathed oftener, and one of the officers for many long months never failed to bathe daily.

Notwithstanding the large amount of moisture from the bath-room and from the cook-house, it passed away readily and rapidly without leaving traces in thick layers of hoar-frost on walls or floor. The attic-room, which naturally received the rising vapor, retained such a small proportion, that, when the heat of advancing summer melted the frost on the inner side of the roof, we had not more than two or three barrels of it to remove. Frost never formed except on windows, and on the washboard to a height of a foot or two from the floor. The beds and blankets were turned down toward the centre of the room one day each week, and oftener when apparently necessary. The only cases of frost at the head of the bed and frozen bedclothing were in connection with the bed of observers, which was almost constantly in use, and in my own bunk, which was in an exposed corner. Both cases received prompt attention, and no recurrence was noted.

The quarters were swept out daily, and every Saturday were thoroughly overhauled for the coming Sunday inspection, the only one of the week. The failure to provide more than half a dozen brooms left us soon without that simple but valuable article, which was ingeniously replaced by brushes in which heavy buffalo-skin did good service.

Exercise was encouraged among the men, but was very rarely enforced. My personal distaste to exercise for its own sake was so marked, that I hesitated to insist on it for others. Sergeant Brainard, who served as the orderly sergeant of the expedition, was instructed by me to use his ingenuity in finding sufficient work of seeming value to keep certain of the men busy in the air an hour daily. He was usually successful with these, and others of their own inclination kept out of doors from one to three hours. The observers in their daily round had enough, if not too much exercise at times. The rule was eight hours on duty and sixteen off, which applied to the three meteorological observers, who were relieved by my astronomer of one tour Sunday, which changed their hours weekly besides giving them a complete day's rest.

Long-continued exercise in the open air while beneficial, is not absolutely essential for all. During the first winter, for a period of three months successively, my out-of-door exercise averaged but fifteen minutes daily, during which it was generally of a very active character, as running at a slow gait. I carefully observed my condition, but could see no resulting injury, being entirely free from sickness. I considered it an experiment, and later took much more exercise, but in winter never exceeded an hour, unless I had *work* to do. During this time I worked steadily six hours daily on records, observations, or in research.

The placing of instruments on Mount Campbell and Cairn Hill was done with the ulterior motive of sending men to read them at regular intervals during the winter. In this manner long walks for some definite object were taken by many of these men, who, fond of hunting or of work, were disinclined to stray and stumble around to no purpose over the floe. The obtaining of ice for drinking and other purposes also insured a certain amount of daily work, particularly during the time the moon was above the horizon, when a store of ice was accumulated for the dark days in the moonless period.

Some surprise has been manifested that this water did not have a deleterious effect on our health, but none was ever noticed. For over eighteen of the twenty-four months at Fort Conger, the only water drank was obtained from the melting of the palæocrystic ice in the harbor. There is no doubt that the ice contained a considerable quantity of saline matter, caused, in my opinion, by infiltration and efflorescence. The potable ice was of such color that a practiced eye at once selected it. The tinge of bluish-white was a shade quite apart from that of the salt-water ice, which had a somewhat deeper shade that bordered on the greens rather than blues.* The ice was melted in a large tank holding a hundred gallons or more, which was provided with pipes running through the upper portion of our cooking-range. The resulting water was used for cooking, bathing, or drinking, though melting ice in a pail in quarters was in general use for the latter purpose. The water, however, contained too much salt to permit of its use for photographic purposes.

Most of our winter amusements were necessarily of a mental character, owing to lack of space for much physical exercise. The library was an excellent one, comprising about seventy-five volumes of Arctic works, many encyclopædias, scientific works, etc., for the studious. There were probably a thousand novels, magazines, and books of a light character.

Cards, chess-boards, backgammon, parchesi, and other games were much in use, but no gambling, save for tobacco, was allowed. One variety entertainment was given, and a semi-monthly newspaper lived for two months only. Hunting was assiduously followed as long as light lasted, and skating was practised until the roughness of the ice rendered it difficult.

One of the party had a violin; and an orguinette, with about *fifty* yards of music, afforded much amusement, being particularly fascinating to our Eskimo, who never wearied grinding out one tune after another.

When these amusements seemed stale, the monotony was

---

* In travelling, opaque, granulated ice, resembling closely pressed snow, could usually be found to a depth of five or six inches on palæocrystic floes.

broken by a series of lectures commenced and generally maintained by me. I lectured some six times the first winter, on Sound, Storms, Magnetism, Poles (geographical and others), Arctic Expeditions, and War Reminiscences, which were supplemented by readings. Lieutenant Lockwood delivered two lectures on Arctic Sledging, and Dr. Pavy one on Africa. The second winter I was assisted in this work by Dr. Pavy, who lectured on Napoleon, and by Sergeant Israel, who gave a series of excellent and instructive lectures on Astronomy.

In addition to this variety and abundance of food, freedom from moisture, personal cleanliness, moderate exercise, regularity of hours and meals, and attempts to promote cheerful amusements, the ordinary medical precautions were followed. The surgeon made regular examinations of the party each Sunday, and reported in writing each month. He was particularly directed to recommend such special and supplementary diet as he might deem needful, and to report promptly any premonitory signs of scurvy. The regulation allowance of lime-juice, one ounce daily, was invariably issued, except when replaced by cider or its discontinuance recommended by the surgeon on account of impaired digestion or for other reasons.

CHAPTER XIII.

SLEDGING IN THE ARCTIC TWILIGHT.

THE disappearance of the sun by no means put an end to our sledging work. After that time various parties were employed in mining coal in Water-course Ravine, and in hauling a portion of it to Depot "A," at Cape Murchison, where some three thousand pounds were accumulated to serve as fuel for sledge parties who might pass the night at that depot. A small quantity was also hauled to the home station.

After consultation with my officers, I decided that the inaction and monotony of our long winter should be postponed as far as possible by the continuance of sledging work after the sun had left us and the Arctic winter commenced. The dangers and privations of this work were undoubtedly great, and such action was contrary to precedent. In these matters elaborate and practical suggestions from our predecessors are not to be lightly disdained or neglected, but it is equally certain that individuals suited by temperament and character for Arctic work, after a certain amount of experience, must not follow too blindly precedent and theory. They should be able to gauge correctly the critical points of the situation, and the limit of endurance to which their men can safely be subjected. Such sound judgment and daring energy are essential before the best and most successful work can be done.

On October 23d, seven days after the departure of the sun, Lieutenant Lockwood, with Brainard, Connell, and Christiansen, with a well-laden dog-sledge, left for Depot "B." Their mission was to construct a large, commodious snow-house, which was to be made thoroughly comfortable, and of sufficient capacity for any sledge-party which would visit it. It is certain that some of the articles selected for house-furnishing were striking, if not unique. My journal gravely sets forth that, in order to properly heat the snow-house, Lieutenant Lockwood was to take a few joints of stove-pipe, a small coal stove, and four hundred pounds of the best fuel which the country afforded—lignite coal from Watercourse Mine. It was surely not according to precedent, and seemed anomalous, if not absurd. But why not coal as well as oil, and a stove as well as a lamp, and so the coal went. It performed admirably then as ever afterward, and if at times the red-hot stove enlarged unduly the roof-flue, it was none the less a cheery, delightful sight and comfort to the storm stayed traveller, and in no wise impaired the strength and stability of the structure.

While Lieutenant Lockwood and party were building the snow-house, Sergeant Gardiner and Private Ellis, with Jens, added a half-ton of coal, mined in Watercourse Ravine, to the supply at Depot "A" (Cape Murchison).

The changing conditions of the ice in Robeson Channel were strongly evidenced by Lieutenant Lockwood's observations during this journey, as compared with previous experiences that autumn. From the summit of Mount Beaufort, on October 26th, Robeson Channel was seen by him to be open in all directions; the only ice to be seen in any quarter was small and unimportant. No floebergs could be discerned, save a few grounded along the shore. It was his opinion, that at that time an Arctic vessel could have steamed, with but little if any trouble, direct from Cape Lieber to at least Repulse Harbor. Previously during September and October the channel had been densely packed with ice. This journey having resulted favorably, I later decided on more important ones.

One great drawback in the autumn work had been our inability to cross Robeson Channel, in order to transport to the eastern shore caches of provisions for the use of the party which I intended to put in the field the next spring in order to determine the configuration of the most northern point of Greenland. It was also very desirable that we should ascertain the quantity and condition of the stores at Thank God Harbor, so as to know what articles and amounts could be drawn from that point for field use, or could be depended on in case a party was detained on that coast. The young ice in September had prevented any attempt to cross Hall Basin by boat, and although the weather had been unprecedentedly cold in October, yet the straits were in no ways fit at any time for an attempt at crossing by sledge. This was shown conclusively by Lieutenant Lockwood's observations on October 26th. In the days following his return the straits jammed with heavy ice, and the temperature remaining steady at about $-7°$ F. ($-21.7°$ C.), it seemed possible to Lieutenant Lockwood that a crossing to Greenland could be made near Cape Beechy, which, being at the narrowest part of Robeson Channel, is the point where the heavy floes drifting from the Polar Sea most readily jam, and, cemented by rapidly forming ice, afford a safe passage to the Greenland coast. I was thoroughly sensible of the extremely hazardous nature of such an attempt, but I consented to the experiment, having full confidence in Lieutenant Lockwood's prudence, and feeling thoroughly assured that his good judgment would cause him to abandon the effort, as specified by his written instructions, at such time as it might seem dangerous to proceed farther. Lieutenant Lockwood left November 2d, the temperature being $-6.5°$ F. ($-21.4°$ C.), with calm, clear weather. He was accompanied by Brainard, Lynn, Biederbick, Saler, Connell, Ellis, and Frederick, all of whom had specially volunteered for the attempt. Fifteen days' rations, with complete camping-gear, were hauled on the eight-man English sledge.

This party was speedily followed by a second, which, composed of Dr. Pavy, Lieutenant Kislingbury, and Sergeant Rice, with both dog-sledges and Jens, left on November 4th to add stores to the depot in Wrangel Bay. The trip from Mount Beaufort to the south of Cape Beechy to Wrangel Bay was made inland, Dr. Pavy thinking that such route would facilitate his movements. The cliffs on the north side of Wrangel Bay were still washed by the open sea, showing that the storms of the previous month had broken up the sea-floe in many places. The quantity of stores which Dr. Pavy was able to add to the depot in Wrangel Bay was so small as to scarcely repay the hardships endured by his party, and the results of the trip emphasized the difficulty and fruitlessness of autumn sledging overland. Dr. Pavy's party reached the station on November 8th, having had no accident, or indeed sufferings, apart from the great hardships which are incidental to all winter sledging in such high latitudes.

The hardiness of the Eskimo dog was illustrated by an incident during this trip. One of the favorites, Gypsy, was in no fit condition to travel, but insisted on following the sledge, and the second day out gave birth to four puppies, which, left in a snow-bank near Cape Beechy until the return of the party, were brought safely to Conger.

Lieutenant Lockwood's party returned on the same day as Dr. Pavy, having been unsuccessful in their efforts to cross Robeson Channel, owing to the open condition of the straits. Judging on his arrival at Cape Beechy that the crossing by the sledge alone would be impracticable, Lieutenant Lockwood decided to take with him the whale-boat, but was compelled to abandon that project as impracticable, as the boat was twenty-eight feet long and the sledge but eleven. In consequence he sent to St. Patrick Bay and brought up by sledge the small, cedar boat Discovery, and on November 5th made a second attempt.

The sky at that time was overcast, and the outlines of objects indistinct, in consequence of which the party experienced many falls in travelling through the snow and over the ice-floes. The party had proceeded but two or three miles into the straits, when they "heard very distinctly the groaning of the moving ice, like a distinct roar or the monotonous groan of a fly-wheel." Lieutenant Lockwood, seeing in the distance a dark line which seemed to indicate open water, moved in advance of the working party, and passed on to a level floe, which he soon found to be in motion. At this point the open condition of the straits, the increased darkness, and the doubtful prospects of success, wisely determined Lieutenant Lockwood to return to Depot "B." An examination of Robeson Channel on the subsequent morning showed a channel of open water of varying width, which was continually changing, according to the movements of the pack.

His return to the station occurred during the spring tides, which, forcing water through the tidal crack, had covered the ice-foot in many places. On several occasions the new ice which had formed over these pools was not sufficiently strong to bear the party, and at times they broke through it, wetting several to the knees. They were frequently obliged to travel on this dangerous ice-foot on account of the steep shore, which was impracticable owing to its occasional drifts and exposed rocks. In the middle of St. Patrick Bay, after the dry ice had been reached, the party was halted by Lieutenant Lockwood, and the greater part of the men changed their foot-gear.

On camping at Depot "A," near Cape Murchison, they found that Private Biederbick had frozen quite severely one of his toes, despite the changes of foot-gear during the day. As it gave him much pain, he was put into a sleeping-bag, and hauled on the sledge to the station. He was soon again fit for duty, as the frost-bite, though severe, was fortunately superficial. Sergeants Brainard, Lynn, and Connell suffered likewise from slight frost-bites, though none of them were serious.

In regard to sledging along the Grinnell Land coast northward, Lieutenant Lockwood says: "High, rocky, precipitous bluffs follow the west contour of the coast-line, broken in by gradually sloping mountain-sides near Watercourse and Shiftrudder Bays. Sledging of any kind is impracticable along this route at any time, except on the ice-foot or main floe. The débris from the cliffs forms an inclined plane extending to the edge of the sea. This slope is only occasionally such as to allow travelling thereon, and even where possible the alternate bare rocks and steep snow-drifts make it extremely laborious."

Along such a bold coast no satisfactory sledging work can be done until the bitter cold of winter has bound fast into a secure and solid mass the sea-floes—the only true Arctic highway.

The temperature remained quite steady at about $-13°$ ($-25.0°$ C.) during the absence of the party. The lowest temperature noted was $-26°$ ($-32.2°$ C.).

Our sledge trips that autumn stand perhaps unparalleled, considering our high latitude, as the sun had been twenty-three days absent when the last party returned to the station.

The results of these winter journeys satisfied me of the inadvisability of sending sledge parties to any considerable distance after the sun has left or before its return. The advantages derived are rarely commensurate with the energy expended. This does not apply to journeys entailing absence of one or

MAKING READY FOR A SLEDGE JOURNEY FROM FORT CONGER.
(*From a photograph.*)

two nights, where parties have a certain and comfortable shelter within reach.

The benefit which came from these journeys was largely moral, and resulted, in a great measure, from the fact that the monotony of our first winter commenced only in the middle of November, and not with the sun's departure a month earlier.

CHAPTER XIV.

OUR FIRST DARK DAYS.

IT is the unknown which awes and terrifies, and so, gazing with a certain dread at the departing sun, the actual experiences of the first dark days came to us as a relief, and not as a hardship. For a time it then seemed that our brooding imaginations had played us false, and that an Arctic night, unbroken for nearly five months, was not so trying after all.

But, as the rapidly fading twilight gave place to darkness, and day after day brought only the gloomy sky and growing cold, we began to realize that it is not so much the conditions of cold and darkness in themselves, which render life in the high north so insupportable, as their eternal reiteration and continuing monotony.

That the long-continued darkness exercised a depressing influence on most of the party was evident to every observing person. Naturally no one was inclined to admit that he was personally affected, but no one escaped this influence. The most marked signs among us were tendency to insomnia, indisposition to exertion, irritability of temper, and other similar symptoms abnormal to our usual characteristics both mental and physical. In my own case, although following a set routine, it was only with difficulty that I could limit my sleeping-hours to a reasonable number, or apply myself steadily and successfully to continued mental work. While free from mental depression, insomnia, and feelings of lassitude which characterized some, yet I was at times affected by irritability of temper, which it required a continued mental struggle to repress. But few were exempt from this symptom. Our faces gradually acquired a pale, yellowish-green color, which was disagreeable to view, and the extent of which was not clearly appreciated until the return of light.

The sun was last seen at the station October 14th, and again reappeared on February 28th, one hundred and thirty-seven days later. There has been much written about Arctic darkness, but the test usually given, that of text legible at noon, conveys to most persons an inadequate idea of its intensity. The sun, indeed, comes near the horizon at midday for a short time, and the effect is apt to be overrated. At Fort Conger stars were to be seen at local noon seven days after the sun had gone for the winter, and so remained visible in a cloudless sky for over four months. In all these days the southern horizon lightened up with more or less glow, the effects of which some have perhaps shown a great tendency to exaggerate, while others have shown an equal disposition to lessen. It is true, that on December 21st a twilight arch of several degrees existed in the latitude of Conger, but the practical benefit from such arch is disputable.* The darkness of midday at Conger was such, for nearly two months in midwinter, that the time could not be told from a watch held up with its face to the south. From this it will be readily understood, that in midwinter the light from the sun at noon is far less than that which is received from the full moon in middle latitudes.

---

* This statement is made with reference to astronomical twilight, which ends when the sun is 18° below the horizon. With reference to what is known as civil twilight, which ends at 6 below, no twilight existed at Conger during December. Apparently opposing statements as to Arctic twilight result from an indiscriminate use of these standards.

Regarding the Arctic night in general, the light is very slightly greater than that of clear nights in middle latitudes, and as the sky is unusually cloudless at Conger, very dark nights were uncommon. Whether it be, as I suspect, from the great freedom of the atmosphere from dust or not, the stars of one fainter magnitude could be seen at Conger than in lower latitudes. The "milky-way," on very bright nights, was so clear and distinct, that frequently on stepping outside the door it gave me the impression of a feeble auroral light, such as is commonly seen. The snow, too, seems to give out a certain amount of fine phosphorescent light. Whether it stores up the light received during the prevalence of the moon or not, and radiates it later, I cannot say.

The light from various sources was such in amount, that only on a few cloudy, stormy days were we ever prevented by darkness from taking our regular exercise. The departure of the sun and the coming of winter weather were nearly coincident. On October 8th the *mean* temperature sank below zero ($-17.8°$ C.), there to remain continuously for six months and a day. For over five months, November to March inclusive, no *single* observation was noted higher than $-3°$ ($-19.4°$ C.). Our lowest October temperature, $-31.1°$ ($-35.1°$C.), occurred on the 18th, three days after the sun left. The mean for that month was $-9.22°$ ($-22.9°$ C.), which has but twice been exceeded.

During the month of October the leisure hours of the men were occupied in banking up the house quite thoroughly. A wall of ice, six feet high, was constructed some three feet from the house, and was rendered wind-proof by a coating of wet snow. The space between the wall and house was later filled in with loose, dry snow, an excellent protection from its great non-conductivity to heat. The second year we improved on the arrangement of the first year, and carried the wall of ice and snow up to the very eaves of the house, a work which added much to our winter's comfort.

October 25th, ten days after the sun had gone, we were much surprised by one of the party making the startling announcement that the sun was to be seen in the southern sky. It proved to be a beautiful mock-sun, which remained visible nearly an hour, its burning colors being watched with attentive interest as the reflected image that revealed the course of our lost luminary. It showed a brilliant disk of blue, yellow, and red, about four degrees above the horizon, with bars of white light extending from its centre upward and downward. I know of no other instance in which this phenomenon has been witnessed after the going of the winter sun.

Our photographer succeeded a few days later, despite the absence of direct sunlight, in making a fair negative, by exposing a sensitive dry plate for an hour, and was similarly successful seventeen days before the return of the sun.

The hunters continued in the field throughout all October, more for exercise than in any well-founded hopes of shooting anything. The existence of game was undoubted, for, during the last three days of the month, two wolves and a fox were seen, and a hare crossed the Dutch Island trail on freshly fallen snow within a mile of the house.

There exists a general impression that the nearer the geographical pole is reached the brighter and more frequent are auroral displays. The region most favored with such phenomena is a belt of country in North America, south of the magnetic pole, in about latitude 60° N., over a thousand miles to the southward of our station.

Some of our displays were grand and magnificent in the extreme, but in general they were lances of white light, having perhaps a faint tinge of golden or citron color, which appeared as moving shafts or spears under the formation known as "merry dancers." The aurora of Grinnell Land is by no means comparable with those of glowing, burning colors, such as are to be seen in Hudson Bay country and Siberia, and some of which have been so vividly portrayed by Kennan in his "Tent Life in Siberia."

Our first winter was marked by displays about twice each week, in which the arch was the most common form after the streamer; magnetic disturbances were rare during colorless and slowly changing forms. The list of auroras will be found among the appendices, but the following brief description covers the most remarkable and striking displays of the early winter.

The aurora of October 28th, although of short duration, was marked by heavy magnetical disturbances, which attained the maximum eight minutes after the last ray faded. The streamers were numerous and very brilliant, despite their colorless character. At one time their shining lances of light converged into a beautiful corona, which seemed to rest, a crown of golden light, on the dark brow of the high cliffs to the southwest.

November 14th: "In the shape of a nebulous mass, much resembling a mass of freshly escaped steam, which appeared to be brilliantly illuminated by reflected rays from a powerful calcium light. Generally colorless, it once showed a delicate rosy tinge for a few moments." Later: "A beautiful and brilliant arch, about 3° wide, formed of twisted, convoluted bands of light, similar to twisted ribbons, extended from the southwest through the zenith to the northeastern horizon. Occasionally well-marked and clearly-defined patches of light detached themselves, as puffs of smoke from a pipe, and drifted fading to the north-northwest. The arch seemed to be continually renewing itself from the southwest to fade at the opposite end." Perhaps a better idea of this peculiar formation may be conveyed by likening the display to an arch having the appearance of a revolving, endless screw. This formation was by no means infrequent, but I have never seen it elsewhere, or known it to be described. The ribbon shape seems an Arctic and unusual form. It was first recorded, I believe, by Whymper in his Alaskan experiences, and later by Nares in 1875.

December 19th: "A particularly fine aurora, like a pillar of glowing fire, from horizon to horizon through the zenith, showing at times a decidedly rosy tint, and later a Nile-green color."

The monotony and unchanging character of Arctic life afford few chances of connected or interesting narrative, so I shall frequently quote freely from my journal, as giving the clearest idea of our life by showing how eagerly apparent trifles are touched and dwelt on.

Other than the departure of the sledge parties which left the station in the early days of November, the most important incidents were the births of the two litters of pups, five of which came on the 2d and five on the 3d of the month. My journal of November 4th says: "Two of the last litter and one of the first have died, and another was eaten by one of the pack. This evening the remaining pups of the last litter were for a time abandoned by their mother, who left them to quarrel with the mother of the other litter, which were in the same room with her. During the temporary absence of the mother, we placed one of her pups with the other litter, but it was pushed away by the indignant parent, who declined any addition to her cares. Finally the deserting mother returned to her puppies."

Another litter came a few days later, and one of the mothers, waiting her opportunity, seized one of the pups of the new litter and was about to devour it when discovered, too late to save its life. It was found to be a common practice for the dogs to seize and devour young pups, but, although the bitches ate readily the litters of others, it never fell under our notice that a mother ever ate one of her own pups.

These dogs were placed in the care of Private Schneider, as our Eskimo were of the opinion that they could not survive. The experiences of our predecessors had shown the difficulty, if not impossibility, of raising litters born in the early winter. Our original teams, however, had been so thinned by dog-disease that I felt the importance of attempting to strengthen them, for at least the second winter, by raising these recruits. Nares also says pertinently, "An Eskimo is anything but a good nurse, and although Frederick is a valuable man in other ways, he cannot be induced to take sufficient care of the young dogs." My experiences were the same, and I selected for the work Private Schneider. He devoted much time and attention to them, and eventually succeeded in raising fifteen puppies, all of which were of great benefit to us in subsequent sledging operations. The disinclination of our puppies to open their eyes on the tenth day more than ever confirmed their keeper in the opinion that the Eskimo dog is an extraordinary animal. Those raised by Schneider were also broken to harness successfully, and driven by him the following summer.

"Our dogs would now never be recognized as the same wolfish, snapping, untamed animals obtained at the Greenland ports. Good care, plenty of food, and kind treatment had filled out their gaunt frames, put them in good working condition, and made them as good-natured, affectionate, and trustful as though they had never been pounded, half starved, and generally abused from their puppyhood upward." Half-starved animals, who have never been kindly spoken to, and who have been cruelly beaten on the slightest pretence, necessarily assume in self-defence a threatening and vicious attitude toward all comers. They were regularly fed, first on alternate days, and then once daily, and we never found it necessary to maltreat and beat them to ensure fair behavior at feeding-time. Indeed feeding-time was the only occasion on which rival dogs would not fight, for long experience had taught them it was a losing game; whichever dog won, both invariably lost their food through neutral and wiser parties.

For a time amusement was afforded us by the discovery of a remarkable double echo, which gave back distinctly the seven syllables contained in the words "taking sea temperatures."

The excitement consequent on the return, November 8th, of the last sledging party for the winter, with Private Biederbick frost-bitten, had not died away, when two days later our second fire occurred. It was the carpenter's tent again, which had been pitched a sufficient distance from the house to ensure the safety of the latter. The fire was as usual the outcome of carelessness, resulting from an attempt to fill a gasoline-lamp without extinguishing it. Sergeant Elison, who was the careless man, paid dearly for his imprudence, as the flaming oil burned severely his hands and face, destroying his beard, eye-brows, and a part of his hair, fortunately without serious after-effects. The temperature was 32° below zero ($-35.6°$ C.) at the time, but the fire organization was promptly on hand, and did good service with the extinguishers. No delay or confusion was experienced by the men in taking the places or performing the duties assigned them by the written instructions, and good order was marked. After the extinguishers were emptied, the remainder of the fire was smothered by blankets. The tent was not destroyed, and but few things of importance were damaged. Fortunately the party engaged in putting out the fire escaped any serious frost-bites, although the cold was intense.

In connection with the question of fire, I made it a point daily to examine the wood-work in the immediate vicinity of the chimneys, which were so arranged as to render the chance of a fire without immediate detection almost impossible. Such wood-work as was exposed to the heat from the chimneys was invariably left bare, so that its condition might be readily seen, which would not have been possible had it been covered by tin or sheet-iron.

Sergeant Brainard's journal of November 11th indicated the opinion of the men as to suitable clothing for ordinary use. He says: "Considerable attention is being given by the men to the manufacture of blanket-clothing; it is considered superior to the ordinary issue if stable-frocks and overalls (thin duck) are worn over to prevent snow from adhering to the rough, woolly surface."

The experiences of the expedition confirmed the opinion of Nares, Payer, Nordenskiold, and many others, that for ordinary use, first-class woollen under-garments, with heavy, woollen clothing, are all that is essential in Arctic service.

The monotony of Arctic life commenced about that time. Different methods to alleviate its discomforts and depressions were broached, none of which were particularly successful, as, indeed, none can be. A tri-weekly school was commenced by me during the month, which was kept up through the entire winter with marked benefit to the men attending. In this work Lieutenant Lockwood relieved me by his cheerful and considerate assistance. Arithmetic, grammar, geography, and meteorology were taught. For a time Dr. Pavy instructed two men in French. The educational qualifications of the men were very good, and there was but one of the party on its original formation who was unable to write, and he acquired that attainment during our stay at Conger.

Lieutenant Lockwood, with the assistance of Sergeant Rice and Private Henry, edited a semi-monthly newspaper, the *Arctic Moon*. Its prospectus, issued on the 14th, excited curiosity and interest until it appeared on the 24th. It lived, however, only for two months, dying for lack of interest, although it served its temporary purpose of amusement and diversion.

It was not until November 14th that the temperature of freezing mercury ($-38.3°$ C.) was noted, and the day following a number of oils and other substances were exposed in a temperature of $-25°$ ($-31.7°$ C.) for the purpose of noting the effect of low temperatures upon them. At a temperature of $-30°$ ($-34°$ C.), tincture of hyoscyamus and oil of peppermint were frozen solid. Coal-oil became of the consistency of syrup at $-25°$ ($-31.7°$ C.), and commenced to show signs of crystallization in places at $-37.4°$ ($-38.6°$ C.). New England rum, ninety per cent. proof, at $-41.7°$ ($-40.9°$ C.) showed a thin coating of slush, and at $-47.4°$ ($-44.1°$ C.) a small amount like syrup remained in the bottom of the vessel, the balance resembling mixed snow and water. At $-49.7°$ ($-45.4°$ C.) the vessel could be inverted without any liquor escaping.

November 17th, the temperature being at $-30°$ ($-34.4°$ C.), the construction of the pendulum piers, which has been elsewhere described, was commenced by us. It was a tedious and trying, though successful job of masonry. A few days later our little dog Gypsy, the brightest and most cunning dog of our teams, lost her last puppy through another mother springing at and killing it. Gypsy appeared to have maternal instincts to a marked degree, and sorrowed long for her lost litter. For a considerable time after this she improved every opportunity, in the absence of their own mothers, to suckle the young in other litters.

Although we were separated so far from our country, yet we could not fail to bear in mind the festivals which we knew were being celebrated by our countrymen. November 24th was duly appointed in orders as a day of thanksgiving and praise. In the morning of that day, I read to the party, as appropriate for the occasion, the ninth selection of Psalms.

Later came a series of races and friendly contests for a few small prizes, which were offered by me to incite general participation. There was scarcely a member of the party who did not participate actively as judge, manager, or contestant.

The snow-shoe race of four hundred yards was won by Sergeant Brainard, pressed hard by Ralston and Gardiner. Later the Eskimo contested with teams of seven dogs each in a race to Dutch Island and return. The half-breed Frederik was first in, being, as the men said, too wily and cunning for the simple-hearted native Jens to contend with. A foot-race of one hundred yards resulted in a dead heat between three, which was eventually won by Ellis. In the afternoon rifle-shooting was tried at a distance of twenty-five yards; a candle set up in a box being the bull's eye. This was won by Private Henry, with Jens and Cross tied, which eventually resulted in the Eskimo winning.

At different times during the day a few auroral streamers of varying brightness shot up and vanished, as if to look on our unaccustomed sports. These mysterious and unearthly visitors from the far south had that day to me a weird and spectral aspect, which sadly belied their name of "merry dancers." The accompanying magnetic disturbances seriously interfered with the pleasure of our observer, who was obliged to quit the group of pleasure-seekers to watch for several hours in the cold magnetic observatory the vibrating needle which swung uneasily to and fro. The day passed quickly and pleasantly, and the unusual amount of out-of-doors exercise gave all a sharp appetite for the excellent meal which followed.

The dinner was the same for the men and officers, except that a small allowance of Sauterne from my private supply garnished the officers' table. Oyster-soup, salmon, ham, cider-ducks, devilled crab, lobster-salad, asparagus, green corn, several kinds of cake and pie, ice-cream, dates, figs, and nuts comprised the *menu*. In addition to a small quantity of punch at noon, a moderate amount of rum was given to the men in the evening, which contributed much to the merriment of the day.

On the 27th, at a temperature of $-35°$ ($-37.2°$ C.), Sergeant Cross froze his right ear while absent about two hours at exercise. This was the only occasion of any such accident during our regular winter exercise, and it probably resulted from a lack of care, although the physique of this man was such, from his habits and services, as to mark him as the individual of the party least calculated to endure hardships and exposure.

About five hundred pounds of musk-meat and birds comprised the fresh meat consumed during November; an allowance of about twelve ounces daily, which during December was increased to nearly a pound.

The decrease of coal burnt during November was over half a ton as against October; a marked gain when considering the greater cold of the latter month, which resulted from the change of stoves in the men's quarters and less work in the carpenter's tent. The December cold demanded more fuel, and the amount burned amounted to eight and a half tons.

The mean temperature for the month of November, $-24.53°$ ($-31.41°$ C.), is the lowest recorded by any Arctic expedition, being over two degrees colder than November, 1853, experienced by Kane at Van Rensselaer Harbor. The highest temperature of the month was 3° below zero ($-19.4°$ C.), and the lowest 46° below ($-43.3°$ C.).

The general health of the party during this time was excellent. Private Long, while in the cook-house, had paid such close attention to his duties that his health suffered somewhat, and necessitated his relief about the middle of October, but he soon regained his usual robust condition.

The next patient was the result of the only serious accident which occurred during the stay of the party at Conger. Sergeant Gardiner, on the last day of November, broke his left leg by falling in the pathway while making a tidal observation. The slope to the tide-gauge was a steep one, and in the dim light of his lantern and the rough condition of the ice he made a misstep, which resulted so unfortunately. Every attention was given to him, Steward Biederbick being particularly devoted in his duties as nurse. Sergeant Gardiner's general health remained good despite his enforced confinement for a couple of months, during which the bone united closely but slowly.

December opened with evidences that the winter solstice was approaching, for the twilight arch at noon was exceedingly fine, though it still afforded an extremely feeble light, which was sufficient to enable occasional journeys to be made to the summit of Bellot Island and to Cairn Hill, in order to read the meteorological instruments there exposed.

On the 1st Sergeants Brainard and Ralston visited the summit of Mount Campbell on Bellot Island for that purpose. They were surprised to find the temperature on the summit, at an elevation of about twenty-one hundred feet, $-8°$ ($-22.2°$ C.), while that at the station was $-27.7°$ ($-33.1°$ C.). A minimum of $-28°$ ($-38.9°$ C.) had occurred upon the mountain since October 31st, against one of $-40.8°$ ($-40.4°$ C.) at the station.

Thermometric tests were made on December 2d and other days, which were based on the assumption that pure mercury freezes at $-37.9°$ ($-38.8°$ C.). From that standard our mercurial thermometers (from Green, N. Y.) rarely showed errors as great as 1° (0.6° C.), but the spirit thermometers read from 2° (1.1° C.) to 4° (2.2° C.) too low. Some instruments showed such great errors (reading invariably too low) that we were unable to use them, as from selected thermometers readings of −80° (−62.2° C.) or lower could have been made.

It seems doubtful if temperatures from alcohol thermometers can be depended on below −60° (−51.1° C.), as at that temperature the standard alcohol from the United States Medical Department, reduced by addition of one-third as much water, showed signs of viscosity, having perceptibly thickened.

On December 5th a lunar eclipse occurred, which was first noted by Lieutenant Kislingbury and Sergeant Jewell. It had unfortunately escaped the notice of our astronomer, and its ending was but unsatisfactorily noted by him, owing to the presence of clouds at that time. As the eclipse was ending, the fleecy clouds which partly concealed the moon, and surrounded it for a considerable time, formed around it to a space of about 8° a most beautiful corona. The large and marked yellow circle which immediately surrounded the moon changed imperceptibly into blue, to be followed again by yellow, and that by red.

A remarkable lunar halo occurred the same day; two almost complete circles of 22° and 46° radius, with two contact arches, both showing clearly prismatic colors. The second contact arch was remarkable in extending beyond the zenith, forming nearly a complete circle.

About the 10th of December was the critical period of our life at Conger, as a number of the men gave indications of being mentally affected by the continual darkness. Their appetites for a time failed, and many signs of gloom, irritation, and depression were displayed. The Eskimo, however, were more seriously affected than any of the men. These symptoms of restlessness and uneasiness were noted by me as early as the 8th, and every effort was made by personal intercourse to restore these Greenlanders to a cheerful mental condition.

On the 13th Jens Edward disappeared, leaving the station in early morning, without eating his breakfast or even taking his seal-skin mittens. The morning was a dark, gloomy one, with threatening aspect, which soon manifested itself in a fall of snow. To ensure striking the right trail, Sergeant Brainard was sent directly north of the station for nearly a half mile, and Sergeant Rice to the south, both parties being provided with lanterns, which would enable them to describe a half-mile circle around the station to determine positively the direction taken by the Eskimo. His tracks were found with some difficulty southward toward Dutch Island and Robeson Channel. Sergeants Brainard and Rice, with Private Whisler, pursued him, followed later by Dr. Pavy and a sledge. He was overtaken near Cape Murchison travelling rapidly northward, but returned to the station without objection, and in time recovered his spirits. No cause for his action in this respect could be ascertained other than his intense desire to return to his home, or place himself in some situation in which, according to the superstitions of Greenland, he could have supernatural knowledge of it.

In the pursuit Sergeant Rice, in one of his many falls in the rough ice-foot of Robeson Channel, seriously injured his shoulder. He was sent back by Dr. Pavy in charge of Private Whisler. The latter, in his extreme zeal to be of assistance, had left the station without orders, and was far too thinly clad for such exposure. The weather was moderately warm ($-29°$ F., $-33.9°$ C.), but the over-exertion, followed by a reaction, so affected him physically and mentally that he would have perished from cold had it not been for Sergeant Rice's judicious and persistent efforts in his behalf. The success of his action

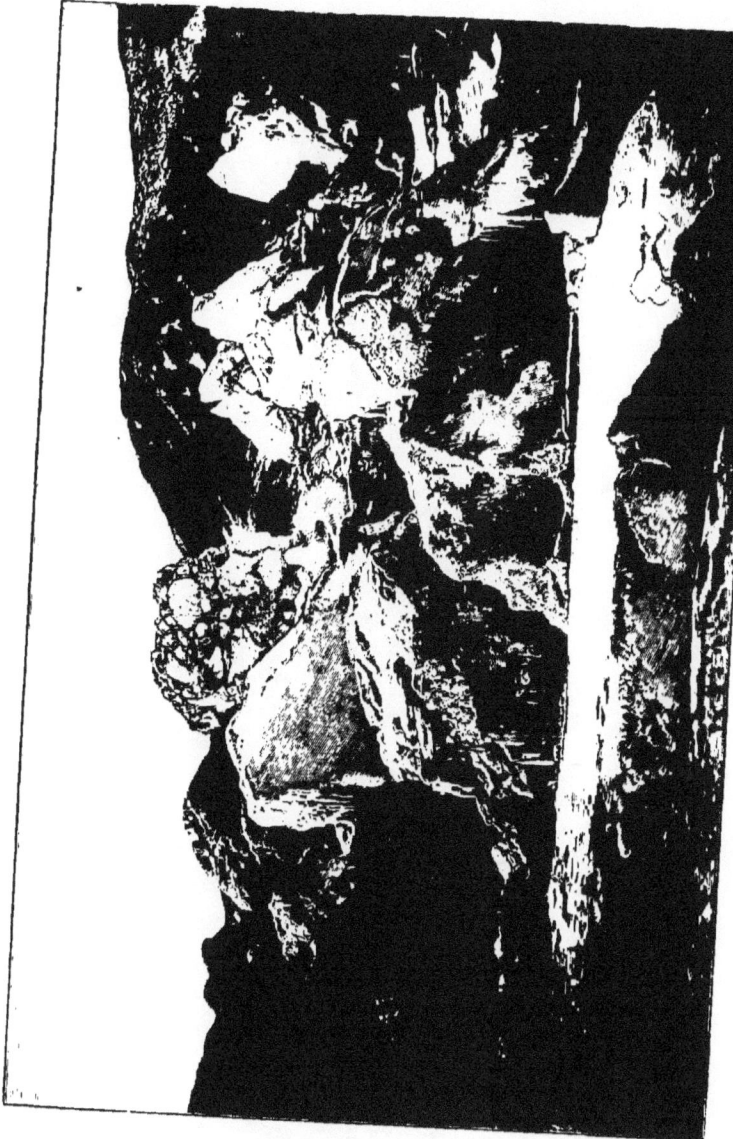

ICE FOOT AND PRESSED-UP ICE, CAPE MURCHISON, ROBESON CHANNEL.

(From a photograph.)

was all the more creditable and surprising, as Sergeant Rice's right arm was entirely useless from his fall.

Sergeant Rice succeeded in getting Whisler within about a mile and a half of the station, when the returning dog-sledge fortunately reached them, and he was soon brought to the station. The exposure affected Private Whisler's mental faculties in much the same manner as was vividly described by Kane in the experiences of his party, when several men eventually perished. It was several hours after his return to the station before Whisler was entirely in his right mind. Eskimo Christiansen, a few days later, seemed to have the same intention of deserting as Jens, but fortunately was dissuaded.

These affairs gave me great uneasiness until the returning sun and the commencement of spring work engaged the attention of the Eskimo, and rendered them more cheerful and contented. In connection with the action of these men, it should be said that the members of the expedition had always treated the Eskimo in the kindest and most considerate manner, carefully avoiding any rough pleasantries with or allusions to them. Inspector Smith had kindly advised me on this subject before leaving Upernivik, informing me of the facility with which the Eskimo, not well acquainted with the English tongue, misunderstood acts and allusions. The generally received opinion as to the extraordinary appetites of the Eskimo was not borne out by the actions of our two natives. The excellent, hearty appetites which they had on joining were never excessive, and were soon equalled by those of our own men. As to seal-blubber, they would not even taste it at Fort Conger, and later, during the retreat, ate it sparingly and with reluctance.

On December 16th our mean temperature for the day was for the first time lower than $-40°$ ($-40°$ C.), being $-40.9°$ ($-40.5°$ C.) corrected. Two days later my journal says: "It is remarkable how our little puppies, that are but six weeks old, endure the cold. They rush out from the lean-to into the open air at a temperature of $-40°$ ($-40°$ C.) and $-45°$ ($-42.8°$ C.), in order to obtain bits from the slop-bucket, and to-night two or three running into the water as it was thrown out, and remaining quiet for a minute, were actually frozen to the spot, and had to be cut out with a hatchet. They appear none the worse for their misadventure."

The winter solstice, although marking our shortest day technically, was by no means the darkest. For a portion of the day the air was filled with falling spiculæ of frost, which were not sufficient to prevent a view of the stars. The outlines of Proteus Point, four-fifths of a mile distant, could be seen. A number of the party visited Dutch Island, among whom was Sergeant Brainard, who, on attaining his twenty-fifth birthday, was, in accordance with the general practice, relieved from duty. The darkest day of the winter, owing to the thick mist and fog, proved to be December 12th, on which the want of light and other unfavorable conditions did not prevent Lieutenant Kislingbury and others from taking their daily walk toward Dutch Island.

My journal of December 21st says: "We have long looked forward to the coming of this day, and its advent is a source of blessing and relief to me. It removes all fear that the winter may not pass safely and comfortably, and so lightens my heart and mind most materially. The blessings of continual health and exemption from serious accidents, except in Gardiner's case, should cause feelings of gratitude to spring up in our hearts toward that Divine Providence which has us all in His keeping. The sun to-night turns northward in its course, and in a few days darkness will give place to returning light, which, as with many other blessings, has never been fully appreciated until it took flight."

CHAPTER XV.

CHRISTMAS AND THE NEW YEAR.

IT appeared surprising that the mere fact of the sun having commenced its northward journey should have such a marked effect upon the spirits of the men as was visible in the days immediately following the winter solstice. It was the most striking illustration of the many instances in connection with our Arctic experiences as to the powerful influence exercised over the physical conditions of the body by the existing mental conditions.

The solstice past, the attention of the expedition was drawn to other considerations incident to the season, the most important of which were the preparations for the proper celebration of the Christmas holidays. It was fortunate that the preparations for Christmas entailed certain work and physical exertion on the part of some of the party, as Sergeant Brainard, who had systematically kept the men at useful labor, completed the last steady outdoor work on the 22d, when the officers' quarters were completely banked up with snow. This labor, with the ordinary routine, sufficed to keep the men from brooding too much over the contrasted conditions as to the coming and past Christmases, and yet kept their minds healthfully on the pleasures of the holidays.

In order that the quarters should be especially neat and tidy for the coming celebration, they were overhauled a day or two in advance, and the floor was thoroughly washed and scraped.

The fact of washing out our quarters may seem an ordinary

circumstance to a person unacquainted with the peculiar conditions of Arctic life, but it was perhaps an unique experience that the sleeping-quarters of an Arctic party were thoroughly washed and scoured in midwinter. Whatever water is brought into the quarters in this manner must necessarily be taken up by the air and deposited elsewhere in the shape of hoar-frost. The fact that water continuously froze on the floor in all our rooms necessitated scraping the floor after washing it. This precaution, with a slight increase in the fires, succeeded in giving us thoroughly clean quarters for our Christmas exercises, without any inconvenience or suffering following.

The preparation of the Christmas dinner was commenced several days in advance, as from its extensive character much extra labor was entailed upon Frederick, who was the regular cook. Unfortunately he burned his arm quite badly on the 22d, but, despite his condition, requested that he be permitted to complete his tour of duty. Long, who was considered the especial cook of the party, with his customary cheerfulness, assisted Frederick in the preparation of this important meal.

The capacity of our excellent cooking-range, with its large ovens and hot-water boilers, was thoroughly tested on Christmas Day. When Frederick, the cook, had planned out a place for cooking the many dishes for the great dinner, he was thrown into a state of dismay on learning that plum-pudding had been added to the list. He came to me, saying that he did not see how he could cook this dish, as his range was taxed to its utmost; and he was much relieved to learn that Mrs. Greely had sent a case of pudding as a Christmas present for the expedition.

The quarters thoroughly cleaned, Sergeants Brainard and Rice took upon themselves the task of elaborately decorating the quarters with such flags, guidons, and other articles as could be used in draping or ornamenting. I refrained from visiting the men's room, until on Christmas eve I was notified that my presence was desired, and on entering I was greatly delighted with the changed appearance of the general quarters. The room, low-studded and unpainted, had never presented a cheerful aspect, even in our days of sunlight, and during the winter season the accumulation of soot from the soft coal burned in the quarters had given it an air of gloom and darkness, which was largely enhanced through the subtle influence of association by the monotony of the long days passed within it. The room was now well lighted, and with its elaborate trimmings had a gay and lively appearance not unlike that presented by army quarters in the far West on like occasions.

I made a few remarks suitable to the festival we were to celebrate and with reference to our peculiar situation, apart from and yet a part of the great civilized world.

I had assigned to Sergeant Rice the grateful task of distributing the Christmas gifts, and he performed his duty with pleasant and well-received remarks befitting each gift and its appropriateness for the recipient. We had neglected to provide ourselves with a Christmas tree, and our new country afforded not even the semblance of a shrub, the largest plant—the creeping Arctic willow—being about a foot long and not over an inch above the surface of the ground. In consequence the presents were spread out on our largest table.

The thoughtful consideration of a few friends and well-wishers of the expedition, some of whom were personally unknown to any of us, had resulted in the donation of many articles both valuable and useful. Every officer and man received a package addressed to him personally, and some were sent for distribution at the discretion of the commanding officer. The idea was a most happy one, and it would have done the generous donors much good could they have known the keen pleasure their gifts made in the hearts of the men who received them. A number of the men, who had lived lives marked by neglect and indifference on the part of the world, were touched even to tears, although they strove man-like to conceal them. The commanding officer received a fan—not needed for Arctic use; and Lieutenant Kislingbury a small dog, which excited the more amusement when he turned away the ridicule by calling out, "O! Schneider, don't you want to buy a dog?" Poor Schneider did not hear the last of it for several days. The prosperity of the joke lay in the fact that Schneider had for many weeks devoted his spare time and attention to the successful raising of our Arctic puppies.

These gifts were supplemented by a number from the commanding officer, which were distributed by lot—some of value and others of an amusing character. A plentiful supply of eggnog, and the removal of the restriction as to the hour of retiring, made the evening a delightful one, and long after the Sabbath and Christmas came together the quarters resounded to hymns, chants, carols, and sentimental songs.

Christmas morning came clear and cold, with a temperature of freezing mercury, which moderated later in the day. The calm air, unstirred by wind, made exercise tolerable, and all sought the harbor-floe for a long walk, in hopes of a marvellous appetite.

At 10 A.M. the Psalms for Christmas were read, to which I added as appropriate the second selection, consisting of the 139th and 140th Psalms. This reading was supplemented by the singing of a hymn and the doxology, led off by Lieutenant Kislingbury. I remember no service in all our Arctic experiences which so affected and impressed the men, unless it was that at our first burial in the winter at Sabine. Our thoughts and tenderest feelings could not but go out to those we had left behind, with doubts and fears as to whether it fared well or ill with them, never distrusting but their hearts were with us in our Arctic Christmas.

Christmas falling on Sunday, no amusements of any kind were attempted, but everyone waited with interest and a certain impatience for the dinner, which was as elaborate as our stores would permit.

The *menu* for the dinner was as follows: Mock-turtle soup, salmon, fricasseed guillemot, spiced musk-ox tongue, crab-salad, roast beef, eider-ducks, tenderloin of musk-ox, potatoes, asparagus, green corn, green peas, cocoanut-pie, jelly-cake, plum-pudding with wine-sauce, several kinds of ice-cream, grapes, cherries, pineapples, dates, figs, nuts, candies, coffee, chocolate. Egg-nog was served to the party in moderate quantities, and an extra allowance of rum was also issued in celebration of the day.

The candies, plum-pudding and cigars were the most appreciated, not only for the satisfaction they afforded the taste, but as being gifts from thoughtful friends. The cigars came from an army lady who knew the weakness of the rank and file for the consoling weed, and the candies were from a leading confectioner of New York City.

On the 26th the men were busy in the preparation for a variety show, which was set for that evening, as Christmas had fallen on Sunday. The Lime-Juice Club announced that they would perform at the Dutch Island Opera House for one night only, and that dog-chariots could be ordered at 10 P.M. The admission fee was in tobacco, the current coin of Grinnell Land.

The first act was a representation of an Indian council, which ended with a war-dance. Nine of the party participated in this scene, which was admirably rendered. Most of the actors had served in the far West, and some had spent months continuously in Indian camps, and so were thoroughly familiar with the parts they portrayed. I doubt very much if a more realistic representation of the wild red-man was ever presented in the Arctic Circle, if elsewhere.

A female impersonation followed, by Schneider, which afforded amusement for the party, but particularly so to the Eskimo. Schneider had provided himself at the Greenland ports with the entire costume of the Eskimo belle, and being a small man, was able to squeeze himself into the garments. As he appeared on the scene with his elaborate make-up and closely-shaven face, one was struck by the excellent resemblance to the Innuit belles whom we had seen in lower latitudes. In his *amowt*, or woman's hood, he brought the largest of his charges, one of the Grinnell Land puppies, who was nearly frightened to death by the applause which greeted his first advent into polite society. Excellent comic songs by Henry were followed by equally amusing imitations of a well-known military character by Connell.

The entire party were prepared for a delightful and interesting literary treat from Sergeant Jewell, who announced that he would give a select reading. It proved to be a well-received jest, which ended the entertainment for the evening. Jewell entered, and after elaborately arranging and opening a large volume, carefully hung up an aneroid barometer and made a special reading of it for the meteorological information of the party.

The full light of the moon came to us again on the 27th, affording a clear and excellent view of the surrounding country, which had been hidden from us for a long time by the intense darkness of the moonless midwinter. We congratulated ourselves that this luminary would remain with us until the reflected rays of the sun would give us again some faint light at midday.

On December 30th my journal says: "I was glad to hear

a very warm and long debate between the party as to the relative merits of the cavalry and infantry arms of the service. This has been the favorite topic among the men, but the despondent humor of the dark days has prevented its recent discussion. The recommencement of these debates proclaims the return of their former good spirits to some of the party." The character of these debates may be imagined from a pertinent statement of Sergeant Brainard, who said that "no argument of any topic of a theoretical character appears to be settled until the owner of the strongest pair of lungs in the expedition is discovered."

December 31st, "The month appears to be ending with very low temperatures. Yesterday and to-day the mercury has been frozen the greater part of the time."

The maximum for December was $-10°$ ($-23.3°$ C.) on the 2d, and the minimum $-52.2°$ ($-46.7°$ C.) on the 24th. The mean of $-32.01°$ ($-35.6°$ C.) has rarely been exceeded in December. The thickness of the new ice was found to be thirty-four inches, an increase of but one inch during the month.

The last day of the year came, and, as at Christmas, the restrictions regarding the hour for retirement were set aside, and the party determined to watch the Old Year out and the New Year in. The watch was enlivened by songs until midnight, being followed afterward by dancing and by a concert from a well-organized calthumpian band, in which the tinware of the expedition played an important part.

The spirits of the party were by no means dampened through an extra allowance of alcoholic liquors. A scrub-race was got up between Biederbick and Schneider to Dutch Island and return, a distance of nearly four miles, in which a small quantity of rum was the hard-earned prize. The men kept up their songs and amusements until three o'clock in the morning.

Later in the day Sergeants Jewell and Lynn visited Mount Campbell to read the instruments, but were unsuccessful in finding them, having taken the wrong ravine on the island. An incident in connection with their return evidenced the great readiness with which, under certain conditions, sounds are heard in Arctic temperatures. I went out of the quarters to listen if I could hear them coming, and from the sound of their voices judged them to be within a short half-mile of the house. Although my extra clothing was only a thin jersey and a light pair of mittens, I concluded I would go out and meet them, the temperature standing at $-28°$ ($-33.3°$ C.). To my surprise, however, I walked nearly two-thirds of the way to Bellot Island before meeting them, and learned on inquiry that they must have been on the hill overlooking Pound Point, and at least two miles from the house when I first heard them.

Of the day my journal says: "Our New Year opens well. It has been a warm day, from $-10°$ ($-23.3°$ C.) to $-30°$ ($-34.4°$ C.), with a touch of wind not at all comfortable. I delayed the service an hour this morning to give the revellers of last night an opportunity for needed rest. It gave me great pleasure to see how bright and cheery the men were last evening. Their good spirits, quiet contentment, and increased appetites ensure us against scurvy this present season. Our unbroken numbers, excellent health, undiminished courage and strength are subjects of deep thankfulness." So, in health, good-will and comfort began our New Year in Grinnell Land.

CHAPTER XVI.

WINTER EVENTS.

OUR Christmas holidays over, matters reverted to the usual routine, and anything novel or unusual was recognized as a relief. Sergeants Brainard and Rice on January 3d repeated the trip of the 1st, succeeded in finding the instruments on Mount Campbell, and made the following report: "The exposed thermometer read, at 4 P.M., $-20°$ ($-28.9°$ C.), being $10°$ ($5.6°$ C.) warmer than at the station; maximum temperature since December 1st, $-13.5°$ ($-25.3°$ C.); minimum, $-44.8°$ ($-42.7°$ C.), being respectively $3.5°$ ($1.9°$ C.) lower and $10.4°$ ($5.8°$ C.) higher than here."

Such discrepancies always appeared in connection with these comparative readings. Nares similarly reported temperatures on Lookout Hill at Floeberg Beach, four hundred and eighty feet high, as being on one occasion $6°$ ($3.3°$ C.), and on another $11°$ ($6.1°$ C.), warmer than at the ship. Dr. Moss at the same place found the temperature some $3°$ ($1.7°$ C.) warmer at the masthead than on the floe. The cause of such differences seems readily explained by assuming it to be radiation which induces the extreme temperatures of Grinnell Land, and as the low temperatures are always in calm weather, the dense cold air has time to seek the lower levels.

If the early days of January came to us with faint light, they brought sharp cold. The mean temperature fell in two days $19°$ ($10.6°$ C.), from $-31.2°$ ($-35.1°$ C.) the 7th to $-50.3°$

(−45.7° C.) on the 9th, and the day following the minimum touched −58.2° (−50.1° C.).

Everything being in readiness, we commenced our pendulum observations on January 6th. During this work regular time observations were necessary twice daily, and the severe cold made the work of the most trying character to our astronomer, Sergeant Israel. He made the observations on the 14th, in temperatures varying from −54° (−47.8° C.) to −56° (−48.8° C.). A few days later, being exposed for a long time to a temperature of −48° (−44.4° C.) in the open observatory, he froze superficially one of his feet. Apart from this the pendulum experiments, though tedious, and involving exposure and suffering, were most fortunately and successfully conducted.

In the meantime the entire quarters had been made as comfortable as was possible. The house had been well banked up with both earth and snow, and all cracks in the men's quarters had been papered over so that no draughts were possible. The men had constructed shelves over their bunks, and had arranged curtains, which insured a certain privacy whenever they sought it. In the officers' room such shelves and conveniences had been erected for each one as were desired. The surgeon had his books, instruments, and such medicines as he wished, on shelves constructed in his corner.

My own domain of eight by eight was in general thrown into the main room, but heavy curtains were so arranged that at night, or whenever I desired privacy, they could be drawn so as to cut off my corner from view. Such little personal trappings as I had taken with me were arranged to the best advantage. On shelves near me were placed my personal books and the excellent Arctic library we were favored with. To save space, my bunk was built on the top of an ammunition-chest, in which the greater part of my clothing was packed.

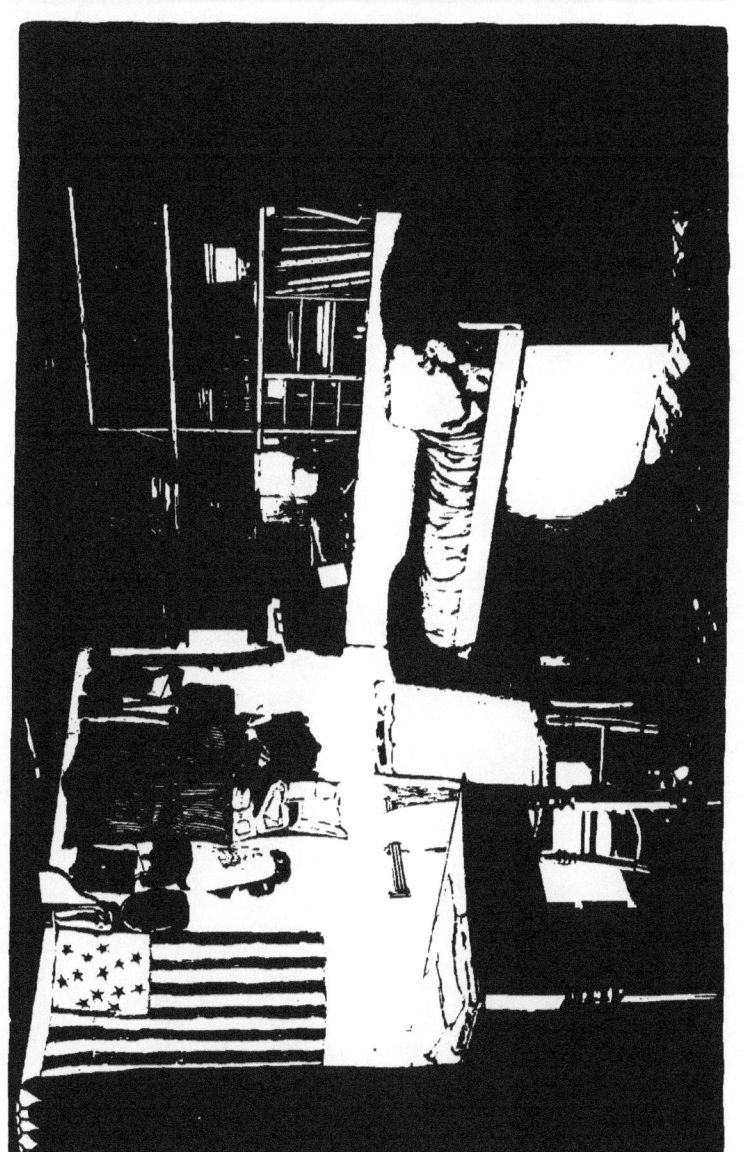

LIEUT. GREELY'S CORNER AT FORT CONGER.
(From a photograph.)

A small desk, a rocking-chair, and some private carpeting added much to my comfort as I daily applied myself to mental work. The ink froze nightly at my head, and the water spilled on carpet or floor at all times turned to ice, but as a compensation the thermometer by day—if day there be without the sun—rose to 90° (38° C.) around my head. Despite these and other drawbacks, it was a comfortable nook to me in that time, and it will always abide in my mind with pleasure, as a place where I did good work myself and planned better for others.

The 16th of January was a day we long remembered at Conger. My journal says: "We have had to-day the most violent storm I have ever experienced, except a hurricane on the summit of Mount Washington." The barometer commenced falling .05 inch hourly at 7 A.M., with calm, cloudy weather. I watched the barometer hourly, the fall increasing until it reached .10 inch an hour at 11 A.M., with a southwest wind of eighteen miles. Observations were then made every fifteen minutes. An hour later the barometer had fallen another tenth of an inch, and the wind, which had suddenly changed to the northeast, attained a velocity of over fifty miles an hour. The air was so full of snow that I ordered the temperature observation to be made by two strong men together, and the tide reading by two others. It was with difficulty that they succeeded in reaching the instruments. It took six of the best men with ropes to make the 1 P.M. readings, when the wind was blowing steadily at fifty-two miles from the northeast, in which quarter it remained. At 2 P.M. the barometer still fell with the same rapidity, and the wind had attained a velocity of sixty-two miles. It was quite impossible to quit the house, and a thermometer was read just outside the southwest door. The wind was then blowing a hurricane, the air full of snow, and the house shook and creaked in an alarming and ominous manner. Every instant

I expected that the roof would be twisted or torn off, and the whole building blown into the open harbor. Such a catastrophe would have left us in desperate straits, and would probably have proved fatal to some of the party. The violence of the wind for over an hour kept us in a state of suspense as to what would be our fate.

The highest registered wind was at 2.15 P.M., northeast, sixty-five miles per hour, but about 2.40 P.M. the wind, which had been blowing steadily, changed into violent gusts, which probably reached eighty or ninety miles an hour. The anemometer-spindle broke short off, and the cups blew several miles into the harbor before they caught and stopped. At 3 P.M. the barometer was at 29.028, a fall of over half an inch (.504) in five hours. The pressure remained nearly steady for three hours longer, but at 4 P.M. the wind had fallen to about forty miles, and observations out of doors were again renewed with some danger and difficulty. If our buildings had not been well banked up with earth and snow, they would have been torn to pieces beyond a doubt. In one respect this storm was an extraordinary one. Payer, in commenting on a statement of Hayes of a storm at $-27°$ ($-32.8°$ C.), says it is probably a typographical error. The general principle that storms do not occur at very low temperatures is sound, and it is equally obvious that during storms the temperature rises rapidly and that observers in the field overrate the velocity of cold, cutting winds. The wind blowing fifty-two miles an hour in this storm, at a temperature of $-13°$ ($25°$ C.), is probably unparalleled. Other remarkable winds at low temperatures occurred January 23, 1882, southeast, thirty-four miles at $-25.2°$ ($-31.8°$ C.), and March 6, 1882, east, twenty-one miles at $-27.2°$ ($32.9°$ C.).

The day following my journal says: "Two days of storm and cloud have passed since the noonday twilight has been seen, and now our eyes note a perceptible change. The southern sky at noon gave us marked assurances of the returning sun. Fine bands of cirrus clouds on the southern horizon were finely colored, the dark-crimson streaks of warm color being overlaid with daffodil-yellows, that shaded gradually into the pearl-grays. Though there has been during the winter a moderate amount of snow, considering the low temperature, yet the hill-tops are now quite bare and show less covering than in October. Yesterday's storm has stripped every exposed place of its usual snow, to pack it in dense, hard drifts in the hollows of the ground and the cracks and other interstices of the harbor-ice. For the first time during our experiences, it would now be possible to cut blocks of snow and build a snow-house. The snow in these low temperatures has none of the soft, fleecy appearance seen in lower latitudes. Each flake, hard and separate as an atom of sand, only unites to its neighbor under stress of force and pressure. It is the snow of our western prairies, only in a more aggravated form, which there, filling a railway cutting, resists so successfully all efforts of trains or snow-ploughs to force a passage."

In nearly a month prior to the storm, only two faint displays of aurora were noted, but in the week following it occurred on four days. In the display of January 19th there was a beautiful auroral arch from horizon to horizon in the magnetic meridian, during the presence of which the needle was greatly disturbed, swinging repeatedly off the scale. The aurora of January 21st was wonderful beyond description, and I have no words in which to convey any adequate idea of the beauty and splendor of the scene. It was a continuous change from arch to streamers, from streamers to patches and ribbons, and back again to arches, which covered the entire heavens for part of the time. It lasted for about twenty-two hours, during which at no moment was the phenomena other than vivid and remarkable. At one time there were three perfect arches, which spanned the southwestern sky from horizon to horizon. The most striking and exact simile, perhaps, would be to liken it to a conflagration of surrounding forests as seen at night from a cleared or open space in their centre. During the display Sergeant Rice exposed a sensitive dry photographic plate toward the aurora without any effect, but the experiment was a doubtful one from the shifting of the light. In general, the aurora was quite colorless, though occasionally red tints were reported. Despite the remarkable duration and extent of the aurora, the magnet was but slightly disturbed. During the display the new moon appeared, a narrow crescent which, strange to say, was exactly the color of blood.

Sir George Nares remarks that, " contrary to the popular belief, the aurora gives us no appreciable light." In our experience the light was considerable on several occasions, and in this case I saw my shadow cast, at a time when the brilliant display was in one quarter of the heavens only. Tromholt says on this point: "The very greatest amount of light which the aurora borealis emitted, or which, in any case, I was able to ascertain during my entire sojourn in Lapland, may be compared to that of the moon two days and a half after full, when 25° above the horizon and the sky is clear."

On the 23d, print, such as is used for leaders, could be read with some difficulty at noon. This test, however, was not a satisfactory one, owing partly to the presence of the moon, but more to the remarkably varying capacity of eyes for this work. A brilliant meteor was observed in the north about 7.35 A.M., which burst into fragments, all colorless except one, which was a brilliant red. No detonation was heard.

On January 29th Lieutenant Kislingbury gave us much

anxiety by a visit to Cape Murchison, during which he was absent for over seven hours, in temperature ranging from $-45°$ ($-42.8°$ C.) to $-54°$ ($-47.8°$ C.). Owing to a previous alarm on account of Lieutenant Kislingbury, I had requested him to note the time of his departure, and the intended direction of his travel, when leaving the house, so as to insure his being found in case of any accident. About 4 P.M. Dr. Pavy entered the station considerably excited, saying he had been to Water-course Bay following the tracks of Lieutenant Kislingbury, who had evidently gone to Cape Murchison, and that, as a light breeze was blowing in the outer harbor, he thought the journey dangerous. Lieutenant Kislingbury's record stated that he had left at 10.30 A.M. "for Dutch Island and perhaps Distant Cape." At 5 P.M., as nothing could be seen of him, the dog-team was harnessed, and a quarter of an hour later Dr. Pavy, with Sergeant Brainard and Eskimo Christiansen, started out. They met Lieutenant Kislingbury about two miles from Dutch Island, suffering somewhat from the trip. He reached the station at 6 P.M. Of course, being warmly clad, he was safe, unless some accident occurred or a wind sprang up, when he must have necessarily suffered from the exposure. As no object was gained by this trip of twenty-five miles in Arctic darkness, I requested that such a long absence should not be repeated until the return of the sun. The road was found to be in excellent condition, and wolf and fox tracks were observed. It eventually transpired that Lieutenant Kislingbury's nose was frozen during the trip, caused, as he said, by riding on the sledge after it reached him.

January 31st: "The presence of a musky piece of beef to-day gave rise to general discussion as to the causes of this flavor to our meat. Such pieces are found but occasionally, and the history of them has been looked into. The weight of evidence favors the belief that immediate dressing of the animal obviates the difficulty." An example the following summer seemed to bear out this opinion: An old bull was killed, which, when running, was said to have exhaled such an odor of musk that it was perceptible at a distance of several hundred yards. It was naturally supposed, though he was immediately dressed, that the meat could not be eaten. To avoid prejudice, I had a quarter served without the knowledge of any one except Sergeant Brainard, and the meat proved free from taint or musky flavor.

Though the glory of the sun had gone, with its wealth of color in halos and sunsets, yet my journal shows that there are other beauties in an Arctic winter than the auroras. Of the many beautiful coronas and paraselenæ, a few will illustrate all. A very beautiful corona, 6° in diameter, was seen the evening of the 30th. It consisted of four concentric circles around the moon, the inner white, the second yellow, the third blue, and the outer red.

On February 1st a lunar halo of 90° was reported, but it had disappeared by the time I was able to leave my bed, and I found two halos of 22° and 46° respectively, which were of exceptional brilliancy and splendor. In the evening of that day a most remarkable lunar halo was visible, the moon at the time being about 25° above the horizon. The circles of 22° and 46° were perfect to the horizon, and were both tipped with contact arches. Six mock-moons were present, two on either side of the true moon, and two above it, all of which showed brilliant prismatic colors, very like the clear, distinct colors seen in rainbows. Spears of light extended from the moon vertically, reaching downward to the horizon and upward to the outer circle. In addition, a narrow streak of clear, white light extended from the moon horizontally on both sides completely around the entire horizon, at an altitude of 25° the same as that of the moon itself. At times a faint mock-moon without rainbow colors was to be seen 90° distant from the moon, being in the north, while the moon itself was in the east, and a second faint one under the moon, so that eight mock-moons were visible at one time. The phenomena, while more marked and of longer continuance, was said to be of the same character as that

Lunar Halo at Fort Conger, February 1, 1882.

noted in the early morning. The display lasted for over an hour, the number of moons varying during the time.

The halo was preceded by an aurora, which was unaccompanied by magnetic disturbances.

At local noon of February 2d, the thermometer on the south side of the tide-house was read without a lantern. The spirit thermometer on the floe, at 5.30 P.M. the same day, read *corrected* —64.8° (—53.8° C.). Regarding extremely low temperatures, I express my opinion that below —60° (51.1° C.) all readings from alcohol thermometers must be viewed with suspicion unless the alcohol used is known positively to be pure. By my observations it was found that three parts pure alcohol to one of water, deposited substances the color and consistency of lard. At a temperature of $-60.4°$ ($-51.3°$ C.), four parts of alcohol to one of water, assumed the consistency of a light syrup, although unchanged in color. This would indicate that, say at $-80°$ or $-90°$, pure alcohol might deposit a sediment.

The following interesting experiments were made as to the effect of low temperatures on various liquids: On February 3d, alcohol, chloroform, brandy, glycerine, ether, nitric acid, and spirits of turpentine, all from standard preparations of the United States Medical Department, were exposed at a temperature of $-55°$. The brandy froze solid in less than an hour, and the nitric acid, beginning to crystallize, formed into a solid substance resembling lard, although the temperature rose to $-47°$. On the 14th of February, in a temperature of $-59.4°$, the spirits of turpentine showed a slight solid sediment, while the main portion of the liquid appeared viscous. Muriatic acid remained unchanged. Sulphuric ether exhibited small crystals suspended midway in the liquid, and a deposit resembling gum camphor partly dissolved. The chloroform showed small spiculæ in suspension near the bottom. Concentrated English rum assumed the consistency of a light syrup, but otherwise remained unchanged.

On the last-named date, medical alcohol and fuel alcohol (the latter near proof) were exposed at a temperature of $-55°$ without undergoing change. At the same time three parts of medical alcohol to one of water were exposed in one vessel, and four parts of alcohol to one of water were exposed in another. In a few hours, at a steady temperature of $-55°$, the first mixture showed a deposit resembling soft lard in color and consistency, while the latter remained unchanged to the eye, but had apparently thickened. The following morning, a temperature of $-60.4°$ having been experienced, the latter liquid had visibly thickened, although no deposit took place. The pure alcohol remained seemingly unchanged.

During this extreme cold weather I observed closely our Eskimo dogs, expecting to see signs of great suffering from cold among them. The only manner in which a calm cold was ever seen to affect them was in causing them at times to lift first one foot and then another from the bare ground as though it burned them. A tent was erected for them, and later the surgeon had some snow-huts excavated, but they never entered the latter, and only sought the shelter of the first during severe wind-storms. One occasionally crept into a closed-up tent, where blankets or clothing could be found.

The favorite sleeping-place was the freshly strewn ashes, and many strove for the top of the ash-barrel, which afforded room for but one. Often have I seen a dog tempted to leave the barrel in order to attack a rival, only to return with a crestfallen look to find his place occupied.

Sometimes failing to dislodge a comrade comfortably ensconced on the coveted barrel, a dog jumped on top of the first comer and curled himself up contentedly. The under dog knew by bitter experience that to quarrel was to lose his bed, and remained until worn out by the weight of his rival. Others sought that portion of the coal pile which was free from snow. Unless they had litters, but one or two of the dogs would ever sleep under cover, and such as did so were put in coventry and harshly treated by the remainder of the pack.

Sergeant Gardiner, much to our gratification, returned to duty early in February, and once again the party of twenty-five were all for active duty. The broken bone had united slowly, but yet much quicker and better than the surgeon anticipated. The continuous absence of sunlight, the lack of exercise, and unvarying monotony of life are all against an invalid in the Arctic regions, but Gardiner's spirits never failed him.

Some experiments were made at this time regarding the freezing of sea-water, which, at a temperature of 28.9° ($-1.7°$ C.), was placed in a barrel banked with snow, the temperature of which was about $-40°$ ($-40°$ C.). On the day following the water was examined, and ice was found to have formed exactly six inches thick on the top, in a mean temperature of $-48.7°$ ($-44.8°$ C.). My journal says: "This result is at variance with Payer's statement, that he has seen the open sea freeze at a similar temperature twelve inches in a day." Subsequently ice formed over the remaining sea-water, from which the covering of ice had been removed the previous day, to the thickness of 5.7 inches in twenty-four hours, at a mean temperature of $-47.8°$ ($-44.3°$ C.).

February 3d, though not the coldest day, was that on which the lowest temperature of the season occurred. The mean temperature was $-52.9°$ ($-48.2°$ C.), with a maximum of $-44.1°$ ($42.3°$ C.) and a minimum of $-62.2°$ ($52.3°$ C.). On the harbor-floe a substandard, which, under similar conditions, read with the thermometer in the shelter, recorded $-63.1°$ ($-52.8°$ C.), or $0.9°$ ($0.5°$ C.) below the regular instrument.

The protective influence of a snow-hut was shown by the fact that on February 5th, after a mean temperature below $-50°$ ($-45.6°$ C.) for five consecutive days, the thermometer inside the tide-house read $-17°$ ($-27.2°$ C.), which was the lowest touched since a door had been put on the snow-house.

February 6th my journal says: "The southern sky at local noon to-day was filled with colors of the most exquisite loveliness, a rich, deep red shading into a remarkable purple." February 6th was the coldest day; the mean temperature being −53.8° (−47.7° C.), although the minimum did not touch −60° (−56° C.). This unusually cold weather was noted in connection with the greatest atmospheric pressure recorded to that time. The barometer touched 30.613 during the day. Despite the remarkably low temperature, Sergeant Brainard was hunting for nearly two hours and saw many hare-tracks.

Jens and Frederik hunted on the following day, seeing hare-tracks but no game. Our first spring animal, a wolf, was seen by Sergeant Rice on the 10th, near Proteus Point. Jens hunted assiduously, but saw no animals until the 15th, when he succeeded in killing a hare, the first game of the season. We were surprised by its weight, which was eleven pounds gross and six when dressed. Its excellent condition showed that, despite the severity of the weather, it had found sufficient and satisfactory food, principally buds of the *Saxifraga oppositifolia*. The animal was densely furred, the long hairs being filled in near the body with a remarkably fine down-like hair. It was entirely white, except a few black hairs at the very tips of its ears.

On the following day Frederik and Jens each shot another of about the same weight as the first killed. This game was welcome as a guarantee for the future, but the meat was not vitally necessary, as on February 17th we had about twenty-three hundred pounds of musk-meat and two hundred guillemots still on hand at the station, besides two musk-cattle cached in Water-course Bay.

February 16th, at midday, the southern horizon showed a bar of gold resting on the Greenland hills, above which the sky was faintly tinged with a Nile-green color, which shaded toward the clear heavens of the zenith into a delicate bright blue. By contrast the northern horizon, entirely clear of clouds, appeared of a distinctive dark blue, which was almost black in its intensity. As the day was so clear, I sent Lieutenant Lockwood and party to read the instruments on Bellot Island, and busied myself in sound experiments at −61.1° (−51.7° C.). Lieutenant Lockwood and men were gone about five hours, but escaped any frost-bites, notwithstanding the very low temperature. He complained much of the many falls from lack of shadows, which prevented them from travelling rapidly, as without such aid hollow and hill are alike to the eye.

The most marked instance of deception from this cause occurred in the experience of Lieutenants Rawson and Egerton, R.N., with a dog-team, when the dogs, unable to detect inequalities in the ice, ran directly over a precipitous floe and fell eight feet, the animals evidently thinking the floe to be entirely level.

At 10 p.m., February 16th, the mercurial thermometers thawed out, after having been frozen continuously for sixteen days and five hours. This is the longest time on record during which mercury has remained frozen. The Alert, in 1876, experienced a similar spell of cold, during which the mercury was solid for twelve continuous days. The longest period of similar temperatures by Kane's record is but five days.

Sergeant Rice, hunting on the 20th, shot at a hare, but did not obtain him. He reported that the hare travelled for a hundred or more yards at a time by jumping on its hind legs, for distances of six to eight feet, never touching the ground with the forepaws. He said he thought it at first an optical illusion, but the tracks confirmed his eyesight, showing the hind feet only to have touched the snow.

The measurement of the sea-ice on February 21st showed a thickness of fifty-two and a half inches, an increase of eight inches in ten days, in a mean temperature of −48.5° (−44.7° C.).

This is an unusually large increase, probably the largest on record, considering the previous thickness of the ice.

Washington's birthday was celebrated by an elaborate dinner and by races and shooting-matches. The snow-shoe walk was won by Biederbick, and rifle-shooting at a hundred yards by Private Long. The return of Lieutenant Lockwood's party from his successful trip to Cape Beechy added to the zest of our celebration. The temperature remained steady at $-44°$ ($-42.°$ C.) during the day, which hardly encouraged out-of-door sports.

The day following Sergeant Elison and Private Whisler were sent to Depot "A" (Cape Murchison) with dog-sledge, to repitch the tent and to put it in good condition for future travellers. Dr. Pavy also accompanied them, and, while they were at work pitching the tent, carried a small load of pemmican and alcohol to the north side of St. Patrick Bay.

A minimum thermometer was exposed at Cape Murchison near the tent, with a view to its being read by all visiting parties. On the same day Sergeant Linn, Connell, and Biederbick visited the mine and got out some five tons of coal, and hauled about five hundred pounds on a Hudson Bay sledge to the edge of the ice-foot in Water-course Bay.

A checker tournament was commenced early in the month, and after a long contest, which created a pleasurable and healthy excitement, terminated on the 24th, the prizes being won by Jewell, Whisler, and Elison.

Lieutenant Kislingbury visited the summit of Mount Campbell on the 25th, and reported that from all appearances the storm of January 16th must have been the most severe at that point for the previous six years. The cairn erected by the English expedition in 1876 was blown over, and the spar surmounted by the iron pipe was broken short off. From Lieutenant Kislingbury's account, the spar and cairn had been lifted by the wind and carried five hundred yards, where wedging between two rocks they were caught fast.

Hunting during the latter part of the month was assiduously pursued with no results. Unfortunately two of the hares, which had been hung up, as it was supposed out of reach of the dogs, disappeared. Suspicion naturally rested on two dogs, who accepted their food from the cooks in a nonchalant manner, which is quite unusual with these animals. This was the first meat thus lost.

February 25th: "The cold weather just passed has been remarkable for its duration as well as its severity, the mean temperature for thirty-five days, January 20th to February 24th inclusive, has been $-47.1°$ ($-43.9°$ C.). During this time the mercury had been frozen solid except for sixty-seven hours. On fifteen other hours the temperature was but a fraction of a degree above the melting point of mercury, but did not continue there sufficiently long to thaw the thermometer. The mercury remained solid for sixteen days and five hours continuously. Until 10 P.M. of the 16th the highest temperature in February was $-43.3°$ ($-41.8°$ C.); the mean of these sixteen days was $-52.3°$ ($-46.8°$ C.). The mean for the same time of the thermometers exposed at the tide-hole was $-54.6°$ ($-48.1°$ C.), showing that the air on the floe was about $2.3°$ ($1.3°$ C.) lower than that in the instrument-shelter, where the thermometers were at a level of forty feet above the sea."

While hunting, on the 25th, Sergeant Brainard found several cross sections of a petrified tree near the station and about nine hundred feet above the sea. The several sections varied from five to eleven inches in diameter, of which the longest, on the surface of the ground, was eighteen inches. A few sections

ARCTIC CLOUDS OVER BELLOT ISLAND.
(*From a photograph.*)

projected from the ground a foot or two. Fragments were strewn around, but no limbs or knots were observed.

Sergeant Brainard, referring to the greenish-yellow tint which had come to all our faces, and which the near approach of the sun rendered very noticeable, says: "A few of our vainest men were observing themselves in a mirror by the noonday light. Much to their gratification their pallor gave a delicate appearance quite unusual to their smoke-begrimed countenances in quarters."

Our last day of winter came, and with it the long expected return of the sun. Lieutenant Kislingbury and Private Whisler climbed Bellot Island and saw the whole disk, but the rest of the party, as the temperature was $-46.6°$ ($-43.7°$ C.), were content with a view of the upper limb from the station. Light clouds veiled its coming as well as its departure, and no shadows were cast, but we could see that it was there. The scene was neither impressive nor magnificent, yet I think all our hearts re-echoed that exclamation of "blessed sun" from the poor Italian of Payer's expedition, while thanking God that to us in health and strength the sun had reappeared, and our first Arctic winter had ended.

Hudson Bay Sledge Pattern. Relief Expedition, 1884.

CHAPTER XVII.

PREPARATIONS FOR SLEDGING.

ACTIVE preparations for spring sledging were commenced early in February, and by the middle of the month the main quarters had been turned into a great workshop for our saddler, tinman, and carpenters. Sledges, boat, cooking-lamps and utensils, sleeping-bags, foot-gear, etc., were in process of invention, manufacture, or repair.

These preparations entailed great circumspection and forethought before they were finally completed. To send out a sledge party for a long Arctic journey demands that careful planning and thorough outfitting which can be successfully done only after a certain amount of field experiences, supplemented by thoughtful consideration of the difficulties to be met with and as to the means best adapted to overcome them. Indeed, not only the success, but the very safety of a party may be put in jeopardy by the neglect of seemingly trifling matters. The dangers which may arise from the dampening of matches was illustrated in the experience of one of our parties in the early spring days, and the leaking or loss of the alcohol-lamp or can in the field would prove a dangerous if not a fatal circumstance.

PREPARATIONS FOR SLEDGING.

The lamps, if not properly made, increase largely the chances of destroying the tent by fire, even if they escape exploding to the great danger of the party.

Sir Edward Belcher, in his first trip, lost an entire day's ration of alcohol, and endangered the tent by the use of a soldered cooking-lamp, from which the filling-tube fell off the first time the lamp was lighted. These and other similar defects are such as can be provided against by care and forethought.

The success of any sledging party depends almost entirely on two important points: First, the adaptability and the state of perfection of the entire travelling-gear; second, the ability of the chief to reduce the constant weights* to a minimum, while retaining everything absolutely essential to the maintenance of perfect health and the performance of satisfactory scientific work.

The retreat of Franklin's expedition proved fatal through these principles being neglected, and, indeed, the lack of success in most cases can be traced, directly or indirectly, to a failure to fulfil these conditions.

It had been my original intention that the greater part of the work of exploration should be done with dogs, of which three full teams had been purchased in Greenland. Of twenty-seven dogs purchased at the Danish ports, only twelve were living at the end of 1881. All the teams had been attacked by disease introduced by the dogs sold to me by the governor of Upernivik, from which sickness the greater part perished. Fortunately there were three private dogs in the expedition, one of which belonged to Dr. Pavy and two had been given to me personally. This enabled me to put into the field two teams of seven dogs each, to which Dr. Pavy added to his

---

* Constant weights are those hauled from beginning to end, such as tentage, sledges, instruments, cooking and other gear.

own team his private dog. Careful attention had resulted in the saving of nine of the puppies born the previous November, but their use in the field that spring was quite out of the question, though I counted, and properly, on making them useful later in the season. This loss of dogs caused me to modify my original plans, in which I had intended that the supporting sledges, drawn by men, should never be absent from the station for more than a week.

The question of sledges was an important and difficult one to settle. The McClintock sledge, which was so strongly endorsed by Payer and the English expedition of 1875, was viewed by me distrustfully, owing to its partial failure with the latter expedition, which used it entirely. Although the enduring powers and strength of my men were remarkable, yet it could not be expected that, as a whole, they should be as strong as the men of 1875, who were selected from the whole of the royal navy. When their picked crews had failed, I could not expect to succeed if I followed the same methods.

The Hudson Bay sledges had been strongly recommended by Dr. Rae, and I finally decided to use that pattern for my supporting sledges on the North Greenland coast, particularly as Lieutenant Beaumont's experience showed the existence of deep, soft snow, in which the McClintock sledge would be substantially useless. In consequence four Hudson Bay sledges were made, which were shod with a light strip of ash fastened to the bottom at either side so as to serve in a measure for runners. In one sledge the strip of ash was shod with steel, but as its use seemed to indicate that the increased friction made shoeing a disadvantage, I unfortunately abandoned my original idea, and sent out the remaining sledges shod only with wood. I should have remembered that Back's voyageurs hauled only a hundred pounds on their sledge, yet the rough travel wore out the runners, and the sledges were nearly broken up till he shod them with steel.

To future explorers in high latitudes, I recommend Hunt's pattern of the St. Michael's sledge as made for the Relief Expedition, 1884, with the important addition of *steel runners*, which should be so arranged as to be attached or detached at pleasure; an extra runner both steel and wooden to be carried on long journeys. This with the Greenland sledge would fulfil any ordinary field conditions, but when a retreat is contemplated or boats are to be hauled, the Melville sledge should replace the McClintock, of which it is an improvement.

Hunt's St. Michael Sledge. Relief Expedition, 1884.

These Hudson Bay sledges, with lashings and coverings complete, each weighing about thirty-five pounds, entailed less weight upon the men than would the McClintock. In addition, the sledge would wear out and not break, while the McClintock sledge, with its mortised stanchions and tight rivets, is a structure that cannot remain long unbroken after its rigid frame is subjected to the violent shocks consequent on travel over very rough ice.

They possessed this further advantage, that as four Hudson Bay sledges replaced one McClintock sledge, whenever the food consumed or placed in caches reduced the weights of the party to any considerable extent, the constant weights would be regularly decreased by abandoning a sledge as soon as its load could be divided between the remaining sledges. In this way it seemed possible to materially reduce the dead weight to be hauled as the party proceeded, a condition essential to marked success, as the strength of all sledge parties must necessarily diminish as they advance. At the farthest point reached, and in the return journey, but thirty-five pounds of sledge would be hauled by the party, as against one hundred and thirty to one hundred and eighty pounds weight involved in hauling a McClintock sledge.

Greenland Dog Sledge.

It was to be expected that long experience should make the Eskimo of Greenland cognizant of the best pattern to be used for such purposes, and so the Greenland sledge was adopted as our pattern for the dog-sledge. The lashings of the Greenland sledge being of seal-skin permit the sledge to be handled in the roughest possible manner without its being materially injured.

The only serious danger of breaking the Greenland sledge is in its runners, which split longitudinally through the row of holes bored to receive the lashings. The upstanders and the runners of our sledges were carefully strengthened by setting in plates of wrought iron, so that the chances of splitting were greatly diminished. The pine slats commonly in use in Greenland were replaced by the best American ash, hickory, or oak. Even with the utmost precaution the slats will be gradually worn out, and finally broken, by the constant pounding and friction on the rubble and hummocky ice. It is consequently essential that two or three extra slats should be carried.

Dr. Pavy had experimented somewhat in regard to the modification of the Greenland sledge pattern with ill suc-

Ancient Eskimo Sledge—Found at Cape Baird 81° 30′ N.

cess, as he reduced the length of sled, and so added to its unmanageableness under difficult conditions. As the shortening theory had failed, it later occurred to me that in the rough rubble ice, which all of the parties were certain of experiencing to a greater or lesser extent, the changed conditions necessitated a longer sledge to avoid the front catching at the bottom of a declivity, and a broader one to prevent upsetting. Eventually the sledges were lengthened some six inches, and were made about three inches broader. This result, it is true, increased the weight of the sledge from ninety-five to one hundred and five pounds, but it was found that the advantages derived were so great that, after once trying the new pattern, no officer was willing to go on a long journey with the old sledge. It is interesting to note that old Eskimo sledges, discovered later at Cape Baird, on the shore of Lake Hazen and elsewhere in Grinnell Land, were proportionally of even greater length than our improved pattern.

The question of the sledging ration was one of vital importance. It is true that the daily allowance of a man should be confined to such amount of food as is barely sufficient to maintain his health and strength, but it is better to err on the side of safety than to incur the serious danger of diminishing the strength of men subjected to such arduous labor and great exposure.

Sir Edward Parry, in 1827, adopted nineteen ounces solid food as his sledging ration, an amount which he found to be entirely insufficient for his men. Dr. Rae in one journey adopted twenty-nine ounces, which was not enough, and later took thirty-four ounces, which was supplemented somewhat by game. Other parties have found thirty-two ounces, when *all* pemmican, enough solids. Convicts at hard labor in England receive fifty ounces solid food—mostly bread and vegetables, however. Payer believes that from forty to forty-five ounces solid food are necessary for a sledging man daily, and he states that McClintock, the great Arctic sledge traveller, allowed from forty to forty-eight ounces. The Arctic expedition under Captain Nares adopted a sledging ration of thirty-eight ounces solid food, an amount, I think, inadequate for the maintenance of strength in an extended trip, unless it consists of pemmican or other highly concentrated substances, such as it is evident most men cannot assimilate properly. The solids of the Nares ration were twenty ounces of meat, fourteen of biscuit, two each of preserved potatoes and sugar, which, with four ounces of fuel, two of rum, an ounce of chocolate, a half ounce each of tea and tobacco, with condiments, made a grand aggregate of $46\frac{7}{20}$ ounces.

I concluded to increase the solids to thirty-nine ounces, and to add an ounce of lime-juice and a half ounce of fuel, by substituting food, etc., for rum. The sledge ration of 1882 was viewed as a tentative one, and, while the parties remained in perfect health and did remarkable work, yet, owing to the general representations, I deemed it necessary, in 1883, to increase it and to modify the character of the food by replacing bread with butter and meat. The ration I finally decided on for the latter year was twenty-two ounces of meat, two of butter, four of vegetables, ten of bread, two of sugar, one-half ounce of milk, one ounce of tea and chocolate, salt one-fourth, and pepper one-twentieth of an ounce. The alcohol allowance of 1882, four and a half ounces after April 30th, (five ounces *before*), was increased the following year to six, as being the smallest amount on which a party of three or four could properly cook their food. The ration of 1883 consisted, besides beverages, of forty and a half ounces of food. Three-fourths of the meat ration were about equal quantities of pemmican, bacon, and frozen musk-meat, while the balance was made up of canned sausage and corned beef.

As a result of my experiences, I would now recommend the same quantity of solid food, but would place the vegetable ration at three ounces preserved potatoes, replacing the other ounce by a half ounce each of milk and of extract of beef. Of the twenty-two ounces of meat, I do not think that more than eleven ounces should be pemmican, the balance to be divided between bacon and fresh meat; the latter to be sliced fine and frozen. In case fresh meat cannot be obtained, it would seem to me well to make the remaining eleven ounces of meat consist of four ounces of bacon and the balance of sausage and canned fresh meat, the latter to be cooked as little as is possible consistent with its preservation.

With the present means of carrying large quantities of fresh meat, it seems unnecessary that any future expedition should be deprived of this invaluable antiscorbutic, and of all men those in the field should be provided with it. Lime-juice pemmican proved to be very unpalatable, and was only eaten under press of hunger.

The use of butter and condensed milk in the field cannot be too highly commended. Tea, the true Arctic drink, should be used for three-fourths of the meals in the field; the balance should consist of coffee in preference to chocolate. It seemed to be generally admitted by our parties that chocolate could not be drank in the field, except at camping, as it seemed to induce thirst during the day if used before the march. The use of extract of tea and extract of coffee would probably reduce the weight of beverages to one-half ounce, and in place might be substituted curry-paste or some other powerful condiment. If extract of tea cannot be used, the tea taken should be compressed.

No rum was ever sent as a sledge ration, but a liberal amount was always furnished as medicine, with authority for it to be used on extraordinary occasions at the discretion of the officer in charge. In outfitting another sledge party I should furnish it with a small quantity of rum, not exceeding an ounce a day, to be used under similar restrictions.

On the above ration of 1882, parties kept the field for forty days in a mean temperature below zero ($-17.8°$ C.), and returned in health and strength; and others for shorter periods in extreme temperatures did arduous work without detriment to health and strength. At depots and on return marches the parties occasionally had an opportunity of an extra allowance, which probably raised the average solids to forty ounces daily. It is not to be assumed, however, that the ration of 1883 is beyond criticism; but, as success commands attention and respect, our experiences are not to be lightly passed by. The acids of limes, milk, and raw meat enter into it, and the peculiar qualities of beef extract and of potatoes supplement them. The variety of diet, and the sufficiency of fuel to properly heat the food, are also important points.

Tobacco was not used as a sledge ration, and each man was expected to carry on his person such as he desired to use. One or two of our men regularly abandoned the habit while serving in the field.

It was a constant practice in establishing supplementary depots for returning parties, to add to them an extra amount of canned fruits, such as pears, apples, cranberries, and also sugar and milk. These articles were most in demand by the hungry and exhausted sledge-men.

Regarding the vexed question of lime-juice, no trouble was experienced in its use as a sledge ration. The amount to be used in advancing was furnished the party frozen into small squares, each of which represented a ration. This ration was most acceptable to the men in the field, and on occasions it was taken in a frozen condition, much to the refreshment and invigoration of those who were in quite an exhausted condition. My surgeon, however, disapproved of this method of taking it, although the immediate result seemed beneficial. The lime-juice for return trips was sent in rubber bags, which, of course, froze solid, but on the return journey the temperature was always high enough to melt it. In any case, as lime-juice thaws at a temperature of about $14°$ ($-10°$ C.), it could be easily brought to a liquid state by keeping it in a sleeping-bag over night.

Alcohol of great strength is the best field fuel, and should be carried in tightly sealed vessels of about two gallons, which not only insures safety by dividing the supply, but enables caches to be frequently made for the return journey and the dropping of empty tins. The soot and smoke from stearine are quite unbearable, and entering the lungs must affect the health in long journeys. A sufficient number of india-rubber bags to carry two gallons of alcohol were taken for ordinary use.

Our cooking utensils were of the simplest character. The lamp and all the cooking vessels were fire-proof, made as far as practicable of single pieces of heavy tin without solder. Careful and systematic experiments caused us to adopt a cooking-lamp having five wicks, but it is evident that the number of wicks to be used must depend on the extent of the heating surface to be exposed to its action.

Speed in cooking and economy of fuel by no means go hand in hand. The successful economy of an alcohol cooking-lamp depends very largely on skilful manipulation of the wicks, which must be pulled up just far enough to allow the heat given forth to be entirely utilized, so that the food is cooked with a minimum amount of alcohol. The best lamp, then, is that which does the greatest amount of work on the allowance of fuel. Our experiments were made in a field-tent in a temperature of $-20°$ ($-28.9°$ C.), and the snow used for melting was at a temperature of $-30°$ ($-34.4°$ C.). These conditions were similar to those in later field work, except that we experimented on snow, which requires more fuel than ice to reduce it to water. The field-lamp in sixteen minutes melted enough snow to produce two and a half quarts of water, and ten minutes later raised it to the boiling-point. At the same time, in an upper vessel, there was made one and a half quart of water, and it was raised to a temperature of

33° (+0.6° C.). Four ounces of alcohol were expended in this work. This agreed well with the results obtained by Payer, who boiled three gallons of water from snow at −13° (−25° C.) to −22° (−38° C.) by an expenditure of twelve ounces of alcohol. Payer does not say, but I suppose his experiments were made in the field. Our small lamp for two men boiled water at an expense of one-eighth ounce alcohol to each pint of water, a greater expenditure than with our large lamp, in accordance with the well-known fact that fuel ration can be decreased as the number to be cooked for is increased. This latter lamp, which, with its frame and cooking-vessel complete, weighed but sixteen ounces, was called by the men the "Tramp's Companion."

The accompanying illustration shows the cooking apparatus. A is a stout, sheet-iron cylinder with perforations for air to reach alcohol lamp E, which fits closely in the bottom of the cylinder. B and C are tin fire-proof vessels with cylinder in centre, which allows heat to rise to D, where bits of iron, laid crosswise on top of C, allow the smoke, with some little heat, to escape.

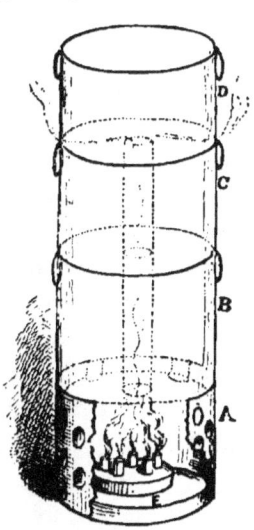

Field Cooking Apparatus.

In this way but little heat is wasted. D inverted fits into A, covering and protecting E while packed. Despite the seemingly frail character of this apparatus, it withstood all tests, and one vessel and lamp, used for two months northward, afterward did service for many months through our retreat and life at Sabine. In preparing future lamps and cooking vessels, the bottoms should be, I think, of tolerably heavy copper.

Contrary to the generally received opinions, fur clothing, even for field services, was not highly valued by the members of my party. It was the general experience that complete double suits of woollen underclothing of the best quality, with the outer clothes of common, thick, woollen material, was all the covering that was necessary to insure comfort in the field. It is important, however, that the surface of the outer garments should have a smooth finish, so as to prevent the adherence of snow to the cloth. In order to avoid this result, the army stable-frocks and overalls, which were made of very light canvas, were worn as outer garments, and proved very satisfactory in this respect; the men, taking them off at night, were able to enter their sleeping-bags with their outer garments in an entirely dry condition. Seal-skin *temiaks*, or jumpers, were found serviceable only in windy weather, and were but little used. Seal-skin trousers were tried by nearly every man in the party, and were discarded by the majority of us, although some adhered to the use of them.

However prudently a man may work, he cannot prevent perspiration from starting while pulling on the sledge or running after it. The moisture thus engendered passes readily through woollen underclothing to finally form as hoar-frost on the exterior surface of the outer garment, from which it can be brushed. But when seal-skin is worn the moisture collects on the inner side, and saturates all the underclothing as well as the seal-skin itself; unless the exertion is steadily continued, the damp seal-skin freezes, and is about as convenient and comfortable as a coat-of-mail. When camp is made, the unfortunate sledge-man is not only obliged to thaw out the seal-skin suit with the heat of his body, but must also dry up the moisture. This operation is not only unhealthy, but it induces cold, makes drafts on his strength, and interferes with his regular sleep. These objections largely disappear when a man can travel leisurely, and refrain from exertions to such an extent as to be free from perspiration, conditions which in Grinnell Land are not possible with successful exploration.

The great trouble in Arctic field service is to protect the person from frost-bite. This is not as difficult as is generally supposed, and whenever frost-bites occur it will be almost invariably found that the officer or men have neglected well-known and strongly emphasized precautions. Inexperience or imprudent carelessness causes nineteen-twentieths of such cases. These remarks have reference particularly to exposure to temperatures above $-30°$ ($-34.6°$ C.), as that amount of cold, from observation, appeared to me to be about the minimum to which men can be exposed for a long time, without the man has extraordinary resisting powers or is most carefully equipped. No man should be put in the field who perspires excessively, or whose circulation is not excellent.

The whole foot and hand gear must be soft, pliable, and never tight enough to in any manner impede the circulation.

Pliability permits that easy and continuous flexure of the joints which in Arctic travel is absolutely essential to maintain warmth. The inner covering of the foot should be some non-conducting material, which not only retains the heat generated by the foot, but permits perspiration to pass through. Nothing is better than heavy, *closely knit*, all-wool socks. Only one pair of socks should be long enough to reach the knee, the others reaching just to and slightly above the ankle-joint. Some preferred to replace the shortest sock by a blanket wrapper, which is only the sock in a clumsy shape. The outer foot-gear may be either moccasins or the Labrador or Greenland boot, which some prefer, owing to its being oil-tanned and capable of resisting, unchanged, *occasional* immersion in water. The moccasins should have light canvas leggings. Both moccasins and boots should be taken, and should be made to order to insure their being large enough, numbers to run from nine to twelve. One pair of each is a *minimum* allowance for each month of sledging that is to be expected of each man.

Failure to obtain moccasins expected from Canada, and inability to procure many boots in Greenland, obliged us to supplement our supply by home manufacture. Canvas boots did not prove a success, but the second winter our saddler, Frederick, extemporized foot-gear which answered admirably all requirements. It consisted of an *ugsuk* skin bottom, so skilfully turned up and sewed that no seam was exposed as a wearing surface, with felt-cloth tops. Inner soles of buffalo, bear, or reindeer skin are very desirable—the hair clipped short—which, taking up the moisture from the socks, keeps the inner sole of boot or moccasin dry. I cannot recommend dog-skin or other skin inner socks for wear in travelling. They undoubtedly are excellent when parties travel very slowly or ride much on the sledge. They should be furnished, however, without fail, for use as sleeping socks.

Woollen mittens (no gloves), with an outer pair of seal-skin, answer for the hands, if supplemented by indispensable woollen wristers, which, extending downward from midway between elbow and wrist, leave fingers and thumb free for use. In low temperatures the bare hand must be always available. The outer seal-skin mittens should have two thumbs, and fit either hand equally well. In the field they should be secured to the coat by lanyards. To lose a mitten is sometimes dangerous.

The head is best protected by a whaler's cap, a leather woollen-lined cap with a turn-down attachment, but individual taste can largely be consulted. Not only is there no satisfactory protection for the face, but face-cloths or preparations, such as glycerine, etc., are dangerous in very low temperatures. During travel, facing a wind—which should very rarely be done—the face is largely protected by a seal-skin covering, which projects several inches in front of the face and resembles a *poke* bonnet. The projecting portion is kept stiff by a small piece of bent whalebone. The face, especially the nose, must be kept from freezing by the frequent application of the warm hand, which is simply placed against the part in danger of freezing, and is never violently rubbed over it. The danger of applying snow of a temperature of $-40°$ ($-40°$ C.) to an already frozen nose, is evident from the mere statement of the case; but when it is rubbed, the snow, being like fine sand, grinds off the cuticle of the nose or face. One of our party, ignorant of this fact, rubbed nearly all the skin from his nose, which swelled greatly and gave him much after-pain and suffering.

Goggles of neutral-tinted glass should always be worn over the eyes during long journeys; otherwise no man is certain of escaping snow-blindness, which entails great pain on the person, extra labor on others, and perhaps causes failure of the journey. It is difficult to enforce this rule, which is equally important on dull or on bright days.

Our sleeping-bags were of well-tanned buffalo-skin, which can be recommended. Sheepskin was tried, and found to make a warmer bag, but they cannot be recommended for long or important journeys. They are not only heavier, but they collect moisture very rapidly, and are soon a mass of ice. The bag should slope gradually, with increasing size from the bottom, which should be large enough to afford comfortable room for the feet, to a broad flap, which can be pulled down over the head by strings running through rings, as shown in the illustration, and then into the sleeping-bag. If lightly covered with strong oiled silk or thin rubber-cloth, it would be much improved, thus preventing the collection of moisture which increases the weight greatly and adds much to the discomfort of the occupants. Each bag should be for two, or at the most three, men. Men sleeping singly suffer much more from cold than in double bags. Our tent-cloths, though excellent, could have been well replaced by light gutta-percha mattresses, which, inflated with air and placed under the bags, would add much to the warmth of the travellers.

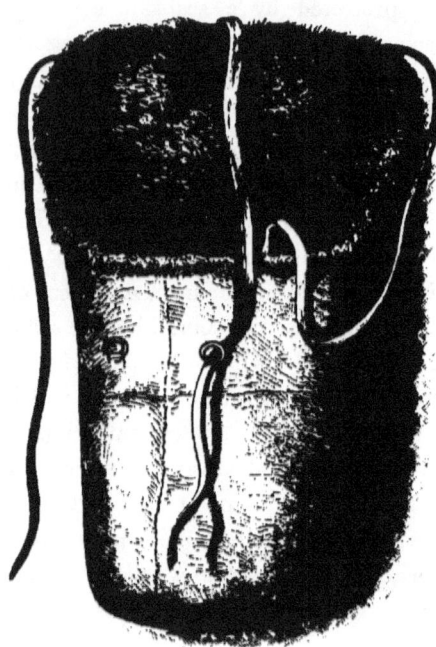

Three-man Buffalo Sleeping-bag.

Common army tents were used by us for field service, and in these were spread rubber tent-cloths, which, made to order for Arctic service, never cracked or split from severity of the cold, as has sometimes occurred in previous expeditions. Regular tent-poles and iron pins were made use of. It seems possible that a rubber tent could be invented which should unite both tent and cloth, and which could be kept upright by a light frame; but tentage in general is a simple question, in regard to which personal preferences can safely be yielded to. The dog or shelter tent should be used when practicable, owing to its extreme lightness, in late spring or early autumn travel.

CHAPTER XVIII.

THANK GOD HARBOR AND HALL'S GRAVE.

LIEUTENANT LOCKWOOD'S WORK.

OUR first spring sledging anticipated the return of the sun by ten days. Lieutenant Lockwood left on February 19th, accompanied by Sergeant Brainard and Eskimo Christiansen, with dog-sledge Antoinette. His orders required him to visit depot "B" near Cape Beechy, and to examine the ice in Robeson Channel, with a view of selecting the best route to be followed in a later trip to Thank God Harbor.

The ice-foot from Fort Conger to Cape Beechy was found to be in excellent condition, the rubble ice being packed with hard snow. The low temperature, $-42°$ ($-41.1°$ C.), caused the sledge to drag with great difficulty, owing to the extraordinary amount of friction. The tent at depot "A" in passing was found to be blown down, probably by the violent gale of January 16th.

The snow-house at depot "B," constructed the previous autumn, was completely concealed by drift snow, which covered the roof of the house several feet deep. In digging out the entrance to the snow-house, the self-registering thermometer, from which I had hoped to obtain the minimum temperature of the winter at Cape Beechy, was unfortunately broken.

Sergeant Brainard, in his field journal, records: "Found a considerable quantity of snow in the snow-house, which had blown down the stovepipe and formed above the stove a cone-shaped mound, which reached nearly to the roof. Working rapidly, in about an hour we had the satisfaction of seeing the house and passage clear and a glowing fire in the little stove. I wonder if we are not the first Arctic travellers who, on such a trip, have had a good coal-fire and a snow-house over it."

On the 20th Lieutenant Lockwood and Sergeant Brainard examined the ice opposite the depot in the direction of Polaris Promontory. They found much hummocky ice intermixed with considerable rubble, conditions which were hardly satisfactory for sledging. While the party were occupied in this reconnoissance, the temperature at the station was $-52.6°$ ($-47°$ C.), but they were so satisfactorily clad that they did not suffer excessively from cold, although they were obliged to watch each other's faces to prevent their freezing under the influence of a light northeast wind.

The following day they examined the ice directly eastward of Cape Beechy, and, passing through a strip of very rough ice not over two hundred yards wide, reached a level palæocrystic floe which afforded excellent sledging. They travelled several miles toward the Greenland coast, and from a high hummock saw that the road for a considerable distance to the eastward was equally favorable. The party returned to Fort Conger on the 22d, in sufficiently early time to participate in the amusements of the day.

The mercury was frozen during their entire absence, and the mean temperature was $-44.7°$ ($-42.6°$ C.) at the station, and probably lower in the field. In these temperatures the party had travelled between sixty and seventy miles in Arctic twilight, for the sun had not returned to us, without frost-bite or mishap. This success augured well for longer and more important journeys. February 28th was marked by the first appearance of the sun, though its slight effect on the temperature was shown by the thermometer recording $-49°$ ($-45°$ C.).

On the following day, in obedience to my instructions, Lieutenant Lockwood, with sledge Antoinette, started for Thank God Harbor by the way of Depot "B." His party consisted of Sergeants Brainard, Jewell, and Eskimo Christiansen.

The main clauses of his orders required that "ten days' allowance of provisions, fuel, and dog-food will be taken from here, which will be supplemented by such additions from Depot "B" (Cape Beechy) as can be carried without materially impeding your progress across Robeson Channel. Your first duty will be to visit the observatory at Thank God Harbor, in order to ascertain exactly what supplies are there available for sledge parties. . . . It is important that the boat-camp, in the ravine about one mile east of Cape Sumner, be visited, and the condition of the whale-boat ascertained. While it is very desirable that the condition of the ice across Newman Bay . . . should be determined, . . . it is left to your judgment to abandon this part of the trip should adverse circumstances arise, or should you think time could be gained for your spring work by so doing. Points should be selected for future depots. . . . You will leave on the Greenland coast all supplies not indispensable to your comfortable and safe return to Cape Beechy. As Sergeant Jewell will probably be charged with the support of your party during the spring, you should communicate freely your views as to the best route and methods to be followed in such work. . . ."

Private Long and Eskimo Jens, with a second dog-team, which carried supplies to Depot "B," were placed under his orders, to support him as far beyond Cape Beechy as would be necessary.

Good travelling and fresh teams enabled them to make the trip to Depot "B," a distance of twenty-eight miles, in five hours and twenty minutes. The night was spent comfortably in the snow-house, and the following morning Lieutenant Lockwood proceeded on his journey, accompanied, until the rubble ice off Cape Beechy was passed, by Private Long. Their stores having been transferred to the Antoinette, the supporting party returned that evening to the home station, and the other toward Greenland.

The load on the sledge Antoinette, on leaving Cape Beechy, was about seven hundred pounds, which enabled the team of

Greenland Coast from Cape Beechy.

eight dogs to travel freely over the palæocrystic floe. An hour and a half's travel brought Lieutenant Lockwood to the farthest point reached by him in his reconnoitering trip ten days previous. Being doubtful as to the condition of the ice in advance, he left one bag of provisions on a prominent hummock, and continued on toward The Gap (a marked indentation central in the bold, high coast which stretches from Cape Lupton to Cape Sumner). Several more hours of sledging over palæocrystic floes, varied by deep snow underlying a weak crust, brought the party to the rubble ice, and an hour later they had the gratification of putting foot on the Greenland shore at Promontory Point (a name given to the bold headland just south of The Gap), where their tent was pitched for the night.

Five and a half hours' travelling south along the Greenland coast, on March 3d, brought them to the observatory, on the plateau above Thank God Harbor, occupied by Bessels and Bryan in 1871-2. Lieutenant Lockwood's experience that day convinced him that no ice-foot properly called existed along that portion of the Greenland coast. In this respect his experiences and opinions were verified by the observations of later parties in both that and the subsequent year. Gentle slopes of snow at times extended to the rows of stranded floebergs, affording level travel, but the difficulty of reaching it and lack of continuity rendered it better to keep out well from the shore.

Level palæocrystic floes of great extent were at times fallen in with, and in the vicinity of Thank God Harbor a considerable number of floebergs were found, most of which were probably grounded, and one of which Sergeant Brainard thought "might well be a remnant of Providence berg."

Considering that it was originally a very light structure, the observatory was in a comparatively fair condition, the sides and one end yet standing; the other end and roof were found broken in pieces, and scattered for several hundred yards in the immediate vicinity. The building affording no shelter, Lieutenant Lockwood decided to construct a snow-house instead of pitching his tent. One was dug out of a huge drift, in two hours' time.

March 4th was spent in taking an inventory of the supplies stored in the dilapidated building. As the temperature was 37° below zero (−38.3° C.), and a fresh northeast wind prevailed, the work was of the most severe character. The stores found agreed in no way with those given in the Polaris record. The English provision-book gave a careful and detailed inventory of articles found by them in 1875, as well as of those consumed by Lieutenant Beaumont's party the subsequent year.

The following articles of serviceable food were found: Six forty-five-pound cans of pemmican, about thirty-five pounds of farina, a half barrel of lime-juice, and a barrel of yellow cornmeal. Ten barrels of hard bread, part made from Graham flour, were found in eatable condition, though some parts were slightly moulded. There were a number of miscellaneous articles in serviceable condition, the most important of which were hatchets, saws, shovels, lead, shot, gunpowder, cartridges for rifle and pistol (calibre fifty), and centre-primed shot-gun cartridges. The English ice-boat was carefully secured, and, as far as could be determined without disturbing it, was in excellent condition. Two of the coverlets left by Lieutenant Beaumont contributed much to the comfort of the sledging party in their snow-house, being a most welcome addition as the temperature fell that night to −51° (−46.1° C.).

The graves of Captain Hall and of the English sailors Hand and Paul were visited and found to be in excellent order. The head-board erected by the Polaris party was so well arranged originally that it still looked quite new, and stress of weather had rendered illegible but few of the letters. The handsome brass tablet erected by the English expedition under Sir George Nares, as a tribute to Captain Hall's memory, stood erect and firm with no signs of decay or weakness in its supports. Lieutenant Lockwood carried and displayed the small national flag made by my wife, which was invariably carried as a sledge flag for the Antoinette.

From the adjoining cairn were obtained and brought to Conger the records left by Captain Stephenson, Lieutenant Beaumont, and other officers of Her Majesty's Navy in 1875-76.

The dreariness and desolation of the country immediately adjoining the anchorage ground of the Polaris was commented on, not only by Lieutenant Lockwood and Sergeant Brainard, but by all others of the expedition who at any time visited it. The surroundings, all agreed, were in marked and disagreeable contrast with the immediate country around Fort Conger.

Lieutenant Lockwood decided to proceed to Cape Sumner over the same route as that followed by Captain Hall in 1870, by the way of Newman Bay. Consequently, later in the day, he examined the country in that direction, finding a level plain whose rocky, gravelly surface was but scantily covered with snow, conditions which promised to make travelling difficult.

This absence of snow as a covering for the ground, not only in Northern Greenland, but in Grinnell Land, was general in our two years' experience, and caused much comment as contrary to expectations.

Sunday, March 5th, proved a beautiful clear morning, with keen frosty air and a temperature, at 7 A.M., of —50.5° (—45.8° C.). The Grinnell Land coast, which had been hidden by low fog the preceding day, stood out clear and distinct far to the westward of them as they turned their backs toward it and started across the low country to Newman Bay. A narrow deep ravine was followed, which, rough and broken, eventually brought them out "on an extensive plain stretching to the east as far as could be seen. We found this little broken by any deep water-courses, though the absence of snow was surprising. The thermometer registered —55.5° (—48.6° C.), and there was quite a perceptible breeze blowing in our faces."

After only six hours' travelling, owing to the extremely low temperature (it had not risen above —50° (—45.6° C.) during the day) and a rapidly falling barometer, Lieutenant Lockwood deemed it the most prudent course to go into camp.

The deepest drift was searched out in a small ravine, where a hole was dug in the snow, which was so shallow that the ground was reached in less than four feet. The tent and poles covered with snow formed its roof, and the party passed a warm night, though cramped exceedingly for room owing to the small size of the house. They had scarcely entered the hut when a snow-storm with brisk wind sprang up, though the temperature at that time was —51° (—46.1° C.). Despite the storm without, the heat of their bodies and the vapor from the alcohol cooking-lamp raised the temperature to an uncomfortable degree, and from the tightness of the house nearly suffocated the party.

Sergeant Brainard in his notes that evening records: "At 11 A.M. the thermometer recorded —55.5° (—48.6° C.) while we were travelling, and a light breeze from the northeast prevailed at the same time. The temperature has remained below —50° (—45.6° C.) during the entire day, and at times we were compelled to keep the warm hand to the face continually in order to prevent it from freezing. Great as are our discomforts, we are congratulating ourselves upon the warmth imparted by our snug snow-den. The temperature has been something almost unknown in the annals of Arctic exploration, and the snow-storm which commenced about the time we entered camp, was accompanied by brisk wind, which in a tent would probably have frost-bitten some of the party severely."

Payer records a sledge journey, March 13, 1874, when temperatures of —47.2° (—44° C.) and —50.8° (—46° C.) were experienced. He says: "I do not believe that we could have passed through the night without the help of grog, in spite of which, boiling hot, we suffered much all through the night from cold and our frozen clothes."

Just before going into camp Sergeant Brainard discovered on that winter's snow the dung of a musk-ox, which he thought could be scarcely a week dropped. He well says: "This should be positive proof that the animal does not migrate south with the sun and return the following year as the sun advances, as many assume to be his habit, but remains in some well-sheltered valley or ravine during the winter darkness, subsisting on whatever comes in his way." This incident, and my personal experience, as well as that of the British expedition, leaves no doubt that the musk-ox is a regular habitant of Grinnell Land and Northern Greenland the entire year.

The morning of March 6th it was necessary for the party to burrow out of their lodging through the snow, as the tunnel had completely filled from the drift of the prevailing storm. The temperature, which had fallen to $-52°$ ($-46.7°C$.) during the night, had then risen to $-36.5°$ ($-38.1°$ C.), but unfortunately a fresh wind had to be faced in travelling.

Despite the continued wind and snow, the party moved onward, and in two hours reached the level expanse of Newman Bay, which was broken to the eastward only by a group of rocks which Lieutenant Lockwood thought might be Howgate Island of the Hall expedition. After four hours' travelling, the strong northerly wind produced such frequent frost-bites that it was deemed best to camp on reaching a favorable snow-drift. They were fortunate enough to find a snow-bank with a vertical front, into which a small entrance two feet wide and three feet high was dug, for four feet, and then the interior was gradually hollowed out until a large roomy chamber was formed. The entrance of the tunnel was covered with the tent, and the alcohol-lamp used for cooking soon raised the temperature of the snow-hut above the freezing point.

The storm broke during the night, and on the morning of the 7th the sky cleared sufficiently for the sun to be seen for a time, but later snow recommenced. After breakfast, at 8 A.M., the temperature outside was $-49.5°$ ($-45.3°$ C.), with a brisk wind from the northeast, and during the day $-52°$ ($-46.7°$ C.) was recorded.

Owing to the continued wind, Lieutenant Lockwood did not deem it safe to travel, and the day was spent in the snow-hut.

The weather still continued very bad on the 8th, though the temperature rose to $-35°$ ($-37.2°$ C.). An attempt was made to proceed on the journey, but the wind increasing in strength caused many frost-bites, as they were facing it, and in consequence the party were obliged to return to their snow-hut.

Immediately after returning, although the hut had been vacated an hour, the following interesting observations of temperature were noted:

Outside the tunnel, $-33°$ ($-36.1°$ C.); on floor inside hut, $+3°$ ($16.1°$ C.); two and one-half feet above floor, $+31°$ ($-0.6°$ C.). Later, when the alcohol-lamp was burning, the temperature reached only $+36°$ ($+2.2°$ C.) inside the hut, but a hole had previously been cut into the roof, which was covered only by a piece of light canvas to serve as a window; candles having been forgotten.

An incident occurred while in the snow-house which illustrated how important a thing a match may be, and how slight a neglect may imperil the lives of a sledge party. Lieutenant Lockwood and Sergeant Jewell had used up or had lost their stock of matches. Both common and wax matches were supplied to and carried by sledge-men, in water-tight cases of rubber. Sergeant Brainard in his field-journal says: "We made the alarming discovery this evening that I was the only one in the party who possessed matches, and those in limited number. An attempt being made to light the wax matches, it was found that they would not burn, the dampness of the house having evidently been communicated to them. Recollecting that I had a box of water-proof matches in a garment which was outside of the snow-house, I procured them, and seating myself on a sleeping-bag, surrounded by my anxious comrades who scarcely dared to breathe, commenced a series of experiments on the new matches. All to no purpose; they refused to burn, as did the wax, and would just ignite the sulphur without even charring the wood. We now began to seriously consider our situation here. We were out of the usual route of travel between Thank God Harbor and Newman Bay, without light and fire, and with temperatures of freezing mercury outside our damp snow-house. We were at least sixty miles from home by the nearest route, and seventy by that we had followed. Could we live three, or even two days, without water, until we could reach Depot "B" (Cape Beechy)? It was finally decided that if to-morrow was a favorable day for travelling we could reach Cape Sumner, and the day following Cape Beechy, and although we would suffer much from thirst yet we would be able to make the journey. The revolver was suggested, and paper was prepared into which it was to be discharged, but one of the party wanted to give the matches another trial. This was done, and match after match ignited only to barely flicker and go out. Jewell finally produced a love-letter, which was very carefully worn in some inside garment, and holding a piece to the next match it caught the flame slowly and immediately communicated it to the alcohol-lamp, one wick of which was allowed to burn until we quit the snow-house." The cause of the matches not lighting eventually proved to be the vitiated, damp atmosphere of the hut.

On the morning of the 9th, with a temperature of $-34°$ ($-36.7°$ C.), the party started for Polaris Boat Camp, near Cape Sumner. In a ravine sloping toward Newman Bay Brainard and Jewell saw four ptarmigan in perfect winter plumage, and Lieutenant Lockwood shot a hare, which stood transfixed with astonishment at Jewell's antics as a beater-in.

As snow was found upon the land the course was at first kept parallel with the bay, so that Reynolds Island was not to be distinguished; but later they took to the floe. The whole surface-ice of Newman Bay was smooth and level, evidently composed of harbor-ice of that season, and the snow upon its surface was packed very hard from the recent storm. Naturally this hard level snow would seem to afford easy sledging, but unfortunately such is not the fact. The dry snow at very low temperatures acts upon steel runners as dry sand, and the friction is simply enormous. The snow retarded greatly their progress, but whenever ice was fallen in with their gait was comparatively rapid. No ice-foot was found along the shore of Newman Bay.

Eight hours' travelling brought them to Boat Camp, where the whale and canvas boats were readily found. The latter boat had six oars, and was substantially in the condition described by the English Arctic reports. The hole in the whale-boat was very small, and otherwise it seemed, on careful examination, to be in excellent order.

The temperature had fallen as they travelled to $-39°$ ($-39.4°$ C.), and was $-40°$ ($-40°$ C.) when Cape Sumner was reached at the end of nine and a half hours' travel. The route from Boat Camp to Sumner was behind a series of stranded bergs, over a snow-slope which could be made practicable for a loaded

"THE ARCTIC HIGHWAY"—RUBBLE AND HUMMOCKY ICE.
(*From a photograph.*)

sledge only by considerable work. Worn out by the day's travel the tent was soon pitched, but their night and morning were wretchedly passed, as the sleeping-bag, saturated with moisture from the high temperature in the snow-hut, was frozen completely solid during the day, and it required the steady exertion of the four men for several hours to unroll it and force themselves within. It was necessary to thaw out this mass of ice by the heat of their bodies. As the temperature had fallen to −40° (−40° C.) this tedious operation was very trying to the chilled, weary men, and their discomfort was not lessened by the cutting, disagreeable wind experienced by them from the exposed position in which their tent was pitched —at the very point of Cape Sumner.

On the morning of March 10th Lieutenant Lockwood, in the exercise of his discretion, concluded not to visit the north side of Newman Bay, as its passage presented no difficulties and he was satisfied that the advance depot for future operations could be established readily either at Boat Camp, Cape Brevoort, or at the mouth of the Gap valley.

The entrance of Newman Bay was crowded with heavy, rough ice, which gave way to small and level floes a few miles inland. Leaving his tent, sleeping-bag, and other articles of future benefit, Lieutenant Lockwood started later across Robeson Channel, in a temperature of −41° (−40.6° C.), and reached Depot "B" in twelve and a half hours. The journey in places was slow and laborious, owing to rubble and hummocky ice, and their discomforts were largely increased by the blinding snowstorm, which for a time shut out even the nearest land.

As a result of his trip, Lieutenant Lockwood concluded that the best route to Cape Sumner was to follow his original tracks eastward until near the Gap, and then follow the Greenland coast to Cape Sumner.

The outcome of this journey was particularly satisfactory. The distance travelled was at least one hundred and thirty-five miles, in a mean temperature, as shown by their observations, of $-42.3°$ ($-41.3°$ C.) during their ten days' absence. The party had perfect health during their entire trip, and no frost-bites were received except slight and superficial ones on the face while travelling. The journey involved extraordinary hardships and sufferings, which demanded no ordinary powers of endurance to meet successfully. The dogs stood the trip very well, except a young animal, about nine months old, who was somewhat tired at times. A not unimportant result was to give Lieutenant Lockwood and the men confidence in their equipment and in their own powers, as compared with other expeditions. The journey from Thank God Harbor to Cape Sumner was made over the same route as that followed by Hall to Cape Brevoort, and entailed the same amount of travel. The journey was made by Captain Hall in six marches, by Lieutenant Lockwood in three, during two of which he was driven by storm to shelter. This comparison is not intended as any reflection on Captain Hall, who from eight years' experience was thoroughly conversant with sledge-work, but to point out the importance of such field-work being done by young men in the most active period of life. Lieutenant Lockwood and his comrades were about thirty years of age, while Captain Hall was over fifty. The entire distance was travelled on foot by the former party, while Captain Hall, from lack of vigor and health, was obliged to keep the sledge.

CHAPTER XIX.

ESTABLISHING DEPOTS.

(DR. PAVY AND SERGEANT BRAINARD.)

WHILE Lieutenant Lockwood was yet absent at Thank God Harbor the sun returned, so it was rendered possible to commence the establishment of depots. The small caches near Mount Parry and the large English depot at Lincoln Bay were sufficient for the use of the party that was detailed to travel north over the Frozen Sea. The North Greenland exploring party was unfortunate in having no nearer base of supplies than Depot "B," which was separated from Greenland by a broad channel nearly twenty miles wide.

To insure the success of work on that shore, I determined on establishing a depot at Polaris Boat Camp near Cape Sumner. To this end Acting Assistant Surgeon Pavy, who had volunteered for spring sledging, was sent, with Sergeant Lynn, Eskimo Jens, and dog-sledge Lilla, on March 5th, to convey a sledge-load of provisions to as northerly a point on the Greenland coast as could be reached in one day's march from Cape Beechy.

The trip to Depot "B" was comfortably made in nine hours in a mean temperature of $-36°$ ($-37.8°$ C.). The sledge load of about seven hundred pounds was dragged by seven dogs. The severe gale which drove Lieutenant Lockwood to camp, after four hours' travelling, likewise detained Dr. Pavy on the

6th in the snow-house near Cape Beechy. The day was spent comfortably, for, although the outside temperature registered −34° (−36.7° C.), yet the interior temperature was raised to +26° (−3.3° C.) by an Eskimo lamp.

On the 7th, after ten hours' severe work in a mean temperature of −38° (−38.9° C.), Dr. Pavy pitched his tent on the floe in Robeson Channel, some two miles from the Greenland coast. During this journey he met with a misfortune through improper packing of the sledge, which resulted in the loss from it of a two-gallon can of alcohol and the breakage and leakage of another. This accident also entailed a couple of hours' delay in an unsuccessful search for the lost alcohol.

March 8th, leaving his tent standing, Dr. Pavy proceeded with his party to the shore, two miles distant, and cached the supplies in a marked break in the coast, midway between Capes Sumner and Lupton, which was designated as the "Gap." The cache, established behind an erratic block, was marked by a signal flag, which Dr. Pavy says was planted "about thirty or forty feet above the ice-foot, its bright red color forming a striking contrast with the slab of Devonic limestone of the neighborhood."

The trip to and from the shore had been made in a storm, but as later in the day it abated, the tent was struck and the party started homeward. They camped on a floe three miles east of Cape Beechy. This day's trip was very severe and uncomfortable, as the temperature varied from −28° (−33.3° C.) to −37° (−38.3° C.) with a northeast wind.

During the night an incident occurred which showed the considerateness and kind heart of our Eskimo Jens Edward. Sergeant Lynn was feeling badly on entering his sleeping-bag, and had fallen asleep before Jens finished his work. The Eskimo, fearing he was sick, was unwilling to disturb him, and decided to sleep outside the bag, without covering other than his fur travelling suit, rather than awaken his comrade to his discomfort. Although the temperature outside the tent sank to −41.7° (− 40.9° C.), the ability of Jens to endure cold was so great that he escaped with but one toe slightly frost-bitten.

The party reached Conger in good condition March 9th. This journey, successfully made in such great cold and strong wind, reflected credit on Dr. Pavy's energy and determination, and that officer gave due credit for their assistance to his subordinates, Lynn and Jens.

On March 13th Sergeant Brainard, with seven men, was ordered to move the small boat Discovery, with such additional supplies as could be hauled, to the depot to be used at or near Cape Sumner. His orders required him to follow the route recommended by Lieutenant Lockwood, and, after securely caching the boat in the Gap, to establish a depot of provisions at such point as could be reached in Newman Bay, the mouth of the Gap valley being preferred. He was also to build a snow-house, if possible, but his absence was not to exceed six days. His closing orders read:

"You are cautioned particularly against travelling in stormy or windy weather, and you will frequently question your party as to their condition, and avoid over-work. I trust your speedy and safe return may be soon noted. You must bear in mind that you start in a temperature of about − 40°, and at an almost unparalleled early season of the year."

The main points of Sergeant Brainard's journey are taken from his field-journal. They started on a clear, calm morning in a temperature of −37.3° (−38.5° C.). The load of over a thousand pounds hauled very hard, "it dragging over the dry, soft snow with about the same noise and resistance as would have been experienced over a sand-bank." In order to make

Depot "B" that day, Sergeant Brainard dropped two hundred pounds of pemmican and moved quite rapidly to Depot "A." There they stopped thirteen minutes to drink some chocolate taken from the station in a rubber bag wrapped in a buffalo robe; the temperature then was $-44°$ ($-42.2°$ C.). After twelve hours' work, during which they travelled twenty-five miles, they reached Depot "B" in an almost exhausted condition. Sergeant Brainard says: "On our arrival the temperature was $-53.5°$ ($-47.5°$ C.). We all retired early, very tired and in a 'broken-up' condition. A few complained during the day of terrible thirst, but there being no remedy for them they had to endure it as best they could. Those who are excessive tobacco-chewers were the most affected."

The party left the snow-house (near Cape Beechy) at 7.30 A.M., March 15th, the temperature standing at $-50.5°$ ($-48.8°$ C.), although it had been down to $-61°$ ($-51.7°$ C.) a few hours previous. A bright, beautiful sunshine with calm air made travelling quite endurable. Four hours and a half of hard work brought them to Cape Beechy and to the rough rubble ice.

Here the very hard work commenced; the broken, jagged pieces of ice afforded a most uncertain and precarious foothold, while the irregularities of the surfaces rendered hauling doubly difficult. By dint of extraordinary exertions the sledge was got through the rubble to a palæocrystic floe, but the rough work necessitated the relashing of the boat on the sledge. This was trying work, not so much for the active handy men, who hauled and pulled at the lashings and so kept warm despite a temperature of $-43.5°$ ($-41.9°$ C.), but to the unemployed, who danced around shivering in desperate efforts to keep their clothes, damp with moisture, from freezing to the rigidity of brass. As they moved on, the uneven, rolling surface of the floe was covered with a light covering of snow, just deep enough to require the men to plough their way and to demand every atom of their strength to pull the sledge through it. Occasionally a bare descending bit of ice came, just enough in extent to force the exhausted men for a few yards into an accelerated pace and give emphasis to the jerk which, as snow came to clog the runners, a moment later brought all up standing. After nearly nine hours of such travel, Sergeant Brainard concluded that the condition of the men was such as to render camping necessary, as continued pulling without food or drink in such low temperatures had quite exhausted them. The temperature, then at $-43.5°$ ($-41.9°$ C.), had not been above $-40°$ ($-40°$ C.) during the march.

An order to camp is obeyed with alacrity, not that it is a comfortable or pleasant thing to do, but because work of any character is preferable to standing quietly around. The only continued comfort for an Arctic sledger is while he is engaged in the drag-ropes hauling a fair load at a moderate pace over a level bit of ice.

With skilled hands the sledge is rapidly unlashed, and while the main party sets up the tent the evening cook is searching out a blue-topped berg, from which to get his ice for tea and stew. The tent is well pitched on a proper site, which preferably is a level snow-covered bit of floe, with a large berg near to the windward to break the force of any sudden gale. If snow cannot be found suited for the site of the tent, it is best that snow be brought and strewed within it. This not only gives a soft bed, but a comparatively warm one, for ice is almost invariably colder than snow.

The rubber tent-cloth spread, the sleeping-bags are brought in and laid down, but to unroll them is a labor of love demanding the strength of a Hercules. The moisture which exhaled the night before from the body, the falling spiculæ of snow formed that morning in the tent, the lingering vapor from the stew, and the drops of spilled tea have all insidiously worked their way deep into the tangled hair, and, turning to ice, have bound fast the tightly rolled buffalo bags. Now they are more like coils of rolled sheet-iron than the supple well-tanned skins they are supposed to be. By great exertions they are finally forced apart, and the wise sledge traveller, be his wisdom from book or experience, seeks them at the earliest moment.

The work of erecting the tent and opening the bags has necessitated the use of the bare hands in a measure, and handling these articles, colder than frozen mercury, is like handling hot iron which burns and cracks men's fingers and hands. The comparatively light work, too, has checked the perspiration, and with stiffening clothing and half-frozen fingers the travellers, other than the cook and commissary sergeant, sit down; and, carefully brushing the snow from their garments, loosen the lashings and take off overalls and foot-gear. They systematically arrange these in the shape in which they can easiest don them, for in five minutes after they are frozen solid. The feet are stripped bare and a pair of fresh socks, warm from the man's breast, are put on and covered at once with a pair of large dog-skin or sheep-skin sleeping-socks. Crawling into their bag their chilled limbs gradually thaw out the frozen skin, and later they acquire warmth when hot tea and stew come to them.

The cook meanwhile has obtained his ice, both for morning and evening meal, and has received from the sergeant the carefully measured allowance of alcohol, which he takes with a dubious shake of the head, as he sees how small the quantity and how much work it is expected to do. His ice cut too coarsely or mixed with too much snow, and the wicks half an inch too high or too low, and the result is a stew mixed with ice, or tea just steaming and uncooked.

The rations, arranged at the station, are served out with the same careful exactness. An ounce too much to-day means shortage to-morrow. The cooking apparatus carefully placed level on a board, he watches it with the utmost caution, for the arrangement is such that carelessness, or perhaps the sudden movement of a man in the bag, may cause a pot to tip and the precious allowance, or a part at least, to be lost. An hour is a moderate time in which to cook the tea, and as the frozen, wretched cook watches it he realizes too keenly the truth of the adage, " A watched pot never boils."

If he has inexperienced comrades they sit up and watch with or aid him, some through a feeling that they must bear a hand, and others because they deem it unbefitting soldiers that their meals should be served them in their beds. They do not realize, until taught by bitter experience, that it is best that all this hardship and suffering should be avoided by all save the cook, and the strength of the party thus be conserved.

The pot finally boils, and instantly it is served to the weary men; some of whom, overcome by the exhausting labors of the day, have dropped off into a sleep, and are doubtful whether to be vexed or pleased that they are recalled to a sense of cold and weariness. The steaming tea and stew are served, the clouds of vapor change to falling snow; the weary men, refreshed by their meal, crawl down in their bags, to be followed by the cook as soon as he can arrange his lamp and pot and tie up the tent securely.

The night, or rather the hours set for sleep, passes slowly. Crowded two or three into one bag, all must be awakened and turn together whenever cramp or cold renders one so uncomfortable that he must change his position. Stiffness, aches, rheumatic pains, cold, and cramps fall to every one's lot to a greater or less extent. Nobody is sorry, save the cook, when the officer calls that unfortunate person, whose only comfort is the reflection that his service passes with that meal, as the cooking is done in turn.

In the morning the same routine is gone through with, modified at times by some depraved article of footgear, which, frozen into metal-like hardness, will not be coaxed or forced on to the foot until it has been taken literally to one's heart and thawed out by the heat of the body. The slowness with which the party breaks camp makes everybody wretched and ill-humored until a short hour's march has thawed travelling gear and human nature into tractable mood.

With the temperature 75° ($-40.7°$ C.) or more below the freezing point of water, it seems to me surprising even now that men can ever do and endure such work and exposure. Only those of perfect health, iron constitution, and marked determination are capable of continued work under such conditions. This account of a march and camp is a fair description (underdrawn if anything) of the experiences of a sledging party favored by fine weather and ordinary travel. When storm and snow come to blind, wet, and buffet the wretched travellers, their miseries cannot be described in words. Such conditions as above must be imagined as the common experience of all Arctic travellers until zero temperatures ($-17.8°$ C.) come with May, bringing other discomforts not much less serious.

On the morning of March 16th, the temperature, which had fallen during the night to $-44°$ ($-42.2°$ C.), had risen to $-40°$ ($-40°$ C.), but a brisk northeast wind rendered travel dangerous. At 9 A.M., however, the wind subsided somewhat, and Sergeant Brainard decided to start. His journal says: "Last night Schneider was very lame, and complained of rheumatic pains and inability to sleep. He was a very indifferent traveller during the entire day. This morning he complains bitterly of the condition of his legs, and is scarcely able to walk about the tent. His condition is so much worse that I consider it the most prudent course to send him back to Depot 'B,' accompanied by Biederbick, who is a capital nurse."

Owing to diminished force, about two hundred pounds were left at this camp, including a day's rations for the return journey. Light drifting snow obliged them to encamp about five miles from the Greenland coast. Sergeant Brainard says: "We fortunately travelled all day over the same palæocrystic floe as yesterday. Our tent is now pitched in a sheltered position, which screens us from the heavily drifting snow, but does not help us with regard to our greatest foe,—the low temperature, which, though at one time as high as $-33°$ ($-35.1°$ C.), has fallen again to $-39°$ ($-39.4°$ C.)."

The morning of the 7th was clear and calm, with a minimum of $-43°$ ($-41.7°$ C.). Says Sergeant Brainard, "Seeing that it is impossible to reach Newman Bay within the time allotted me, owing to the greatly reduced strength of the sledge-party and the increasing roughness of the ice, I decided to leave our tent standing, and to transport the boat and supplies to Depot 'E,' established by Dr. Pavy a few days before in the Gap. That done we would return to Fort Conger."

A little over four hours' travel brought them to the cache. Brainard continues: "We placed the boat beside a huge rock and fastened her down securely with boxes, rocks, etc., first placing hard bread, medical knapsack, etc., under her to prevent them from being blown away. We began the excavation of snow-house, but the increasing wind compelled us to abandon the work and seek our own safety." They were none too soon, for "the storm meanwhile increasing in violence obliterated entirely our trail at times, and prevented us from seeing more than a few yards in advance. The wind was fortunately at our backs, but frequent frost-bites of noses and cheeks were experienced before we reached the tent, in an exhausted state, after nearly eight hours' absence. 5.30 P.M.," says the field-journal, "we are now sitting in our sleeping-bags, with all sleeping-gear on, receiving hot chocolate from the cook. We congratulate ourselves on reaching the tent as we did, for the wind has increased to a gale, and the air is so full of drifting snow that objects a hundred yards distant cannot be distinguished. St. Patrick was honored this evening by a few songs from 'The Wild Irishman.'" Singing songs when sheltered only by a light tent from a drifting gale and a temperature lower than $-40°$ ($-40°$ C.) was a fair sample of the indomitable spirit and unvarying cheerfulness of the men of the Lady Franklin Bay Expedition.

On March 18th, the morning temperature of $-43.2°$ ($-41.8°$ C.) rose before starting homewards to $-41°$ ($-40.6°$ C.). After six hours' travel camp was made, in order that a few hours' work should be devoted to collecting at that point some scattered stores near by. The drifting snow of the preceding day had forced itself into their travelling-gear, and Sergeant Brainard says: "Our buffalo sleeping-bags are so badly frozen that at this camp the men were compelled to thaw themselves into them or go without sleep. They chose the former evil without giving it much thought, and passed a most wretched night in consequence." The next day they reached Depot "B," where Schneider and Beiderbick were found in good condition. On the 20th they returned to Fort Conger thoroughly worn out, but in excellent spirits.

This sledge journey was a remarkable one, and exhibited not only Sergeant Brainard's executive ability and good judgment in a strong light, but also proved the mettle and strength of the general party. This journey involved an average daily march of about seventeen miles for six successive days in a mean temperature of $-41°$ ($-40.6°$ C.). Notwithstanding the inability of one man to withstand the hard work in such extreme cold, the trip was successful; and all, including Schneider, returned well, though troubled with slight frost-bites.

The lowest mean temperature experienced by McClintock in his ten sledge journeys was $-30°$ ($-34.4°$ C.), when in twenty-five days he made, with a dog-team, the same average distance as this party, and at a correspondingly early time of the year.

Devil's Head (The Bellows Valley).
[*June*, 1884.]

CHAPTER XX.

NORTHWARD OVER THE FROZEN SEA.

(DR. PAVY'S NORTHERN JOURNEY.)

A FEW days later Dr. Pavy was sent northward in an attempt to reach land to the northward of Cape Joseph Henry. From his experience gained along the Grinnell Land coast the preceding autumn, he was convinced that he would be able to proceed a long distance northward over the Polar Ocean, and was confident that land would eventually be discovered in that direction. While doubtful of the existence of land to the southward of the eighty-fifth parallel, I considered it important that no chance of geographical success should be neglected, and consequently assigned one of my dog-teams to Dr. Pavy for this special work. He was given the services of Sergeant Rice, the photographer of the expedition, who had also volunteered for the trip, and Eskimo Jens Edward. These two men, selected by Dr. Pavy as his assistants, were gifted with remarkable physical powers and such aptitude of resource as particularly fitted them for the work.

The most important clauses of my instructions to Dr. Pavy read: "The details of your journey and the route to be followed northward from Lincoln Bay are left to your judgment and arrangement. I deem it important, however, to invite your especial attention to the route across Feilden Peninsula and James Ross Bay to Cape Hecla. While overland travel is usually objectionable, the experiences of the English expedition, 1875-76, as well as that of your own journeys, indicate that travelling is thus facilitated when the party can avoid any considerable distance of the polar pack. . . . 4th. You are to bear in mind that in no instance must your party be separated; that the exact location of depots must be made known to each member; that no advance must be made beyond such time as, on full allowance, one-half of your provisions have been consumed; and that in case of any considerable movement of the ice, or on the appearance of any lanes of water, you must at once seek the main-land. . . . 6th. In case no land is reached, one day must be devoted at your most northerly point to determining your position with the greatest care, and in obtaining detailed information as to the depth of the sea, the temperature of the water, the tidal currents, the thickness of the new ice, and any other available data. Whenever you are obliged to rest your team a day, similar observations should be made. . . . 9th. A careful lookout will be kept for driftwood, and if any fragments that could possibly have belonged to a ship be noted, it must be brought to the station . . . for identification. It is possible that some tidings of the Jeannette may thus be obtained. In accordance with your wishes, no special anxiety will be felt for your party until June 1st. Trusting that your earnest enthusiasm for polar exploration, united to your practical experience, . . . will insure all possible success, and wishing beyond all your safe return, I am, etc."

The party left on March 19th with a team of excellent dogs. It seemed to me, then, an excellent opportunity of ascertaining the capabilities of a dog-team, by noting the constant weights of the sledge, the weight of the dogs on going and returning, and the food issued to them daily. Through a misunderstand-

240 THREE YEARS OF ARCTIC SERVICE.

ing of my instructions the dogs were not weighed after returning, nor were the constant weights determined.

Dr. Pavy's team had been used for the purpose of facilitating

Dr. Pavy's Party Starting North, March 19, 1882.
[*From photograph by Sergt. Rice.*]

Lieutenant Lockwood's work on the North Greenland coast, and to assist this section Sergeant Jewell was in turn detached, with the dog-sledge Antoinette, driven by Eskimo Christiansen, which was to serve as a supporting sledge as far as Lincoln Bay, where the remains of the English depot of 1875 served as a base for Dr. Pavy's subsequent operations. Sergeant Jewell, on his return, was to bring south to Depot "B" two hundred pounds of Australian beef and certain small stores.

In order that Sergeant Jewell might carry as large a load as possible, he was provided with no tent, but was directed to avail himself at Depot "B" of the snow-house, and while journeying from that point to Lincoln Bay and return he was to shelter himself by snow-house or "dug-out."

The party left in a temperature of $-25°$ ($-31.7°$ C.), and the trip northward was comfortably made in about that mean temperature, although while at Depot "B" a temperature of $-41°$ ($-40.6°$ C.) was recorded. From Cape Beechy to the north side of Wrangel Bay the ice was largely rubble and rough hummocks, which made progress slow and tedious, and necessitated three days' journey where two had been estimated.

Sergeant Jewell left Lincoln Bay for Depot "B" on the 23d, having been furnished with but one hundred and sixty-four pounds of beef instead of two hundred as ordered in writing. His journey southward was made under very trying conditions and in very low temperatures. On leaving Lincoln Bay the temperature stood at about $-40°$ ($-40.6°$ C.), but fell steadily during the day, and registered $-53°$ ($-47.2°$ C.) during the night. He was fortunate in finding large snow-drifts just south of Wrangel Bay, where he passed a tolerably comfortable night in a snow-hut. The following day, travelling in temperatures which ranged from $-45°$ ($-42.8°$ C.) to $-49°$ ($-45°$ C.), he reached Depot "B," where orders had been sent him to carry out instructions from Lieutenant Lockwood regarding the transportation of stores from Depot "B" to the Greenland coast.

From March 25th to 30th Sergeant Jewell, assisted for a portion of the time by Private Ellis, was engaged with his sledge in accumulating stores on the Greenland coast. There was no day on which the temperature did not fall as low as —40° (—40° C.), and on four days —50° (—45.6° C.) and —51° (—46.1° C.) were recorded. The mean temperature in which this work was done was about —40° (—40° C.).

On March 27th Sergeant Jewell was deprived of the services of Private Ellis, who, when sent to aid him from the home station, to Depot "B," had unfortunately wet his feet from tidal overflow during the journey. Not exercising the proper precaution of changing his foot-gear, Ellis' imprudence resulted in his being seriously, though superficially, frost-bitten. Notwithstanding his condition, he made a journey, March 25th and 26th, from Depot "B" to the Greenland coast and back, and then, in order not to interfere with the work, insisted on Sergeant Jewell permitting him to return to the station alone. Private Ellis showed remarkable fortitude and determination during the whole affair, which was especially creditable to him.

On the 30th, the barometer having fallen below 29.00 and fearing a violent storm, Sergeant Jewell prudently concluded it best to return to the station, rather than to venture another trip to the Greenland coast.

In the performance of this extraordinary work Sergeant Jewell showed an endurance and fortitude which surprised many, as his physique was but medium. He justified every confidence placed in his faithfulness, energy, and judgment then and afterward. He crossed Robeson Channel six times during March, and ten times during his service—more frequently than any other member of the expedition, except Eskimo Christiansen.

In connection with his own trip to Lincoln Bay, Dr. Pavy reported that north of Cape Beechy the ice-foot became so encumbered with grounded floe-bergs that his party was compelled to take to the floe-ice, notwithstanding its difficult character. On leaving the shore they passed footprints of recent origin, made by a well-grown bear who was travelling south.

Dr. Pavy passed his cache in Wrangel Bay without visiting it, but proceeded to the depot near Mount Parry, on reaching which the tracks of the bear were again fallen in with. The bear had evidently stopped for lunch, and had shown discrimination in his selection of the food. The sacks of bread had been torn open, and the bags torn into shreds, but the bread was left untasted. The pemmican covering had been stripped off, and about two-thirds of it (some seventy pounds in quantity) had been eaten.

After Sergeant Jewell left, on the 23d, a comfortable snow-house was built, to serve as their headquarters until the last load of provisions to be used in the northern trip had been carried beyond Black Cape.

At this camp Old Sneak—one of the team—displayed his faculty for avoiding work. When in harness he did his duty, for he well knew that Jens' keen eye was on him, and that his slackened trace would be followed by the driver's lash, thrown with such force and precision as to make the thick fur fly from any selected spot. When the food had been given out Sneak was on hand, as always on similar occasions, but the loaded sledge with the team in harness waited on him alone. A thorough search failed to find him, and fearing that some article left behind in the snow-hut might suffer from him, Jens entered the house to secure the food, and there found the truant quietly awaiting their departure.

On March 24th, having perfected his arrangements, Dr. Pavy started north, but a southeast breeze with a temperature of $-36.5°$ ($-38.1°$ C.) drove the party to camp near Cape Union, where they were storm-stayed for twenty-two hours.

Dr. Pavy expressed the opinion, that in the vicinity of Cape Union, owing to the escarpment of the cliffs, the coast could never be practicable for fall travelling, as in places dogs could not travel, and in others the conditions were such as to be impracticable even for men. Three times in one day his party was driven from the ice-foot, and once was compelled to lower the sledge by the dog-traces over a high and perpendicular ice-foot. Though the ice was level in most places, yet a thin crust of snow, mixed with the salty efflorescence from the sea-ice, impaired the progress of the party by the extreme friction it caused the sledges.

At 3 p.m. of the 25th the temperature moderated to $-27°$ ($-32.8°$ C.), and enabled them to resume their journey, but the ice was found exceedingly broken and uneven, and in one place for a hundred yards the sledge and load had to be transported by hand.

In connection with this day's journey Dr. Pavy says: "I will farther say, that to my belief the Eskimo are indispensable for extended sledge journeys. Their experience in managing dogs, and the apparent facility with which they can drive at once over difficulties where the best of their inexperienced Caucasian pupils will fail or labor for long hours, put the usefulness of their services out of the question. Moreover, their endurance to cold will allow them to perform the many duties of a driver with bare hands, and in half of the time that it would take to freeze ours. The history of Arctic work, from Wrangel to this day, will bear witness to the fact that all dog-sledging expeditions that have used natives as drivers, or perhaps their best substitutes (I mean men trained for years to the work), have succeeded with comparative ease. I think that Sir George Nares, on his homeward journey, must have reflected more fully on the usefulness of dogs and their drivers."

I can scarcely concur in the ideas thus put forward by Dr. Pavy in his official report. My opinion in this respect was also shared by Lieutenant Lockwood and Sergeant Brainard, who made the only successful explorations with dog-sledges during our two years' services. The utility of the Eskimo dog as an Arctic draught animal is beyond doubt; an opinion in which I am sure Sir George Nares and his experienced officers will heartily concur. But when it is stated that the Eskimo is indispensable for extended sledge journeys, I must thoroughly dissent. The valuable Arctic papers for the expedition of 1875 contain the opinion of Baron von Wrangel "On the best means of reaching the Pole," in which he advocates the employment of dogs " and active and courageous drivers." The note attached to that paper, whether Wrangel's or the accomplished editor's, well says that success would be doubtful with Eskimo or Tchouktschi drivers—men without courage or activity. Our Eskimo drivers could not be excelled in their race for bravery, energy, and activity, but Lockwood and Brainard would never have reached their farthest point had they depended on the courage and activity of their dog-driver, whom it was needful to incite to continued exertions. This is no reflection upon the courage of these men, who are unable to appreciate the object of these journeys, and who are necessarily depressed on outward marches owing to the diminishing supply of food, which to them forbodes hardships and sufferings, if not dangers.

The most perilous and remarkable sledge journeys in connection with the British expedition of 1875 and 1876 were made without the aid or assistance of Eskimo drivers. At the very point where Dr. Pavy's party was then struggling, and under similar unfavorable ice conditions, was made the memorable sledge journey, March 12 to 15, 1876, in which those heroic officers, Lieutenants Rawson and Egerton, R.N., displayed such fortitude, endurance, and unselfish energy in their efforts to save the life of a Danish dog-driver from the Greenland settlements. These young English officers gave of their heat and life to save this denizen of an Arctic coast. Later the same officers, with no Eskimo, but with British sailors, made successfully, in temperatures as low as $-42°$ ($-41.1°$ C.), the trip from Floeberg Beach to Discovery Harbor and back in ten sledging days—journeys which compare favorably with our own successful work.

In our own expedition the successful raising, breaking, and training for field services of our Eskimo dogs born at Conger were due to the intelligent and zealous efforts of Private Schneider, who, after an experience of several months, drove nearly as well as an Eskimo.

The ability of the Eskimo to endure privation and hardships has been greatly overrated. Successful resistance to conditions of cold and privation by men is not so much a matter of race and original habitat, but depends to a greater extent than is usually acknowledged upon the moral force and mental determination of the individual. The subsequent experience at Cape Sabine in the case of Eskimo and Caucasian, with the same food and in pursuit of the same object—game or relief for the party—instances this. In the trip toward Littleton Island Sergeant Rice returned in fair physical condition, while Eskimo Jens was completely exhausted. The same relative difference in their condition was noted between Sergeant Long and Eskimo Christiansen on their return from the unsuccessful hunt for game in Alexandra Harbor. Another illustrative instance between Rice and Jens occurred in this very trip of Dr. Pavy's.

The 26th to 28th were occupied in the moving of a second load from Lincoln Bay to Black Cape, the party experiencing temperatures from $-11.5°$ ($-24.2°$ C.) to $-44°$ ($-42.2°$ C.), and on the 29th reached Lincoln Bay again. The first glaze on the snow from the heat of the sun was noted on the 28th, the highest temperature noted having been —11.5° (24.2° C.), and on the 29th the party discarded their *jumpers* as too warm while travelling. On March 30th the temperature, which had stood at —52° (—46.7° C.) the previous night, rose to —8.5° (—22.5° C.). As a severe storm with drifting snow prevailed, the party remained comfortably in the hut during the day, improving the delay by drying and repairing their boots and clothing.

On the evening of March 31st the party, in a temperature of —38.8° (—39.3° C.), left Lincoln Bay with its last load northward, and when within a short distance of Cape Union the right runner of the sledge broke longitudinally through the lashing holes. Sergeant Rice offered to return to Conger for a new runner, and started at once, accompanied by Eskimo Jens; the temperature then being —42° (—41.1° C.). They took a small spirit-lamp to melt ice with, a small quantity of preserved meat and chocolate for a lunch, and also the steel shoe of the runner. The journey was made to Depot "B," about four miles south of Cape Beechy, in one march. Between the cape and depot Rice says that Jens, for whom he had repeatedly stopped, was so exhausted that, despite all persuasion, he was obliged to stop within a few hundred yards of the depot, and he reached that point fifteen minutes after Rice's arrival. Sergeant Rice modestly said: "Doubtless Jens' exhaustion was due to the greater exertions he made, and worry he had undergone in getting the dogs, with broken sledge, back to Lincoln Bay, for I am sure that his powers of endurance are greater than my own." The march from Lincoln Bay to Depot "B" occupied nineteen hours, and involved at least forty miles' travelling, and possibly farther, owing to the extremely tortuous path they were obliged to pursue. The party reached

Conger on the 3d, at 7 A.M., and, being furnished with a new runner, left on the 4th.

The presence of Lieutenant Lockwood enabled me to send the runner to Cape Beechy, relieving Rice and Jens thus far, but beyond that point they were obliged to carry it. In returning, the trip was made from Depot "B" to Lincoln Bay in nineteen hours, they following the inside route by the way of Wrangel Bay, where the depot of provisions left the previous autumn was found in good condition, unvisited by the bear.

Dr. Pavy, during the absence of Rice and Jens, travelled a short distance inland over the high hills to the westward of Lincoln Bay, in the hopes of discovering whether an inland route could not be found which would allow a party to travel at any time from Wrangel Bay to Floeberg Beach.

Dr. Pavy says: "At the highest point reached, which I estimated to be about two thousand feet, I had a magnificent view, especially overland. From the head of Lincoln Bay several valleys could be seen, which, succeeding to each other, appeared to lead toward Wrangel Bay. In another direction, northeast, I could distinctly see a succession of sloping hills cut with ravines and valleys. I think it is possible to reach the coast at the entrance of some of the numerous openings near Floeberg Beach." Between the United States range and a lower chain of mountains nearer to the coast, Dr. Pavy thought it probable that a long and extensive valley existed trending from the northeast to the southwest.

Lincoln Bay was finally left on the evening of April 6th, the party selecting night travel, as was generally recommended to field parties. High winds drove them to camp part of the 7th and until the evening of the 8th, when on starting, "the wind," Dr. Pavy says, "was blowing such a gale that in places, over good ice glazed by snow, it pushed the sledge faster than the dogs could run." On this day the temperature rose to +4.8° (−15.2° C.), being the same day on which the temperature was first observed to be above zero at the home station.

The party was delayed by high winds on the 10th, which drove them to camp, and on the following day the rough and difficult ice obliged them to move their load by hand nearly a thousand yards. The temperature was so mild on the 10th that Rice and Jens slept out-of-doors, though Dr. Pavy occupied the snow-house.

The Alert winter-quarters were reached on April 11th. Of the approach Dr. Pavy says : " A heavy lead-colored sky, contrasting fearfully with the whiteness of the freshly drifted snow, lent to the surrounding landscape a gloomy appearance. From a distance we could see a large cairn on top of the Alert's lookout, and lower, on the brow of a smaller hill, some dark object, which at first we took for a cache, but was soon found to be the tomb of Petersen. Beneath the large stone that covers the remains of the Danish interpreter a hare had taken up his residence, strangely associating the fact of his presence with the words of the epitaph engraved on a copper plate at the head of the tomb, 'He shall wash me, and I shall be as white as snow.'"

From the lookout hill at the Alert quarters, as far as could be seen, the pack consisted of crowded masses of rough and hummocky ice similar to that described by the officers of the Alert. Dr. Pavy was of the opinion that the ice in that neighborhood had broken up and that the coast-water had been possibly navigable the preceding autumn, but at great risk and danger.

Referring to the grounded bergs, which in 1875–76 protected the Alert from the destructive pressure of the polar pack, he says : " This spring no floe-berg could be seen around the place where the Alert must have dropped her anchor in

1875. No signs of palæocrystic ice were observed closer than about a mile and a half from the coast."

The temperature then was above zero (−17.8° C.), and for them, heavily clothed, the weather was so warm that when travelling, even in shirt-sleeves, they perspired freely.

Referring to the cairn at the Alert winter-quarters, Dr. Pavy says: " About five feet from the ground a large iron cylinder, sealed probably by the engineers of the ship, and in which are secured the documents of the British expedition, is so firmly held by an enormous weight of stones that it would be necessary to tear down half of the monument to get at its contents. . . . We contented ourselves with leaving our record in an air-tight rubber match-box, well secured with heavy rocks by the side of the English documents." The party were impressed by the thick body of snow which covered the surrounding country, in marked contrast to the ground in the vicinity of Conger which was scarcely concealed. The signal flagstaff, with attached halliards, at Cape Sheridan, was still standing in as firm a condition as when erected in 1875.

The danger of travelling along that coast was instanced by the fact that on returning to Black Cape for a second load of stores, not only were the provisions scattered around several hundred yards from the point where they were cached, but the ice-foot was covered with many stones which had fallen from the cliffs during a violent gale, and on the place formerly occupied by their tent several heavy blocks of slate were lying. Dr. Pavy says: " From Cape Union to Floeberg Beach parties travelling during the windy days are continually exposed to the fall of stones from the ragged and disintegrating tops."

The ice continued as a palæocrystic pack from Cape Sheridan to Harley Spit, and thence to View Point, so that following a direct course they found good travel generally, though deep snow-softened by the sun at times impeded their progress. View Point was reached on the morning of the 15th, and Dr. Pavy says he was then "more fully supplied (with stores) than I had expected to be when leaving Fort Conger." The party for a couple of days were favored with calm, beautiful weather and high temperatures. At Conical Hill, on the 16th, many traces of musk-oxen, and fresh tracks of the lemming, ptarmigan, hare, and fox were observed.

From a high hill in Feilden Peninsula the ice in James Ross Bay was seen to be in good condition. My instructions to cross Feilden Peninsula not being mandatory, Dr. Pavy decided, on account of the bare ground in some places and soft snow in others, to follow the coast to Cape Joseph Henry. This decision, though it seemed wise at the time, eventually proved fatal to the success of the journey, as had James Ross Bay been crossed, and the land quitted in the vicinity of Cape Hecla, six miles north of Henry, the party would probably have avoided their polar drift, which resulted in the loss of the greater part of their stores and the complete abandonment of their expedition.

These remarks are made not to reflect on Dr. Pavy's judgment, which doubtless caused him to select the route apparently the easiest, but to emphasize the great importance of following, as far as practicable, a coast line, so that the broken and distorted ice of the Polar Sea may be avoided as long as possible. My opinion entertained then still holds, that to the northward of Capes Hecla, Columbia, or May the ice of the Polar Sea is not as rough and broken as in the entrance to Robeson Channel between Capes Joseph Henry and Bryant. Dr. Pavy remarks of the country near View Point, that it presented numerous signs of animal life, and more abundant vegetation than in any other place seen by him north of Discovery Harbor.

Level new ice afforded excellent travel from View Point to

the neighborhood of Cape Joseph Henry. The character of the palæocrystic ice from Harley Spit to Conical Hill was set forth as consisting of: "Circular, nearly level floes of small dimension, the largest perhaps a mile and a half in extent, at the edges of which was a fringe of bergs and hummocks. Between them were ditches or crevices from five to fifty yards wide, which must have been at some time filled with young ice. These hollows, originally from three to seven feet deep, were now shallow, and in places nearly filled with a mixture of freshwater ice and frozen snow." These floes showed the powerful influence of the polar sun for several summers, and "in every place where the recently fallen snow had blown off the ice was fresh and good for cooking."

Near Cape Joseph Henry the new ice showed that when the sea closed the preceding autumn a belt of open water, free from heavy ice and at least two miles in width, extended along that coast. To the northward of Cape Joseph Henry, however, it decreased in width, and ran along the coast to the westward toward Cape Columbia as a very narrow strip.

During the 18th and 19th of April a severe storm prevailed, which confined them to their tent, the temperature varying from $-5.5°$ ($-20.8°$ C.) to $-12°$ ($-24.4°$ C.). There is but little doubt that this storm had a marked influence in the disintegration of the polar pack which occurred a few days after.

During the 20th and 21st the party succeeded in transporting their stores to a point on the polar pack about four miles north of Cape Joseph Henry, but were forced to desist from their work by a violent storm from the south-southeast on the 21st, which continued as a severe gale during the night, the wind being estimated at forty miles from the southeast.

At that point they had, from a high floeberg, an excellent view of the polar pack, the appearance of which was discouraging in the extreme. "East of the line of massive cliffs of Cape Joseph Henry the Polar Sea was of such rough appearance that no sledge, even lightly loaded, could have made any progress over its disordered surface. It was nothing but an inextricable maze of huge bergs and enormous hummocks, piled up in a similar manner as when travelled over by Commander Markham. Directly north of Cape Henry and a certain distance from us, perhaps three or four miles, the confusion of the ice was the same, discouraging in its compactness." To the northeast this line of thick-ribbed ice "also prevailed, but to the northwest and due north of Cape Hecla seemed to be of a less ponderous character." Indeed, the conditions were so favorable that the route in that direction was determined on; as, "besides the advantage of stumbling over a less dense pack, we could also add the advantage of establishing a depot (at Cape Hecla) for our return," and of determining the exact route after "a good view from the summit of the high cliffs of Hecla."

On moving northward on the 23d, Eskimo Jens suddenly called out "Water!" which Dr. Pavy thought to be a false alarm; but a half hour brought them to a point where, from a high berg, was seen extending "to the coast (toward Cape Hecla) an open channel a mile wide, in which floated small and rare pieces of ice. For three or four miles—as far as the perspective allowed—the eye could follow them. Here, on account of the convexity of the floes, the line of water seemed to close at the entrance of James Ross Bay against a margin of ice, and about the meridian of Crozier Island. To the west this opening increased in width past Cape Hecla, extending as far as we could see from hummocks thirty feet high. From the side of the pack where we stood, following the edges of our floes and several larger ones above, it took a more northerly direction. Here again, as to the southeast, a convex curve of the pack . . . closed to the view its northern extension." Eskimo Jens, notwithstanding their critical condition, was greatly delighted and much affected by the appearance of a fiord seal (*Phoca hispida*), without doubt the most northerly seal ever observed.

As Dr. Pavy had left his compass behind in the tent, he could not determine the movement of their floe except with reference to marks on the shore, but it was evident later that the pack was moving to the northward into an open portion of the Polar Sea, as new lines of coast gradually opened to the westward, including three capes, the farthest of which was thought to be Cape Columbia. To the east and northeast, at a considerable distance, Eskimo Jens declared there were unmistakable signs of open water. Such a condition of the ice indicated clearly a marked disintegration of the polar pack, and in case of a severe southerly gale and large water-spaces to the northward the situation would have been critical. Dr. Pavy believed that the water did not extend farther than the coast of Feilden Peninsula, and that the pack was still touching Cape Joseph Henry; an opinion to which Eskimo Jens objected, claiming that water extended along the coasts of James Ross Bay and Feilden Peninsula.

This state of affairs, as well as the limiting clause of Dr. Pavy's orders, prevented him from attempting to proceed northward over the disintegrated pack. He consequently decided to return at once to Cape Joseph Henry. Taking only indispensable effects, and sufficient provisions to feed the party for a few days, they started in haste for the cape, but on arriving opposite it, found open water of three-quarters of a mile in extent between them and the land. On returning to their old camp for some farther stores, the water-space toward Cape Hecla was found to have increased in width to about three miles, while the water-clouds to the north and northeast had increased in amount and distinctness.

The farthest latitude attained by this party is given by Dr. Pavy as 82° 56′, it being estimated, as no observations for time, magnetic declination or latitude were made at any period during his absence.

Dr. Pavy then thought of reaching land, and, travelling westward for fifteen days, of endeavoring to extend Lieutenant Aldrich's explorations to the southwest.

A grinding, roaring noise, indicated that the pack was crowding against the lower coast, and in consequence, the sledge was hastily loaded with the most indispensable effects, and with food enough to enable the party to reach Harley Spit. Abandoning his tent, provisions, and part of his scientific instruments, Dr. Pavy succeeded in reaching Cape Henry, where the pack was grinding against the high, perpendicular ice-foot. The pack stopped motionless against the shore, which enabled them to scramble successfully over the rough, high floebergs which made the ice-foot almost inaccessible. At the edge of the ice-foot it was necessary to unload, and hoist the dogs and articles over its vertical edge.

Dr. Pavy concluded it would be unwise to return for the articles abandoned, as the pack was liable to move northward again, since in the offing it was drifting south. He immediately started southward, impressed with the idea "that Robeson Channel was open, and that great haste was necessary," fearing that the ice toward Cape Sheridan would also break up and seriously delay their progress homeward.

At noon, April 24th, the party camped at View Point, where a record was left in the old English cairn, and in the evening of the following day they reached Harley Spit. At 7 A.M. of the 26th the party was again in the snow-house at Black Cape.

"From Cape Sheridan, south of the palæocrystic pack, the ice was broken, in motion, and in many places separated by large lanes of water." The next morning the wind blew from the south, and caused an opening to the north of Black Cape " between the solid ice of Robeson Channel and the loose floes above—a space of about a mile wide, and of which the transversal end disappeared

Dr. Pavy and Jens Skinning Seal.
[*Fort Conger*, *May*, 1882.]

two or three miles from the coast." The party, however, travelled southward over solid ice to Lincoln Bay, where for two days an effort was made to find an inland route between that and Wrangel Bay, which probably failed through their going too far to the west and north. The party was favored with excellent weather, with no wind and high temperatures, from this time forward.

Depot "B" was reached on May 1st, and the following day

the party arrived at Fort Conger, having the same excellent health during their arduous journey of six weeks' duration they had always enjoyed. Rations of lime-juice were daily issued during their outward journey, until the supply was abandoned on the pack, and their field-ration proved sufficient for the maintenance of their strength and health.

Dr. Pavy commended the intelligence, judgment, and perseverance of Sergeant Rice, and the efficiency and faithfulness of Eskimo Jens Edward.

Despite steady and unremitting labor and the possession of health and strength, this attempt to travel over the Frozen Sea failed through natural causes; but, as Dr. Pavy says, it "determined the important fact that last fall open water could have been found as far as Cape Sheridan, and from Conical Hill perhaps to Cape Columbia; and proved, by our experience, that even in such high latitudes the pack may be in motion at an early period of the year, perhaps at any time. I am firmly convinced that, but for our misfortune in finding open water, we could, without greatly distancing Commander Markham, have reached perhaps the latitude of 84° N."

In speaking of the rough character of the ice of the Polar Sea, Dr. Pavy does justice to the courage, endurance, and energy of his gallant predecessors: "If such was the ice over which the British dragged heavy loads and cumbersome boats, instead of being astonished at the small distances daily travelled, on the contrary I sympathize with them in their sufferings, admire their perseverance, and applaud heartily their pluck and gallantry." He farther states his belief that Commander Markham in no way exaggerated his hardships, an opinion, it is hardly necessary to say, which is shared by every person who has ever seen palæocrystic ice or known the trials of Arctic sledging.

CHAPTER XXI.

CHANDLER FIORD.

I HAD long considered it possible that the interior of Grinnell Land could be penetrated successfully; that the land itself was of limited extent, and that it could be readily crossed. This opinion was clearly set forth in my instructions to Dr. Pavy at the time of his unsuccessful trip, in September, 1881, into Archer Fiord, whence he was compelled to return by open water. In those instructions I pointed out the experiences of Lieutenant Archer, R.N., in Beatrix Bay, and the comparatively low ground to the southwest of Archer Fiord seen by that officer, as showing the possibility of travel in that direction.

My letter of the preceding September farther said: "The object of your journey is to determine, if possible, the existence or non-existence of the sea or other water to the westward or southward of Mount Neville. It seems to me quite probable that such water exists at no great distance. Lieutenant Archer, R.N., who viewed the country from an elevation of thirty-eight hundred feet, says: 'No single high hill or mountain was visible at any great distance to the westward, while mountain ranges extended northward from magnetic bearings 72° N., and southward from 72° S.' Sir Edward Belcher found islands about three hundred miles to the south-southwestward of that point. Lieutenant Aldrich, R.N., in 85° 33′ W., reported that the coast of Grinnell Land turned south as far as could be seen. These facts, with Sir J. D. Hooker's discovery that 'the vegetation of this meridian of the polar area is entirely Greenlandic, showing no more relation than does Greenland itself to the flora of the American polar islands,' argue a land, and especially to the westward, of limited extent."

There were two possible routes, both nearer to Conger than Beatrix Bay, which had been left untried by Captain Stephenson, R.N.; one by the way of Conybeare Bay, and the other through Black Rock Vale. In order to gain some knowledge as to the practicability of the former route, which was preferred by me as affording travel over the floe, I decided on a preliminary trip.

On April 19th, Sergeant Cross and Private Bender, with a Hudson Bay sledge, left Conger with instructions to penetrate as far into Conybeare Bay as possible, in a journey which should entail an absence of not exceeding twelve or fourteen hours from the depot, established on the shores of Sun Bay. They carried with them, as far as the depot, certain supplies, which were subsequently to be used by any party travelling in that direction. They returned on the 22d, having succeeded in reaching a point in Conybeare Bay opposite to the west end of Miller Island, but, owing to the prevalence of snow and fog to the westward, they had been unable to determine whether the bay extended far in that direction. Travelling in the bay was heavy and discouraging.

Although fully impressed with the importance of an Arctic commander's remaining at his station or ship, the condition of affairs at this time was so favorable that I decided to absent myself for a period of fifteen days. Full instructions were given to Sergeant Israel as to what should be done in case of special contingencies in connection with the sledging parties to the northward.

Fearing the difficulties of inland travel, and believing there was in sledge travel a point at which extra rations became a burden and hindrance, I decided to reduce the weights as far as possible, and to limit my rations to twenty days at the longest. The means of transportation were to be two Hudson Bay sledges, one of which was to be drawn as far as was convenient and then abandoned. The weights of these sledges were not to exceed, with their loads, four hundred and fifty pounds on leaving the depot at Sun Bay, which would be a comparatively light load for myself and the three men, who were to accompany me.

A four-man shelter-tent, after the pattern known during our civil war as the "dog-tent," was made for us, which, complete, weighed about eleven pounds. Our cooking-lamp with its apparatus, including plates, cups, etc., weighed only six pounds, and another light lamp weighing a pound was taken for the use of any man who might possibly be detached.

Privates Biederbick, Connell, and Whisler were selected to accompany me, but owing to Private Biederbick's suffering exceedingly from toothache, he was replaced at the last moment, somewhat against my inclinations, by Bender, who, although exceedingly anxious for field services, had been pronounced by the surgeon unfit for it. In order to save the strength of my party on starting, Sergeant Cross and Private Long were taken one march beyond the depot in Sun Bay.

At 12.30 A.M. of the 26th the party left Conger, the temperature then standing at $-7°$ ($-21.7°$ C.).

At 6.18 A.M. the tent on the shore of Basil Norris Bay was reached, the distance as travelled along the winding ice-foot being sixteen miles. The ice proved to be of excellent character for travel, having recently formed of the overflow of the spring tides from the tidal cracks. The only difficulty experienced was in crossing occasionally from the outer to the inner ice-foot, which, necessitating travel over very rough ice, was

LIEUT. GREELY AND PARTY STARTING FOR EXPLORATION OF GRINNELL LAND, APRIL, 1882.

(*From a photograph.*)

exceedingly difficult, and resulted in the injury of one of our sledges.

At 9 P.M. that evening we started over the low "divide" to Sun Bay, where we were delayed for a few minutes in an attempt to kill a wolf which was seen near. The gun had been left behind, but we had two revolvers, with one of which Private Connell fired at the wolf without success. We travelled at a free gait and soon rounded Stony Cape, where we for the first time looked into Conybeare Bay. The ice formed from the tidal overflow in Sun Bay afforded excellent travelling, which continued until we passed the several spurs of Stony Cape, when we found the ice-foot very much broken up and in a difficult condition for travel ; our sledges continually overturning, at times one man had to hold them right side up.

Private Whisler and myself were dragging one of the sledges, which, being of an improved pattern, did excellent work. The second, Old Veteran, dragged by three men, was of such an inferior pattern as to cause an enormous amount of friction and entailed corresponding exertions to advance it.

At 2 A.M. we stopped for tea, on the complaint of some of the men who were exceedingly thirsty. It may well be remarked here, that during this trip the men who were especially addicted to the use of tobacco seemed to experience thirst to a greater extent than those who refrained from its use. Whether this was a result of the habit, or was a coincidence, I cannot say. The cooking-lamp did not work satisfactorily, and it was an hour and a quarter before we were again on the road.

While delaying for this tea the temperature fell to $-14°$ ($-25.6°$ C.), the lowest experienced by us during the journey. It was my own experience that the suffering from the cold while delaying for this lunch was so marked as to destroy the effects of the tea when obtained. I decided in consequence of this brief experience that lunches were inadvisable, and that the best plan to follow would be to march as far as was practicable without taking food; and then, be the distance great or small, to regularly encamp and obtain proper rest and food before proceeding farther.

The surface of Conybeare Bay was covered by deep snow, which was in that most trying condition for a traveller, glazed over by a crust which was just thick enough not to bear the weight of a man, but sufficiently so to prevent walking except by lifting the foot quite above the snow. A short experience of that kind of travelling decided us to quit the snow-covered floe and to follow closely the ice-foot, which, though entailing a greater length of travel, would afford more rapid progress with a lesser expenditure of strength and time.

The ice-foot proved alternately good and bad, until at 6.35 A.M. we camped opposite a gorge which was nearly due north of the west end of Miller Island. What was thought to be a low point of that island extended about half a mile to the westward of us, but this was determined later in the year by Lieutenant Lockwood to be a separate island.

A comfortable camp was made between the shore and a row of forced-up hummocks, which left a level space of snow between them and the high barren cliffs that rose above us to a height of nearly two thousand feet. Between the cliffs proper and our camp was a high ridge of about six hundred feet in elevation, of peculiar form, which had evidently been separated from the main cliffs by the erosion of water and the action of frost. The outlying spur of the ridge was cut off by ravines fully two hundred feet deep, which ran one to the east and the other to the west, leaving a narrow passage-way with high rock-walls on either side. The distance travelled in this march was fifteen miles.

Sergeants Cross and Long, who had been of assistance to us, turned back the following morning from this camp, carrying with them to the depot in Sun Bay a two-man sleeping-bag. That evening, the temperature standing at $-4.2°$ ($-20.1°$ C.), arrangements were made for our farther journey by equalizing, as far as practicable, the loads between the two sledges. We cached at that point one day's rations for our return trip, and also nearly a gallon of alcohol which we feared would be lost through a leak in the tin caused by the overturning of the sledge.

At 9 P.M. we started westward, following closely the ice-foot, which was generally good, taking breathing spells of three minutes for each hour's travelling. At 1 A.M. the temperature sank to $-8°$ ($-22.2°$ C.), with a clear sky and nearly calm weather. At 3 A.M. we reached a point where the shore made a semi-circular bend to the northward, more than doubling the distance to the next point. In the centre of the curve opened up a valley which extended some distance inland. To avoid the long detour by way of the shore, I decided to strike directly across the bay to the next prominent point. On reaching the centre of the bay a second valley was seen running at right angles to the first. From our new stand-point the valley which ran to the north-northwest seemed to extend about fifteen miles, gradually narrowing, while the second, to the east-northeast, soon closed in an abrupt ravine. The two valleys united a few miles from the ice-foot in one broad opening some three miles wide, bounded on each side by high hills.

The travelling across the floe was exceedingly tiresome, owing to the deep snow and thick crust, and, despite several changes of places in the drag-ropes and a number of short rests, the party reached the other side in an exhausted condition. This result sprang partly from the continual breaking through of the crust, and partly from the extraordinary amount of friction of the Old Veteran.

We reached the coast again at about 4.10 A.M., and immediately encamped. The distance travelled during this march was estimated at sixteen miles.

On examining the sledges I decided to abandon the Old Veteran, being satisfied that its farther retention would materially retard our progress.

While we were at this camp Private Connell visited the mouth of the valley running to the northwest. He found vegetation to be abundant, and reported that during the summer months a river evidently flows into the bay from the valley. At that point he also noted four wolves, and with them a musk-ox, the first of the season. Leading to the valley he also found what appeared to be a musk-ox trail (similar to the buffalo trails of the "Far West"), which indicated plainly that the valley was a winter resort for these animals.

While at that camp (No. 3) surprise was expressed by nearly all at the great length of the bay. Lieutenant Archer, looking into it from Stony Cape, had judged it to be ten miles long, and I thought it to be about fifteen miles. Looking over the distance we had already travelled, we concluded it to be fully forty miles from Stony Cape to the extreme southwest point, where we believed the end to be. It was evident that the nearest land to the westward was very high, as its apparent elevation had undergone slight change, although we were some sixteen miles nearer it than at Stony Cape. Doubtless the point where we were camped was thought by Lieutenant Archer to have been the end of the bay, an opinion in which I would have concurred on leaving Stony Cape.

The temperature fell to $-4°$ ($-20°$ C.) at this camp, and on calling the cook it stood at zero ($-17.8°$ C.). When packing the single Hudson Bay sledge, it was found necessary to abandon a pair of snow-shoes and a spade; in addition, we cached a day's ration for our return journey.

We started westward at 9.30 P.M. with a falling temperature, −8° (−22.2° C.), clear sky and light easterly wind.

The deep interest with which we had hitherto pursued our journey was now greatly intensified. The eye of civilized man

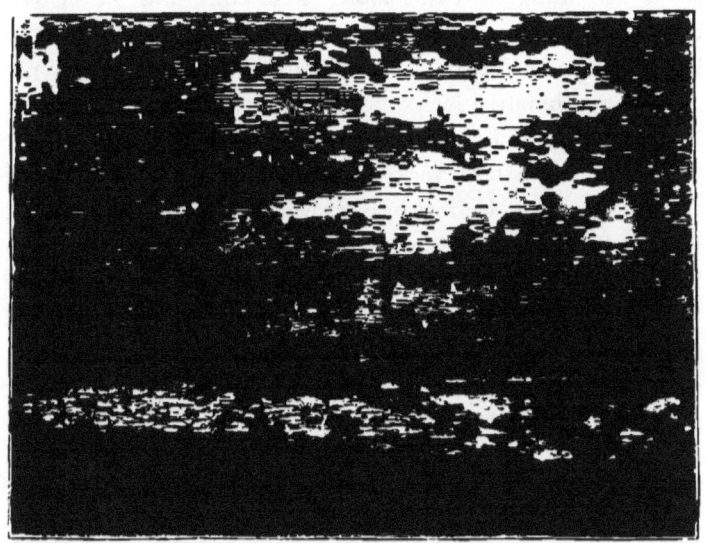

Chandler Fiord looking east from Camp 3, Miller Island in centre.
[*From photograph.*]

had not seen, nor his foot trodden, the ground over which we were travelling. A strong, earnest desire to press forward at our best gait seized us all. As we neared each projecting spur of the high headlands, our eagerness to see what was beyond became so intense at times as to be painful. Each point reached, and a new landscape in sight, we found our pleasure not unalloyed, for ever in advance was yet a point which cut off a portion of the horizon and caused a certain disappointment.

Our travelling was for a time along the ice-foot at the base of very high and precipitous cliffs, evidently of schistose slate. They rose as sheer precipices, over two thousand feet above the level of the bay—solid rock, without a vestige of vegetation to cover their nakedness. Indeed, the only vegetation seen for some ten miles, travelling along these cliffs, was on an outlying spur of clayey earth at the point where our previous camp had been made. In one place a narrow cleft, apparently not more than a hundred feet wide and over a thousand feet deep, broke the continuity of the crest of the cliffs.

It would have been very dangerous to camp at the base of these crags, as the ice-foot was strewn with many fallen rocks. Even as we travelled along several masses fell hundreds upon hundreds of feet, until checked by the ice-foot at the edge of the shore. At one place a rock, which must have weighed several tons, was lying on a large palæocrystic floe about a half mile from the shore. I visited and examined it, thinking it might have been brought from some other cliffs, but it was apparently of the same formation as those near by. It is worthy of remark, that this was the farthest point at which palæocrystic floes were seen in this bay—good evidence that they drifted from the polar ocean. After following a fair ice-foot nearly three hours, we tried the snow-covered floe, and, finding that the crust would bear us, kept well out from the shore and turned our course to the southwest, which seemed to be the true end of the fiord.

At that time directly in front of us was an abrupt rocky promontory, the most prominent headland in the bay, whose elevation was nearly three thousand feet. Between this bold headland and the cliffs along which we were travelling a valley seemed to break in to the northward. To the southwest there was a second prominent mountain, with other breaks to the northward of it, which showed that, if the main fiord did not extend in that direction, a bay must at least exist, which possibly trended to the northwest. Owing to this uncertain condition of affairs, and in order to save time, I left the drag-ropes and directed the party to travel for the nearest headland. On reaching that point one of the party was to make tea, while another should travel to the north for half an hour, if unable sooner to determine the prospects for an advance in that direction.

Leaving the party at 12.30 A.M., I travelled toward the southwest. After going some three hundred yards over fair travelling, I fell in with smooth and bluish ice, evidently of fresh water, which was covered with a hard, thin layer of snow affording the best of travel.

In order not to delay the sledge, I took up a slow dog-trot, hoping to reach the land to the southwest and determine the extent of the bay in that direction. Just at that time an opening to the north came in view, disclosing a narrow bay, or fiord, which extended a long distance. At its apparent head, some ten or twelve miles distant, a broad band of glittering ice showed up plainly, which I supposed to be the front of a large glacier. Beyond it were low hills on either side, while in the distant background snow-clad mountains of the hog-back character appeared. The bay discovered by Lieutenant Archer, gradually enlarging, had now developed into an extensive and important fiord. In attaching to it later the name of Chandler, I desired to show in a faint way my appreciation of the great energy shown, and serious responsibility assumed by Mr. Chandler, in fitting out the Relief Expedition of 1884.

Both sides of the northern arm of the fiord in the foreground were shut in by huge precipitous cliffs. It seemed quite evident that our line of future travel would lay in that direction, but I hastened on with an increased desire of determining the extent of the southern arm of the fiord without delaying my companions. My spring exercise, which had almost entirely consisted in running at a slow gait, now proved of marked benefit to me, and in an hour's alternate run and walk I must have travelled, at a low estimate, five or six miles. When I stopped I found myself in the centre of a nearly circular bay, which I designated Ida Bay. From the south to the northwest the shore was yet some two miles distant, but to the northward there was a projecting point not more than a mile from me. The bay was shaped somewhat like an ellipse, with the major axis from the southwest to the northeast, and about five miles by three in size. The bold promontory, which at the bifurcation of the fiord consisted of huge, precipitous crags, sloped backward to the west into comparatively low ground, leaving gentle valleys of upland between it and the prominent mountains that were seen at the head of the bay. The promontory first mentioned was about twenty-five hundred feet high, but, owing to the grandeur of the surrounding scenery, was hardly as impressive on near approach as at a distance.

The ravines to the westward, though narrow, yet gave indications of easy gradient, and travelling, if difficult, seemed possible through them. The low land to the southward was a marked feature of the country, and indicated an easy route for overland travel. My field journal says: "In that direction the land was comparatively low, with several small ravines and valleys until the hills rose again (to the eastward) in high bluffs, which, facing the new bay, also cut off from my view any portion of Miller Island to the eastward." (It was evident from Lieutenant Lockwood's discoveries of the ensuing year, that the river running through Musk-ox Valley, must empty into Ida Bay through one of the ravines seen by me.) From the point I reached, the coast line of the bay was seen to be continuous, and no chance of farther travel over ice appeared possible.

I took a few bearings and made a rough sketch, which delayed me a few minutes. During this time I was chilled through, as my clothing was saturated from perspiration caused by rapid travelling; the temperature was $-8.5°$ ($-22.5°$ C.). Starting back, rapid travel soon warmed me up. I met Private Connell, about a mile from the sledge, coming to meet me, as the men were somewhat alarmed at my long absence.

The party, on reaching the promontory, had made good use of their time. As soon as the sledge stopped Whisler had travelled up the fiord to the next point, finding excellent ice for travel and the best of prospects ahead. Connell had cooked a comfortable lunch for the party. Bender had improved the delay by repairing most ingeniously the sledge, which had been split by the rough ice. He succeeded in rendering it thoroughly serviceable, as well as in reducing its friction. The helpfulness of my men was particularly marked in this instance, as this work had been done by them without any special instructions to that effect. On my arrival at the sledge it was found repaired, repacked, and ready for instant travel, while a cup of warm tea was waiting for me. I delayed the sledge for a few minutes to take the warm drink, and then started to the northward.

We kept directly up the arm of the fiord, as the ice-foot was poor and ill-marked, and the outer ice afforded perfect travel. It was evident from the character of the ice that we were approaching the mouth of a river, or discharging glacier; for, in place of opaque, whitish ice, we found the surface of the fiord covered with layers of fresh-water ice of great clearness and marked beauty. Its delicate blue contrasted sharply with the underlying strata of the sea-ice. In places the overlying freshwater ice was at least six feet thick, composed of several clearly defined strata. There was no doubt the river, or glacier, discharging its water at low tide over the surface and damming below, had formed these strata at different periods.

As we travelled up the fiord, the cliffs which bounded it gradually decreased in height, and a low hilly country beyond opened up, while the snow-capped peaks of the United States mountains became more prominently and clearly outlined.

The day was beautiful—with a sky of perfect blue, no wind, and a very steady temperature, from $-2°$ ($-18.9°$ C.) to $-8°$ ($-22.2°$ C.). As we approached the ice a very light wind from the northeast was experienced, which appeared to us as the cold air descending from a glacier.

The glacier front, as we thought it to be, was scarcely a mile distant, and we were anxious to proceed, but I deemed it prudent to refrain from overwork.

We went into camp at 7 A.M. (No. 4) after eight hours' work, during which we had travelled twenty-one miles, exclusive of the side trips.

My field journal says: "To-day's discoveries change Conybeare Bay into a fiord (Chandler Fiord). It is quite certain that the site of camp No. 3 where the two valleys united, is that which was thought to be the end of the bay by Lieutenant Archer's party. This is evident, not only from the appearance of the country from Stony Cape, which conveyed the same impression to me, but also from the bearings given on his map. Archer Fiord to the southward of Miller Island was completely shut off by the south side of Conybeare Bay just after leaving camp No. 3, so that the greater part of to-day's travel has been over a part of the fiord which could not possibly have been seen by Lieutenant Archer. The arm of the fiord opens to the north, a direction to an observing eye from the eastward, the most unlikely. This arm, about five miles wide at its southern extremity, narrows gradually to three miles at our present camp. On the eastern side the cliffs are continuous—sheer precipices—save occasional breaks, or notches, which are in no manner practicable. The general elevation is never less than one thousand, and sometimes as great as fifteen hundred, feet. On the west side, the cliffs, while attaining a general elevation of about two thousand feet (decreasing gradually from three thousand feet at Promontory Point to fifteen hundred at our present camp), have occasional gorges of no great size, which never attain to the dignity of ravines. Possibly at one gorge they could be scaled, but it would be decidedly hazardous. Our journey of twenty-one miles is a remarkable day's travel, which never could have been made except by reason of the extraordinary conditions of the ice. I have worked all day in the drag-ropes, except during the time taken for some eight miles extra travel, and am quite worn out this morning from lack of sleep through pain in my left foot, caused by breaking through the snow, covering a tidal crack, into the sharp-pointed ice beneath, while pulling heavily. The instep appears to be badly bruised, and I suffer much from it to-day, although at the time it did not appear to be so serious. I regretted to break in on Connell's sleep after a long march, but I felt the necessity of getting both latitude and time sights at this point."

CHAPTER XXII.

LAKE HAZEN.

IT was evident that we were at the head of Chandler Fiord, and farther progress must be over the glacier or through some adjacent valley. The evening was a perfect one for Arctic travel—calm, clear, with a temperature of $-4°$ ($-20°$ C.). Leaving a day's rations safely cached on shore near camp No. 4, an hour's steady travel over the best of ice brought us to what we had thought a glacier front. It proved to be an ice-dam, which rose fifteen feet above the level of the ice at its base, but, as the constant formation of ice at that point had raised the base, its top must have been twenty-five feet above the sea. From the vertical front occasional small streams of fresh water were trickling, which afforded us, for the first time during the trip, sufficient liquid to entirely quench our thirst.

A brief examination of the ice showed that we were at the junction of tide-water and a fresh-water river flowing from the interior. The stream runs through a valley about a mile wide, hemmed in by high cliffs, and discharges in summer over gentle rapids, or at the level of the sea, but the first heavy frost, forming heavy ice over the fiord, creates a dam which is gradually overflown by the open river behind. By the end of winter results an ice-dam, a mile in width, and twenty-five feet in height.

The river-ice was found level and smooth, affording such excellent travelling that the traction of the sledge was not felt. In consequence I dropped the drag-belt for the day.

During the first hour's travelling occasional shallow pools of fresh water were found on the surface of the ice, which were an especial pleasure to Whisler, who frequently dropped the drag-belt to enjoy the clear cold water. The ice was a delicate whitish-blue, very clear, and in places so transparent for three or four feet that several overlying strata, twisted and distorted, could be seen.

The river proved to be very crooked, and though in most places we were able to travel directly from point to point, some slight detours were rendered necessary in order to avoid wetting our foot-gear in the occasional water-pools.

Two hours' travelling brought us to a small rocky island in the centre of the river, which had been prominent for the previous ten miles, and which first seemed to be a projecting point. It proved to be five hundred feet by three hundred in size, of about thirty feet in elevation, with a level, smooth top. It had evidently been subjected to glacial action in previous ages, but showed no signs of such in recent years. Considerable vegetation, such as saxifrage, *dryas*, a number of grasses, and occasional willows, was found.

The travelling improved as we advanced up the river, and my field journal says: "The sledge runs very easily, offering no impediment to the men's travelling freely, and, although myself moving at my best gait, I was unable to get two hundred yards' start of them in an hour's travelling. In many places we slid along without taking our feet from the ice for a hundred yards at a time. The river fills the entire valley and is of a varying width from one and a half to four miles. Hills are becoming considerably lower on both sides, while the mountains in the background are rapidly rising into great prominence. Though winding very much, the general direction of the river is nearly northwest. We camped at about 3 A.M., after some eighteen miles' travel over the best road I have ever seen within the Arctic Circle. I have made to-day's trip a short one, partly on account of the great pain from my foot, and partly because yesterday's long journey, with the side marches and the little rest owing to observations, was very trying to the party. It seems to me that a long rest will gain time in the end. Many tracks of musk-oxen have been seen to-day along the river's edge, and a few on the ice, all comparatively fresh."

While Bender was cooking, Connell and Whisler, with their usual energy, were out looking over the adjoining country. Whisler brought in some common moss, which was quite green. Connell reported that from an adjacent hill he had a fine view to the northward, in which direction the mountains showed up very prominently. He also saw many musk-ox trails, running from the direction of the mountains to the southward.

April 30th we started at 3 P.M. The temperature was comparatively high, being +4° (−15.6° C.) under the influence of the sun, though it had been down to −8° (−22.2° C.). A light northerly wind was accompanied by a few delicate cirri, the first clouds of any character seen since leaving Conger.

The excellent condition of the ice, and the rapidity of our travel, was instanced by the experience of Whisler, who, delaying at camp about five minutes, was unable in an hour's time to catch us, although travelling at his best gait. We were fortunate enough to find several pools of water on the surface of the ice, which were refreshing in the extreme.

At times the course of the river was very tortuous, and in an hour we travelled first north, then northwest, afterward to the west, and eventually to the north again, though my journal says: "We have the great advantage of being able to travel most of the time from point to point in a straight line, which greatly facilitates our progress, for if we were obliged to follow the shores of the river the distance would be more than doubled."

We passed one place where the river flowed between a narrow gorge of only eighty yards in width with high, precipitous cliffs. While resting in this gorge we could plainly hear the noise of the water flowing under the ice. Occasionally we struck snow with hard crust, which, though affording excellent travel, was so inferior to the ice that it cut our gait down sometimes as low as two and a half miles an hour. The elevation of the river above the sea increased more rapidly during this day than the preceding one. Fresh tracks of the musk-ox, fox, hare, and lemming were seen along the shore.

At 7 P.M. we were astonished beyond measure at reaching a point where the stream was open. I was almost inclined to doubt the evidence of my own eyes, and, indeed, rubbed them once before answering the inquiry of one of the men as to what that was. The open river, about fifty yards wide and of clear water, was a rapidly running stream of an average depth of two feet. This stream was bounded on both sides by thick, clear ice of ten feet in thickness.

We travelled alongside the open river, keeping to the bordering ice-walls, which decreased in thickness and eventually disappeared entirely at a point where the stream doubtless remains open the entire year. Here we were driven to the hill-side, where the deep snow and sharp projecting rocks made travel slow, and rendered the task of keeping the sledge upright a severe one. A couple of hundred yards farther and a sharp turn brought in sight a scene which we shall all remember to our dying day. Before us was an immense ice-bound lake. Its snowy covering reflected "diamond dust," from the midnight sun, and at our feet was a broad pool of open blue water which fed the river. To the northward some eight or ten miles—its base at the northern edge of the lake (Hazen)—a partly snow-clad range of high hills (Garfield range) appeared, behind and above which the hog-back, snow-clad summits of the United States mountains rose with their stern, unchanging splendor. To right and left on the southern shore low, rounded hills, bare, as a rule, of snow, extended far to east and west, until in reality or perspective they joined the curving mountains to the north. The scene was one of great beauty and impressiveness.

The excitement and enthusiasm which our new discoveries had engendered here culminated, for our vantage ground was such that all seemed revealed and no point hidden. Connell, who had continually lamented the frozen foot which turned him back from the trip to North Greenland, declared enthusiastically that he would not have missed the scene and discoveries for all the Polar Sea.

Although the march had not exceeded ten miles, I concluded to camp where water was to be had, and in order to determine in which direction our steps could be turned to best advantage. We accordingly bivouacked at the junction of Ruggles River (temporarily so called) and Lake Hazen.

As we were about entering camp, a dark-colored bird, about the size of a plover, flew swiftly by us from behind and disappeared. It was neither snow-bunting or ptarmigan, as all agreed. Wolf, fox, lemming, hare, musk-ox, and ptarmigan tracks were all seen during the day.

At this camp, No. 5, I obtained a fair set of time observations, and quite wore out myself and the rest of the party by sitting up for latitude observations. I succeeded in obtaining a set of subpolar observations, which were not perfect, owing to the prevalence of light cirrus clouds and the altitude of the sun, which was at midnight only 7° above the horizon. In the time between the two observations Private Connell travelled about five miles to the eastward along the lake, and from his extreme point, a hill of moderate elevation, he could see the end of the lake. The mountains in that direction, he said, decreased in elevation, finally terminating in hog-back hills to the southward.

Private Bender was sent to the northward to cross the lake and examine the valley opposite, which seemed to be of considerable size and appeared to have a glacier in its northern termination. He returned after four hours' travel, and reported the opposite valley to be unimportant. Near the northern shore he had discovered the existence of a long, narrow island (John's island) of considerable elevation, which, from our camp, appeared to be part of the main-land.

The night was a clear, beautiful one, with only a breath of wind and the temperature $-3°$ ($-19.4°$ C.), so that, while Connell and myself occupied the sheep-skin bag within the dog-tent, Whisler and Bender slept on the outer ground.

Numerous tracks of ptarmigan and hares were seen in the vicinity of our camp, and while I was making the midnight observations a ptarmigan came within twenty-five feet of us, but flew away before our work was completed. At 5 A.M. I was awakened by the calling of a ptarmigan, which seemed to be challenging another bird that answered within a few feet of me. I called to Whisler, who had the revolver, to shoot the bird. He reported that it was perched on the ridge-pole about two feet above my head. As he was a good marksman, I told him to take very careful aim and shoot it; but Connell, who was in the bag with me, displayed such a marked lack of confidence in Whisler's marksmanship, that in deference to his doubts I directed Whisler not to fire, and so the bird escaped.

My journal of May 1st says: "Early this morning I started

east, and, ascending a hill four miles distant from the camp, observed to the eastward of the lake hog-back hills, which were of considerably lower elevation than the mountains to the north. Two ptarmigan alighted on the hill, one of which came within five or six yards of me, giving utterance to frequent calls, which were interrupted every few seconds by other notes sounding like a challenge. I stood perfectly quiet and admired his plumage of pure white, spotted only by the crimson-red of his eyelids; when tired of examining me he leisurely flew away.

"There appear to be a number of glaciers on the north side of the lake, but the bad light, with the sun beyond them, rendered it impossible to speak with certainty.

"Willow, as well as grass, was quite plentiful. Old willow shrubs in small quantities were seen, and I doubt not, in case of necessity, enough for cooking purposes could be found.

"There was very little snow to be seen over the hills on the south side of the lake, but the mountains which separated the lake on the north side from the snowy range were partly snow-clad, similar to those in the vicinity of Conger. The lake was packed with hard, level snow of about a foot in depth, which was covered with a strong crust. The *sastrugi* showed prevailing northeast winds.

"There is in the snow-covered mountains to the northward a twin peak; two cones running together, that to the eastward being of slightly lower elevation than the one to the westward; both are pure white, distant from thirty-five to forty miles, and about five thousand feet high.

"My attempt to obtain time observations this morning were but partly successful, owing to obscuring clouds. It seems strange that the heavens over the lake to the westward, and, indeed, in every direction except toward Robeson Channel, are cloudless and bright."

We got into our sleeping-bags at 4.30 A.M., and turned out at eleven o'clock for latitude observations, which were again poor and unsatisfactory, owing to the covered sky.

While breakfast was being prepared, Whisler reported that he had seen fish six or seven inches long in the lake; Connell, with pin-hook and line, tried fishing unsuccessfully.

Whisler, who had visited the hills to the westward of Ruggles River, reported a number of musk-oxen in sight, with evidences of a larger number in that direction. While absent he shot a ptarmigan.

At 2 P.M., May 2d, we started to the westward along the south shore of Lake Hazen. We were obliged to make a detour into the lake to pass around the open water which feeds the river, and which extends unfrozen for about one hundred and fifty yards into the lake.

What appeared to be a glacier on the north side opened up to view, but after a careful examination with the telescope we decided it to be only snow.

The men travelled along the lake shore, while I left them at various times to examine the character of the country to the southward, over which I travelled about a mile distant from and parallel to the lake. It was found invariably to consist " of small hills, from none of which was the view extensive." The ascent to the southward was very gradual, and no high land in that quarter was visible. Much grass, many willows, and other vegetation abounded, while, to my surprise, not more than a quarter of the ground was then covered by snow. Several hours of this travelling, from its rough character, proved very injurious to my lame foot, which was protected against the stones only by moccasins, and I returned to the lake. During a portion of the day the men travelled in snow-shoes, which were of service, although they were not much accustomed to their use.

Along the shore we fell in with two hares, one of which Whisler shot with a revolver, while the second, though wounded, escaped. In pursuing it Whisler saw a third hare, and struck a trail over which a number of musk-oxen had lately travelled.

Five hours' march brought us to a "remarkable ridge of pebbles and smooth stones, which extend for a hundred yards or more along the shore, with their bases at the high-water mark. In some cases the ridges were twelve feet above the level of the surrounding ground. While it is possible that ice or snow might form a part of them, it is hardly probable, as none was seen anywhere in connection with them, they being merely high parallel ridges of pebbles. The direction of *sastrugi* on the lake shows prevailing northeasterly winds, and these ridges were situated so that the winds would have full force over them. After a careful examination I have come to the conclusion that they have been formed during severe gales from the northeast quarter, which must force the ice violently against this shore during the summer or early autumn." This opinion was confirmed by direct evidence the following summer.

After nearly seven hours' travel we camped, having made probably sixteen or seventeen miles, although the men insisted that it was over twenty.

My field journal that morning says: " During to-day's travelling I found along the entire shore of the lake four distinct ridges of pebbles, thus affording suitable evidence that the water has attained four different levels in separate years. The highest ridge was the outside one, nearest the lake, and is about six or seven feet above the level of the ice, which is fully fifty yards distant. There is no ice-foot along the lake, as none is to be expected, but the ice is grounded and fixed fast to the shore at the very edge, and as the water falls it slopes gradually toward the centre of the lake, occasionally separated from the main body of ice by deep, narrow cracks. The sloping of the ice rendered it necessary in following the contours of the shore to keep about a hundred yards out from its edge, where the snow-crust was stronger and better than elsewhere. Any attempt to proceed toward the centre of the lake invariably resulted in the party breaking through the crust, which made our progress slow and difficult.

"Opposite our present camp, on the northwest side of the lake, we have seen during the afternoon travel what is evidently a large glacier. It was hidden from view farther to the east by a projection of the land on its eastern side, where several small mountains are situated."

We had a good rest at camp No. 7, where we spent twelve hours, being delayed somewhat by the bad behavior of the cooking-lamp. The temperature sank to zero ($-17.8°$ C.) during the night, which, in connection with a light wind, made it uncomfortably cool, but in the early morning the wind died away, rendering travel delightful.

While the men were packing the sledge on May 2d, I walked rapidly along the shore to the next point, in order to examine the country, and determine whether it would be best to proceed westward to the end of the lake, or northward to the glacier which had been in sight since the previous day.

On reaching the point I was not entirely satisfied that I could see the end of the lake, although the men on arrival maintained that it was in view. My field journal says: "I feel confident from the break in the land to the southwest, between the mountain range in the north and the low hills to the south, that there must be a valley or pass leading westward."

As the distance clearly seen to the westward was at least twelve miles, and it was doubtful if we could reach it by the day's travel, I decided to cross the lake to the glacier and determine something of its size and character. I also hoped that from the adjoining mountains something more satisfactory could be seen of the topography of the country to the southwest. We consequently turned north to cross Lake Hazen. In a short distance the travel was found of the worst possible character, the crust being just too weak to support the weight of a man. In consequence the men put on snow-shoes, of which there were three pairs, while I followed the sledge. After six hours' travelling, during which we had marched twelve miles from our previous camp, we stopped inshore from the lake a scant mile and made camp No. 8. We were then three miles east of Henrietta Nesmith glacier, which I named for my wife.

The snow-covered ground rose so gradually, from the level of the lake, that we were not conscious of having reached it until we were some distance inland. I unwisely decided to camp there, expecting to obtain our ice from the lake near-by. As soon as camp was reached, Connell and Bender arranged the tent and commenced preparations for supper. We were all quite exhausted by the difficult travelling, but I decided to visit the glacier front at once, fearing that I should be prevented by some unforeseen contingency the following morning. Private Whisler asked also to visit it and obtain ice for cooking purposes for supper, as the ice near-by was very dirty and unfit for use. I advised him not to do so, owing to the great distance. He started directly for the main front by the way of a small bay, through which the water from the glacier reaches Lake Hazen. I decided to follow up along the base of four small mountains to the eastward of the glacier, as they seemed to abut against it and afford a route by which I could reach its surface.

While *en route* I found a large pasture-ground, where muskoxen had broken the crust and scraped away the snow to reach the willows, grass, and saxifrages which grew plentifully at that place. Traces of musk-oxen, from a day to weeks old, were met with. In different places there were direct signs that some of the crust had been broken since the last storm, other portions prior to the last storm, and still others long before that time. The evidences were marked and clear that this point was a pasture-ground much frequented by these animals.

Hare and wolf tracks were quite frequent in the vicinity, but there were none of the fox, although traces were seen that morning in crossing the lake. It was a matter of surprise to me, despite these marked evidences of considerable numbers of musk-oxen on the north side of the lake, and similar traces of equal numbers on the south side, that at no place was the track of a musk-ox to be found at the edge of the lake or on the main floe. This would seem to show a disinclination to cross any extent of ice, as was the case along the Ruggles River, where the foot-tracks on the river-ice were near the very edge.

I had hoped to find the top or crown of the glacier flush with and pressing against some point of the mountains, so as to permit an examination of it, but such was not the case. From the central medial line the crown sloped down gradually to either side, and near the mountains the angle of descent was sharper, but at a distance of a hundred yards from the mountain it stopped, leaving a perpendicular wall of ice twenty-five to thirty feet high. With considerable difficulty I climbed the steep mountain-side, which was covered with coarse, yielding sand, until I was far above the edge, and apparently on the same level as the opposite central crown of the glacier, which was about four hundred yards from the centre of the main or discharging front. My barometer then read 28.89. Descending the precipitous cliffs, I then stood at the eastern base four hundred yards lower down the glacier than the point opposite my station on the hill. The barometer then read 29.49. The difference of the two elevations was not far from five hundred and twenty feet. I estimated the height of the vertical front of the glacier at that place to be one hundred and fifty to one hundred and seventy-five feet. This gave the glacier a very large slope of three hundred and sixty to three hundred and eighty feet in a distance of four hundred yards, which seemed to indicate an enormous thickness of the ice in rear.

Henrietta Nesmith Glacier.
[*Showing eastern edge crowding against the mountains.*]

During the day's march the glacier had gradually grown from a narrow line of ice to a sharply defined bank, which from camp, two or three miles distant, appeared to be perhaps twenty-five feet high. A nearer approach, causing it to tower into enormous proportions, awakened my wonder and admiration, which continually increased as I examined it critically from its front, and came to have a just idea of its magnitude. The face, convex, or crescent-shaped, was about five miles from hill to hill—a mass of sheer, solid ice, averaging about one hundred and seventy-five feet in height, though in one place as low as one hundred and again as high as two hundred feet.

My field journal says: "The top of it was a pure dead-white, densely opaque, resembling in a marked manner the surface of loaf-sugar, or broken and unpolished white marble. Lower down it shaded into a color bordering on blue, the whole very much resembling floebergs. In general, the color of the ice, which lay in detached piles at the foot, was a delicate blue, shading closely on the white, but in certain places strata of a faint yellowish color were to be seen. These strata were invariably confined to certain points, and formed a very inconsiderable portion of the visible front. Their color while in the glacier itself gave the appearance of a delicately tinted roseshade, which, as I have said, changed to a faint yellowish on close examination. There were three large deeply-worn gullies or channels on the surface of the glacier, one at the centre and one near each side, which showed that in the summer and autumn very considerable streams of water must be discharged from the surface of the glacier. The side gullies were of inconsiderable size compared with the central one. The lowest part of the crown of the glacier was at a point where water of the largest discharging channel had worn deeply into the ice, leaving its elevation not more than a hundred feet.

I saw several moraines on the southwestern side, but was too much worn out by travel in the deep snow in front of the glacier to visit them. The next morning Connell visited and examined them. The following description was obtained immediately on his return:

The moraines were three in number, situated near the western face of the glacier, and nearly parallel to each other. They were composed of black sand mixed with coarse pebbles and occasional boulders of small size. No large blocks of stone were visible. No. 1, about twenty yards in length and fifteen feet high, extended in a gentle curve from a point within about five yards of the glacier front to a point twenty yards distant from the base of the high hill to the westward, against which the side of the glacier pressed. The nearest point of the moraine was so close to the glacier front that the falling ice covered a portion of it.

No. 2 was likewise fifteen feet high, about seventy yards long, and generally parallel to and about ten yards distant from No. 1. No. 3 was about twenty feet high, a hundred yards long, parallel to, and thirty yards distant from No. 2. The front of each moraine was nearly perpendicular, but the rear portion (that part nearest the glacier) gently sloping.

The appearance of the moraines seemed to indicate that within a moderately late period the western spur of the glacier must have advanced and retrograded three separate times, the period of retrogradation in each case being more marked than that of progression, as shown by the greater size and importance of the moraines, as the distance from the present front increased.

Careful observations resulted in no satisfactory evidence as to whether the glacier is at present progressing or retrograding. I think it hardly possible that in late years it could have extended any considerable distance farther than its present front. This opinion seemed reasonable, not only from the presence of the moraines, but because the hills immediately adjacent to and in front of the glacier, and but slightly above the level of the lake, showed plants and lichens which were common to the entire country, such as purple saxifrage, Arctic willow, *dryas*, and the poppy. Over the lower grounds immense quantities of sand were scattered, probably deposited from the summer streams, which were so intermixed with the snow that it was impossible to tell where the land ended and the lake commenced.

No yellow strata of ice, such as had been seen near the centre, were visible in the western half of the glacier. We had heard masses of ice falling frequently during the night, and a considerable quantity broke and fell from the front while Connell was opposite that discharging stream, which is a little east of the centre front at the lowest point of the crown.

The ice when undetached had presented at its great height a light yellow shade, but newly fallen it was found on examination by Connell to be of a fine pink tinge, quite marked in the masses. A small watercourse runs at certain seasons of the year from the western side along the front between the glacier and the moraines. Although covered with level ice, no running water could be heard by Connell, nor could any be obtained by digging with a hunting-knife. It is possible that this watercourse may come from some discharging brook of main importance, which, being on the western slope of the glacier, could not be seen from an exterior standpoint.

Three similar watercourses were discovered by me some distance in front of the main brook, which discharged from the centre of the crown of the glacier. It occurred to me as being possible that the western brook might discharge from under the glacier, as frequently occurs in the Greenland fiords.

This summer surface-discharge seemed singular to me, and I examined all the watercourses which appeared to be entirely dry and with but little ice, but the deep snow might have easily concealed some stream of water under the surface-ice.

Private Bender left at the same time as Connell, with orders to ascend, if possible, one of the adjacent mountains, in order to examine the country to the westward. He was unable to ascend to the summit of either, as the base and side of the mountains were covered with soft, yielding sand, laying at such an angle as rendered an ascent to the top hopeless. It seemed probable from his account that this sand was a deposit resulting from the grinding of the mountain-side by the glacier at some former time. From the highest point reached by him he was unable to see any considerable distance up the glacier, owing to intervening mountains. To the southwest he could see some twenty-five miles or more. The lake appeared to end in a small, nearly land-locked bay some fifteen miles distant, beyond which nothing could be seen except a succession of low, rounded hills. The same description of country existed to the southward, although the hills were slightly higher. No high mountains were visible in either quarter. There appeared a decided break in the country to the westward of Lake Hazen, as the ice-clad mountains to the north of us very abruptly gave place to low hills. A few mountains to the westward were partly snow-clad, the most prominent of which was a pyramid-shaped mountain some twenty miles distant, that had been our landmark ever since the lake had been reached, and which now bears the name of Whisler. Unfortunately I neglected to send a barometer with Bender, so the exact elevation of the point reached by him is uncertain, but he thought it to be not far from two thousand feet.

On returning from Henrietta Nesmith glacier to camp on the north side of Lake Hazen, May 3d, I noticed an atmospheric phenomenon which seemed to me unique; it was a beautiful mock-sun, accompanied by clearly defined prismatic colors, at a distance of 120° from the sun. This phenomenon was seen in the only quarter of the heavens which at that time was covered with light clouds, being nearly south of the glacier, which was at my back.

I since find this phenomenon mentioned by Flammarion as being especially remarkable and rare. He says: "Sometimes the solar rays experience two successive reflections upon the vertical surfaces of one of the prisms. There is then visible, at 120° from the sun, a white image more or less diffuse, which has received the name of *paranthelion*. The horizontal bars of the ice-crystals reflect also the solar light, but in an upward direction, which prevents the spectator from perceiving it unless he be upon the summit of a steep mountain, or in the car of a balloon, above the cloud containing the icy particles. It will be readily admitted that these conditions can rarely be fulfilled; but MM. Barrae and Bixio were fortunately able to realize them on July 27, 1850. The image of the sun thus reflected appears almost as luminous as the sun itself. Bravois suggested for this phenomenon, at once so remarkable and so rare, the name of *pseudohelion*."

May 4th, we built a cairn on a prominent hill about two miles east of the glacier, and three hundred feet above the lake, in which was deposited a notice of our visit. The cairn is about five feet high and is quite prominent from the eastward, but in other directions does not show up until near at hand.

I succeeded in obtaining a good set of time observations, but did not deem it advisable to wait for latitude. The high temperature of the air at that time ($-11°$ F., $-11.7°$ C.), and the fact of the country to the westward being open, decided me to return at once to Conger and attempt a second trip later in the year. It was evident that if we turned our faces to the westward we could travel no farther than we had already seen, and the high temperature caused me to fear that the river would break up behind us, in which case our return to Conger would be a matter of extreme difficulty, if not considerable danger.

We consequently took a direct course across the lake for the mouth of Ruggles River, and after eight hours' steady travelling arrived there in an exhausted condition.

The desire to reach a point where water could be obtained and fuel saved was the only incentive which enabled us to make this journey in a single march. The lake could have been crossed in a single day with no other sledge than a Hudson Bay, as, while the surface of the crust frequently broke under one of the party, the sledge never stopped during our entire march. I estimated the distance at twenty miles, though the men insisted it must have been at least twenty-five. We were obliged to make occasional detours from a straight line of travel, owing to the character of the ice and snow fallen in with.

While crossing the lake a number of cracks were found, and it frequently occurred that the ice sank an inch or two whenever the party passing a crack reached other ice. It seemed evident from this that the glacier streams which discharged into the lake must be frozen quite or entirely up during the winter. The supply of the lake being thus cut off, there is a difference between the winter and summer levels not far from six or seven feet, and the ice gradually sinks as the water fails.

The tracks of wolves at the camp indicated a visit during our absence, but the ptarmigan which we had cached under snow-blocks was still undisturbed.

Time observations were taken, and the next morning, after caching fourteen cans of beef, we started at seven o'clock and travelled with the utmost rapidity until noon, when I stopped for latitude, and decided to make camp No. 9 at that point. The distance travelled in this march was estimated at seventeen miles. Our journey lay along the open river for a time, and I took a number of observations to determine its discharge. The river at that point was seventy-five yards wide and two feet deep, with a rocky bottom. From the mean of these observations, the current of the river was determined to be over three hundred and fifty feet a minute, or about four miles an hour.

During the day, as we were marching, four musk-oxen were seen on the hill to the east, and later, after making camp, six others observed to the southeast. It seemed possible to us that they attained the summit of these hills from the valley visited by Connell at camp No. 3. It is evident that they could not reach the river directly, as the cliffs were far too precipitous.

A long rest of twelve hours put our feet in good condition for our next march, which began at midnight of May 4th to 5th.

A few scattered snow-flakes and a very high temperature of $+31°$ ($-0.6°$ C.) seemed to threaten bad weather, the first of the journey. During the day we passed a very small island near the eastern shore, which had not been noticed by us on our outward trip. Another small island was discovered near the western shore some distance lower down the river. It was some fifty yards across by a hundred yards long, with an elevation of ten to fifteen feet above the river. It consisted almost entirely of gravel, with but scanty vegetation. The number of water-pools on the ice had increased since our upward journey, and detours were occasionally necessary to pass them. They finally drove us to the eastern shore near the large island discovered in our outward journey.

We passed the ice-dam on the eastern end, where there were large ridges of heavy ice in front of and parallel to the main dam. A careful examination of this ice-dam left me of the opinion that there were no natural falls at this point, but that it was simply a dam of ice formed from natural causes during the winter. Bender was here detached with a knapsack to take up the cache left at camp No. 4, while we proceeded, and after seven hours' travelling made camp No. 10 on the ice in Chandler Fiord.

After an hour, as breakfast was ready, and Private Bender not in sight, Whisler was sent to meet him. A slight fog had risen in the meantime, which was quite thick and rendered it possible to see only a short distance. Connell, going a few hundred yards from camp, kept Whisler in sight, while I in turn kept Connell in sight. Finally Bender arrived, nearly two hours behind us. He had lost himself in the fog, and, strange to say, had turned his face up the stream and recrossed the dam before he found out where he was. Finding himself on the wrong shore, he waited for the fog to clear before trying it again. He informed me that on the western side the river had commenced breaking up, and in one place a water-hole over a hundred feet in length had formed. The ice-dam to the extreme west was nearly level with the land, which explains why so much smooth fresh-water ice was found on that side and but little or none on the east.

The weather was so warm that I slept with open tent and flap.

We left camp No. 11 that morning about 8.30. Camped at 7.08 P.M., May 6th, between camps 1 and 2. Whisler's eyes pained him very much from snow-blindness, and he could scarcely see. I dropped wine of opium in them.

On May 7th we started about 4.30 A.M., and in five hours reached the tent at Basil Norris Bay, where we rested a few minutes to melt ice for water. Leaving here all our supply of food, except enough for a single meal, we reached French Cape a little before noon, quite worn out with our seven hours' travel.

Two hours were spent in preparing a meal, after which the threatening weather was such that I decided to attempt to reach the home station, although we were very much exhausted. We left at 1.45 P.M., at which time a strong easterly wind prevailed, followed a short time later by occasional light snow.

After a little over two hours' travelling, Connell complained of severe cramps in his legs and knees, and a few minutes after was obliged to give out and quit the drag-belt. I endeavored to prevail upon him to get on the sledge, which he begged permission not to do, saying he was able to hobble into camp by himself. Stopping occasionally to keep Connell in view, as I was unwilling to permit him to get out of our sight during the wind and snow in his exhausted condition, we were finally met a half mile from the station by Schneider and Henry, one of whom took my place in the drag-belt, while the other went out to meet and assist Connell. A few minutes later Doctor Pavy and Jens came with the dog-sledge, which was sent to bring Connell in. We reached Conger at 7.20 P.M., having travelled thirteen hours and a distance of nearly thirty miles since making our last camp.

This sledge journey was an exceedingly fruitful one in its results. It disclosed physical conditions in the interior of Grinnell Land hitherto unsuspected. The absence of discharging glaciers, which had excited remark on account of the extreme latitude of Grinnell Land, was now explained by the discovery of a broken, rugged country, intersected by a system of fiords and lakes, which readily drains, during the short Arctic summer, the inconsiderable snow-fall. The valleys, bare of snow, give birth to vegetation, luxuriant for the latitude, which serves as pasturage for considerable game. The presence of the glaciers, bursting through the Garfield range, proved the existence of an ice-cap on the northern part of Grinnell Land, and inferentially a radically different topography from the country in the vicinity of Discovery Harbor and Lake Hazen.

This journey involved over two hundred and fifty miles' travel, which was made in twelve days. The rate of travel compares favorably even with McClintock's most extraordinary journeys. The system of reasonable journeys, and immediate travel after necessary rest, ample and nourishing food, exceedingly light equipment, and smooth ice, all favored and facilitated rapid progress. To these conditions were united others essential to successful sledging—the hearty co-operation, great persistency, and untiring energy of the enlisted men of the party.

Icebergs, from a Photograph.

LIEUTENANT JAMES B. LOCKWOOD.

(*The leader to the Furthest North.*)

CHAPTER XXIII.

THE FARTHEST NORTH.—CONGER TO CAPE BRYANT.

[LIEUTENANT LOCKWOOD.]

WHILE the journeys described in the immediately preceding chapters were being made, the exploration of the North Greenland coast was being conducted under the efficient and active leadership of Lieutenant James B. Lockwood. The advance sledge was to be hauled by dogs, with Eskimo Christiansen as driver, and one enlisted man (preferably Sergeant Brainard) was to be selected, at Lieutenant Lockwood's discretion, from the most energetic of the supporting party at its farthest. Until the selection was made, Sergeant Jewell was to be with the dog-sledge. The supporting sledges—four of the Hudson Bay pattern—were to be hauled by Sergeants Brainard, Lynn, Ralston, Elison, Corporal Salor, Privates Biederbick, Connell, Frederick, Henry, and Whisler.

The weight of these men averaged 176 pounds; ranging from Whisler, 156, to Henry, 203. The average amount of extra clothing was ten pounds per man, consisting of sleeping-gear, extra socks, mittens, and jumpers. The clothing in wear was generally double suits of underclothing—one woollen and one blanket—three pairs socks, with outer ordinary wool clothing, over which a light duck suit was worn to keep the snow from adhering to the wool. A few only wore outer clothing of skin. The foot-gear was made up of moccasins, and Greenland, Labrador, and canvas boots; enough being taken to furnish each man with two pairs.

Sergeant Brainard, in charge of the sledges Hayes, Kane, Hall, and Beaumont, left the station April 3d, in a temperature of $-29°$ ($-34°$ C.). They dragged on leaving seventy-eight pounds per man, which was to be increased slightly at Depots "A" and "B," and on leaving their base of supplies, in Newman Bay, was to be as near two hundred pounds as the state of the ice would permit them to haul. This accorded with my views, that the extreme hard work of sledging should be gradually reached in order to avoid overwork, which is most probable in the early days of strength and enthusiasm.

A few remarks bearing on the dangers of sledging, and the importance of caution and discretion, were made to the men on leaving. A general salute was given the party near the station, and I accompanied them with the puppy-team as far as Dutch Island.

Lieutenant Lockwood had remained at the station to perfect some personal arrangements, and left the following day. His team nominally was of eight dogs, averaging sixty-two pounds weight; but one dog, weighing forty pounds, never hauled the food she ate.

Lieutenant Lockwood's orders read: "You are charged with the full control and arrangement of the most important sledging and geographical work of this expedition—of exploring the northeast coast of Greenland. I am not unaware of the difficult position in which you are necessarily placed from our inability to lay out suitable depots to the northeast during the past autumn, from the limited number of your supporting parties, and from your working with a wide strait covered with ice separating you from your base of supplies and field of operations. The energy and discretion already displayed, united to your endurance and experience (tested by nearly two hundred miles of field work this season, with temperatures lower than 90° below the freezing-point), give me strong assurance of success. . . . Memoranda showing the location of supplies to the northward will be furnished you. The object of this work will be to explore the coast of Greenland near Cape Britannia. Should you be fortunate enough to pass beyond that point, you will proceed in such direction as you think will best carry out the objects of the expedition—the extension of knowledge regarding lands within the Arctic Circle. . . . At your farthest, one day must be spent in determining your position . . . and in making such other observations as will be practicable. It is particularly desired that the period and character of the tides be noted, if any way possible. From the farthest land, specimens of the various rocks, vegetation, etc., should be obtained. . . . While it is desirable that Lieutenant Beaumont's cairns be visited, you are to make no considerable detours for such purposes. . . . The depots should be carefully noted and secured; each member of the party should be shown their exact location. . . . Your attention is invited to the danger of pursuing your journey beyond such point as your provisions are half consumed, and to remaining or venturing any distance from the land after lanes of water have once shown themselves."

The depot at Cape Beechy, with those established on the Greenland coast during March, was sufficiently supplied to enable Lieutenant Lockwood's main party to haul their supplementary supplies from Depot "B" at one load. This left to him the collection at Polaris Boat Camp, in Newman Bay, of the stores at Depot "E" and on the floe in Robeson Channel.

The supporting party camped at Depot "A," near Cape

Murchison, where Lieutenant Kislingbury had thoughtfully preceded them and arranged the tent for their reception. The temperature on arriving was —32° (—35.6° C.), which fell to —41° (—40.6° C.), making their first night a severe one, though it was passed satisfactorily. Their loads were there increased to ninety pounds per man.

They reached Depot " B," April 4th, in six hours' travel, and camped in the snow-house, at which point they were joined by Lieutenant Lockwood, who left Conger that evening, with the dog-sledge.

On the evening of the 5th the entire party left Depot " B," hauling a hundred and thirty pounds to each man and a hundred to each dog. Cape Beechy was reached after about four and a half hours' travel, as Sergeant Brainard says, comparing the time with that made in his previous journey: "An hour and twenty minutes in favor of the Hudson Bay sledge with one hundred and thirty pounds, as against the McClintock with one hundred pounds. The work performed by these (Hudson Bay) sledges is very gratifying to us, the friction being much less than with the English sledge."

Whisler complaining of illness, the party camped after seven hours' travel. Here the field sledge-ration commenced, the alcohol (fuel) allowance (five ounces) of which was not considered satisfactory, barely melting the frozen meat. The fuel allowance of the British expedition, 1875, was four ounces. As the English allowance had been unsatisfactory at times, after consultation with my officers I fixed our ration at four and a half ounces, which was increased, under certain circumstances, to five. Subsequently six ounces were fixed on as a proper ration, and that amount proved satisfactory.

At this camp, Brainard says: "Ralston, cook; temperature about —40° (—40° C.); his duties were rendered very trying on account of having frozen his fingers during the operation of the morning meal. Our sleeping-bags were like iron, and sleep was out of the question; our teeth were clattering and clashing together in a most dangerous manner. Connell froze one of his toes in the sleeping-bag; it is very sore and considerably swollen, but he, however, intends to retain his place in the drag-ropes; Henry suffering with rheumatism, and says he cannot proceed, and so has been ordered to return to the station. So much for huge men for Arctic service."

The temperature fell as low as $-48.8°$ ($-44.9°$ C.). The party escaped serious frost-bites, except Connell, who was badly frost-bitten on the ball of his foot. Lieutenant Lockwood says: "Henry was suffering from rheumatism, and thought he would have to be hauled back if he went any farther, so I directed him to return to the station. Connell thought he was able to go on; was willing and anxious to try at any rate."

They moved forward from this camp on the evening of April 6th. After Connell had limped along painfully for an hour, he was so done up that Lieutenant Lockwood says: "He had fallen out of the drag-ropes, being hardly able to get along at all. He reluctantly agreed to going back. Leaving the main party to proceed, I left my load and took Connell to Cape Beechy," from which point he thought he could proceed by himself. During the day they fell in with several strips of rubble from young ice, in which the Hudson Bay sledges, entirely unsuitable for such ice, were frequently overturned. The rough, pointed ice damaged the sledges, and other mishaps made travel correspondingly slow and laborious. Lieutenant Lockwood being absent with Connell, Brainard camped, owing to high wind, after seven and a half hours' travelling.

Here Brainard was cook, in a temperature of $-27°$ ($-32.8°$ C.), with a brisk wind. His field journal says: "This morning the functions of cook are particularly disagreeable, with a strong wind threatening to carry away our tent, and in addition I have to face the scowling countenances of my companions, who gloomily take their breakfasts in the small pannikins. The obvious cause of these half-angry faces is the lack of meat, for which hard bread was substituted. Ritenbenk, the king-dog, ably assisted by Gypsy, the queen, entered the tent while we were sleeping, and carried away the meat already prepared for our evening meal. As no allowance for thieving dogs was made in our scale of provisions, we are compelled to fast until the next meal."

From this camp Lieutenant Lockwood started in advance to do work with the dog-sledge, leaving Sergeant Brainard again in charge of the supporting parties. This arrangement continued until Cape Bryant was reached, as Lieutenant Lockwood employed his time, with the more rapid dog-sledge, in alternately advancing his own load and in assisting the man-sledges.

Shortly after starting the brisk wind developed into a severe storm, which drove Brainard to camp in less than three hours.

Salor and Biederbick, through a misunderstanding, allowed themselves to become separated from the main party, and had to be hunted up in the furious storm by Sergeant Brainard, who finally came upon them, burrowed in a snow-bank, with only a rubber blanket to protect them. He succeeded in bringing them safely to the tent, where the rest of the party were anxiously awaiting them, alarmed as to their safety.

The storm increased to a violent gale, the wind reaching, it was estimated, sixty miles an hour, from which they were partly sheltered by huge bergs immediately to the windward, or their tents would not have stood for a moment. The barometer rose in twenty-one hours over six-tenths of an inch, and the temperature 26° (14.4° C.). The wretchedness of the party was extreme, as the drifting snow, weighting down their already crowded tents, cramped them excessively, and rendered the proper preparation of their meals impossible.

Finally, on the evening of April 9th, the storm abated, when Sergeant Brainard says: "We are anxious to quit this miserable place at any price. We have been in the sleeping-bags about forty-five hours, suffering discomforts that words would fail to convey any idea of, and which can only be appreciated by those who have had a similar experience."

Lieutenant Lockwood was caught by the same storm near Cape Sumner. In passing that point he says:

"Here, instead of the protection I had anticipated from the bluffs, we encountered a series of blasts and whirlwinds of snow, disagreeable in the extreme, and making it difficult to keep the sledge from sliding sideways into the pits formed by the snow adjoining every mass of ice." Reaching a large snow-drift, he continues: "We dug a small hole in the snow-bank and crawled inside," where "how long exactly we remained I don't know; I was glad to leave even before the storm had ceased. . . . We had no light except from some cracks, which closed and opened continuously through some unknown agency, occasionally new cracks forming. This movement was accompanied by a noise which was rather alarming, until I found that our abode didn't decrease in size thereby. On crawling out when the storm had ended, the dogs were almost concealed from view by the snow which had drifted over them."

Near Cape Sumner the supporting party met Lieutenant Lockwood returning to their assistance. The travelling that night was fairly good, and the men were somewhat cheered by the sight of the sun, which then was above the horizon at midnight. After passing Cape Sumner there was so much rubble and broken ice that, on arriving at Polaris Boat Camp, after ten hours' travel, the sledge Beaumont had been so badly injured as to be useless, the bottom being completely worn out by friction over sharply pointed ice.

Violent squalls were experienced at Boat Camp, which broke the poles and blew down the tent, driving the parties eventually to snow-burrows. The wind was so violent that, while at work, the men were frequently blown over, and one gust lifted the dog-sledge, with its load of two hundred pounds, bodily from the ground. The sledge struck Ralston on the forehead, knocking him several yards and injuring him severely. An attempt to cook supper resulted only in the loss of the fuel, and the party lunched on hard bread and frozen meat. Brainard, who was an uncomplaining man of great endurance, says: "We imagine that no other party in the Arctic regions has ever passed through discomforts similar to those experienced by us during the past few hours, which have left us in a miserably forlorn and dejected condition."

The party were at this camp forty hours before they were able to obtain a satisfactory meal. The air-holes in the snow-houses continually filled with drifting snow, and on an attempt to cook a meal the alcohol lamp refused to burn on account of the vitiated atmosphere. As the air-holes filled up as rapidly as made, they immediately dug out the entrance, when Whisler fainted, and others suffered wretchedly from the confinement in such bad air.

As Whisler complained of severe lung pains and commenced spitting blood, and Biederbick was suffering with bladder trouble, Lieutenant Lockwood decided to send them back to Conger. Biederbick, despite his wretched condition, assured Lieutenant Lockwood that he would be responsible for Whisler's safe return to Conger, where they arrived in fair condition April 13th. Connell and Henry had reached the station on the 8th. During Henry's return, which was slightly in advance of Connell, the only personal encounter with a wolf was experienced. He reported that on entering the tunnel to the snow-house a huge wolf met him, and running over his back escaped. Later he claimed to have seen three wolves and that two of them followed him to Dutch Island. Connell met a wolf between Cape Beechy and Depot "B."

An Arctic Wolf, killed near Fort Conger.
[*From a photograph.*]

The party were employed until the 16th in accumulating at Boat Camp the stores of Depot "E" and those on the floe in Robeson Channel, which was accomplished under very difficult and discouraging circumstances.

A succession of violent gales rendered it almost impossible for the party to do work of any kind. Their tents were repeatedly blown down, their travelling-gear scattered, their sleeping-bags so badly frozen that at times the strength of four men was required to open them; and, worse than all, the conditions were such that the proper preparation of their meals was nearly impossible. A new peril also threatened them along the Greenland coast south of Cape Sumner. Sergeant Brainard says: "From the high cliff, huge rocks were blown which came crashing down to the very edge of the floe, endangering our lives and warning us that travelling on the ice-foot was too dangerous to be persisted in. In passing a narrow ravine a beautiful cascade of snow was seen, being formed by the wind rushing violently down a narrow, rocky cut in the face of an abrupt cliff, carrying with it a small and constant amount of fine snow, which leaped from rock to rock, resembling a silver mountain stream falling from a series of ledges."

While this work was progressing, Lieutenant Lockwood, fearing that the runners of the dog-sledge would not last because of the rough ice, returned to Fort Conger and obtained an extra set, which were taken along for emergencies.

While at Boat Camp violent storms, and the scattered condition of the stores, prevented constant watch over the dogs, and they succeeded in stealing about forty pounds of bacon and beef. Fortunately the large amount of stores transported to that point prevented any inconvenience from this loss, which otherwise might have had very serious results. The necessity of packing the meat for the journey in light muslin bags facilitated the theft.

Examining the sledges after this work, Lieutenant Lockwood decided that two were unserviceable, which left but two for further work. He expected to obtain a third at Cape Beechy, but, on visiting that depot, discovered that it had been so misplaced that, owing to the snow, he was unable to find it. In place of the injured sledges, the Nares was extemporized from the extra dog-sledge runners and slats.

One of the violent gales wrenched the cedar boat, cached by Sergeant Brainard at the Gap, from its bed and rendered it un-

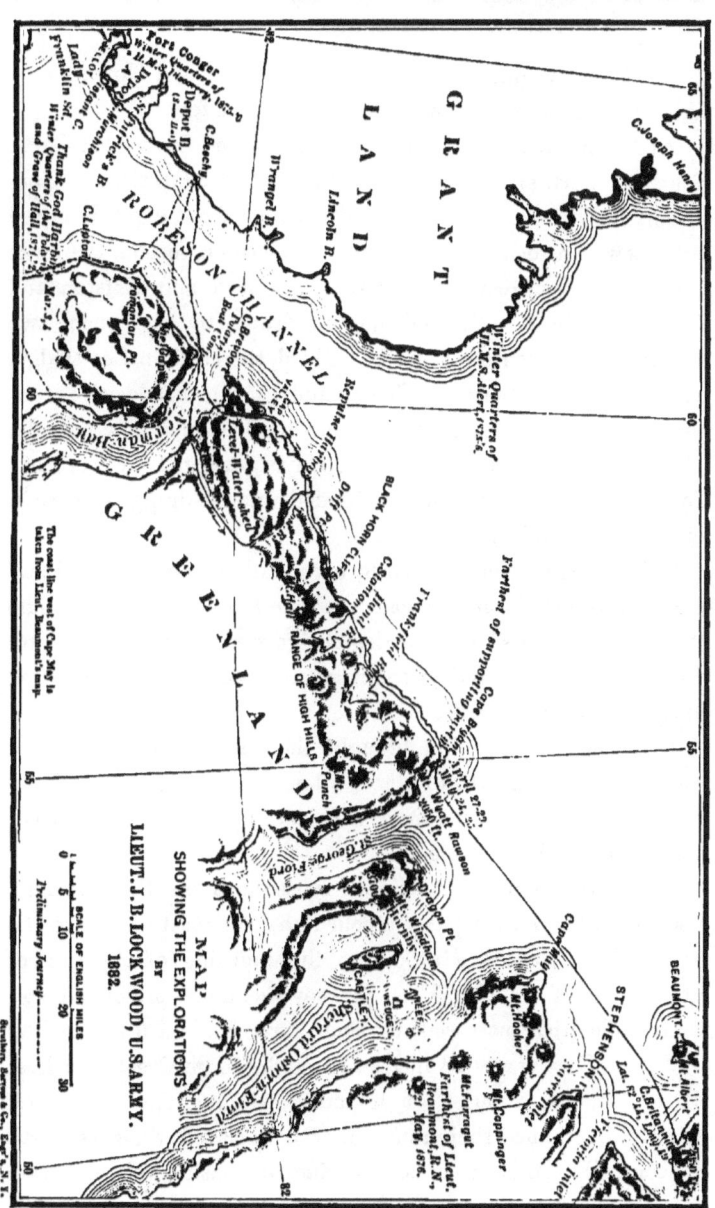

serviceable; it must have been lifted bodily and blown a considerable distance, as it was found on the ice-foot.

At 10 P.M. of April 16th, the party started from Boat Camp for their northern trip, taking three hundred rations. Lieutenant Lockwood was in advance, hauling about eight hundred pounds with a team of eight dogs. Then came, second, the large sledge Nares, drawn by Sergeants Brainard and Ralston and Corporal Salor; estimated amount drawn by each man, two hundred and seventeen pounds. Third, the Hudson Bay sledge, Hall, drawn by Sergeant Jewell and Private Frederick; estimated amount dragged by each, one hundred and fifty pounds. Fourth, the Hudson Bay sledge, Hayes, dragged by Sergeant Lynn and Corporal Elison; estimated amount dragged by each, one hundred and fifty pounds.

The average weight drawn by each man was one hundred and eighty-two pounds, and by each dog one hundred pounds. The "constant weights" of the dog-sledge were two hundred and forty-three pounds, and of the remaining sledges three hundred and seventy-five pounds.

Eight hours' travelling brought the party to what was supposed to be the mouth of Gap Valley, but it eventually proved to be a ravine (Rocky Gorge) considerably farther to the eastward. Here they camped.

After tremendous exertions, consequent on the overland travelling, the entire party reached the sea-coast a little to the eastward of Repulse Harbor, on the morning of April 22d, after five days' travel. Their journey was much prolonged, and their difficulties increased, by their error in regard to the Gap Valley. They travelled instead through Gorge Creek and Lost River Cañons, a series of tortuous, winding ravines, which greatly lengthened their route, as well as taxed their strength by compelling them to cross a divide of considerable elevation above the sea. On the 20th of April the temperature in these ravines fell to −40° (−40° C.), an unprecedentedly low temperature for such a late season of the year.

The character of the route passed over is shown by the following extracts from Lieutenant Lockwood's diary. On the 17th of April he reconnoitred Rocky Gorge, the grade of which was at first easy. The following day he says: "We came to the narrow gorge referred to. Its vertical sides were but a few feet apart; under foot the stones were exposed. Passing this the stream-bed widened and ran between sloping hills, but we encountered at the same time deep, soft snow. This was the general character of the travelling—ravines with soft snow, varied by gorges at intervals, with exposed stones and fragments of rocks. The stream is very tortuous, but the grade very slight its entire length, except when interrupted here and there by low banks of drifted snow. Its general course, as near as I could judge, is southwest."

"April 18th we came to a fork of the ravine coming in from the north; the first branch of the main stream which seemed to offer a practicable route to the north. One or two had been passed, but they were so narrow and steep—mere gullies—as to forbid the assumption that they formed part of Lieutenant Beaumont's route. It was the route of this officer, as laid down on his map, that I was endeavoring to follow. However, I continued on, but a few hundred yards beyond, seeing the stream bearing decidedly to the east, I left the sledge, and, ascending a low slope to the left, soon found myself in a 'divide' very similar to the 'divides' of the western prairies. To the north the 'breaks' of water-courses running in that direction could be seen. On the slope alluded to I saw a bird, to which Frederik gives the Eskimo name for eagle; was unable to get a shot. . . . A short distance beyond found myself on a level plain, its broad expanse stretching out for miles all around. The weather was overcast, threatening snow, but I could see the 'breaks' to the north, and after an hour's travelling reached them—the snow affording very good travelling—to find myself in a water-course quite broad and offering a very good route; the snow was generally hard; but few stones were exposed to view through it. The general course of the stream seems northwest; it is very picturesque. About 7.15 A.M. I came to what looks like a gateway opening into a street, a cañon running east and west, and so level that it was with many doubts I concluded *to the left* was down stream (Lost River)."

On April 20th, in a reconnoissance to determine his exact location, he says: "After proceeding half a mile the cañon changed into a wide valley, bordered by sloping hills, which, at a little distance back, assumed the proportion of mountains. Passing the point of a hill, which hid the view ahead like a cape, the valley was seen to continue on in a direction a little north of west until closed up entirely, apparently by a low range of hills. At 11.45 A.M. we reached this place, and found a narrow gap. I here delayed thirty minutes and ascended a hill, but could see little save another valley-like expanse ahead, which seemed to turn to the north. In half an hour more we were opposite this opening to the north, and saw the floebergs lining the long-looked-for coast. On our right and left were low, sloping points about half a mile distant from each other; behind us was a semi-circle of hills and mountains, and before us a level delta of bare stones. A few feet more in the elevation of the polar basin would make a bay of this place; it was doubtless the bed of one some time in the past."

Proceeding toward the sea Lieutenant Lockwood says:

"About a half mile from the coast I found an old piece of

drift-wood about six feet long, four inches wide, and four inches thick, pine or fir apparently, and evidently split from the body or branch of a tree. It was partially buried."

Sergeant Brainard's field notes speak of the journey as painfully laborious. April 18th he says: "Men all very tired; Jewell especially appears badly used up, although he displayed plenty of pluck in remaining in the drag-ropes to the last moment." They were obliged to double up their crews, travel three to five times over the road, and he continued, "to add to our discomforts, aside from the severe strain of tramping through snow knee-deep and more, there was a high wind with snow blowing directly in our faces. . . . Besides, the crust breaks just as we put our weight on the drag-ropes for a strong pull; this taxes the strength severely, and will soon break down the hard workers." April 19th: "The sledge often sinks to the slats, making it necessary to resort to standing pulls. . . . Nares, the improvised sledge, dragging on slats almost constantly, but Hudson Bays glide over snow without sinking much."

The lime-juice pemmican, so highly recommended by theoretical authorities, proved very distasteful, and could only be eaten raw; and, then, between the frozen lime-juice and solid meat their lips and mouths became sore.

Brainard writes: "The majority of the party complain of sleeping cold, and the rest assert that they obtain no sleep at all. This no doubt is owing to the condition of the sleeping-bags, which were frozen so badly on camping this morning that three men were required to unroll them, and we were obliged to thaw ourselves gradually into them." April 21st: "We encountered sand-bars and gravel-beds, which could not be avoided, and necessarily our labor was very severe and tedious, and frequent standing pulls became necessary. This with a northeast wind of about twenty miles an hour. . . . Advanced the remaining Hudson Bay sledge in face of a terrific gale, which drove the flying snow against our faces with a force and power equal to handfuls of gravel thrown by the strongest arm. This caused a painful smarting sensation, so intense as to be one of our most disagreeable experiences. The party is much worn out by the extra work. I think eight hours' labor sufficient, and hereafter will confine myself strictly to that, except under special circumstances."

On the morning of April 22d the entire party again camped together, in the face of a raging storm, on the lee side of some huge floebergs a short distance to the eastward of Repulse Harbor. Lieutenant Lockwood's party, despairing of getting their large tent to stand, pitched their small shelter-tent, which would hardly hold them on account of the rapidly drifting snow which soon covered it. "While at supper," says Lieutenant Lockwood, "some of the dogs thought my bag a good place to rest, and we returned to find it covered with snow. Remained in bag the rest of the day, missing supper in the large tent."

Sergeant Brainard, enumerating other discomforts, says:

"Our position while sleeping (?) is necessarily very cramped, the sleeping-bags being at half-mast, *i.e.*, our bodies on the ground and our legs run up against the tent-pole, and even then only about half our bodies can be inserted. Wind is estimated at forty miles per hour. The trials of an Arctic cook are numerous and irksome, sorely trying to the patience and temper of those called to that office. After the fierce storm had slightly abated, 'Shorty' (Frederick) found the cooking apparatus all correct except the fuel, which was outside under a huge drift. The deep drifts not only covered the sides of the tent, but also completely closed the entrance, making it necessary for him to tunnel his way through to get outside, where a new difficulty arose. The fuel was under four feet of snow, which also covered the shovels. Despite the high wind that, sweeping around the berg, threatened to blow him away, he was not a moment discouraged; but, with bare hands, commenced manfully digging into the hard drift, occasionally uttering a deep groan, and calling down maledictions on Arctic work in general. His meal, however, was an excellent one, and, after getting warmed thoroughly over the lamp while cooking, he seemed to forget all his recent troubles, and the bright side of his usually genial nature came bubbling to the surface."

"The storm raged till early morning of the 23d. . . . The dogs ate up all the bacon left, about twenty pounds, and about half as much English beef, during our sleep. It was packed on the Nares, and out of their reach it was thought."

A runner of the dog-sledge broke near this camp, and in moving forward, on April 23d, it was necessary to replace it by exchanging runners with the Nares. Sergeant Elison succeeded in repairing the runner for the Nares, but it gave way completely in a rough place, and the load was moved forward by lashing together the two Hudson Bay sledges and putting on it the loads previously carried by the three sledges. This improvised sledge was hauled only with great effort, as it dragged like a harrow. They camped about a mile west of Black Horn Cliffs, at a point where they were driven from the ice-foot to the main floe, to reach which they were obliged to cut a route for a half mile or more through adjacent rubble-ice.

"At and beyond Drift Point," says Lieutenant Lockwood, "the snow-slopes and soft snow were met with, and it became necessary to 'double-up,' *i.e.*, advance by half loads."

Sergeant Brainard's field notes of the same march record:

"Not far from camp I found a seal-hole newly made, and

traces of that animal in the snow which had lately fallen, showing that he had become alarmed at our approach, and had sought safety under the ice. . . . After passing Drift Point we encountered snow-slopes, which made progress slow and tedious, and drove the party in despair alternately to the tangled rubble-ice and the sharp, difficult snow-drifts. The slopes are formed by the snow blowing from a rather abrupt hill to a ridge of gigantic floe-bergs grounded at its base, filling entirely the intervening space, except next the bergs themselves, where the eddying wind prevents the snow from drifting in. These clefts, from fifteen to twenty feet deep, and at a sharp incline, make the snow-slopes very dangerous surface to travel over, as the sledge is liable at any move to escape the control of those who are hauling it and slide into this deep space, even if it does not drag down the unfortunate sledge-men."

Sergeant Brainard's experiences illustrate the great distance at which high land can be seen on clear days. From the eastern end of Black Horn Cliffs, on April 24th, he says: "The clear pellucid nature of the atmosphere was such that Capes Sheridan, Union and Black Cape, as well as several points in the United States range of mountains were seen, the distance being nearly fifty miles. . . . Temperature 11° (−15.6° C.). The hot blazing sun is thawing the surface of the black, dirty snow near the cliffs, and in consequence our moccasins are completely wet through."

About this time my letter was read to the party by Lieutenant Lockwood, in which I promised a conditional reward of $900 and upward, contingent on making a northing surpassing any ever before attained. Lieutenant Lockwood offered fifty per cent. additional reward. The amount was to be distributed in such proportions as Lieutenant Lockwood should judge each man's work merited. I doubt if the question of reward ever entered into any man's thoughts during all the extraordinary suffering and exposure to which this journey subjected him, but it seemed a proper intimation that success would be in some way rewarded.

The Appropriation Committee of the House of Representatives, on a statement of the case by me, after my return, reported favorably as to the assumption of both these rewards, and Congress so enacted.

They started on their tenth march, April 24th. I quote from Lieutenant Lockwood's journal: "Opposite Black Horn Cliffs, and extending a short distance this (the west) side, was a clear, smooth floe of ice (formed last year, I suppose), over which, with a heavy wind on our backs, we made rapid progress. When opposite the farther (eastern) end of the cliffs, and some distance from shore, farther advance was stopped by a considerable mass of rubble-ice." Finally, I found a route—somewhat circuitous—to the shore without much difficulty, and continued on over a smooth, level floe (last year's [?]), which extended half way to the gorge. The rest of the way a good route was found on a hard, gently sloping snow-slope, inside the line of bergs and hummocks which here commenced to fringe the shore. I saw two ptarmigan in winter plumage along here. I found no cairn or provisions, though I went half a mile beyond the gorge. The violent wind made my return slow and very uncomfortable."

They camped east of and close to the Black Horn Cliffs.

On the morning of April 25th the party were delayed a few hours by the illness of Eskimo Frederik, who complained of stomach trouble. Lieutenant Lockwood finally managed to get him as far as Rest Gorge, about two and a half miles to the eastward of Black Horn Cliffs, where he put him in the sleeping-bag and gave him a drink of whiskey. There they camped.

Sergeant Brainard writes: "We have no way of knowing exactly what ails him, and he has no way of making known his wishes except by sighs, which is a very unsatisfactory method of talking. Not knowing of any other remedy, a huge drink of hot brandy was given him, and we soon had the satisfaction of learning that he was sleeping soundly, which report was afterward confirmed by hearing him snore loud and deep enough to almost cause the ice-foot to vibrate; hopes were then entertained of his speedy recovery. . . . The map of this coast made by Lieutenant Beaumont is a model of accuracy and correctness . . . as far as we are able to discover. The two sledges Hayes and Hall are now almost worn out and very hard to drag."

During the afternoon Ralston and Jewell succeeded in finding the English cache at Stanton Gorge; it was marked by a cairn on a hill somewhat back from the coast, and in a position which did not show up well to the westward.

"Before starting," (April 26th) says Lieutenant Lockwood, "we built a cairn here, and left one day's rations for entire party and the dogs, and also everything in the way of clothing, foot-gear, etc., that could be spared.

"At Stanton Gorge, Sergeant Ralston showed me Beaumont's cache, which was situated upon a 'shoulder' of the mountains about a hundred feet high. This cache consisted of forty rations, fifty-six pounds sweet pemmican, ten pounds bacon, and a metal box containing the hard bread, potatoes, etc.; also a can of rum which Sergeant Ralston had brought down to Rest Gorge the previous day. I built up the cairn again, and left a record of my movements to date, and took the rations to the ice-foot, in order that they might be convenient to the dog-sledge on its return, for I thought it desirable to take them on to Cape Bryant."

That evening the party camped near Frankfield Bay, when Lieutenant Lockwood records: "The route from last camp led us, as far as Cape Stanton, inside a line of floebergs on a snow-slope quite steep in places, but generally hard on the surface, and offering fair travelling. As an exception, however, it should be stated that there is an ice-foot for some little distance at Stanton Gorge. The travelling over Hand Bay was also quite good."

At this camp writes Brainard:

"Temperature −23.5° (−30.8° C.). Very few of the party obtained any sleep, owing to low temperature and frozen sleeping-bag, in which much frost and dampness has accumulated the past few days."

At 7 A.M., April 27th, the party left their camp opposite Mount Lowe and marched to Cape Bryant.

Lieutenant Lockwood says: "Travelling rather heavy (over snow-covered ice-foot). At 9.25 A.M. reached east shore of Frankfield Bay. On the way the snow was generally hard and good. From here the only route, or at least the best route forward, was over the foot of a hill, the ascent rather steep, and the slope quite so; the snow on it had packed hard and smooth."

"I saw four ptarmigan and killed three with the shot-gun. Frederik had, some time before, when by himself, killed two with the pistol. This pistol, which had a wooden stock, similar to a gun's, fixed to it, was habitually carried on the sledge."

"The travelling since leaving Frankfield Bay has been along a low fore shore, excepting two or three indentations of the coast where we crossed old floes. Along the shore we travelled over a snow-covered ice-foot, or what is generally called an ice-foot (?); sometimes *good* and sometimes *bad*, never *very* bad. Over the floes referred to it was generally quite fair."

The main party reached Cape Bryant, 8 P.M., April 27th,

temperature —14° (—25.6° C.), after over eleven hours' steady work in the drag-ropes. Not only were they all nearly worn down by the exhausting effects of previous hard work and exposure, but Sergeants Brainard and Ralston had been suffering from snow-blindness, and Private Frederick from an injured knee. The party consequently remained at Cape Bryant April 28th, recuperating and preparing for further work.

Lieutenant Lockwood decided to send back the supporting party, and advance with the dog-sledge and two men. He writes:

"Personally inspected the Hudson Bay sledges, and was confirmed in the declaration of all the men that they were entirely unserviceable for further use. One I cut up and made slats for the dog-sledge; the other was repaired sufficiently to carry the *constant weights* of Sergeant Lynn's party on their return to Boat Camp."

"After this I built a cairn on the slope of the hill, perhaps a quarter mile from the shore, and deposited inside the forty English rations, all our own that were surplus, the gun, etc., and everything I thought we could do without. I also left a record. Sergeant Brainard suffered severely from snow-blindness during the day and had to remain in the tent."

"Cape Britannia was dimly visible; later in the day it was quite distinct. The view is so well represented in Lieutenant Beaumont's journal, that I will not attempt to describe it. Sergeants Brainard, Ralston, and Elison went along the coast to the south to find Lieutenant Beaumont's cache, or cairn, but were unsuccessful."

From the summit of Cape Fulford, which was visited by Sergeants Ralston, Elison, and himself, Sergeant Brainard says: "The east side of Sherard Osborn Fiord, with its mountains and capes, was distinctly outlined, and appeared much nearer than the distance given on the map. The appearance of the ice in the fiord encouraged us very much. Its surface has an undulating appearance peculiar to ice which seldom breaks up, and is studded here and there by small hummocks." The zeal and activity of the members of this party could not be more strikingly illustrated than by their tramp of twelve miles on a resting day, in such a country, in order to familiarize themselves with their surroundings.

The journey of Lieutenant Lockwood's supporting party, which here terminated, was an extraordinary one, considering the character of the ice, the loads drawn, the stormy weather, and the temperatures to which they were subjected. In his noted journeys, made about six hundred miles farther south and over ordinary ice, the famous sledge-traveller, McClintock, averaged only two and a quarter miles daily more than this party.

The experiences of McClintock, more varied than of any other Arctic explorer, show the advisability of sledging with dogs. In seven journeys, covering over three thousand miles, his men travelled eleven and one-third miles daily. With both men and dogs he later averaged twelve and a half miles daily, and with dogs alone twenty-four miles daily. The comparison between the man-system, under an officer of extraordinary energy—Lieutenant Beaumont—and the mixed system, which I followed perforce, should also be convincing in favor of dogs. Lieutenant Beaumont made his trip from Discovery Harbor (Fort Conger) to Cape Bryant in thirty-one marches, travelling via Floeberg Beach, and with a mean temperature of $-13°$ ($-25°$ C.), ranging from $14°$ (-10 C.) to $-45°$ ($-42.8°$ C.). He travelled one hundred and eighty-three miles to make his distance of one hundred and thirty-four miles.

Lieutenant Lockwood's supporting party travelled from Conger (Discovery Harbor) to Cape Bryant, via Polaris Boat Camp and

Gorge Creek, in eighteen marches, with temperatures ranging from 14.5° (−9.7° C.) to −48.8° (−44.9° C.), and a mean of −11° (−23.9° C.). They marched about one hundred and sixty miles to pass over their route of one hundred and twenty-one miles.

The difference between the six miles made daily by Lieutenant Beaumont's men and nine by Sergeant Brainard and his associates resulted from the contrasted loads, especially the constant weights. It was the unanimous opinion of my men that they were worked up to their last pound of strength, and that the weight of two hundred and twenty-five pounds per man, hauled by Beaumont from Repulse Harbor, would have broken them down.

Of the two hundred and twenty-five pounds hauled by Beaumont's seven men, ninety-five and one-half pounds per man figured as constant weights, which they not only hauled to Bryant, but part of the way back. The constant weights of Sergeant Brainard and six men were sixty-two and a half pounds on leaving Cape Sumner, which would not have exceeded seventy pounds per man if Lieutenant Lockwood, with his baggage, had joined them. The total weight drawn by each man was one hundred and eighty-two pounds. Consequently on starting Lieutenant Beaumont's men hauled forty-three pounds each more than the men of Lieutenant Lockwood's supporting party, twenty-five pounds of which were constant weights.

The abandonment of one sledge and caching certain useless articles reduced the constant weights of our men to forty-seven pounds at Black Horn Cliffs. They were farther assisted on their totals by Lieutenant Lockwood with the dog-sledge, on special occasions where bad travel obliged doubling up, which somewhat reduced their labor.

Lieutenant Lockwood marched with dog-sledge from Conger to Bryant in thirteen journeys. He travelled two hundred and ninety miles, although the distance was but one hundred and twenty-one miles, the remaining travel being in doubling up or in side journeys. His actual marches averaged eleven hours each, during which he made twenty-two miles daily.

Fourteen to fifteen hours of daily work and exposure, in storm with driving snow, or with clear, balmy air, and zero temperatures, brought them to Bryant at that early day, and made success seem certain.

CHAPTER XXIV.

THE FARTHEST NORTH.—CAPE BRYANT TO CAPE WASHINGTON.

JOURNEY OF LIEUTENANT LOCKWOOD AND SERGEANT BRAINARD.

MAY 29th Sergeant Lynn turned back for Polaris Boat Camp with the supporting party, while Lieutenant Lockwood, with Brainard and Christiansen, turned his face northward over the frozen sea.

"I selected Sergeant Brainard to accompany Frederik and myself," says Lieutenant Lockwood, "and made up a list of seventy-five rations, sufficient for twenty-five days' absence from Bryant, viz.:

	Pounds.
Pemmican (lime-juice)	40
Musk-meat (frozen in tins)	34
Sausage and English beef	17
Beans, Boston baked	19
Potatoes, evaporated	5
Cranberry sauce (three cans)	4½
Tea	2
Chocolate	3
Sugar	10
Lime-juice (frozen in cakes)	2¼
Hard bread	60
Milk	1½
Alcohol	19
Total	227⅛

"The constant weights, etc., consisted of 1 'A' tent, poles and pins; 2 sleeping-bags (one buffalo and one dog-skin), 1 cooking-lamp, 1 rubber blanket, 1 axe, 1 spade, 1 hatchet, 1 pistol, 1 sextant, 1 sledge-runner (extra), 1 shelter-tent, 1 small cooking-lamp (extra), 2 pairs of snow-shoes, 1 catch-all bag, containing ammunition, cups, plates, spoons, sounding-line and lead, brush, record-cases, tin funnel, measure cup, chopping-board, etc.; 3 clothesbags (individual weights given elsewhere), and sledge (80 pounds). Total constant weights, 256 pounds.

"Dog pemmican (3 sacks) 300 pounds; total amount drawn by 8 dogs, 783⅓ pounds; or an average for each dog at starting of (about) 98 pounds.

"At 4.47 P.M. I left with dog-sledge, Sergeant Brainard, and Frederik (Eskimo), taking a course toward Cape May. The weather continued delightful. Found the floes quite hard and level, interrupted only by occasional low detached hummocks, on which the drifted snow made our progress very satisfactory. When nearly opposite Dragon Point, however, the snow-crust seemed to weaken, and the sledge frequently sank to the slats, requiring our united exertions to move it."

Brainard's field notes say: "The dogs, not being accustomed to hauling such heavy weights, sit down as soon as the runners cut through the crust, . . . and complacently watch us, with a puzzled expression, . . . until we lift the sledge bodily and place it on the firm crust."

On April 30th, Lieutenant Lockwood, at "1 A.M., camped opposite Dragon Point, the dogs being much exhausted by such a heavy load. The clearest day I have yet seen; no wind. Temperature lower than usual. 4 A.M.: Finished supper. 4.20 A.M.: Thermometer, 1° (−16.7° C.); barometer, 29.35. Halts during march for relashing, about thirty minutes in all. Lieutenant Beaumont's sketches and descriptions of this section are very good, as well as I could judge by the eye."

At 5.22 P.M. he again started, and soon found "the dragging

very heavy and fatiguing, snow sometimes knee-deep, the sledge coming to a stand-still repeatedly. On these occasions the dogs complacently sit on their haunches and observe the operation of pulling it out, which falls to us. After dropping half the load the travelling seemed to improve, due, possibly, to a slight change of direction, which brought us on a line with Cape Britannia. Sergeant Brainard quite over his snow-blindness. We find the lime-juice pemmican very unsatisfactory, and eat it only with great reluctance. Cape Britannia is very distinct, due, probably, to the remarkable refraction of the atmosphere. Beaumont Island presented the appearance of one island on top of another, the first inverted. 4.15 A.M.: Turned in."

At 4.25 P.M., May 1st, they started with whole load, but Lieutenant Lockwood soon dropped half with Brainard, and, going on himself, "stopped at an old floeberg, and, taking off load, sent sledge back for remainder. Character of the ice better, so that I have determined to try hauling everything at once. The floes in sight very large, broken at long intervals with ranges of low hummocks; isolated mounds scattered here and there. All covered with snow. The floes in places are slightly undulating. 7.48 P.M.: Thermometer, $-1°(-18.3°C.)$."

Lieutenant Lockwood during that march gave up all idea of visiting Cape May, as he found the roads better to the north, and travelled direct for Cape Britannia. He camped "hardly more than five miles from Cape May. The large floe last referred to extends north as far as I could see. Supper consisted of tea, lime-juice pemmican, hard bread, and a stew (?) of beans and cracker-dust; the allowance of alcohol only sufficient to melt the ice and warm the water; the stew was cold. 9.15 A.M.: Turned in."

"Brainard and I didn't sleep much. The Eskimo invariably snores two minutes after he composes himself to rest. Took a number of compass bearings of different points very carefully, and was disappointed to find the instrument no better than before. I had spent some time yesterday in trying to mend it. There seems to be a want of magnetism."

They started north at 8 p.m., May 2d, but twenty standing pulls in as many minutes obliged them to drop half the load. Shortly after Lieutenant Lockwood " attempted a sketch of Stephenson Island—an island to all appearances from here. Saw wolf and fox tracks going north some distance back. Noticed a line of hummocky ice extending from Beaumont Island in the direction of Cape May. Doubled up just in time, the travelling since,

Stephenson Island from Cape Britannia.
[*From sketch by Lt. Lockwood.*]

up to this spot, being soft and deep, sometimes nearly up to the knees. 10.45 p.m. came to a crack in the ice, which seemed to follow the lines of hummocky ice referred to. This crack, when first met, was in width the length of a tent-pole, and full of free water and 'sludge' about two feet, as I remember, below the level of the edge of the ice. Following it south a few hundred feet, we found two or three cracks, but only two feet or a little more wide, so there was no difficulty in crossing. This place was at the intersection (approximate) of a line from Cape Britannia to Cape Bryant with another between Cape May and Beaumont Island. This being a good opportunity to get the depth, I sent Frederik back for Sergeant Brainard and the load—the lead and line not being with me."

"May 3d, 1.07 A.M.: Dog-team back again. The dogs always travel much faster going back or forward over a trail. Selecting a good spot, I gave Sergeant Brainard the line; it ran out its full length without touching bottom. I then attached in succession four coils of seal-thong, a long piece of rope, and finally Frederik's whip; all with the same result, no bottom. Having nothing now left but the traces of the dogs, we began drawing the line back, while considering if these should be risked. I had attempted to measure it *exactly* by arm-lengths as it went down, but found this inconvenient and decided to wait till we got it all out. We drew out the whip and part of the rope, when the latter suddenly parted, and of course the rest was lost. The rope was about half an inch in diameter, and would hardly be thought the first part of the line to give way. The approximate length of line below surface is as follows: Rope, including whip, 148 feet; four coils thong, 240 feet; four cod-lines, each 108 feet—432; total, 820 feet. Weight of lead six pounds. Thus, besides the loss of the line, all farther attempts at sounding were prevented."

Of the tidal crack Sergeant Brainard's notes say: "At this point (the first reached) the crack opens about six feet wide, and branches a short distance to the north into three distinct openings, each of about the same width as the main one. This would seem to indicate that some strong current from the Greenland shore existed, for this is firm ice apparently wrenched apart by some strong movement of the sea."

Lieutenant Lockwood writes: "At 2 A.M. proceeded en route with half load. In the course of a quarter of an hour passed a narrow line or belt of low hummocks seemingly parallel to the ice-crack. After this was an immense level floe, which extended

to the right and left and ahead as far as I could see; it was difficult to perceive the smallest break or unevenness in its great expanse. At 3 A.M. met a little mound of snow-ice, which, as it saved the melting of snow for water, I camped alongside of. Bearings from this camp: Beaumont Island east-southeast; Cape Britannia southeast by south; Stephenson Island southwest by south; Cape May northwest by west (all magnetic). At 5.30 P.M. thermometer 19 (—7.2°C.)." These bearings were from a pocket-compass that Lieutenant Lockwood used after finding the prismatic compass to be unserviceable.

They started at 6 P.M., May 3d, and at "8.28–8.35 P.M. stopped for rest at a line of very low, hummocky ice, which sweeps in a curve to the northeast on one hand, and on the other to the southwest toward Cape May. The floe we now saw before us was an unbroken expanse of level snow, and seemed to continue thus and occupy the whole space between Beaumont and Stephenson Islands and Cape Britannia, reminding me very much of the plains of the West; crust quite hard and firm, enabling us to carry everything at once. At 9.35 P.M., intersection of route with a line between Beaumont and Stephenson Islands."

After fourteen hours' travel, during which they travelled thirty miles to make good fourteen, the party camped within about five miles of Cape Britannia.

Sergeant Brainard at this camp records: "Cape Britannia is now within our grasp. . . . We got into our damp, cheerless sleeping-bag with lighter hearts and in a more amiable frame of mind than for weeks. Even the dusky Greenlander has imbibed some of our spirit (doubtless inspired somewhat by Lieutenant Lockwood's recent promise of a hundred crowns if he reached Cape Britannia), and, sitting up in his dog-skin bag, takes mental note of everything which passes, with a delighted grin overspreading his shining, good-natured countenance. . . . Stephenson Island is a very high rocky mass, oblong in shape, with nearly vertical cliffs, notched here and there by deep ravines, from two of which pass small glaciers, one nearly discharging. The remainder of the coast to Britannia is broken and mountainous, with two or three glaciers."

"The dogs during our sleep got at the pemmican, which was buried as usual under the sledge, and ate their allowance for two and a half days." *

An hour and a half of good travel, on May 5th, brought them to land before untrodden by man, and thenceforward everything was doubly new.

"At 7.53 P.M.: Reached Cape Britannia; the line of demarcation between the floe and the shore-ice was very slight, and only indicated by one or more indistinct cracks. After pitching the tent on the ice-foot, we proceeded to build a cairn about seven feet high, twenty or thirty yards above, on the side of a little ravine just below the cliff. In it I deposited a record of my journey, five days' rations, three days' dog-food, the extra sledge-runner, shelter-tent, little lamp, and the snow-shoes. The last three articles were brought along in case the snow east of Cape Bryant was too deep to allow the dog-sledge to travel. I now judged we could get along without them. After this I took an observation for latitude. Frederik came in with a ptarmigan; it had commenced to change its plumage; some of the feathers were black."

"May 5th, 1 A.M.: Thermometer, 2° (−16°.7 C.); barometer, 29.52; calm. Sergeant Brainard and I started for the top of the cape or mountain. We followed the water-course referred to; the ascent was quite steep, with several intermediate crests or

---

* All quoted passages are from Lieutenant Lockwood's field journal, unless otherwise stated.

ridges, each seeming from below to be the top. At 2.35 A.M. reached the summit. Thermometer, 14½° (−9°.7 C.); barometer, 27.32; windy. We were apparently on an island; its most northern limit ended in a bold headland, Cape Frederick, a half dozen miles distant. Away to the northeast, or a little south of it, was a bold headland—some fifteen or twenty miles off— the termination of a promontory or island stretching to the north. Between it and me were the projecting capes of three similar bodies of land, farther to the right—all separated by great fiords (Nordenskjöld and Chipp Inlets) stretching to the south, and overlapping one another, so that little could be seen

Beaumont Island from Cape Britannia.
[*From sketch by Lt. Lockwood.*]

to the south of them but a confused mass of snow-covered peaks. Glancing around toward the north and west, the eye rested on nothing but the ice-pack till Beaumont Island was reached; after that the mountains near Cape Bryant.

Stephenson Island is evidently an island (previously doubtful), for the opening of a fiord (Nares) that separates it from Cape May can be seen, and on its east is an immense fiord (Victoria) running to the south. The two fiords are to appearances connected; no land visible at the head of the large one. To the east the coast trends to the southeast, forming with the south side of Britannia coast an immense funnel, ending in a fiord. All to the south is an indistinct mass of snow-covered mountains. We built a cairn on the summit (one thousand nine hundred and fifty feet above the sea) and deposited a record."

Brainard says: "Recent traces of hares, foxes, lemmings, and older traces of musk-oxen discovered. . . . The abrupt, rugged nature of the cliffs to the westward would not admit of their being scaled, so we followed a deep, narrow ravine to the southward. . . . In the interior a succession of lofty mountain peaks were visible, some of great elevation. They were not arranged in a chain, but formed an irregular, ill-defined mass. Deep snow covered their summits, and an occasional glacier of moderate dimensions could be seen struggling toward the sea from out of the chaotic mass of snow-capped mountains."

The twentieth march, on May 5th, enabled them to round Cape Frederick and camp opposite Nordenskjöld Inlet. Travel was first along an excellent ice-foot, but heavy ice, crowded against the high, abrupt cliffs, soon drove them to the main floe. During their march a deep, grinding noise indicated movement of the floe-ice, the Eskimo being positive such was the case. Lieutenant Lockwood going seaward to investigate, "saw the tide-crack, evidently a continuation of the one crossed west of Britannia." Beyond Cape Frederick they struck "last year's ice; it continued some distance and reached to the north several hundred yards from shore. From Cape Frederick the tide-crack continued toward Cape Emory, curving to the right *en route*. It was plainly marked by a line of heaped-up, hummocky ice, and by being the line separating the smooth and generally level floes inside from the rough pack without. . . . All inside the ice-crack seems one unbroken floe, smooth and level, assuming an undulating surface in most places near the ice-crack, caused by ranges of hummocky ice covered with snow-drifts." Lieutenant Lockwood got as the result of his latitude observations 82° 51′ N.

Near this camp Brainard says: "An exclamation from Christiansen caused us to look around and halt the sledge. We were astonished to observe unmistakable signs of open water—the bright rays of the sun playing over the rippling surface of an open pool. . . . At the point we examined, it was about a hundred yards wide, and looked as if it had been kept open during the winter, as none of the débris had attained any considerable thickness. Christiansen visited the pool later for seal, but saw no signs of any. Fresh fox and hare tracks seen by me near Cape Frederick. After camping, the dogs were running about like ravenous wolves, gnawing at everything, and badly chewed and splintered the thermometer-box before it could be secured. The ptarmigan lately shot was placed on the ridge-pole for safety. A hasty rush of feet, and a heavy body striking violently against the tent, caused us to rush out to investigate this commotion. The ptarmigan was missing. A few feathers in his bloody jaws marked the king-dog, Ritenbenk, as the thief, notwithstanding his bland look of innocence." Brainard's moccasins here gave out, after thirty-three days' steady wear.

Their twenty-first march carried the party to Cape Benét, the western entrance of Mascart Inlet, which was reached 11.33 P.M., May 6th, after over ten hours' travel, which exhausted both men and dogs. During the march the tidal crack was frequently seen and varied from one to a hundred yards in width, being "covered with new ice, except when broken by pools or lanes." Markham Island was apparently separated from the main-land to the northeast by a narrow, deep fiord. Brainard noticed three small glaciers on the shores of Chipp and Nordenskjöld Inlets which nearly reached the sea.

The following notes of Sergeant Brainard are of interest in connection with Lieutenant Lockwood's statement, that no distinctly palæocrystic ice was seen to the northward or eastward of Cape May:

"The ice met with on this coast appears to be of an entirely different character from the large floes and floebergs so familiar to the traveller on the Grinnell Land coast. The hummocks are all of small size, and no large floes or bergs are met with. Huge masses of ice form a wall which rises along the shore at

Looking into Chipp Inlet.
[*From sketch by Lieutenant Lockwood.*]

all prominent headlands. It is most likely formed from large quantities of rubble-ice being forced up by the tremendous pressure of the polar pack, and subsequently cemented by the summer sun into a compact mass resembling one immense block of ice."

This camp proved prolific in animal life, thus indicating a luxuriant vegetation near. Two ptarmigan were flying around, a hare was captured, and traces of foxes and lemmings observed.

Tracks of a passing bear, going to the northeast, were seen on the ice-foot, and "abundant traces of musk-oxen were discovered, proving that these animals frequent this place in considerable numbers, though the indications were not of recent date."

"The only excitement and recreation," says Sergeant Brainard, "experienced since leaving Bryant occurred this morning shortly after arriving in camp. It happened in this way: While cutting ice for cooking purposes, I saw a hare on the slope just above me, and fired twice without effect. Frederik, evidently very much disgusted at my lack of marksmanship, took the gun and wounded him twice, and immediately followed up his advantage with a shower of stones and Eskimo epithets. After an exciting chase of over half an hour along the rocky slope, in which the lieutenant and myself joined, the hare was captured."

Before starting that evening three days' rations were cached.

The twenty-second march carried them, May 7th, to Low Point, 83° 07′ N., which was of equal latitude with the most northerly land ever before reached—Cape Columbia, Grinnell Land, by Lieutenant Aldrich, R.N., 1876. Soft, deep snow, sometimes to their thighs, made it the worst and most exhausting travelling since leaving Brevoort Peninsula. Distant Cape was passed, "a grand headland of dark-looking rocks forming a huge cliff," and far in advance appeared Cape Ramsay, which at first was thought to be an island, but the thick snow which had fallen during the whole march rendered it uncertain. The only sign of life was a snow-bunting, the first seen, although they had been heard before. The tidal crack was open along their route the whole day. Lieutenant Lockwood says: "Brainard and I very tired; we both remarked a frequent feeling of lassitude and weakness of late."

A fine march (the twenty-third), during which the dogs trotted at times, brought them, in seventeen miles' travel, to

Pocket Bay, east of Cape Mohn, 83° 10′ N. The fine travelling encouraged the travellers, notwithstanding the high wind and drifting snow. The land, which had been running due east, now trended decidedly to the north, the much desired direction. A lemming was caught during the march in Jewell Inlet, about 83° 9′ N.

"At this camp," says Sergeant Brainard, " the thieving propensities of our canine friends were developed to an unusual degree. While we were sleeping they burst off the strings, entered the tent, and stole our provision-bag and hare. They were so elated over the success of their raid that they forgot their caution, and their retreat was not effected without considerable noise, which awoke us. Everything was recovered, except a quarter of the hare, which Ritenbenk contended was his lawful share of the game. His control as king-dog was admirable, for the rest of the half-starved pack watched him quietly as he ate the hare."

On May 10th the explorers crossed De Long Fiord, constructing, in passing, small cairns on the northern and southern points. They were able to travel only by the wind, which was directly at their backs, part of the time, as the coast was hidden by a violent snow storm. The coast from Cape Hoffmeyer north was a low, sloping shore, giving place in a short mile inland to a "grand line of cliffs."

After nine and a half hours' march in high, cold winds and drifting snow, during which they travelled twenty-two miles, the party camped on Mary Murray Island, 83° 19′ N., 42° 21′ W.

This island, shaped like a shoe, proved to be "a narrow, rocky ridge projecting a few hundred feet above the level of the ice, its top inaccessible except in a few places." From it three capes, the farthest probably Cape Washington, could be seen.

The violence of the gale delayed them at this camp sixty-three and a half hours. Latitude and time observations were obtained.

Animal life existed, as several snow-buntings flew around, hare tracks were noticed, and an unfortunate lemming was captured by the dogs. It was difficult to say whether the party were the most disturbed through mental anxiety and disappointment as to farther advance or by physical suffering from cold and exposure. The high wind, with the very low mean temperature of 8° (−13.3 C.), reduced their feet "to a condition," says Sergeant Brainard, "not unlike a cake of ice. We frequently changed our foot-gear, and rubbed our feet briskly with the warm hand, but to no purpose." This unprecedented experience was attributed to camping on bare ice, but it more probably resulted from insufficient food, as they ate only at intervals of fifteen, twenty-four, and nineteen hours, so as to enable them to travel yet farther.

Their twenty-fifth and last march is thus described by Lieutenant Lockwood:

"May 13th, 12.30 A.M.: Thermometer, 11° (−11.7° C.); barometer, 29.30. Northwest wind and snow, but the cape ahead could be seen, and anything is preferable to cold feet, which we have endured for sixty-two hours."

"Started at 1.45 A.M. after building a small cairn near-by. The north cape of Wild Fiord disappeared from view shortly after starting, but the travelling was very good near shore over 'blue top floe,' and at 3.45 A.M. the cape was reached. Here, and along the line of cliffs beyond which it terminates, immense masses of bergs and hummocks were pressed so closely to the foot of the cliffs that it was necessary to get outside on the floe. A tortuous way was found to the top of this ice-wall, and the sledge then lowered, by means of the traces, some fifteen feet or more. For some distance we worked our way slowly through a mass of rubble-ice, with the constant use of the axe, and crossed two or three small lanes of water; and beyond travelled for a few hundred yards on a 'clear' floe of last year's ice, when, at 5.30–6.15 A.M., we were stopped by another lead or lane of water. The sun being discernible, I took an observation, and at the same time sent Frederik to find a crossing. (This crossing, says Sergeant Brainard, was dangerous, owing to thin and rotten ice.) One being found, we continued over a floe of last year's ice at quite a rapid gait on a line generally parallel to the cliffs. Presently the weather clearing, a large, wide inlet (Weyprecht Inlet), with the cliffs and mountains on its farther side, opened up to view, forming a grand panorama, the most remarkable yet observed. To the right oblique the line of cliffs ended in a cape, from which the coast turned abruptly to the south and then ran in a curve toward the southeast, forming the western shore of the inlet. Directly ahead was a pyramid-shaped island (Lockwood Island) of considerable altitude, which seemed to touch the line of cliffs back of it, which ran almost north and south, ending in a cape (Cape Kane) to the northeast of our position, and on the other hand gradually curving back to the southeast and forming the eastern side of the inlet. A little to the right of the island referred to is another (Brainard Island), *apparently* of a cone shape. The land to their rear towered up to an enormous height, and formed a mountain certainly not less than four thousand feet in height, completely dwarfing the islands and cliffs beneath. The tide-crack, which we were now on the outside of, ran in a great curve between the two capes, at the extremities of the inlet, and was marked by a wall of ice-hummocks. Inside was a level surface of snow, covering a floe which extended from shore to shore, and outside alternate masses of rubble and smooth floes of last year's ice."

Ten hours' work carried them only sixteen miles, and, worn out by travel through deep snow, they made their farthest camp at the north end of Lockwood Island, which, by circum-meridian and subpolar observations reduced by Gauss' method, was determined to be in 83° 23.8′ N., the highest latitude ever attained by man.

Of this event Sergeant Brainard's field notes say: "We have reached a higher latitude than ever before reached by mortal man, and on a land farther north than was supposed by many to exist. We unfurled the glorious Stars and Stripes to the exhilarating northern breezes with an exultation impossible to describe."

For three centuries England had held the honors of the farthest north. The latitude of Hudson, 80° 23′, in 1607, gave way to Phipps, who reached 80° 48′ N. in 1773. Scoresby, the elder, in 1806, reached 81° 12′ 42″ N.; and, twenty-one years later, came Parry's memorable journey, during which he reached 82° 45′. These latitudes were all attained in the Greenland Sea. Inglefield opened to the world the Smith Sound route, and in 1871 Meyer reached 82° 09′, the highest on *land*, and Payer, a year later, almost equalled Meyer by his sledge-journey to Cape Fligely (82° 07′), Franz Josef Land. In 1876 Aldrich surpassed Parry's famous latitude, and reached Cape Columbia, 83° 07′ N., only to be surpassed on *sea*, a few weeks later, by Markham, 83° 20′ 26″ N., during that journey over the Great Frozen Sea in which such energy, persistency, and courage were exhibited by the officers and men of the Royal Navy.

Now Lockwood, profiting by the labors and experiences of his "kin across the sea," surpassed their efforts of three centuries by land and ocean. And with Lockwood's name should be associated that of his inseparable sledge-companion, Brainard, without whose efficient aid and restless energy, as Lockwood said, the work could not have been accomplished.

So, with proper pride, they looked that day from their vantage-ground of the farthest north (Lockwood Island) to the desolate cape which, until surpassed in coming ages, may well bear the grand name of Washington.

CHAPTER XXV.

LOCKWOOD ISLAND AND RETURN.

OF his plans, at Lockwood Island, Lieutenant Lockwood says: "The rations being almost exhausted, I decided to make this cape my *farthest*, and to devote the little time we could stay to determining accurately my position, if the weather would allow, which seemed doubtful. . . . We built a large, conspicuous cairn, about six feet high and the same in width at the base, on the lower of two benches. It is about thirty feet above the level of the ice-foot, and about the same number of yards distant from it, and just this side of a picturesque mass of rocks which crowns the cliffs. In the cairn I afterward deposited a record of my journey to date, and also the thermometer (minimum registering). I regret that the instrument only reads to $-65°-53°.9$. C., it was set at $+14°-10°$ C. After repitching the tent Sergeant Brainard and I returned to the cairn, and collected in that vicinity specimens of the rocks and vegetation of the country, the sergeant making almost all the collection."

"We ascended without difficulty to a small *fringe* of rocks, which seemed from below to form the top, but found it only a kind of terrace of the main elevation which lay before us. The ascent, at first very gradual, became steeper as we went up, but we had no difficulty, as for some distance below the summit the surface is covered with small stones, as uniform in size, position, etc., as those of a macadamized road. Reached the top at 3.45 P.M. and unfurled the American flag (Mrs. Greely's) to the breeze in latitude 83° 24′ N.; longitude 40° 46′ W.

"The summit is a small plateau, narrow, but extending back to the south to broken, snow-covered heights. It commanded a very extended view in every direction. The barometer, being out of order, was not brought along, so I did not get the altitude.

"To the northeast (about) projected a rocky headland (Cape Kane) to the north, and at its foot I could perceive another low shore projecting out and forming a cape some distance beyond, Cape Washington, doubtless separated from the first by a fiord (Hunt Fiord), as the first was from the promontory on which we stood.* The fiord just to the east of Conger Inlet extended south till shut out by the mountains south of us, but it presented every appearance of connecting in that direction with the fiord last crossed (Weyprecht). The horizon beyond, on the land side, was concealed by numberless snow-covered mountains, one profile overlapping another, and all so merged together, on account of their universal covering of snow, that it was impossible to detect the topography of the region. To the north lay an unbroken expanse of ice, interrupted only by the horizon. Could see no land anywhere between the two extreme capes, Washington and Alexander Ramsay, referred to, though I looked long and carefully, as did Sergeant Brainard. Delayed on top

---

* On map facing page 325, the sketch of Lieutenant Lockwood's entitled "Next Point beyond Farthest" shows Cape Washington to the left with Cape Kane in foreground: "Farthest from the West," discloses Lockwood and Brainard Islands against a high background, the west shore of Conger Inlet.

twenty minutes; left a short record in a small tin box under a few small stones (there were no large ones)."

Sergeant Brainard's field notes contain: "Several snow-buntings seen flying around the tent. The geological and botanical specimens were limited in number—the former owing to their weight, and the latter owing to scarcity of vegetation and trouble in securing it. Numerous traces of foxes, lemmings, hare, and ptarmigan at this point.

"The lately fallen snow has entirely disappeared, except oc-

Cape Alexander Ramsay.
[*From sketch by Lieutenant Lockwood.*]

casional drifts in ravines, leaving only the bare rocks and scanty stunted vegetation, which render the aspect a dreary and desolate one. The peculiar formation of the country, as well as the rocks, etc., presents certain characteristics, which give rise to the conjecture that in remote ages volcanic action was not unknown to these regions. To extend our rations sixteen hours between meals is at present our established rule.

"We now ascended the summit of the cape (Lockwood Island),

which was from two thousand six hundred to three thousand feet elevation above the sea, and displayed our flags. About eight miles to the northeast a point of land (Cape Kane) is visible, similar to the one on which we are now standing, with an intervening fiord (Conger) which probably communicates with the one to the westward, making this an island. Another point (Cape Washington), about fifteen miles away, projects farther to the north than the intermediate one. In the distance, looking past these points, is a low blue line stretching away to the northward. Owing to haze in that direction it could not with safety be pronounced land, although at first it gave one that impression. The interior was a confused mass of snow-capped peaks, and the country much broken by entering fiords. Toward the North the Polar Ocean, a vast expanse of snow and broken ice, lay before us. For sixty miles our vision extended uninterruptedly, and within it no signs of land appeared. The ice appeared to be rubble, the absence of the large palæocrystic floes being remarked on."

"As I awoke," says Lieutenant Lockwood, "a small piece of pemmican (our only remaining dog-food) was slowly but surely moving out of the tent. The phenomenon astonished me, and, rubbing my eyes, I looked more carefully, and saw Ritenbenk's head without his body, and found that his teeth, fixed in one corner of the sack, were the motive power. His eyes were fixed steadily on me, but head, eyes, and teeth vanished as I looked. He had burrowed a hole through the snow and had inserted his head just far enough into the tent to lay hold of a corner of the sack. The whole pack are ravenous, and eat anything and everything, which means substantially nothing in this case."

On the evening of May 16th, Lieutenant Lockwood and party left for Conger, and in nine marches reached Cape Bryant.

Apart from snow-blindness and bad travelling, the following are the most important incidents: Records were deposited at Mary Murray Island, Capes Hoffmeyer, Mohn, Neumayer, and Britannia. At the first cape snow-buntings and fox-tracks were numerous. Weyprecht and De Long Fiords were "of immense extent and have many lateral branches. The head of the last could not be seen; a long way up is an island."

At Low Point, 83° 07' N., Lieutenant Lockwood stopped "to observe a glacier some distance inland to the eastward. This (Buys Ballot) glacier had all the appearance of a large mound-shaped hill covered with snow, with a continous wall of green

Elison Island.
[*From a sketch by Lieutenant Lockwood.*]

ice all along the side toward the sea. The wall must have been of considerable height."

Sergeant Brainard says of it: "A glacier with smooth rounded surface, not unlike an inverted saucer in shape, and with a nearly vertical face two hundred feet high. We passed it in a snow-storm, going northward. Temperature low, but a cached thermometer and broken barometer have simplified our meteorological observations." At Cape Benet two ptarmigan flew by, and many tracks of foxes and hares were observed. Stopped opposite Elison Island and made a sketch of it. Nordenskjöld Inlet "runs a long distance inward, as straight as a canal—no land visible at its head."

Brainard says: "Lieutenant Lockwood intended going around Britannia to the eastward, but short provisions and deep snow in that direction prevented." The extra runner and small cooking-lamp were left at Cape Britannia for "next year." At that point old traces of musk-oxen were seen, and geological and botanical specimens obtained. Snow-shoes were put on on leaving that camp, and Lieutenant Lockwood says: "Regrets at leaving them behind haunted me every day while travelling north. Nothwithstanding it was my first attempt, the relief was wonderful. We wore them almost continuously afterward, and had no difficulty in keeping ahead of the dogs to encourage them." Brainard also says: "Snow-shoes found to be very advantageous. Unfortunately we have only two pairs of them. Christiansen frequently breaks through the crust to his hips and is dragged out by upstanders and dogs. . . . Used surface ice (fifteen miles northeast of Cape May) for cooking purposes, it being entirely free from saline matter. Owing to scarcity of fuel we gnaw our frozen cakes of lime-juice when thirsty. Crossed tide-crack to-day: it is now frozen so thick it cannot be broken with a tent-pole. Saw a remarkable parhelion, five bright mock suns with prismatic colors, and a purple bar uniting four of them." North of St. George's Fiord many tracks of foxes going both north and south were met with.

Victoria Inlet, sketched from Britannia, was seen, in passing, to be a broad deep fiord, with no visible head, which presented a magnificent aspect, with the high cliffs of Nares Land to the east.

The last camp before reaching Cape Bryant, Brainard's notes say: "In their mad rush to secure their breakfast the dogs nearly upset the tent. Their wolfish propensities were aroused, and neither blows nor Eskimo imprecations were of avail until food was thrown them."

At Cape Bryant Lieutenant Lockwood attempted to obtain tidal readings in a crack one-quarter of a mile from shore, in water from one hundred and three to one hundred and fourteen feet deep, but finally abandoned the attempt as fruitless. Sergeant Brainard's journal says: "Crustaceans were obtained from the bottom, adhering to the stone. The rock when drawn to the surface did not appear to have been in contact with gravel or mud. The strong movement of the line to the eastward would seem to indicate a current in that direction. Our dogs are evidently preparing for war. They tore open the ammunition-bag, bit several metallic shot-gun cartridges through and spoiled a dozen. I killed two snow-buntings for specimens."

At Cape Bryant Lieutenant Lockwood cached for "next year's work:" Pemmican, 98 lbs.; bacon, 7 lbs.; hard bread, 47 lbs.; alcohol, 18½ lbs.; dried beans, 18½ lbs.; chocolate, 4 lbs.; tea, 1¾ lbs.; stearine, about 15 lbs.; snow-knife, medicines, and fifteen shot-gun cartridges.

The distance from Cape Bryant to Polaris Boat Camp was passed over in six marches. Sergeant Brainard discovered Lieutenant Beaumont's cache at Bryant. The pemmican, spirits of wine, and tent were missing, probably covered with snow; but an Enfield rifle, cartridges, and a few articles of underwear and sledging-gear were found. Near it Lieutenant Lockwood shot a ptarmigan "on a floeberg, quite remarkable for its size and the regularity of its shape. It was thirty feet high by fifty long and broad, square in form, with undulating surface to its snow-covered top. *Salt* icicles hung from its south side. The ice composing it was very homogeneous. How such a mass could be pushed up until it touched the ice-foot is a mystery." Near Cape Stanton he says: "The ice to the north seemed very rough; no extensive floes visible. . . . The changed appearance of the floebergs is a subject of daily remark. Well-known floebergs were so much dwindled down in size as to be hardly recognizable."

At Repulse Harbor they opened Lieutenant Beaumont's cairn. Sergeant Brainard well says: "Poor fellows! their history at this period, when the whole party, scurvy-stricken, were turned back by open water from their attempt to reach the Alert, is related in this record by Lieutenant Beaumont in a touching and pathetic manner."

In 1876, Lieutenant Beaumont, after a journey of successful exploration, pushed with extraordinary energy until the breakdown of his sledge-crew by scurvy on the eastern shore of Sherard Osborn Fiord, found himself compelled to turn backward with his disabled crew. After a severe and exhausting march along the North Greenland coast, during which his men sickened and weakened daily, he reached Repulse Harbor with his party in an almost helpless condition.

With a laudable desire that his work should live after him, Lieutenant Beaumont left at Repulse Harbor a record of his successful geographical explorations, and further says: "Out of seven men forming the whole party, two, William Jenkins and Charles Paul, are absolutely helpless, having to be dressed and carried to and from the sledge. Another, Peter Craig, is just able to walk very slowly. Wilson Dobing is gradually approaching the stage when he will no longer be able to pull, and Frank Jones, though he has unmistakable signs of the same disease, has not become worse until the last few days. Severe work made the stiffness a little more felt; the two last, together with Alexander Gray and Lieutenant Beaumont (who, as yet, is well in health), are the four working hands upon whom the burden of the work falls entirely. Both Dobing and Jones are working with great spirit and determination; Craig has shown much courage in holding out so long, and all have done their best."

Uncertain as to the best course to follow in his desperate strait, Lieutenant Beaumont boldly decided to cross Robeson Channel to the Alert, where relief was certain, but, in doubt as to the possibility of making the trip, he wrote:

"I, Lewis A. Beaumont, who wrote the preceding record, having weighed over very carefully the whole matter, firmly believe that, to the best of my belief and knowledge, I have taken the right course and hopefully trust, with God's help, to carry it out.

"It is my intention, immediately on reaching the Alert, to procure assistance for those at Polaris Bay (believing that they are too few to manage the twenty-foot ice-boat), either from that ship or the Discovery."

Rotten ice and open pools drove him back, but he did not despair and turned his face southward, adding:

"We have been out on the ice, and, after having successfully passed the shore hummocks and the first floe, we came to open water and last year's ice decaying fast. Though we could have got round it, I did not feel justified in running so great a risk as it would be to arrive on the other side eight days later with three helpless men and more open water; so, having no choice left, we are starting for Polaris Bay immediately."

Still later, when affairs were yet worse, he wrote:

"REPULSE HARBOR DEPOT, June 13, 1876.

"Three of us have returned from the camp, half mile south, to fetch the remainder of the provisions. Dobing has failed altogether this morning.

"Jones is much worse, and cannot last more than two or three days.

Repulse R. Dep't June 13th 1876

3 of us have returned from the Camp of the ½ mile south to fetch the remainder of the provisions – During has failed altogether this morning. Jones is much worse and cents last more than two or 3 days. Craig is nearly helpless; therefore we cannot hope to reach Petaria Bay without assistance. 2 men cannot do it – So we will go as far as we can & live as long as we can. God help us

LH Beaumont

"Craig is nearly helpless; therefore we cannot hope to reach Polaris Bay without assistance. Two men cannot do it, so we will go as far as we can and live as long as we can. God help us.

"L. A. BEAUMONT."

This brilliant record of British courage, discipline, devotion to duty, and endurance must ever affect deeply all who may read its full details. To the men of the Lady Franklin Bay Expedition, who justly appreciated the terrible contingencies of the situation, and who dared similar dangers, this story, as told by the gallant Beaumont, was full of deep and thrilling interest.

The trip from Repulse Harbor through Gap Valley was made in a little over eleven hours. A wonderful snow-grotto was found in Gap Valley, being, says Brainard, "about a hundred yards long with an entrance ten feet in diameter. It was supported by small columns, and the vaulted roof was covered with fine, feathery frost-work, more beautiful than any which had ever before charmed my eyes." Near here he "found several rocks containing fossils."

Sergeants Lynn, Ralston, and Elison were found well at Polaris Boat Camp. They had reached that place in six marches from Cape Bryant, travelling as rapidly with their light sledge as Lieutenant Lockwood had done. Frederik, Jewell, and Salor had returned to Fort Conger. The party at Boat Camp had experienced a succession of violent gales which made life wretched and uncomfortable. The only exciting event had been the visit of two bears, May 17th, which came from Newman Bay and passed southward from Cape Sumner while the party were asleep. A few ptarmigan and a fox were the only other signs of animal life during the twenty-five days' monotonous stay.

LIEUT. LOCKWOOD, BRAINARD, AND CHRISTIANSEN RETURNING FROM 83° 24′ N.
(*From a photograph.*)

Lieutenant Lockwood left there four hundred pounds of rations and some other supplies for the next year's work, and in fourteen hours' travel crossed Robeson Channel to Cape Beechy in face of a violent snow-storm. It was quite remarkable that, travelling on this day in which no sun was seen, the party were badly affected with snow-blindness through not using goggles. Two of them had to be led into Conger, where the entire party arrived June 1st, after an absence of sixty days. Apart from snow-blindness they were all strong, healthy, and sound.

This sledge-trip must stand as one of the greatest in Arctic history, considering not only the high latitude and the low mean temperature in which it was made, but also the length of the journey and the results flowing therefrom. The mean temperature for the forty-three days' outward travel was below zero Fahrenheit—one of the lowest means on record for an extended trip. The party were absent sixty days, and experienced no serious frost-bites, although subjected frequently to temperatures from $-31°$ ($-35°$ C.) to $-49°$ ($-45°$ C.). During that time Lieutenant Lockwood made with the dog-sledge forty-six marches, and travelled (one thousand and seventy statute miles) nine hundred and twenty-eight geographical miles—an average of over twenty geographical miles to a march. His outward journey of two hundred and seventy-six miles entailed travel of four hundred and seventy miles, owing to the necessity of doubling up and assisting the man-sledges. The outward rate of travel was 2.1 miles, and inward 2.3 miles per hour.

His discoveries extended to a point ninety-five miles along the north Greenland coast beyond the farthest ever seen by his predecessors, to which should be added about thirty miles of coast-line between Capes May and Britannia not visible to Lieutenant Beaumont. The results of his journey, then, consist not in the mere honor of displaying the Stars and Stripes four miles nearer the geographical Pole than the flag of any other nation, but in adding one hundred and twenty-five miles of coast (not including several hundred miles of inland fiords) to Greenland, and in extending the main-land, over a degree of latitude, from Cape May northward to Cape Washington.

The domain added to Physical Geography may thus be summarily described: From Cape Bryant to Cape Washington the coast-line is a series of high, rocky, and precipitous promontories, probably the north projection of islands in many cases, with intervening inlets. This afforded but little coast-journeying, and necessitated the constant crossing of fiords with accompanying bad travel.

The inlets, with "no visible land at the head of several of them, were very much like immense canals, and gave the whole coast the appearance of Greenland between Upernavik and Disco." One inlet from the summit of Britannia Island appeared to run nearly parallel to the coast, making "islands of all the promontories to the north." As far as seen "the interior seemed very high and was . . . a maze of mountain-peaks, with universal covering of snow, merging into and overlapping one another. . . . From Lockwood Island I saw mountains to the east, perhaps twenty or thirty miles distant, and a high mountainous country doubtless exists all along this coast for some distance to the south, the shore-lines of the fiords invariably being at the base of steep cliffs and mountains."

The tide-crack, as it was called, is a very remarkable division between the somewhat hummocky floes of the Polar Ocean and the level ice of the inlets, varying from a few feet to several hundred yards in width. It was seen from near Cape May to Lockwood Island—and later off Cape Bryant—and stretched from headland to headland in gentle curves. Near

Cape Frederick moving ice was detected. I agree with Lieutenant Lockwood that it was caused by "the outside polar pack having constantly more or less motion." This cause seems most probable, as the drift of the Tegetthoff, Dijmphna, and Jeannette in different parts of the Polar Basin, and Nordenskjöld's experiences at Mossell Bay show beyond a doubt that open water-spaces exist in the Polar Ocean, and its main ice moves the entire winter. The drift of Dr. Pavy near Cape Joseph Henry, and of Brainard at Black Horn Cliffs, both in April and in different years, prove the uncertain unification of the polar pack, even in early spring when floe-ice is most solid.

The existence of last-year's ice to the northward of Cape Britannia indicates that in unusually favorable years there is a possibility of a well-found ship pushing along the northwestern coast of Greenland, as Maclure did along Banks Land; probably, too, to meet the same fate as the Investigator in Mercy Bay.

The age of the tide at Conger and the exceptional depth of the sea north of Cape May (one hundred and thirty-seven fathoms and no bottom) augur to my mind the inconsiderable extension of Greenland to the northward (say to the eighty-fifth parallel) and the presence there of a deep sea as compared with the shallow basin north of Grinnell Land. Indeed, I doubt not there is a very considerable land to the north of the Parry Islands, which, entirely ice-clad, throws off to the east the immense palæocrystic floes and floebergs which crowd down on Grinnell Land and thence southwestward to Banks Land. In a limited way the same conditions prevail near the North as toward the South Pole. This opinion indicates my belief that Carpenter has advanced the correct theory as to the formation of this ice, and that Moss was right in believing the salt in it to be by infiltration and efflorescence.

Lieutenant Lockwood's success might have been greater if

the dogs, purchased in Greenland, had been exempt from disease. Other causes militated against him, for which I was responsible. Had I not been tempted to send a party north of Cape Joseph Henry, when the mere honor of the Farthest North seemed within our grasp, the North Greenland expedition would have been pushed at least fifty miles beyond Cape Washington. Had Lieutenant Lockwood carried snow-shoes beyond Britannia, he would undoubtedly have reached Cape Washington. If I had sent northward Hudson Bay sledges, steel shod, a few miles at least would have been added to this unprecedented latitude. With our wits sharpened by our first year's experience, and with our energies turned in one direction Lieutenant Lockwood and I concurred in thinking that he could proceed a hundred miles beyond Lockwood Island. His extraordinary journey to Black Horn Cliffs, when he was turned back by open water, in 1883, proves that this opinion had sound premises. In 1882 Lieutenant Lockwood's opinions were in entire accord with my own, and our mistakes, which only add to his credit for this successful work, are touched on only for the benefit of posterity and our successors in Polar exploration.

This journey has been erroneously thought by some to have opened up again the Smith Sound Route. Such is not the case, for no nation will willingly spend $500,000 for a *possible* chance of planting their national ensign a hundred miles northeastward of Cape Washington. I say possible chance, for on the coincidence of favorable ice-navigation, solidity of the pack, perfect outfitting of a sledge-party, good judgment, and indomitable energy of leader and men depends the hope of success of any party who strive to beat, on the Greenland coast, the latitude of Lockwood and Brainard.

CHAPTER XXVI.

SPRINGTIME AND SUMMER.

OUR winter had been one of unprecedented severity—the mean temperature for the one hundred and thirty-one days without the sun being $-32.3°$ ($-35.7°$ C.). Spring opened, however, much warmer, and its March mean of $-29.9°$ ($-34.4°$ C.) was particularly mild.

Apart from the sledge journeys, the following items extracted from my journal cover the most important incidents of our spring life in 1882:

"March 2d.—Sergeant Rice and party went to Watercourse Bay for the two musk cattle cached last autumn. They found only the bones hanging to the tripod, the meat having been picked by cunning foxes through the snow-drifts forming by it.

"I have been running for exercise lately, and, from two hundred and fifty yards the first day, now run three thousand yards without stopping. Shortness of breath and stiffness were at first experienced, but have now passed away. This experience varies from the facts noted by Nares, where violent exercise, even with healthy men, was followed by blood-spitting."

"7th.—Lieutenant Kislingbury, hunting to-day, wounded a hare through the hind leg. It hopped steadily away, and was followed two miles before he got a shot, when a ball was put through the stomach. In two miles' further chase it lost a cupful of entrails. A third ball broke both fore-paws, when the animal, jumping to reach a high rock, fell over a cliff for nearly two hundred feet. When picked up it still showed signs of life. Such tenacity of life on the part of so timid and weak an animal was surprising."

"March 8th.—I learned to-day that one of the officers had lately neglected to take his lime-juice regularly. On questioning him he said he thought its beneficial effect as to scurvy would be destroyed if it was persistently taken. I felt obliged to insist on the same rule in this matter for officers as men,— no exemption except for medical causes."

"10th.—The black bulb, in the sun, recorded to-day, for the first time, 11.8° (−11.2° C.)."

"23d.—Our first lemming was caught to-day. The ends of its black hairs were pure white, giving it a peculiar pepper-and-salt appearance."

"25th.—To-day, with its mean temperature of −40.5° (−40.3° C.), is the coldest of the month. The minimum was −46.8° (−43.8° C.)."

"26th.—Private Bender was re-enlisted to-day, his term of service having expired yesterday."

"29th.—The barometer touched 28.988, the lowest point reached since our arrival. The day is, however, clear and calm."

"April 3d.—Sergeant Rice saw icicles pendent upon a floe and from the cliffs with southern exposure. The highest temperature has been −7° (−21.7° C.) He brought in a fox, probably poisoned."

"8th.—The sun is now above the horizon at midnight. To-day the temperature rose at 5 P.M. to 1.2° (−17.1° C.) after having been below zero (−17.8° C.) for one hundred and sixty consecutive days. Private Henry saw a wolf at Depot "B," April 6th, and two followed Connell and him to Distant Cape yesterday."

"April 11th.—The snow on the black roof melted freely under the influence of the sun. Lieutenant Kislingbury saw an eagle, and its scream was heard by Sergeant Gardiner." This was probably the same eagle which was seen by Lieutenant Lockwood and Eskimo Frederik in St. Patrick Bay, April 4th.

"13th.—Long killed a ptarmigan near the coal-mine."

"14th.—Gardiner heard a snow-bird, the first of the season."

"16th.—Cross, hunting to-day, saw a fox."

"22d.—The maximum at The Bellows since October 12th has been 15° ($-9.4°$ C.), against 13.9° ($-10.1°$ C.) at Conger."

"29th.—Two snowy owls were seen to-day by Lieutenant Kislingbury."

"May 3d.—An incident, which caused much amusement, occurred while I was in the field, in which Lieutenant Kislingbury played a part. One of the men had suffered terribly for nearly a week with toothache, which permitted him neither to eat nor sleep. Lieutenant Kislingbury was the only officer at the station, and the man begged him to pull his tooth, which the Lieutenant consented to do, with the understanding that the afflicted man should himself adjust the forceps. This done, Lieutenant K., by main strength pulled the tooth, fortunately without breaking the man's jaw. To their consternation, however, the tooth pulled was perfectly sound, while the aching one still remained. The men have suffered considerably from toothache during the past year." It is especially important that all recruits for Arctic service should have perfect teeth.

"5th.—Schneider, with his team of seven puppies only five months old, made their first long trip at this time. They made a round trip of over fifty miles in twenty hours, hauling from forty to sixty pounds per dog. They are now considered fit for light field work." These dogs, raised with so much care and trouble, proved of great value in subsequent explorations.

On May 14th, in accordance with Long's request, I sent him and Whisler to visit the English depôt in Archer Fiord. Long had been debarred from extended trips, owing to the uncertain

Long and Whisler returning from Archer Fiord, May, 1882.
[*From a photograph.*]

state of his health, and by the advice of the doctor. They took a Hudson Bay sledge and snow-shoes, and were absent but four days and two hours, during which time they travelled about sixty-five miles. Long travelled some distance farther than Whisler and visited Hillock Depôt where the rations left by Lieutenant Archer, R.N., were found in good order, except the bread which was mouldy.

On May 9th Dr. Pavy was ordered to proceed with dog-team the following day to Repulse Harbor, to communicate with Lieutenant Lockwood's party, but Jewell, Salor, and Frederick returned to the station that day bringing a report of Lieutenant Lockwood's movements. The order was consequently amended and Dr. Pavy visited instead Sergeant Lynn's party at Polaris Boat Camp, taking them some delicacies from the station. He returned on the 16th, coming in accordance with his orders by way of Thank God Harbor, from which he brought three cans of pemmican, a grindstone, and several books.

May 16th, seal-holes were observed near Distant Cape, and two days later a seal (*Phoca barbata*) was seen. Five of this species were subsequently killed during the month—four by Jens and one by Connell. The largest was eight feet two inches long and weighed four hundred pounds gross. One of the seals had evidently been injured by a bear, as he was badly scratched and one of his flippers had been bitten off. The seals were flayed by Jens and the skins kept for specimens, but the meat, except the liver and other choice bits, was fed to the dogs.

Seal-hunting was a matter of pride and interest to Jens, and he pursued it as long as the condition of the ice would permit. He used a blind, a large piece of white cloth, which was mounted on a miniature sled so as to cover it entirely from view. The hunter crawling cautiously on the ice, pushes the sled before him, watching the seal through a small hole in the cloth. A support on the sled affords a rest for his rifle when the hunter is sufficiently near to be certain of killing the seal.

"May 15th.—I saw to-day a patch of moss quite green; temperature $16°$ ($-8.9°$ C.)."

"May 19th.—I visited the coal-mine to-day, going overland. In the deep, soft snow were many tracks of foxes and lemmings. In certain places a fox had been digging for lemmings, there being frequently holes a foot deep. In one case the fox had dug down vertically eighteen inches, and then tunnelled after the lemming for a long distance. I obtained from the slate above the coal about fifty fine specimens of fossils. The work was too dangerous to be long pursued, as huge masses on the overhanging cliffs had been detached by this melting weather, and were ready to separate and fall. Several fell while I was present. The coal seam is two hundred yards long and extends eight feet above the level and an unknown distance below the surface of the creek which flows by it in summer. It seems probable that the stream has worn its way through the friable slate and soft coal, leaving the present narrow deep cañon with walls of slate and coal. Near by the main seam is another of less extent. An immense quantity of coal could be easily mined. I saw what I took to be an Iceland gull (*Larus leucopterus*). I at first thought it the Burgomaster, but it was so small and the pale blue mantle was so marked that I consider its identity certain. I saw a trickling stream to-day, from which possibly two gallons an hour were flowing. Several such have been seen within the past few days in very favorable localities. Up to this time the maximum temperature has been only 23.8° (−4.6° C). Connell caught a lemming to-day.

"May 21st.—An Iceland gull, evidently a straggler, was seen to-day; probably the same bird observed by me on the 19th.

"May 25th.—Lieutenant Kislingbury brought in an owl's egg, which was somewhat larger than, though closely resembling, the white egg of a hen. Sergeant Israel found it very palatable. The male bird showed signs of fight when the egg was taken, while the female looked on from about a hundred yards. The first owl observed was on April 29th; since then one or more have been frequently seen. The nest is a mere hole hollowed out on the summit of a commanding knoll, and furnished with a few scattered feathers, grass, etc.

"Long planted half of the garden to-day." Lettuce, cabbage,

Coal Seam showing above Watercourse Creek.
[*From a Photograph.*]

radishes, etc., were experimented with unsuccessfully, owing, I think, to the alkalies in the soil.

On May 25th I sent Sergeant Israel, Connell and Jens with a dog-team to ascertain whether Lake Hazen was practicable by an overland route through The Bellows.

The following is a summary of Sergeant Israel's report:

Seven hours' march brought them to the depôt at head of Basil Norris Bay. Traces of game were seen, and several musk-oxen travelling westward on Sun Peninsula.

Camp No. 2 was made after five and a half hours' work, about a mile and a half southeast of Devil's Head, in a latitude which was later determined to be 81° 46' N. The valley at first was almost entirely bare of snow, but later they were obliged to put on snow-shoes. "At this camp," says Israel, "we found a considerable quantity of coal, some wood, and numerous pieces of a substance resembling resin. The valley had recently been crossed by a herd of musk-oxen. . . . Connell found a musk-ox skull, apparently of great age."

Camp No. 3 was made just north of a projecting spur from the west, which nearly crossed the valley. Longitude, by observation, 6' 10.4" W. of Conger (in time); latitude, 81° 47' N.; magnetic declination, 102° 10' W. From an adjacent hill fourteen musk-oxen were seen, of which "Connell shot two cows and a yearling. After driving off the rest of the herd we skinned these." Two hours' travel on May 28th brought them to a place where the valley narrowed rapidly, with steep mountains to the west. Connell was sent up a mountain, but saw only an occasional peak to the west, owing to cloudy weather. He ascended fourteen hundred feet above the valley, which was at that point about three hundred and twenty feet above the sea. Israel "proceeded up the valley about three miles. The valley at this point splits into two narrow ravines, one extending up a mountain-side for a mile, and the other terminating in the same manner after extending to the north about three miles. As there is no turn in either of these passes there can be no doubt that the valley ends here instead of communicating with another running in from the east as I at first thought."

Returning to the point where Connell had ascended the mountain the latitude (by observation) was determined to be 81° 54' N., longitude (D. R.) 7' 44.4" W. of Conger (in time). About three miles north of Devil's Head the valley was measured with the following results: "Width, 4,280 feet; height of cliffs, west, 1,999 feet; east, 825 feet." In returning, lack of snow forced them to carry load and sledge for considerable distances. The upper portion of the ravines, which were said by Sergeant Israel to be filled with snow, must have been filled with glaciers, for the amount of water seen later in Bellows River was by far too great to have come from any snow in the valley. The musk-oxen killed by Connell were later brought to the station by Sergeant Rice, who was sent with Schneider and Jens into The Bellows.

Decoration Day at Conger, 1882.
[*From a Photograph.*]

"May 28th.—The temperature at 9 A.M. reached 32.5° (0.3° C.) having been continuously below the freezing-point for nine months less two days."

"May 30th.—It being Decoration Day, we observed it as a general holiday. Happily we have no graves of our own but on this occasion, Frederick and Long were inspired with the thoughtful idea of decorating the head-boards of the dead of the British Arctic Expedition, set up at this place in 1876. In default of regular flowers they made an elaborate artificial bouquet, which, with our camp colors, were tastefully draped over the head-boards." These marks of appreciation and honor to our dead predecessors must be considered of greater value thus coming from the rank and file of the expedition than if the initiative had been taken by the officers.

June was opened by the safe return of Lieutenant Lockwood and his party, who were not long contented to remain at the station. On June 10th Lockwood, Brainard, and Frederik left under orders for a trip down Archer Fiord and returned on the 15th. In addition to six hundred and fifty pounds of dressed meat from three musk-oxen killed by them, they brought in the English Hillock Depôt of eighty-four rations, the bread being bad. It was evident that the rations left in bags by Lieutenant Archer, R.N., had been consumed by animals. Lieutenant Lockwood was turned back from Hillock Depot by the immense quantity of water covering the floe in Archer Fiord.

Of Eskimo relics Sergeant Brainard says: "I found at the head of Sun Bay the sites of fifteen Eskimo summer tents, evidently occupied during their hunting season. Near the head of Basil Norris Bay I discovered fifteen other circles slightly larger than the first. I picked up numerous bone and a few wood relics of these hardy people, but nothing metallic was seen. Those I collected were worked, drilled, and bored, but large numbers of split bones, probably of the seal and musk-ox, were strewn around."

My journal says of these relics: "The most important is of

worked porous bone, six and one-half inches wide, one and one-half inch thick, and eighteen and one-half inches long. Evidently it is a part of a native sledge and of the cellular bone of the whale, as described by Kane. One side was covered with lichens (of which I recognized at once seven separate kinds), and was so affected by exposure as to be almost unrecognizable as bone. The reverse side, however, showed plainly the marks of the knife. No less than forty-two circular holes had been bored through or into (so as to connect with other holes) this piece. On both sides appeared mortices into which dowels, extending from this piece to others, could be inserted. In addition, one end was thinned down so that it would overlap a second similar piece without increasing the thickness. Two bones forming a peculiar harpoon were found, which are so fastened together that when used the head remains in the seal, while the shoulder, as it may be called, is by a pull separated from it, forming with the seal-thong (by which it remains connected with the head) a hinge by which the animal can be towed without pulling out the lance. It is like the harpoon of the Danish Eskimo. There are several other parts of hunting-gear. A dog-trace fastening (whale's tooth probably) appears much fresher and is in far better condition than any other article discovered. One very small article is of walrus ivory. Sergeant Brainard says that fully a ton of bones could be gathered from one of the encampments. There was only one place resembling a house, about six feet square, of large flat stones, the roof of which had fallen in."

Various other signs of the presence of Eskimo encampments were noted in the vicinity of Discovery Harbor. On June 5th Connell found the bone handle of a skinning-knife at the site of what was thought to be a lookout on a high cliff above Dutch Island. I later visited the place, and a careful search resulted in the discovery of a toggle for dog-traces made of walrus ivory, a spear-point of narwhal's horn about nine inches long, many bones of hare and lemming, and one which might have been human, though the doctor could not state positively, as it seemed too porous. In addition, a piece of pine (?) wood carefully worked, two inches long, an inch wide, and an eighth of an inch in thickness. In one end and one side were two small wooden pins, which had evidently been used in fastening other pieces to it. On June 15th, I found on a low plateau near Fort Conger, south of Cascade Ravine an ancient Eskimo cache. June 20th, Connell dug up, near Proteus Point, part of a stone lamp and various articles of hunting-gear made from walrus ivory. One of the most interesting articles we discovered was a piece of birch bark admirably preserved.

June 21st, I discovered an Eskimo cache on the plateau near the Sugar Loaf, and two days later Private Henry found at Distant Cape, about two hundred feet above the sea, part of a bone shoe of a sledge-runner on which were six or seven different kinds of lichen. July 2d, Sergeant Brainard found, near Dutch Island, the site of an Eskimo summer encampment, where he unearthed several parts of hunting implements made of the bone of the whale, and a spear-point of a narwhal's horn. A few days later he picked up the bone handle of a knife, another spear-point, and the shoe of a sledge-runner.

Though no permanent huts were to be found near Conger, yet the many traces indicate that for years the Eskimo must have frequented the shores of Discovery Bay, and later discoveries proved their winter residence in the interior.

On June 10th Connell killed two musk-oxen near the station, and this led to the discovery of seven others, who, strange to say, were gathered on the very summit of Sugar Loaf, about eighteen hundred feet above the sea. A party sent out killed them all and captured alive four young calves, which were found with them. The calves were brought in by the men on their heads from the top of the mountain, at which point Dr. Pavy picked up a fossil shell. Every effort was made to raise the calves, which soon became tame and tractable. They ate milk, corn-meal, and almost any food that was given them. They grew finely, except one whose throat was torn open by the dogs. In a short time they became very fond of Long and Frederick, who generally cared for them, and would follow them around and put their noses into the men's pockets for food. I

Musk Calves at Conger, Four Months Old.
[*From a Photograph.*]

had intended to send them to the United States by the visiting vessel of 1882. When the long nights came it was impracticable to give them exercise, and probably from this cause, despite our care, they died.

On June 19th I succeeded in having the launch moved from her winter bed on the ice-foot into the tidal crack.

One of the most surprising peculiarities of Grinnell Land was the unusually early date on which flowers came into blossom.

June 1st the purple saxifrage (*Saxifraga oppositifolia*) was in bloom, and three days later the catkins of the willow (*Salix arctica*), followed the next day by the sorrel (*Oxyria reniformis*). On the eleventh *Cochlearia fenestrata* blossomed, and ten days later the Arctic poppy (*Papaver nudicaule*). On the latter date I discovered on the summit of the Sugar Loaf reindeer moss (*Cladonia rangiferina*), one of the few places in which it was found growing near Fort Conger. That 1882 was not an exceptionally early year was shown by 1883, when, giving personal attention to the subject I discovered six varieties in bloom by June 6th. At Thank God Harbor, in 1872, saxifrage was in bloom by June 3d.

The following are the earliest flowers found in bloom by Nordenskjöld: Pitlekaj, 67° 05′ N., 187° W., *Cochlearia fenestrata*, June 23, 1879; Treurenberg Bay, Spitzbergen, 79° 57′ N., *Saxifraga oppositifolia*, June 22, 1861, and the same plant at Wahlenburg Bay, Northeast Land, 79° 46′ N., June 15, 1873. Kumlein reports that in early July, 1878, at Cumberland Sound, about 67° N., only four plants were in blossom.

Of the birds of Grinnell Land, the rock ptarmigan (*Lagopus rupestris*) is a winter denizen. The owl (*Nyctea scandiaca*) and snow bunting (*Plectrophanes nivalis*) had been with us since April, while a stray eagle (*Haliætus albicilla*) and Iceland gull (*Larus leucopterus*) had also been observed.

On June 3d the ravines commenced discharging generally into the bay, and on the same day the geese (*Bernicla brenta*) arrived, accompanied by one of the robber gulls, the long-tailed skua (*Stercorarius longicaudatus*). In the order named appeared later the burgomaster (*Larus glaucus*), dovekie (*Uria grylle*), knot (*Tringa canutus*), king duck (*Somateria spectabilis*), long-tailed duck (*Harelda glacialis*), eider duck (*Somateria mollissima*), tern (*Sterna macrura*), and turnstone (*Strepsilas interpres*).

It was remarkable how wild and wary were the members of

the feathered tribe which came to us in summer. Only by great caution and patience could our hunters get within gunshot, and then many specimens were lost by falling in the sea where strong currents and heavy ice prevented their recovery.

In the Appendices will be found papers treating more fully than is convenient here the subjects of botany and ornithology.

CHAPTER XXVII.

SUMMER EXPLORATIONS.

[LIEUTENANT GREELY'S JOURNEY.]

LATE in June sledging over the sea-floe was ended, and nothing but summer routine was possible in the vicinity of the station.

I decided to personally renew the explorations of the interior of Grinnell Land. With this view Private Biederbick was sent to the depot at Basil Norris Bay, with orders to penetrate as far into Black Rock Vale as it was possible for him to do, and return in a single march. He travelled some sixteen miles up the valley discovering a lake of considerable size, temporarily named Lake Heintzelman, which discharges into the sea through a river of the valley. He reported travel to be practicable for some distance by wagon, the manner in which I contemplated pursuing this work.

Later Sergeant Lynn with Private Bender were sent into the valley with orders to ascertain whether the northern end of Lake Hazen could be reached by that route. They took with them from the Basil Norris Depot a dog-tent, and light sleeping-bag, to be left a day's march outward. They were absent four days and succeeded in reaching a high hill from which four glaciers could be seen, and a lake which they believed to be Lake Hazen. They were doubtful whether a wagon could be hauled over the country successfully.

I decided, however, to make the attempt, and left Fort Conger on June 24th with Lynn, Biederbick, Salor, and Whisler. I travelled as far as the depot in Basil Norris Bay with the dog-sledge Antoinette. The harbor floe had lately been covered with much water, which left the surface of the ice sharp and pointed. The dogs' feet were badly cut owing to the forgetfulness of the driver to take sealskin boots for them. These boots are very necessary in travelling over sharp ice at any season or hard snow at very low temperatures. Considerable difficulty was experienced in reaching safely the southwestern shore of Discovery Bay, owing to the many water-holes in the main floe.

While the party were cooking dinner I obtained latitude observations, and later examined the sites of the Eskimo summer encampments, which were on a plateau about twenty feet above tide-water. There were large piles of bones mostly of the seal, which had been split evidently for the marrow. A few pieces of worked bone and wood were found, and also the slat of an ancient Eskimo sledge.

Our travelling outfit, taken from the depot, was of limited character and quantity; consisting of bread, pemmican, corned beef, tea, chocolate, sugar, milk, salt, pepper, and alcohol, and sleeping-bags. The plan of march contemplated two men hauling the fore-wheels of a light wagon, on which the main load was packed. Two others carried knapsacks containing loads of about twenty pounds, and at intervals these men changed work with those pulling the wagon.

I carried myself the scientific instruments, including telescope, prismatic compass, sextant, etc., and employed my time in examining, as fully as possible, the country over which we passed. At one low ridge, before Black Rock Valley was reached, I found by digging that the alluvial soil was composed of various strata of a fine lignite coal and of sand. The coal evidently had been brought to that point and deposited by the floods from the river in The Bellows.

Nearly three hours' work brought us to the "Knife Edge," a remarkable formation on the western side of Black Rock Vale. On the east side is a high round bluff of peculiar formation known as Bifurcation Cape, which separates The Bellows and Black Rock Vale. The river was nearly forty yards wide and

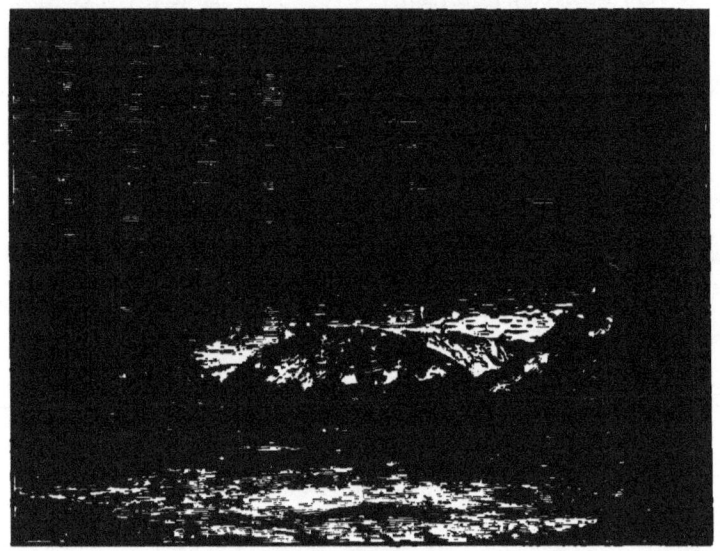

Bifurcation Cape, separating Bellows and Black Rock Valleys.
[*From a Photograph.*]

eighteen inches deep at the entrance of the latter valley. From the very entrance of Black Rock Vale we had virgin ground for exploration, untrodden by our English predecessors.

After thirteen hours' travelling from our home station we camped on the northeastern side of Lake Heintzelman, at the point where the dog-tent had been left by Sergeant Lynn.

On the shores of this lake Biederbick found a pair of reindeer antlers, and I picked up a piece of close-grained wood, apparently pine, two and a half feet long and nearly an inch in diameter. A musk-ox was seen near this point, but at too great a distance to be pursued. Indeed, hunting was quite apart from the object of the journey, as fresh meat in great quantity was yet on hand at our home station.

In a ravine near the camp were two trees, probably coniferous, partly covered by earth. One was ten feet long and sixteen inches in diameter, and originally had two branches. The second tree was six feet long and twelve inches in diameter. They were about one hundred and fifty yards distant from Lake Heintzelman, and fully twenty feet above its level. Two-thirds of both trees were imbedded in the ground, and it was only with considerable labor that they were dug out. It seemed evident from their position that they must have been brought there as drift-wood, and gradually covered up by the earth washing down from the adjacent hill-side. Their presence, at an elevation probably three hundred feet above and eight or ten miles distant from the sea, shows without much doubt that within a tolerably recent period this valley has been an arm of the sea. Up to this point, and, indeed, for a short distance beyond, marine shells on the surface of the ground were quite common. While at this camp (No. 1) several flies were noted.

During this march no snow was seen except on the adjacent mountain-tops. Lake Heintzelman was covered, except a narrow margin of water, by thick honeycombed ice. The presence of such ice in summer indicates the permanency of a lake.

After nearly twelve hours' rest we moved onward, and at noon, stopping a few moments, I obtained latitude observations in the centre of the valley. At that time a high warm wind was blowing from the interior, and the temperature was considerably above 40° (5° C.).

As the wagon showed signs of weakness and the west side of the river was less rough than that on which we were travelling, we attempted, just above Lake Heintzelman, to cross the river, but found the water too deep for safe fording. Geese, musk-oxen, and a wolf were observed on the march, none of which were we able to obtain.

Seven hours' travelling over very rough ground "dished" a wheel, and lunch was taken while repairs were being made. About this time I saw many musk-oxen, fifteen in one herd, and three in another. In the vicinity of this spot the remains of dead willow existed in sufficient quantities to enable us to cook our tea with it.

About 5.30 P.M. we again camped, after nearly eight hours' travel, during which we made about sixteen miles. The valley at that time was a mile wide with tolerably level ground on either side of the river, which flowed first to one and then to the other side of the valley. Above the main level of the valley were occasional projecting plateaus—mesa lands or benches— which were some forty to fifty feet above the level of the river, but apart from these projecting benches it was shut in by high steep cliffs, of an elevation varying from fifteen hundred to two thousand feet. In its whole extent the valley was entirely barren of snow, and in most places was covered with a comparatively luxuriant vegetation. This consisted generally of willow, saxifrages, and dryas, though where the river widened, in occasional places, grasses or sedges to a height of ten or twelve inches were frequently noticed.

The only snow visible were drifts near or on the very summits of the cliffs, which encompassed the valley. In occasional places these drifts fed inconsiderable brooks, which in course of years had worn narrow beds through the scanty soil to the rocks which underlaid it. It would have been possible to scale these cliffs only at such points as the water-courses had worn their way. My journal says: "Lake Heintzelman is about a mile and one-fourth wide at its lower, and three-fourths of a mile at its upper end, substantially filling the whole valley from cliff to cliff. The river from the lake to our present camp averages about two and a half feet in depth, and varies from twenty to forty yards in width."

Twelve hours' rest at Camp No. 2 put us in good condition. We cached one day's rations for the returning party and moved on, seeing some skuas and a wolf. A short distance farther, owing to the rough country, we were obliged to cross the river, which was done with some difficulty, as it was nearly two feet deep with a soft bottom. Shortly after two musk-oxen were seen, on the side of the river we had just left.

My field journal says: "The country now opens into a fine level valley about a mile and a half wide, covered in the main by a very considerable quantity of grass, which in its manner of growth and appearance resembles the bunch grass of our western prairies. In addition there are many young willows, saxifrages, dryas, etc. Enough dead willows can be gathered at almost any spot for the requirements of any sledge party."

A short march brought us to the junction of two streams, one of which flowed from the continuation of Black Rock Vale and the second from a valley to the left, nearly at right angles to that in which we were travelling. I decided to follow the latter valley, as it ran nearly in a western direction, and so must eventually bring us to Lake Hazen.

As travelling was bad and slow, while the party were following the main valley, I climbed a high hill, of about nine hundred feet elevation above the river, which promised a good view of the western country. Unfortunately other hills of nearly the same elevation cut off part of the prospect. I was able, however, to see a portion of the hog-backs to the northwest, which I designated as the United States Mountains, and a partly snow-covered range, somewhat to the southward of them, which I had named Garfield the preceding spring.

A fine hare, still in fur of perfect white, visited me while I was making my observations, and examined me curiously at a distance of a few yards. As I was not armed he escaped, but even had I been, I should have hesitated about killing an animal which, having such great natural timidity, had placed so much confidence in my kind intentions.

Crossing the main valley I reached the summit of the hill to the westward, which proved to be a divide of the water-sheds of the region, that to the west draining into Lake Hazen. The elevation of this divide was about 1,390 feet. From it I had a beautiful view to the westward, which showed four lakes between me and the eastern end of Lake Hazen. A glacier on the north side of Lake Hazen was also plainly visible to the naked eye, and showed up finely through the telescope. I there caught a butterfly, and saw three skuas, two bumble-bees, and many flies (of three kinds), which, my field journal says, "are not as plentiful as yesterday."

A very strong wind with high temperature, about 45° (7.2° C.), interfered somewhat with my success in obtaining a set of circum-meridian observations, as the hill was totally bare of shelter. The latitude proved to be 81° 49' N.

As I passed down the divide to the westward, other lakes came into view, making eight in all seen during that day's march. After eleven hours' travelling, on the shoulder of a hill adjacent to Lake Appleby we made Camp No. 3, June 27th.

I quote from my field notes: "Private Biederbick saw two tern, of which one was shot, and a long-tailed duck. In addition, a flock of birds from twelve to fifteen in number, resembling snipe, but unlike any other species seen by him, were observed, and also a butterfly. About a mile southwest of the divide Biederbick picked up a piece of lignite coal, which resembles that of The Bellows and of the mine in Watercourse Bay. It seems somewhat remarkable that this coal is so widely spread over the country and that we should find it on the watershed of Lake Hazen. I have observed reindeer moss in two places, of quite stunted growth, however. Private Whisler saw three long-tailed ducks and killed one, which, with the tern, flavors excellently our stew.

"I find that we are surrounded by a system of small lakes, which, draining from one into another, form a complete chain and finally discharge into Lake Hazen. The lake of highest elevation, temporarily named Rogers, drains into Lake Appleby, and that into Lake Biederbick.

"The chain of lakes discovered are permanent, as without exception they have a large central section of ice, the winter ice having melted this summer only at the edges.

"I have obtained time observations and bearings of the sun, from which the variation at this point is approximately 103.5° W. From the summit of the hill above the camp I can see part of Lake Hazen and the west end of John's Island. Quite a number of glaciers are in view, pressing through the gaps in the Garfield range, and what I take to be the higher part of Henrietta Nesmith glacier is seen in rear of the mountains.

"Later, Whisler, who had been hunting toward Lake Hazen, saw six long-tailed ducks and shot one. Lynn saw nine musk-oxen within two miles of the camp."

I decided to examine the small lakes to the eastward, but in trying to reach the main ice in Lake Appleby, so as to cross it and avoid a long detour, I broke through its edge, and wet myself to my thighs, and later sent Biederbick in my place, while drying my clothing. He returned after several hours' absence, bringing a rough drawing of the lake system as observed by him. He reported having seen about sixty long-tailed ducks, several flocks of turnstones, several king ducks, Brent geese, and a tern.

While at this camp, No. 3, we obtained but little sleep, owing to the large swarms of flies, which worried us very much. Biederbick and I slept in the dog-tent, but the great heat and the annoying flies broke our rest and made us thoroughly uncomfortable. On rising at 2 A.M. the temperature was found to be very high, 48° (8.9° C.), with a minimum of 47° (7.8° C.) since the preceding evening. We felt certain the temperature must have touched 50° (10° C.), which is a torrid heat for Grinnell Land. Dead willows were very plentiful in the vicinity of our camp, and we were able to cook entirely with them, and so reserve our small stock of alcohol.

In early morning the conditions of light were so favorable that from the hill-top, the outlines of five glaciers were plainly visible in the Garfield mountains.

At 3.30 A.M., June 28th, when we again started westward, the air was uncomfortably hot, with a temperature of 53° (11.7 C.). During this day's travel I found small pieces of lignite coal to be quite plentiful along the shores of Lake Kilbourne. In this lake also there were many small minnows from three-quarters to an inch and a half in length, several of which I caught. We crossed, between Lakes Kilbourne and Craig, a stream two hundred yards long and thirty feet wide, with an average depth of nine inches, which connected the two lakes.

Finding the distance very much increased by following the shores of the lakes, I decided to strike direct across the country, and in seven hours reached the mouth of the river by which the lake system drains into Lake Hazen. Within a half mile of Lake Hazen I picked up a large reindeer horn.

As we were preparing to cross the stream a pair of long-tailed ducks was seen in the river, and both birds were wounded by Biederbick at the first shot. The male being the worst hit could not fly, and as ammunition was scarce Biederbick waited to get them together to kill them at a single shot. The female bird would fly away a short distance and then return to the mate in the stream. Attracted by her calls a second male came and settled in the water and was fiercely attacked by the first. The birds were so carried away by anger and passion as to lose all fear of man, their natural enemy, and allowed us unnoticed to approach to the river's edge within a few yards of them. During the fight which followed between the males the three were easily killed at a shot.

The river was crossed with considerable difficulty, it being quite wide with a muddy bottom, and we were obliged to carry most of the articles across on our backs, which was only done by wetting ourselves to our thighs. As the temperature of the water was but slightly above the freezing-point, our bath in it was by no means pleasant. While crossing the river a flock of king ducks and twelve musk-cattle were seen. Our route now followed the south shore of Lake Hazen.

The wagon, in the men's vernacular, was a " man-killer," and the rough, uneven road not only wrenched the men sadly by the sudden heavy jerks and joltings, but also threatened to break the vehicle down completely. By loading the knapsacks to their utmost capacity, and through the system of caching each day rations for the return journey the load on the wagon was considerably reduced. Frequent changes from knapsack to wagon work enabled fair progress to be made.

Marching a few miles farther two islands, parallel with each other and with the south shore, were discovered in Lake Hazen, one a mile and the other about half a mile long. Opposite them I made camp No. 4, having travelled about twenty miles in ten hours.

In order to save fuel, the party scattered to collect drift-wood along the edge of the lake, which consisted chiefly of dried willows, but Corporal Salor brought in with his willows two small pieces of unworked pine wood. Sergeant Lynn, while gathering fuel, saw six musk-cattle on the northeast side of the lake, and near Camp Burgomaster—gulls, terns, geese, turnstones, a purple sand-piper, and many skuas were also observed.

During the day's march I noticed considerable reindeer-moss of somewhat stunted growth. Only very rarely had specimens been seen in the vicinity of Discovery Harbor, and even these beds near Lake Hazen were insufficient for pasturage.

The weather was so warm that all slept in the open air, disdaining our only covering—a dog-tent, into which four men could barely crowd.

On starting, at 12.30 A.M., June 28th, the temperature stood at 53° (11.7° C.), with a minimum of 46.5° (8.1° C.) since the preceding evening. While travelling along the lake I saw two ptarmigan, which were shot by Biederbick. One was in winter plumage of perfect white, but the other had slightly changed its snowy coat, being beautifully marked with delicate hues of browns and yellows which shaded into black.

Near by I discovered the former site of an old summer encampment of the Eskimos. It was situated about twenty feet above the level of Lake Hazen, and just over the brow of a low divide which separated the main lake from a slough, which had evidently in years past formed an arm of the lake itself. Searching carefully about a number of bones were found, and also pieces of unworked wood, besides a decayed sledge-slat of pine or fir. The circles indicated that four tents had been pitched at this place. The surroundings of the encampment were marked by luxuriant vegetation of grass, sorrel, poppies, and other plants. Some specimens of the sorrel in this locality must have been from eight to ten inches in height, and they grew in such quantities that we plucked them by the handful.

A short distance beyond the encampment the party were enlivened by the appearance of a young hare, which we concluded to catch, as he took refuge in a mass of rocks. After quite an exciting chase by the whole party, I succeeded in seizing him. The high temperature then appeared, by our feelings, to be about 100° (38° C.), though probably about 60° (15° C.) by the thermometer, and these extraordinary exertions caused profuse perspiration, which saturated our clothing.

A short distance above this point, while passing around the sandy shores of a bay extending inland from the lake, I found two bone shoes for the runners of a sledge. There were five pieces of worked bone (of the whale), and the two runners were complete, except a small piece, about two inches long, which was missing from the end of one. The runners were imbedded about a quarter of an inch deep in sandy loam, which had gradually been deposited around them in past years by water from the lake. As found they were about two and a half feet below the highest level of the lake, as shown by the bordering fringe of gravel and drift-wood. It appeared surprising, at first, that they had not been buried entirely by the sand. While this might augur their recent abandonment, yet the fact that they were more or less covered, on their exposed parts, with mosses and lichens would contradict that theory. It seemed probable that high winds, sweeping along the level beach, would gradually uncover articles once completely buried, especially as the light covering, when dry, drifted. The deposit of sandy loam was an extensive and level one, such as, from its appearance, had naturally formed from the action of the lake while yet under the surface of the water. The gradual subsidence of the lake in winter and the melting of the ice-foot the following summer left these articles undisturbed, while carrying away the wood.

In making noon observations at camp No. 5, which I reached some time in advance of the men, I found that my sextant case had evidently been stepped on the night before, and one of the shades broken and the instrument possibly injured. Later, on returning to the station, the injury was found to be such as did not impair the value of my observations. A poor set of latitude observations were obtained, owing to a very high gale, which had suddenly sprung up from the southwest, and also to the obscuration of the sun.

Camp No. 5 was established at the junction of Lake Hazen and Ruggles River, the place discovered by me the preceding April. The cache then left was found undisturbed.

On arriving at this camp it presented a delightful and pleasant aspect. The sky was partly covered with true cumulus clouds, quite rare in Arctic heavens; the sun marked with checkered bars of sunshine and shadow the babbling river, the large blue pool, and its noisy occupants; the temperature was high, and the gay yellow poppies and other flowers drew to them gaudy butterflies. If one but turned his back to the central ice of Lake Hazen, and the bursting glaciers from the ice-clad mountains northward of the Garfield Range, and gazed southward to the low brown hills faintly tinged with olive-green, he could well imagine himself in the roaring forties instead of eight degrees from the geographical pole. Four long-tailed ducks were noisily swimming and feeding at the junction of the river, and many turnstones, with a few skuas and terns, were flying about. The whole hills on either side were tinged with green from the fresh leaves of the young willow and an occasional bed of dryas and saxifrages. At this point, and in its immediate vicinity, a large number of butterflies were seen, of which there were apparently three different species. They were so active and distrustful, however, that I succeeded in capturing but one during the day.

Having some leisure time before the arrival of the wagon, I examined carefully the surroundings of the camp. The flora appeared to be the same as that existing in the vicinity of Discovery Harbor, with the exception of two flowers, which were different from any others I had seen. Specimens were procured and carefully arranged, but unfortunately were spoiled during my return trip by being soaked beyond recognition while fording the many streams.

It is to be regretted that I had paid but little attention to Arctic flora, and in the press of other matters neglected to make a description of these plants. Another plant, of the heath family, was found in very large quantities, one or two specimens of which were sent back safely to Conger.

I was surprised greatly in discovering, against a vertical bank facing Ruggles River, three abandoned Eskimo huts, which doubtless had been occupied in the far past as permanent abodes. These houses were built from large fine pieces of slate, which were readily obtainable from the adjoining rocks. Many pieces of this slate, as large as three feet by two feet, were lying around, the thickness of which varied from three-fourths of an inch to an inch and a half. The Eskimo had utilized the steep, precipitous bank, against which the back of the houses rested and in which the chimneys were built.

The houses were six feet wide and ten feet long, though possibly they may have been longer, as the walls most distant from the bank had fallen and partly disappeared, through being undermined by the river. The side walls of the structure were about three feet in height. Apparently the whole house had been covered with large pieces of slate, which served as a roof, for many such pieces were found in the interior space, which was partly filled by them. It is probable that the width of the houses depended on the size of the pieces of slate which could be used as a covering. No signs of a ridge-pole, or a wooden support to the roof, were to be seen. We carefully removed the flat slabs, and, digging among the dirt and moss, which was of considerable depth, found many relics and bones, which were most numerous near the chimney, or fireplace. Bones of the musk-ox, hare, and of various birds (and at least one kind of fish) were found in great abundance. Among other articles were three combs of walrus ivory, one of which had ornamental work on it, and whalebone fish-hooks (?), a bone needle (?), and pieces of whalebone, a shoe for a sledge-runner, and a number of other worked articles of bone and wood, the use of which were unknown. A selection was made from the bones, in order that it might be determined what species of animals had been killed by the Eskimo who had occupied this place. A piece of dog-skin of considerable size was also dug out, which had rotted to such an extent that it fell to pieces when handled.

The main party arrived at camp at 2 P.M., after more than thirteen hours' steady work, during which we had travelled about twenty-three miles.

A southwest wind prevailed all day, with cumulus clouds and a very high temperature, which I estimated to be 45° (7.2° C.) at 6 P.M., just after time observations had been made under disadvantageous circumstances.

At 2.45 A.M., June 29th, we started westward, with a very high temperature of 50° (10° C.). The equal altitudes, for which I had delayed so long at the camp, were not obtained, owing to cloudy weather.

During the night Private Biederbick, from one of the adjacent hills, saw a large herd of musk-oxen, fully thirty in number, besides many calves. In the morning nine others were seen on the same divide, but to the west of Ruggles River, which indicated their being different animals from those seen during the night. A number of terns and long-tailed ducks were also flying along the open water. Ruggles River, somewhat to my surprise, was but little higher than in the preceding May, being knee-deep, with a rocky bottom, at the shallowest point, where we crossed.

After crossing the stream, about fifty yards from its mouth and the same distance from Lake Hazen, on our direct route, the remains of an Eskimo habitation were discovered by Private Whisler, I think. Its entrance passage, facing to the north toward Lake Hazen, was twelve feet long and three in width. About half way between the mouth of the entrance and the main hut was an opening to the right, a circular space which was five feet in diameter. It seems probable that this might have been the storehouse, or possibly have been intended for the use of dogs in winter. The main room was seventeen feet and four inches long by nine feet in width, being in the shape of an ellipse, the major axis of which was at right angles to the entrance passage.

One peculiarity of the house was the existence of two fireplaces, one in the east and one in the south end, both of which had been built outward so as to take up no part of the space of the room. The sides of the entire habitation were low walls of sodded earth, which were lined inside by flat, thin slate, the tops of which, on an average, were elevated about two feet above the level of the interior floor. The interior next to the walls was raised above the centre, forming a ledge, or bench, which, covered with flat slabs of slate, was probably used for sleeping purposes, similarly to the wooden platforms in vogue among the Danish Eskimo.

An hour was occupied in carefully examining these remains

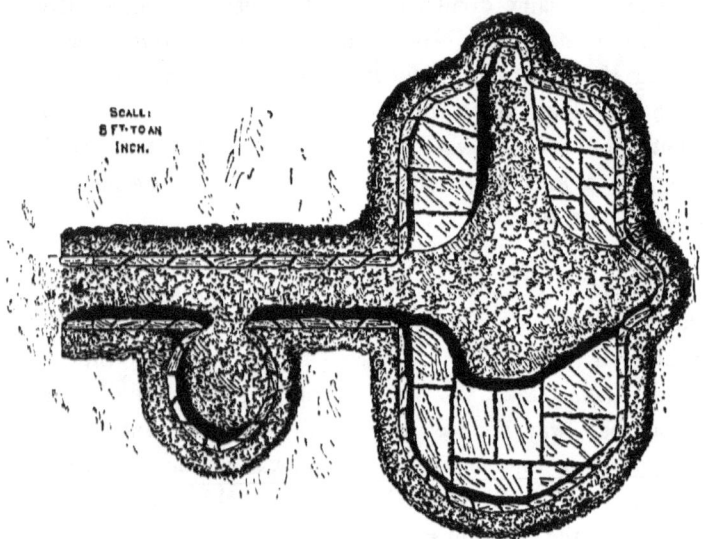

Plan of Eskimo House, Junction of Hazen Lake and Ruggles River.
[*From drawing by Lieutenant Greely, June, 1882.*]

and in digging in and about them at every place where it seemed probable that anything could be found.

Near this was the remains of what seemed to be a second habitation, of the same character, but of smaller dimensions. Near the end of the house was found what I at first took to be a grave. It was a place about four feet long by two wide, filled with moss and other vegetation of luxuriant growth, around the margin of which was a row of upright flat slate rocks which projected slightly above the surface of the vegetation. With much trouble we dug out the moss and the hard earth under it to the depth of a foot, when we found that the bottom was covered with flat slate stones. One or two of these were pulled up with considerable difficulty, but the only object which rewarded our labor was a small piece of worked bone, which had evidently been left there by accident. The conclusion to which we came after the examination, was that it had possibly been the provision cache, which was thus arranged to secure the meat from the dogs, but of this we felt by no means certain.

In the two houses and in the immediate vicinity we collected about forty pieces of wood and worked bone. Among other articles were one large and two small narwhal horns, two walrus-ivory toggles for dog-traces, such as are now used by the Greenlanders; an arrow-head, two bone handles, a skinning-knife with bone handle and iron blade, a bear's tooth, whalebone shoes for the runners of two sledges, and a wooden upstander with a carefully made and well-fitted bone top. Several sledge-bars, some of bone and others of wood, and a complete wooden sledge-runner, which was very heavy, being five feet long, nine inches high, and over two inches thick, were also discovered.

Among other pieces of wood was a pole, nine feet long and about two inches in diameter, of a hard, close-grained, coniferous wood, probably fir or hard pine. Parts of two wooden sledge-runners were badly rotted, but one was yet in fair condition.

There were several articles of worked bone whose use I could not surmise, and the character of which were unknown to our own Eskimo. The bone articles were of walrus, narwhal, and whalebone, the first being the predominating material, from which small articles had been made. Musk-ox and hare bones were very plentiful.

"It appears evident," my journal says, "that these Eskimo

had dogs, sledges, arrows, and skinning knives, and fed on musk-oxen, seals, hares, and occasionally fish. While this habitation does not appear to have been covered with stones, as were those found by me on the east side of the river, yet the arrangements indicate more than a summer encampment."

It is more than probable that these habitations were covered with skin roofs, which must have been secured in a different manner from the Greenland method, as no circles of stone were found. The construction of these houses certainly entailed a large amount of work. In quitting them, the roof and its supports must have been entirely removed. It is possible that the long pole found may have been used in some manner as a support for the roof. It is extraordinary that, in abandoning this country, they should have left behind the pole and the sledges, which were very valuable, unless, indeed, their dogs perished there. The depth at which the dog-toggles and other bone articles were discovered indicate their having been left by accident where found, as they were covered by débris, which evidently accumulated during the occupancy of these huts.

The surroundings were carefully examined for graves, as during the occupancy, covering at least two years, of habitations of such size it was likely some one must have died. No traces of any human remains could be found, nor, indeed, of the dogs; but, in the case of the latter, their uncared for remains would have been devoured and their bones removed by foxes or wolves. It is pertinent to remark that musk-ox or other expected bones were rarely found in Grinnell Land.

Nearly an hour was spent in the examination of these remains, after which we started westward. From an adjacent hill I plainly saw that the valley north of John's Island, visited by Bender in April, was filled with a glacier, the front of which, however, is three or four miles distant from the lake. Examining the valley with a telescope, it was plain that the glacier discharges into Lake Hazen by a river opposite the eastern end of John's Island, or behind a range of low hills near by, but the former seemed to be the more probable point. A second glacier, a little farther to the westward and about five miles distant from the lake, probably discharges by a river opposite the middle of the same island.

During this day's march I found a large reindeer's antler, and Corporal Salor saw a bumble-bee and a "devil's darning-needle." Butterflies were very numerous, as many as fifty being seen during the day. After six hours' travelling I stopped the party for lunch, during which I took a set of circum-meridian observations and compass bearings of the important points. The place where we lunched was also the farthest for Salor and Whisler, who were turned back to the home station, as their farther presence would have been of no benefit to us. With this view their blanket sleeping-bag had been left at camp No. 5, to which they returned during this march.

The weather during the day was excessively hot, and we suffered extremely. The attached thermometer of the aneroid barometer, which was carried always in the shade, stood at 74° (23.3° C.), and the exposed thermometer, though swung repeatedly for seven minutes in the air, could not be got to read lower than 73° (22.8° C.). This temperature was certainly a very remarkable one to be experienced in such a high latitude, but I am confident as to its reliability within one or two degrees.

After eleven hours' marching we made camp No. 6, on the eastern bank of Cobb River, a narrow, rapid stream about two feet deep, which drains the country to the southward.

The day's march carried us farther along the shores of Lake Hazen than I had reached in May, and now a new, undiscovered country was gradually opening to our view.

While dinner was being prepared I ascended a hill to the southward, which was by barometer four hundred feet higher than the plateau on which we camped. From this point I could plainly see that Cobb River for about four miles flows from the south, and by a break in the hills I judged its upper portion to come from the east, thus draining the country to the southeast. To the southward the hills gradually rose to an elevation of two thousand feet, but in all the extent of country within sight there was no snow or ice, except such as was to be seen in the centre of Lake Hazen, or visible in the form of glaciers flowing down through the valleys of the Garfield Range.

On an adjacent hill, about three hundred feet above and commanding an extensive view of the lake, I found an Eskimo meat cache, near which were signs of fire, although no burnt fragments of any kind remained, probably having been swept away by the high winds.

My field notes say: "During our day's travel the wagon-wheel has dished twice, and is in bad condition, but we hope to get it a long distance to the westward, though we shall undoubtedly be obliged to pack all our effects in returning. Several musk-cattle and a number of hares have been seen to-day, though we have not been fortunate enough to obtain either. The musk-cattle did not appear to mind revolver shots at forty or fifty yards. The birds seem to be disappearing, as we have seen only a duck and a goose during the day.

"At 4 P.M. the temperature of the air was 67° (19.4° C.) in the shade. In order to determine it correctly, I plunged the thermometer in the river, and was surprised at the temperature of the water being 45° (7.2° C.). The only inference to be drawn is that the river must flow a long distance from the supply of snow which feeds it. The thermometer, after being taken from the river and carefully wiped, rose slowly in the shade to 64° (17.8° C.), which must be accepted as correct. The very high temperature of the air to-day explains the temperature of the river, and we cannot do otherwise than believe that the temperature of the interior of Grinnell Land must be considerably higher in summer, and correspondingly lower in winter, than the coast regions.*

"Vegetation is very luxuriant at certain spots passed to-day, but in the immediate vicinity of our camp the willow was scarce, and so supper was cooked with alcohol. We were able to collect sufficient wood to cook our morning meal."

Longitude observations and magnetic bearings were made at camp No. 6, on Cobb River, from which the declination was 108° W. A small cairn was erected at the camp, in which was cached a day's rations for our returning journey, and about 4 A.M., June 30th, we started westward, the temperature of the air being 49° (9.4° C.), and that of the river 45.5° (7.5° C.).

Two herds of musk-oxen, of four and five heads respectively, were seen just after leaving camp, and later three other herds, aggregating thirty-one head. Four revolver shots were fired into a large bull within a distance of twenty feet, by Sergeant Lynn, but the animal escaped.

We had much trouble with our wagon, the wheel dishing frequently, and after about six hours' labor, during which frequent stops were made to repair it, I concluded that nothing was to be done but abandon the vehicle and travel with packs. With a view to this contingency, knapsacks had been brought with us.

On one occasion, while the wagon was being repaired, I had a

---

* In connection with the high temperature experienced by us, it is well to note that on the same date the temperature rose to 51.2° (10.7° C.) at Conger, which was the highest ever there experienced, except the temperature of 53° (11.7° C.) two days following. The temperature inland was consequently about 20° (11° C.) higher than on the shores of Discovery Bay.

fine view of Henrietta Nesmith glacier, which was directly north of us. The glacier was examined carefully with field-glass and telescope. The main glacier is formed from five streams of ice pressing downward from the ice-cap in the rear of the Garfield Range. A tributary of the glacier flows in from the west about four miles above the snout, and the second and third from the northwest about seven and ten miles respectively inward. The main stream of ice comes nearly from the north, being separated from the last tributary by a rounded mountain spur which cuts off the horizon in that direction, but in all other quarters was an ice-horizon which covered thirteen degrees of azimuth. A number of bare peaks showed up on its eastern side, which defined plainly its limits in that direction, at least near the lake. The discolored strata, observed by me in May, in the face of the glacier is now fully explained, being the abraded soil from mountain spurs at the confluence of the main stream of ice and the tributary branches. Under slightly changed conditions the faint streak of earthy sediment would be supplemented by well-defined medial moraines, no traces of which could be observed, though careful search was made for them by telescope.

The break-down of our wagon was a great draw-back to our success. We had travelled over a hundred miles from Conger, and I expected to make an equal distance farther to the west. With packs our distance must be now quite limited, but we accommodated ourselves to the new order of affairs.

After a hearty lunch I directed Lynn and Biederbick each to take what they thought they could carry, and I did the same. Lynn took forty-five pounds, Biederbick fifty-seven pounds, and I thirty-one pounds, as our regular loads. My load was smaller than the others, through my inability to put anything additional in it, or on my knapsack, for fear of injuring my sextant. Besides the combined loads, a bag of hard bread weighing over thirty-seven pounds was taken, which was to be carried alternately by Lynn and Biederbick, who were occasionally relieved by me. By this arrangement Lynn carried half the time eighty-two pounds, and Biederbick ninety-four pounds, while I occasionally carried sixty-eight. These loads, if they could be carried, enabled us to start with sixteen days' rations of twenty-nine ounces solid food—insufficient for proper nutrition, but we thought we could make it do. We took no tent, but simply a blanket sleeping-bag large enough for the three, and no clothing besides that in wear, except dry stockings.

Opposite Wagon Hill, where the wheels were abandoned, were two small islands, one of which was named Dyas Island. Having so arranged the articles abandoned that they would be safe from foxes, and placed the wagon so prominently that it could be easily found, we shouldered our packs and again turned our faces to "unknown regions."

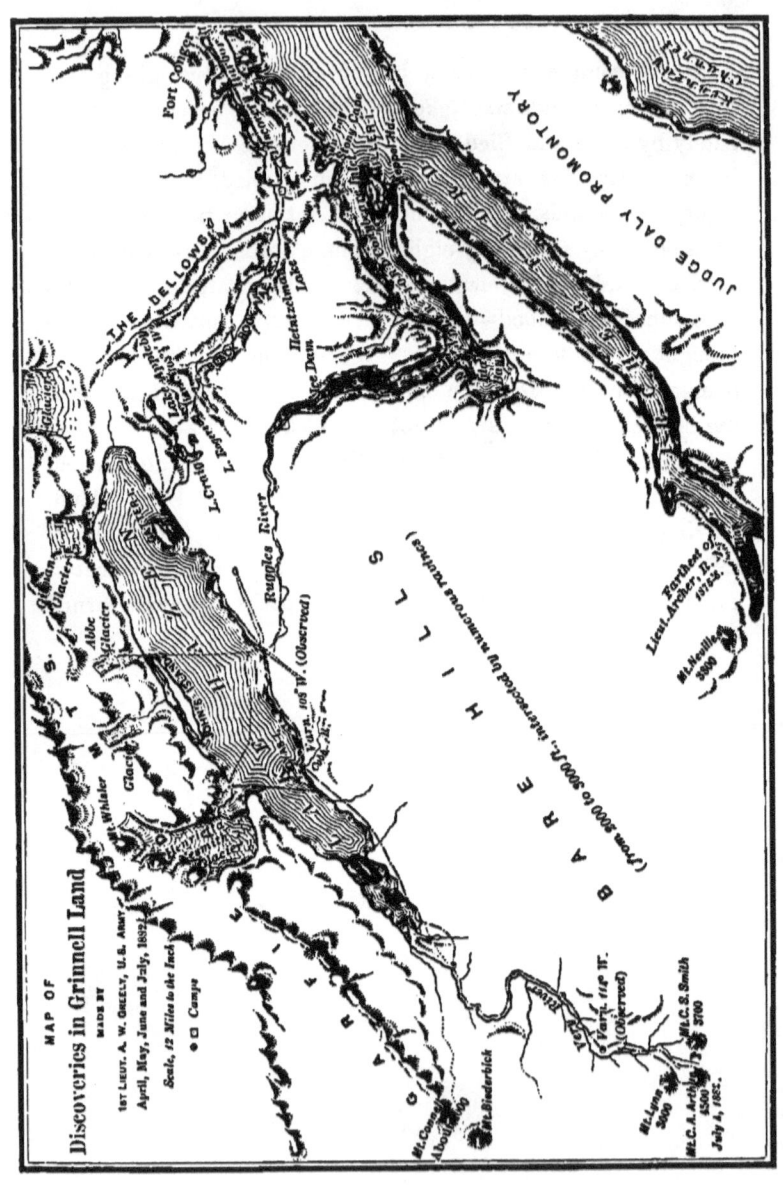

CHAPTER XXVIII.

SUMMER EXPLORATIONS (*Concluded*).

WE soon crossed a river, an important tributary of the lake, about a hundred yards wide and eighteen inches deep, flowing with great rapidity. We were wet above our knees, much to our subsequent discomfort in travelling.

Ten musk-cattle were seen shortly after, on one of which the revolver was tried without effect. This herd was grazing in the vicinity of several summer ponds which had formed on the plateau a short distance from Lake Hazen. The vegetation was the most rank I have seen in the polar regions. Grass in considerable quantity grew at the margin of these shallow lakes to the height of eighteen or twenty inches.

The heavy loads, and the rough character of the country over which we travelled, exhausted us about ten hours after leaving camp No. 6, during which time we had marched seventeen miles. It was evident that Biederbick, and possibly Lynn, was overloaded. The former, ambitious to do his very best, sadly overtaxed his strength during the day. We accordingly made camp No. 7 near Lake Hazen.

Being anxious as to our prospects, I walked some four miles to the westward to the summit of a very prominent hill, whence could be seen a break in the low hills indicating a valley, from which issues a river that empties into the northwest end of Lake Hazen. The Garfield Range appeared to end a short distance to the westward, there being seen beyond Mount Whisler only one mountain, of considerable less elevation (Mount Connell).

During this side trip I found a piece of untanned reindeer-skin, two inches by one inch in size, with a piece of sinew still attached to the inner side. The hair was firmly attached to the skin, and the whole piece was in an excellent state of preservation. My journal says: "It does not seem to me that it could have been in its present place over four or five years. One of the edges seems to have been cut with a knife. There was no snow in the valley where it was found."

We cached at camp No. 7 a day's return rations and all our alcohol, as the small cooking-lamp had been lost since leaving the wagon, and so lightened our load about twenty-three pounds. We readjusted the weights, also, as far as practicable, Lynn carrying forty-seven to sixty-eight pounds and Biederbick fifty-one to seventy-two pounds, there being a package of twenty-one pounds which was carried by them alternately.

We came to another river, twenty-five yards wide and two feet deep, which we succeeded in crossing near the lake, where it was a quarter of a mile wide and so shallow that the water did not go over our boot-tops. Light rain commenced shortly after, and, to avoid being soaked, we rested under the side of a large rock and protected ourselves by stretching the sleeping-bag over our shoulders for some twenty minutes. Crossing a high, rocky hill we came to a broad valley, where a wide, swift river, knee-deep, flows into Lake Hazen from the south. In crossing this river we were wet to our thighs and left in a very uncomfortable condition, as the water was icy cold.

We saw shortly afterward a herd of fourteen musk-cattle, which were too wild to be easily approached.

Leaving this valley we reached the summit of a broad, high ridge, some four hundred feet above the level of Lake Hazen.

This afforded a fine view of a second valley (Very Valley), which, though two or three miles wide, seemed narrow on account of the lofty, precipitous hills which enclose it.

We descended into Very Valley with great difficulty, owing to the precipitous sides, and made camp No. 8 near the river which was flowing through its centre, which I had named Very River. I camped early, after eleven miles' march, as Biederbick showed signs of illness and was quite worn out with his heavy load, although I relieved him a little at times. He thought that if we rested a while he would be able to proceed. The work was very trying on Lynn and myself, and we were but little less exhausted than Biederbick.

My journal says: "We are camped about two hundred yards south of Very River—a broad stream which divides into many channels opposite us, leaving an island of considerable size which I have named Biederbick Island. About four hundred yards up the river from the camp the streams flow into one channel, which, in its half mile of width, shows no break or flats. A second river runs parallel to it, and from the high cliffs back of our camp was seen to be separated from Very River for six or seven miles by a narrow ridge, which was some three hundred feet in elevation. This second river, named Adams, rises to the northwestward, and evidently drains the country in that quarter, as it flows through a break between the Garfield Range and a distant range of mountains to the west, which I have called Conger Mountains. This unites with Very River a mile or more to the westward of Lake Hazen. The valley of Very River, as seen from here, is about twelve miles long and averages one and a half miles in width. While the hills southward of Very River are but three hundred feet high, those to the northward of Adams River rise up sharply to an elevation of a thousand feet or more. Back of these high hills appears the Garfield Range, through occasional depressions of which are visible the hog-back peaks of the United States Mountains covered with eternal snow or ice."

Our stay at camp No. 8 was very uncomfortable, as occasional light rain fell for seven hours, which saturated us, we having no protection except a blanket sleeping-bag covered with light canvas. I delayed until 6 P.M., hoping for latitude and time observations, as well as the improvement of Biederbick, but was disappointed in all respects. I finally decided to send him to Conger, and proceed with Sergeant Lynn.

Biederbick was ordered to return to the wagon, where he could protect himself with the shelter-tent, and was furnished with a fire-proof tin and cup for cooking utensils. At each cache he was to leave a note of his condition. "I feel doubtful," says my journal, "about permitting him to return alone, as we are a great distance from the home station, but he insists upon his ability to reach it safely, and begs that his sickness may not interfere with the success of my journey."

Just as I was leaving the camp the clouds broke, and I succeeded in getting an indifferent set of time observations. While at this work we saw five birds, which I examined carefully through a glass, as did Sergeant Lynn. We decided that they were of the plover family, and were not golden plover, but from the rings around their necks we concluded they were the ringed species. Their plumage was ashy gray, with a well-marked white band around the neck, and I should have considered them the ringed-neck plover, *Aegialitis semipalmata*, but as that species was not probable, I concluded they must be *Aegialitis hiaticula*.

Starting from camp No. 8, Lynn carried sixty-four pounds and I forty-seven, which gave us ten days' short rations. After an hour's travelling, while taking bearings, I found that the fire-proof cup for cooking purposes had been lost by me, through the strap of the haversack becoming loose. Sergeant Lynn went back to find it, and, after an absence of nearly two hours, returned unsuccessful. He found on the way a nest of five small eggs, which he cached for our return. We supposed them to be of the plovers seen by us, though somewhat doubtful of it, as they seemed too large for so small a bird, being over an inch long.

While he was gone I collected a quantity of dry willows, with which I succeeded in drying a portion of my wet clothing.

We marched but nine miles, and at 1 A.M., of July 7th, we made camp No. 9 on a plateau overlooking Very River, where we were driven on account of quite heavy rain falling, evidently the western edge of a rain-storm which was well marked toward Lake Hazen. While camping eight musk-oxen were seen on the northwest side of the river.

We remained in our bags ten hours, getting but little sleep, owing to our clothing, which was very damp and in places saturated. Quitting our sleeping-bag, and ascertaining that our butter-can was fire-proof, we hunted up wood, and in a few minutes had a warm stew of pemmican.

Cloudy weather interfered with satisfactory circum-meridian observations at this camp.

At noon of the 2d we travelled along the valley on a broad plateau, which was about half way between Very River and the high, precipitous cliffs to the southward. An hour's march brought us to a point where a fine landscape was in view. My journal says: "A broad cañon-like ravine shows up to the northeastward, through which flows a river that evidently rises in the country west of Mount Whisler. Through the low space of the ravine snow-clad hills and mountains show up beyond Mount Whisler. The last mountain rises sharply above the high cliffs to the northward of Very River. In one ravine the front of a large glacier was visible to the westward of Mount Whisler." We saw here five herds of musk-cattle, aggregating thirty-one head, one herd of which had several calves.

A few miles farther the valley narrowed, and I thought it advisable to stop for tea, as we had taken none in the early morning, and the character of the country appeared about changing, so that dead willow might eventually disappear. While tea was being made I walked ahead to a prominent point. My journal says: "The stones are very sharp and thick, and the banks of the river very precipitous. In one place the stream comes up to the plateau, and a fresh landslide of two hundred yards has recently fallen into the river, which at that point seems very deep. At the point reached by me the stream nearly fills the valley, a quarter of a mile in width. The river flows now from the south, much to my disappointment, and, from the configuration of the hills and country ahead, it seems to me to derive its source from a second lake like Lake Hazen. Beyond this point we had hoped the branch would flow from the south and the main stream from the northwest. At times we have already been driven to precipitous hills, and again, owing to their steepness, into the edge of the river itself, to make progress."

Tea over, we started southward, with the temperature at 40° (4.4° C.). As fog had set in we were unable to see the country to the westward. A short distance beyond we met with a large tributary coming into the river from the east, a rapidly running stream from two to three feet deep. We followed up this river for a quarter of a mile, but the chances of crossing did not improve, and we were driven to ford it, which was done with difficulty. The current was so strong, and the bottom so rough, that thrown on some protruding rocks, I was not only soaked to the waist, but sprained my right wrist slightly. Sergeant Lynn, crossing in another place, escaped with few bruises, but was soaked to the thighs. My journal says: "The stream, from its gradient, cannot come from any great distance, although the volume of water in it is very great."

About a mile beyond this tributary we came to a place where we were unable to follow the river, owing to the abrupt character of the banks, and to proceed farther it would be necessary to scale a very precipitous hill. The fog had turned to rain, and we were in such an uncomfortable and wretched condition that I concluded it would be best to make camp No. 10, although we had travelled less than eleven miles.

We obtained seven hours' unsatisfactory rest at this camp, and after a luncheon of bread and pemmican, washed down with ice-water, cached a day's provisions for our return journey and started onward. My sprained wrist pained me greatly, scarcely permitted me to make notes, and interfered seriously with my progress over the crest of the hill, which was so steep that it could only be climbed with great exertions.

During this march we saw a ptarmigan and heard a snowbird, the last birds toward the interior.

The day's travel was made over a wretched route, as the river filled the whole of the narrow valley, except in occasional places where rapid tributaries entered the main stream. Our pathway lay either over projecting ledges at the edge of the river, or along steep hills of loose, broken rocks which were scarcely passable. Several tributaries were passed during the day, and at the junction of one we were driven by rain to the sleeping-bag for a short time.

Six hours' travel from camp No. 10 we put foot on the first snow found, or indeed seen, by us, except on very high hill-tops, since leaving Fort Conger. It was a mass of ice overlain with snow, seemingly the beginning of a small glacier. A few miles farther the country was more open, the hills became lower, and the valley widened. Snow in considerable quantities was now frequently met with, and, finding a comparatively dry spot on a high plateau, we made camp No. 11, after over eight hours' march, during which we travelled eighteen miles. I was just in time to get a poor set of circum-meridian observations. We were much exhausted by our exertions, as we had travelled at our best gait despite the rough road, hoping and expecting hourly to reach the summit of Grinnell Land.

Frequent rain, which in some places froze as it fell, kept us in our bag for seventeen hours. The confinement, while affording us considerable rest, was very severe, owing to the low temperature, and the fact that sleeping-bag and clothing had now been constantly wet for three days. We had no fuel with which to warm our food, but as it was the 4th of July, we celebrated the day by a half gill of rum and lime-juice combined, and after eating a piece of pemmican and hard bread travelled on, caching a day's provisions for our return. Before leaving the clouds fortunately broke, and I was able to obtain observations for magnetic variation, which proved to be 114° W.

Crossing another tributary we found the main river largely reduced in size, and the greater part of the country covered with wet snow, underlain with mud and water. After about three hours' travel, having reached a dry spot on the summit of a small hill, which was like an oasis in a desert of snow, we dropped at that point our sleeping-bag, and everything but glasses, compass, and a lunch, and started to ascend a high mountain which was in view a few miles to the southwest.

We found the walking very heavy, the snow nearly knee-deep, with water half a foot to a foot deep under the surface of the snow. Occasionally we were able to find a bare spot of ground where soft mud about two or three inches deep was equally as trying as the snow.

At the base of the mountain, which I named Mount C. A. Arthur, the river divided into two large brooks, one of which sprang from a deep ravine in the very heart of the mountain, and the other from a narrow valley between this mountain and Mount Lynn to the northward. At the junction of these brooks, which was reached at 11 A.M., the barometer stood at 27.17. After two hours' steady climbing, I reached the summit of the mountain in a thoroughly worn-out condition. The barometer stood at 25.35, indicating an ascent of over eighteen hundred feet, and an elevation above the sea of forty-five hundred feet.*

The travelling was of such an exhausting character that Sergeant Lynn was unable to follow me, and after wading about a half mile in snow four feet deep, underlain with water two feet deep, he was so worn out that I sent him back to the junction of the brooks, where he was ordered to await my return. In my tired condition I could never have reached the top, except as a matter of honor and duty. Frequently I crawled on my hands and knees a long distance; at one time as far as a quarter of a mile. At times I threw the glasses ahead of me, so as to make it certain I should proceed. When about fifteen hundred feet below the summit of the mountain, travelling improved, as the underlying water disappeared.

When I was about a half mile from the top farther progress

---

* I think Mount Arthur the highest mountain in Grinnell Land, it being by barometrical measurement fifty feet above the highest peak of the Victoria Range ascended by Lieutenant Lockwood. Mount Grant has a greater height on the late Admiralty chart, but on somewhat doubtful authority, as it was never visited; and Nares, on his original map, says, "estimated height about three thousand feet."

seemed impossible. My strength failed me, my sight dimmed, and my throat became parched and thirst intolerable, while perspiration poured off me profusely. I revived myself by rest, and by eating snow, a doubtful expedient even in summer. After that I could walk only a hundred, and later fifty, steps at a time, but finally the summit was reached.

As I had been travelling for over five hours with my boots filled with ice-water, kept at the lowest temperature by the snow, I found, on reaching the summit of the mountain, that my left foot had lost all sense of feeling, and that there was but little sensation in my right. Knowing the danger of perishing by freezing, I kept moving steadily, as that was my only safety.

The summit of the mountain was a level, unbroken expanse of snow, about a half mile in diameter. I was unable to get any satisfactory compass bearings, as when sitting down to the compass no peak could be seen in any direction. I had no snow-knife or other instrument with which to erect a pedestal. I attempted to take bearings standing, but all were unsatisfactory, and in consequence I located everything with relation to the sun. When within nine hundred feet of the top, at the base of the main cone, the surrounding hills were so high that no view beyond them was possible, but from the very summit the view was a remarkable and extensive one. There was no doubt of my being on the crest of Grinnell Land, where the farther side drained to the western Polar Sea.

My journal says: "The whole country seems spread out before me as on a map. A second chain of mountains (Conger Mountains) is seen extending to the westward as the prolongation of the Garfield Range. They are separated by a break of eight or ten miles from Mount Whisler, which is the most westerly of the Garfield Chain. Northward of the Conger and Garfield Ranges are a confused mass of hog-back mountains, all entirely snow-clad, which I include in the designation of United States Mountains. The valley northward of Mount Whisler extends to the eastward about half way to Henrietta Nesmith glacier, and from that point to the eastward the rest of the Garfield Range is crowded closely against the United States Mountains, evidently being the only obstacle which prevents the glacial ice-cap from overflowing the country to the southward. The overlapping, rounded tops of ice-clad mountains can be distinguished for at least twenty miles to the northeastward beyond the Henrietta Nesmith glacier, which must be nearly forty miles distant itself.

"To the westward the valley between the Conger and United States Mountains opens out or widens in that direction. The mountains themselves, after extending a great distance, trend gradually to the northwestward, probably terminating in the Challenger range of Aldrich.

"With the following exceptions, there is visible as far as the eye can reach, say fifty miles, only low, rounded hills intersected with numerous ravines, which, outside of a radius of ten to fifteen miles from Mount Arthur, are generally bare of snow. By low hills are meant those from fifteen hundred to twenty-five hundred feet high. Did not the country in all directions resemble to the eye that which I had just travelled over from Lake Hazen, I might think it a plateau country, as was supposed by Lieutenant Archer. The most important exception is from the west-southwest to southwest, where a depression in the hills discloses a range of partly snow-clad mountains, distant not less than, and perhaps much over, seventy-five miles. I cannot but think this depression drains the western country into a channel or strait between the near hills and the distant mountains, and that the range is situated on a separate land."

The north and south ends of the range were cut off from

view by the hills, but it can not in any way be joined to the Conger Range. Again, due southward was seen, about forty miles distant, a prominent mountain rising sharply on its eastern point and showing a flat top, which extended westward and gradually (perhaps from perspective) merged into the low hill.

In the southeast there was a prominent peak, with a few illy-defined snow-clad mountains, evidently the western slope of the Victoria and Albert Range.

Eastward appeared what I took to be Mount Neville, of Archer, while the very top of a slightly lower peak to its north was clearly visible, the lower part, however, covered from view by a pencil or low bank of level clouds, which seemed to lie along Archer Fiord and extend a great distance to the westward. This low line of clouds was doubtless mist rising from the face of the southern ice-cap, similar to the veil of mist seen a few days later in front of Henrietta Nesmith glacier. Its presence prevented my discovering this ice-cap, which was so successfully traced by Lieutenant Lockwood the following year. Except this low-lying cloud, the air was very clear, in the condition known to meteorologists as visibility.

It was evident to me that no sea could be reached that trip, and that farther travel would add nothing to our knowledge of the country, as we could hardly hope to proceed farther than twenty miles at the most.

During the twenty minutes I was on the summit a cold northwest wind sprang up, which chilled me through and warned me to leave. Constant movement was necessary to prevent me from freezing, and, as it was, my damp clothing was covered with thick hoar-frost in a few moments.

I had ascended the southeast side of the mountain, where the gradient was easiest, but I decided to descend on the north side by a direct route toward Mount Lynn. Near the base of the mountain I found a remarkable line of almost vertical snow-banks and drifts, the front of which ranged from a hundred to a hundred and fifty feet in height. Being worn out with fatigue and cold, and to save a long detour, I concluded to chance a bad fall by descending the drifts, and so slid down at a place a hundred feet high, fortunately landing in deep, soft snow.

The first bare ground reached was about nine hundred feet below the summit, the barometer reading 26.05, which made the snow-line about thirty-eight hundred feet above the level of the sea. No earth capable of vegetation was seen on any part of the mountain or at its base, although on the southern side of Mount Lynn lichens and purple saxifrage (*Saxifraga oppositifolia*) were seen.

I rejoined Sergeant Lynn at 2.20 P.M., and my left foot, without sensation for a couple of hours, was vigorously treated by Lynn until the circulation and sensation returned.

Our flag was displayed from the summit of Mount Arthur, but as the rum and lime-juice were carried by Lynn, we were obliged to drink the health of the President, Our Country, and the Day at the base of the mountain instead of on the summit, as we had planned. A small cairn was erected on the side of Mount Lynn, about forty yards above the junction of the creeks, and carefully inserted in one of my shoulder-straps was left a brief record of our visit to the mountain.

We reached the camp quitted that morning, after twelve hours' absence, exceedingly fatigued by twenty miles' travel and very uncomfortable with wet clothing and cold feet. I succeeded in obtaining a set of equal altitudes that evening and the following morning, which, with the latitude obtained near the camp, satisfactorily determined our position.

I desired to examine the country to the eastward before returning to Fort Conger, but the condition of our foot-gear precluded this work. Lynn's boots were in a very dilapidated condition, and my own were but little better, so, after a few hours' sleep, we turned our faces toward home. Two hours' travel carried us beyond the last snow, where tracks and traces of musk-cattle were observed, one calf being among the number, and near by the first live willows were seen. This proves that the musk-ox crosses at times to the western shore of Grinnell Land, even if he has not migrated to Greenland from the Parry Islands by way of the western instead of the southern shores of Grinnell Land. Many butterflies were observed during the day. At one point we were delighted by the sight of four beautiful snow-clad peaks, visible to the northwestward through a break in the low hills. A snow-bunting was also heard, the only species of bird found until Lake Hazen was again reached.

After nine hours' steady and rapid travel we made camp No. 13, "having travelled about twenty-two miles over an exceedingly rough road. Our very light loads have enabled us to pass by routes impracticable with heavy packs. What is left of our boots has hardened through alternate soaking and drying until they are like cast-iron. Lynn's ankles are very badly galled; my own less so. We are now camped opposite a large tributary of the Very River, which was not seen by us on our outward trip, owing to fog veiling it as we passed. It flows from the westward, and has been temporarily named W. H. Lewis River. Through its broad valley a number of partly snow-covered mountains are visible. We are now enjoying a bright sun, which, for the first time in five days, permits us to dry our clothing. We are also eating our first warm food in four days.

"After taking a set of time observations we had dinner, and since then have devoted some time to repairing our clothing, which is badly torn. I visited the river-side a short time since, with a vague idea of crossing and examining the opposite valley, but Very River was so deep and swift that I dared not venture into it. It was perhaps as well we could not cross, as our boots are now worn so thin that the stones seriously bruise our feet.

"I am much surprised at the large amount and the luxuriant character of the vegetation in this valley. There are extensive patches of thriving green willow, which cover the ground for hundreds of square yards. In other places saxifrages, dryas, Arctic poppies, and bunch-grass are equally abundant. Dead willow is to be found in large quantities, some of which is two inches thick at the base.

"The steep cliffs on the western side of Very River are shaded in various tinges of green, which, well marked, prove the existence of willows or luxuriant mosses on the shoulders of their sharp slopes.

"We are now stretched out on a spot of dry sand, with bright sun, no wind, the temperature about 50° (10° C.), plenty of grass and water, and a bright fire before us. The green hills, fertile valley, and mountains devoid of snow, except upon their very summits, rather impress me with a feeling that I am camping in one of our Western Territories, and not in latitude 81° 30′. N."

On July 6th we travelled steadily for over nine hours, and succeeded in covering the same distance as was made in two of our outward marches. Our camp was made very near camp No. 7. We passed an unsatisfactory night, however, as we had necessarily wet our lower clothing in fording the many streams, and a high cold gale blew all night. I was so worn out and uncomfortable that I slept only while breakfast was being cooked, perhaps three-fourths of an hour.

From our camp the Henrietta Nesmith glacier presented a beautiful appearance. It was concealed from view the greater part of the time by a veil of rising vapor, which, driven by the high wind eastward, allowed the ice to show up most picturesquely through the torn rifts of the forming cloud.

July 7th we passed the abandoned wagon, where a note from Biederbick reported his arrival and departure in fair condition. We took what was possible from the wagon, and in twelve hours, by taking all short cuts possible, reached the junction of Ruggles River and Lake Hazen. We travelled a steady gait up hill and down, over bad road or good, determined to take no rest until we should retrace the distance travelled in two days' outward journey.

On reaching that river I found it had risen considerably since we went west, and now was of such a depth, with so swift a current, that it was not pleasant to think of fording it.

During the day Lynn had carried seventy pounds' weight, and I about sixty-five. My zeal for science was sadly tried this day by a patent plant-press, in which were carried botanical specimens. In whatever conceivable manner I arranged the press, it speedily admonished me that it would carry easier in any other position. I once turned it over to Lynn, and took in its place five times its weight, but, after watching his despair for several miles, received it back, and did penance the rest of the march. At the end of the day, sad and bruised, I took out the plants and laid the press carefully on a boulder, where it probably remains to this day.

Of the relics at Ruggles River, Salor and Whisler had been ordered to take as many back to Conger as they could carry. We found remaining from one hundred and fifty to two hundred pounds' weight, which, unfortunately, was on the wrong side of the river. Stripping off our lower clothing and taking about a hundred pounds' weight, I entered the river first, finding the current so strong, that if I had not been weighted down I could scarcely have crossed. The water reached my hips, and

was at a temperature of 32.6° (0.3° C), just above freezing. I had intended recrossing the river to bring over the balance of the relics, but I was unwilling to venture back into such water and strong current in the face of a southwest gale, and was equally disinclined to expose Lynn to danger and discomfort. I ordered him to secure, on a high spot of land, all the relics he could not carry in one load, and to cross with the rest. In consequence we left two runners (one of which, of heavy coniferous wood, was about six feet long, eight inches high, and two and a half inches thick), two poles, a reindeer antler, and several worked pieces of pine wood.

We got, at the earliest moment, into our sleeping-bag where we passed a bad night, getting but little rest and less sleep. Our wet clothing, the low temperature, and high wind made us wretchedly cold and uncomfortable. To add to our discomfort, occasionally dashes of rain wet our sleeping-bag and prevented our clothing from drying out.

I decided to abandon all unnecessary food and other articles at Ruggles River, in order to carry to Conger, a hundred miles distant, the relics we had found. We started about 1 A.M., July 8th, heavily laden with whalebone, etc. At times the route along the lake-shore was so winding that we travelled inland to shorten the distance, and, in so doing, discovered several considerable lakes about a mile to the south, which drain into Lake Hazen through small brooks. During the day several musk-cattle and ducks were seen, and a young turnstone was caught by me.

The day's work was a very hard one, as each of us was carrying between sixty and seventy pounds, and the country passed over was quite rough in places. Rain fell occasionally during the march, wetting our clothing sufficiently to chill us thoroughly when clearing weather and strong wind followed.

Several of the small valleys, in the vicinity of the discovered lakes, were filled with luxuriant vegetation, among which frequent large beds of heather, with their delicate white flowers, were particularly noticeable. This species was seen in no other portion of the country, except in a favorable spot on Bellot Island.

At one point, I found convincing evidence as to the formation of the ridges of gravel which had puzzled me in my discoveries the preceding spring: The main ice of the lake had been forced by a high northeast wind against the shore, and masses of broken ice, from twenty to thirty feet high, had been pushed up on the shelving beach, forcing a ridge of gravel before it.

Nearly ten hours' travel brought us to the river which drained the chain of lakes into Lake Hazen, and there we camped on the farther side, so worn out by previous hardships, that we had made but a little greater distance than on a single outward march. In crossing the stream we were wet to our hips, and went to our bags in a wretched condition, having barely enough fuel to warm our tea. The weather had been so bad, that in eight days we had dry clothing but once, and our camps were now situated so that we were obliged to ford streams and wet our clothing anew just at the end of each march. The temperature of the river was 33° (0.6° C.).

From a high hill, adjacent to camp, I examined carefully the country to the eastward of Lake Hazen, which was plainly visible. I had intended, in returning, to explore in that direction, but our boots were now in such a plight that it was doubtful if they would hold together until we reached Conger. The east end of the lake was about six miles distant, and had a regularly defined coast-line, which could hardly have concealed by its contours any moderately-sized arm of the lake.

"It is therefore evident," says my field journal, "that Bender must have discovered new lakes, which he mistook for the extension of Lake Hazen. The country east of Lake Hazen slopes gradually to a high ridge, beyond which is a break which I now take to be the Bellows, but which may be an intervening valley containing the lakes and glaciers referred to by Bender. A small stream, which escaped our observation when going west, now shows up at the eastern end of the lake.

"I am extremely puzzled to understand how Gilman glacier and its neighbor to the east discharge their surplus water. A well-marked line of low hills, at least two hundred feet in height, cuts them off from Lake Hazen, but I scanned with the telescope the entire range in vain, for anything looking like a break. The hills were but seven to nine miles distant, and the telescope an excellent one. Lynn used the glass with the same result. It is evident the glaciers must discharge into the lake in some way. It is possible they feed lakes lying among the hills, and that they may be those seen by Bender."

On the evening of July 8th we left the sleeping-bag but little refreshed by our sleep, which had been frequently broken by our cold and comfortless condition. We took but a portion of the food, and started on without waiting for tea, eating as we went. Travelled in a straight line for the head of Black Rock Vale, in doing which two new lakes were discovered by us, both of considerable size, with much ice in the centre.

After five hours' travelling we reached a broad sloping valley, well covered with vegetation, through which a small brook of gentle gradient drained into Black Rock Vale. Fuel being found, we stopped for tea. While at this camp we endeavored, without success, to catch a half-fledged duckling, whose mother could not be seen, and observed a large burgomaster gull flying toward Lake Hazen.

The broad valley, as we travelled on, narrowed into a small ravine with such precipitous sides and rocky bottom that we could scarcely travel through it. This cañon was a short one, and led us into Black Rock Vale at a point just above camp No. 2, which was reached after ten hours' wearisome travel.

Just before reaching this camp a number of places were passed which evidently had served as sites for summer encampments for the Eskimos. We were in too exhausted a condition to make more than a cursory examination, but I noted that there were about a dozen circles along our immediate route.

After three hours' rest, without sleep, in our bag at camp No. 17, we decided to start for the depot in Basil Norris Bay, as the weather became very threatening. On leaving, we abandoned sleeping-bag, beef, hard bread, and hatchet, placing them in a cairn. When we reached the centre of Lake Heintzelman, camp No. 1, we were so worn out that we were obliged to stop and lunch on the stores there deposited. My journal says: "Our feet are in very bad condition, as our boots are almost in pieces. Each sharp stone bruises and hurts my feet. Lynn's have been in a similar condition for several days, and he has suffered much more than I from this cause. One of his boots has only a part of the inner sole left, and he has to choose his ground carefully. His ankles are very badly chafed, and I am certain that every step for several days must have caused him pain. He has never complained, nor even intimated that he was tired and would like to camp early. His cheerful spirit and endurance are extraordinary."

During this march a violent dust-storm drove us to shelter under a high bank. The wind was from the southeast and of a most violent character, and blew in such gusts that at times we could make no headway against it. A good lunch refreshed us, but, in order to reach Discovery Bay, we dropped everything except our Eskimo relics and scientific instruments. As we neared the junction of our valley and the Bellows, the wind, which had lulled, recommenced blowing in a violent manner, and the previously high temperature gave place to a falling one.

We reached the mouth of Black Rock Vale in eight hours' travelling, but were disappointed to find the river so high and the current so swift as to be apparently impassable. There was cached at that point certain Eskimo relics and other articles, from which it was evident to us that Salor and Whisler had been compelled to retrace their steps up the valley and pass around Lake Heintzelman, a detour of fifteen miles.

The stream seemed so dangerous that I concluded to try the Bellows, and see if that river could be forded a mile or two up the valley. If so, we could take a straight line for Conger across the mountains, by way of Lake Alexandra. We left everything but my sextant and a lunch, and started up the Bellows; but, after an hour's travel, the river was yet so broad and deep, with a muddy bottom, as to render its crossing dangerous. We then returned to the river in Black Rock Vale. On reaching its banks we were utterly exhausted by our long march, as we had travelled continuously twenty-one out of the preceding twenty-four hours, and had slept but a few hours for three days. We were also chilled by the high southeast gale and low temperatures, and were obliged to lie down under a bit of sheltering ground, where we were protected from the wind, for ten minutes' rest, to recuperate our strength before we made the attempt to cross the roaring torrent.

Stripping off our boots and socks so as to have dry foot-gear after crossing, Lynn ventured first into the stream, and had gone but two or three paces when he plunged in up to his shoulders, and in a second more completely disappeared, overcome by the strength of the current. I ran down the bank a few yards, expecting to plunge in and rescue him, but he scrambled out, fortunately on the opposite side. He presented such a forlorn and utterly comical appearance that I could not help laughing at him, although an instant before I had been apprehensive for his safety, and knew that a similar experience was in store for me. I ventured very carefully into the water in another place, and by extreme caution succeeded in keeping my feet until I reached a point where Lynn was able to give me a hand and help me out. I was soaked to my breast, and had been obliged to hold my chronometer and field-book above my head to insure their safety.

We stopped long enough to put on our socks, and started at our best gait for the depot. The wind was blowing some thirty miles an hour, and the temperature was about 33° (0.6° C.), just above the freezing-point. I was so chilled and benumbed that I had to resort to running to keep life in me, but I found myself too exhausted to continue it. I then tried running slowly for a hundred paces, alternating by walking an equal distance. A mile of this experience reduced me to a slow, feeble walk. Lynn was so exhausted and worn out that I feared he might fall by the way, as he had to stop and sit down every hundred yards. I kept on at my best gait to reach the depot, so as to have sleeping-bag and warm drink ready for him on his arrival, or to bring it to him if he should fail.

I reached the depot at 11 p.m., of July 9th, after twenty-seven hours' travelling, so exhausted that I was scarcely able to stand. In five minutes' time, however, the alcohol-lamp was heating a pot of water, and near it stood butter, baked beans, hard bread, with coffee and milk, ready for the boiling water. I dragged out the sleeping-bag, and, putting it near the lamp, went out to watch for Lynn, who was coming along slowly. Learning that he was yet able to walk, I stripped off my wet clothing, and when he arrived, a quarter of an hour later, I was in the bag, with a hot supper ready for him.

On July 10th we started for Fort Conger, the weather being cloudy, cold, and raw, with a northwest wind. To our dismay Basil Norris Bay was entirely open, and we were very uneasy until two hours' travelling brought us to a point where we were able to cross on the floe-ice directly to French Cape, wading through many water-pools on the way. From that point to Musk-ox Bay we followed the shore or ice-foot as opportunity offered. The rotten ice frequently broke, and the muddy shore, lined with stranded ice, afforded the worst of travel. Our lower extremities were soon wet, and a drizzling rain saturated the rest of our clothing. On arriving at Musk-ox Bay we found it open, and, to avoid a long detour inward, struck out on the harbor-floe, which we found to be in a wretchedly rotten and unsafe condition. We were obliged to travel nearly half way to Bellot Island before we rounded the bay, and frequently were forced to wade through ice-cold water to the depth of our thighs, and cross many unsafe floes. With great difficulty, and after encountering serious perils, we reached the northeast point of Musk-ox Bay, where snow-squalls and bad weather rendered our travel uncomfortable until our arrival at Conger.

The outward journey entailed one hundred and eighty-two miles' travel, and the homeward ten miles less—an aggregate of three hundred and fifty-two miles in nineteen marches. This average of seventeen and a half miles to a march may seem small to those who have vague ideas as to the rough, rugged character of the country over which we journeyed.

Though Sergeant Lynn was a man of fine physique and iron endurance, yet my journal shows we were in such an exhausted condition on our return that it was many days before either of us could do active work. Lynn's feet were greatly swollen and badly bruised, and his ankles were so deeply galled that it was a month before the sores healed. He afterward acknowledged that his feet had pained him excessively during the last three days of our trip. My own sufferings came later, for, two days after our return, when I expected to be quite well, my feet swelled, and the muscles of the ankles and feet became stiff, tense, and sore, and remained so for many days.

This July journey was a continuation of my explorations in April, and the results were:

1. The satisfactory, if not complete, determination of the extent of North Grinnell Land.

2. The outlining of the extraordinary and previously unsuspected physical conditions of the interior of that country.

3. The discovery of numerous valleys covered with comparatively luxuriant vegetation, which afford sufficient pasturage for large numbers of musk-oxen.

The area of newly discovered land which fell under my observation was not far from five thousand square miles, of which over one-half was determined with sufficient accuracy to enable me to pass positively on its physical geography. This area closely coincides with that of the entire land discoveries of the British expedition of 1875-76.

The question of the physical geography of the interior of Grinnell Land was set at rest, and, inferentially, in connection with Nordenskjöld's discoveries, that of Greenland. My discoveries accord closely, though not entirely, with the very acute opinions advanced by Sir Joseph Hooker. The intimate relations between the physical sciences is forcibly illustrated by this ability of a highly trained and accomplished specialist to state from a handful of plants the insularity or continental configuration of a land and its physical condition.

Hooker, in treating of the flora of Grinnell Land, said in 1877: "These facts seem to indicate that vegetation may be more abundant in the interior of Greenland than is supposed, and that the glacier-bound coast-ranges of that country may protect a comparatively fertile interior. . . . We are almost driven to conclude that Grinnell Land, as well as Greenland, are, instead of ice-capped, merely ice-girt islands."

Nordenskjöld also believed that comparatively fertile valleys might be found in the interior of Greenland, and sought for them nearly seven hundred miles south of the point where I discovered them in Grinnell Land.

His failure to find such resulted from the unexpected orographical features of the country, the surface resembling an inverted saucer, a nearly level top with a very gradual slope to the sides. The whole ice-cap question turns on this point, which explains the reason the borders of Grinnell Land and its fertile belt are free from inland ice: this fertile belt, one hundred and fifty miles long and forty wide, extends from Robeson and Kennedy Channels to Greely Fiord and the western Polar Ocean. Its iceless condition depends entirely on its physical configurations. The abrupt, broken character of the country makes it impossible for the winter's scanty snow to cover it. Long, narrow, and numerous valleys not only offer the greatest amount of bare soil at favorable angles to the heating rays of the constant summer sun, but also serve as natural beds, with steep gradients, for the torrents from melting snows. The summer rivers drain rapidly the surplus water, and long before autumn and sharply freezing weather come, the land is generally free from snow, and the large rivers have dwindled to brooks. The deep intersecting fiords not only receive the discharging rivers, but, from their frozen surfaces, furnish large quantities of saline efflorescence, which mixing with the land-snow facilitates greatly its disappearance in the coming spring.

Where such conditions, as above enumerated, do not prevail in Grinnell Land, ice-caps are found similar to the inland ice of

Greenland, traversed by Nordenskiold. The Garfield Range cutting off the snows of the United States Mountains from draining into Lake Hazen, an ice-cap exists there probably not far from three thousand miles in area. There is but little doubt the Challenger Mountains bound this ice-cap to the northwest, and that its northern face drains through Clements Markham Inlet and the many ravines which Aldrich speaks of as running far inland from the bays on the shores of the Polar Sea.

Similarly the *mer de glace* Agassiz covers the country to the westward of the Victoria and Albert Range, and its northern limit coincides with the commencement of a country where favoring valleys and fiords drain its melting ice. I have no doubt this southern glacial ice-cap covers many thousand square miles, and that its offshoots, besides the glaciers of Rawlings, Dobbin, Allman, and Franklin Pierce Bays, are to be found at the head of every considerable brook, or its connecting valley, in Kennedy Channel, Kane Sea, and Hayes Sound.

Similar physical conditions must govern the distribution of the inland ice in Greenland, and I doubt not that from Thank God Harbor one can travel eastward to St. George Fiord, and probably thence, through inlets and connecting valleys, over the coast of Greenland to the east coast. Such a trip I had planned, but was obliged to abandon it for want of dogs. The absence of any coast-glaciers north of Petermann Fiord, the extreme inland extension of Victoria, Nares, Sherard Osborn, and other inlets, as well as the comparative freedom of the bordering coasts from snow are all significant facts.

The actual determination of the northern edge of the inland ice of Greenland would have been a valuable contribution to Arctic geography, which would have fittingly supplemented the discovery of such extraordinary physical conditions as resulted from our summer explorations in Grinnell Land.

CHAPTER XXIX.

LAUNCH TRIPS, ETC.

DURING my absence in the interior affairs had passed quietly at the home station. The hunters had assiduously kept the field, but the scarcity of large game, and the shyness of the birds, made it profitable only as exercise and employment. Unfortunately the hot days of June spoiled a large quantity of meat, which became fly-blown, although carefully watched. A future party, by all means, should excavate a cellar for game, whenever the amount on hand is considerable.

On July 12th winter again threatened, for thin ice formed in places over the harbor in early morning and late evening. Although the sun was yet above the horizon at midnight, the temperature fell to 29° (−1.7° C.), a very low reading so near midsummer. The weather moderated, and a genuine rain came three days later.

On July 6th Schneider shot a Sabine gull, a rare bird, the first of the species at Conger, and probably the most northern specimen ever obtained. It was in company with long-tailed skuas, while the examples seen by Bessels were with the tern.

Near the end of the month a hunting party, under Sergeant Brainard, visited Cape Beechy. They killed eight musk-oxen, twenty-four geese, and two goslings. The geese were moulting in Beechy Lake, and the hunters found it necessary to strip and swim to the central ice to secure their game.

Whisler and Henry, at the same time, were sent across country to bring from Black Rock Vale the Eskimo relics cached by me. Passing to the westward of Lake Alexandra, they discovered, some distance beyond, a lake one-half, and a second one-third, the size of Lake Alexandra, into which they drained, thus forming a chain. In the two lakes nearest the sea, fish were seen, the largest about four inches long. A fourth lake exists near the Bellows, and drains into that valley. They shot during their absence two musk-oxen and a hare. As no officer cared to make the trip, Sergeant Brainard was sent with the jolly-boat to Basil Norris Bay for this meat. Unfortunately one animal had spoiled, but the other, with two shot by Brainard's party, was brought in.

These cattle, with one killed near the station by Jens, averaged three hundred and seventy-seven pounds dressed, a contrast to sixteen weighed in June, which averaged but little over two hundred pounds.

On July 20th Dr. Pavy's contract as surgeon of the expedition was renewed, the conditions being slightly changed in his interest, and at his request. The oath was formally administered, and the contract witnessed by Lieutenant Lockwood.

The ice had commenced to break up on July 9th, on which day the harbor partly cleared, and later the water increased rapidly in Hall Basin. Private Ellis, on July 22d, positively claimed that he saw a walrus off Distant Cape, which indicated much open water southward, and augured well for the coming of the visiting steamer. The storm of July 28th, during which the wind reached forty-eight miles an hour from the southeast, broke up much of the ice in the straits, and left open water south of a line drawn from Cape Murchison to Petermann Fiord.

Discovery Harbor was unusually clear of ice the last half of July, and boating was much indulged in. Schneider saw, July 29th, near the station, a small fish, resembling a salmon, which may have come down from Lake Alexandra. A few days later I saw two minnows, about an inch long, in the harbor.

The conditions in Hall's basin remaining favorable, I decided to run the launch southward around Cape Lieber, to determine the state of the ice in Kennedy Channel, and with the hope of seeing to the southward the visiting steamer, which all expected daily. We left August 7th, at 10 A.M., and two hours and a half later landed Lieutenant Kislingbury, Sergeants Brainard and Israel, who were to explore the vicinity of Cape Baird during our absence.

As the tide had commenced setting some light ice southward, I did not care to venture too far, and so landed, about 3 P.M., just north of Cape Craycroft. Here I cached a barrel of bread and a hundred pounds of meat, which I had brought out to supplement the small stores at Cape Baird, in case of delay.

From an elevation of about two hundred feet Kennedy Channel was carefully examined with a glass. Cape Constitution and the eastern half of Franklin Island could be plainly seen, but no ice, except a rare and occasional floeberg. It was evident that Kennedy Channel was freer from ice than in August, 1881. Doubts were expressed as to whether a ship had been sent, for it seemed certain that she would have run up during the southwesterly gales. During an hour's stay the men occupied their spare time in obtaining fossils, the presence of which had been detected by Sergeant Gardiner. This place was again visited, and the report of Sergeant Gardiner on fossils forms an appendix. Sergeant Brainard also found later many fossils and a petrified forest near Cape Baird.

On our return, the eastern entrance of Discovery Harbor was found to be packed with ice, and, running in to the westward of Bellot Island, we reached shore near Proteus Point with great trouble.

The party at Cape Baird had examined the country thoroughly. The only land-game was a dirty yellowish-white fox, which had also been seen from the launch. Sergeant Brainard, who seemed intuitively to locate such places, discovered the sites of eighteen Eskimo summer tents, and gathered near them a large number of relics. The circles varied from five to fifteen feet in diameter. There were two upstanders, runners, bone

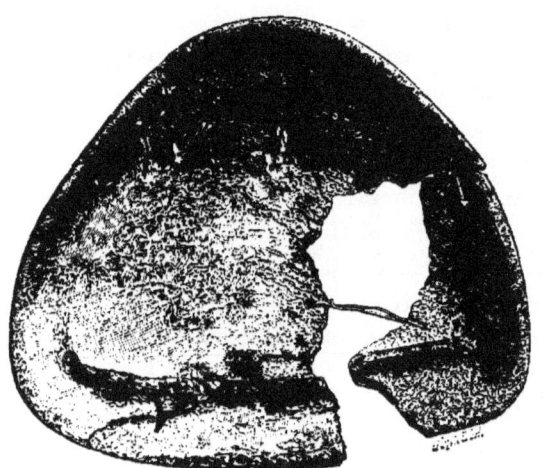

Eskimo Stone Lamp, Found near Cape Baird, 81° 30′ N.
[*From a photograph.*]

shoes, cross-bars, etc., making a complete sledge; a very large stone (steatite probably) lamp, fifteen inches across, was broken in five pieces, and had been still used fastened together by seal thongs. There was also a bone spear-head, and other relics of like material, the use of which was unknown to our Danish Eskimo.

Our trip to Cape Craycroft was a disappointing one, in that it gave no tidings of the relief steamer. The causes which delayed her are plain from the report of Mr. Beebe, which shows too conclusively a misapprehension of the situation. From Beebe's statements it appears that the Neptune remained about nine days in Pandora Harbor, the time being partly spent in hunting. "During our stay there of a week," he says, "riding out a succession of *southwesterly gales*, much trouble was experienced, our anchor being lost, etc. . . . On August 7th the water-casks were filled, and we resumed our way northward."

It is well known that strong *southwesterly* winds insure the most favorable conditions (indeed, during a bad ice-year the only conditions) under which Smith Sound and Kane Sea can be navigated. Since the Neptune spent her time in a retired harbor, losing her anchors under a wind which undoubtedly cleared from ice the whole west side of Kane Sea, we can now easily understand why she failed to reach Conger in 1882.

I had still some hopes of the ship, but, as Archer Fiord was open, I felt obliged to send the launch Lady Greely, under Lieutenant Lockwood, to examine the head of the fiord, with a view to future exploration in that direction. He left on August 13th, with orders to be absent not exceeding three days. He followed the southern shore outward, in order to obtain game. "The north shore," he says, "is at the foot of a continuous line of steep cliffs, while the southern is a glassy slope rising gradually to the hills some miles back. In places, however, these hills approach the shore, and here and there the mountain streams have formed great gaps and declivities. . . . Ella Bay is walled in on both sides by steep and high cliffs, which, extending inland, form a valley."

Unfortunately, at the head of Ella Bay the launch was run upon a large shoal at high tide, and was left high and dry.

This gave Lieutenant Lockwood great uneasiness, and he was unable to absent himself from the launch more than two or three hours. As soon as the launch could be got off he was obliged to return, which was done without farther mishap. During the trip a large amount of game was obtained, comprising twelve musk-oxen, weighing twenty-four hundred pounds; twenty-four geese, three hares, twenty ptarmigans, and forty-five smaller birds. In the waters at the head of Ella Bay there were many large yellow jelly-fish, one of which, over six inches in diameter, was brought to the station.

A large bone, apparently of a Greenland whale, was discovered at the head, and a very large piece of driftwood at the south shore, of the bay. The bone was three and a half feet in length, a foot in diameter, was partly petrified and weighed eighty-five pounds. A small glacier was noticed in Beatrix Bay, and two others on the south side of Archer Fiord. Traces of summer encampments of Eskimo were observed here and there on the shores of Ella Bay. A visit to Hillock Depot proved that the provisions cached in bags by Lieutenant Archer, R.N., had been eaten by foxes or wolves.

About thirty more head of musk-oxen were seen on the south side of the fiord, but they were not disturbed, on account of the quantity of meat already on board and the uncertainty of our coal lasting for the return journey.

Sergeant Brainard, who had charge of the fresh meat, records that up to this date fifty-two musk-oxen had been obtained in 1882, averaging two hundred and forty-three pounds each of dressed meat.

Private Long, on August 12th, distinguished himself as a hunter. My journal of the following day says:

"Long returned at 6 P.M., having been gone twenty-two hours hunting. His prolonged absence caused much alarm, as he was alone. Several parties had been sent out to search for him, when he was met returning. He had fallen in with a herd of musk-oxen in the valley, about two miles above the head of St. Patrick Bay. He had sixteen rounds of ammunition at starting, and, shortly after, fired two at an owl. With the remaining ammunition he killed eight musk-oxen, and wounded two others; four escaped. He had delayed to skin the eight before returning to the station, in order that the meat should not taint. He saw three large falcons (*Falco candicans*), the first that have been observed by us."

Long's record as a hunter had always been a fine one, but this success first particularly called my attention to his extraordinary qualities in that direction. He never afterward, even under most critical circumstances, failed to show the same patience, coolness, and skill as on this occasion.

My journal says:

"August 14th.—Lieutenant Kislingbury, having volunteered for the work, left, with the Valorous, to obtain the meat at the head of St. Patrick Bay, intending to pass around Distant Cape to Cape Murchison by boat, but he was obliged to return, owing to the ice crowded against the shore between Dutch Island and Distant Cape. He left again at noon, with four men, to put the meat on tripods off the ground, where it will be safe until it can be brought in by sledge."

"August 15th.—Lieutenant Kislingbury and party came back this afternoon, having remained over night in St. Patrick Valley. The meat is securely cached—hung on poles in stone huts which they constructed. The three cattle lately killed by Brainard and Cross were visited, and are in good condition. Falcons were seen, but not near enough for a shot to be obtained."

On August 19th Lieutenant Lockwood was ordered, with the launch, to Ida Bay, the southwestern point of Chandler Fiord, leaving en route Dr. Pavy and Sergeant Elison at Cape Baird, whence they were to visit Carl Ritter Bay on foot, in the hope that some signs of a ship might be noted. The trip was made without serious difficulty, until densely packed ice was fallen in with in Chandler Fiord some miles to the westward of Miller Island. The launch reached with difficulty a point within a mile of the northern extension of the fiord.

Chandler Fiord looking Westward, Ida Bay to Extreme Left.
[*From a photograph.*]

Sergeant Israel, our astronomer, landed at several places, and made sufficiently extended astronomical and trigonometrical observations to accurately determine the configuration of the southern part of the fiord. A small, rocky islet was discovered just to the west of Miller Island, which in April had seemed to me to be a prolongation of the latter island. Several photographs were taken, and two musk-oxen were obtained.

In a ravine on the southern side of Chandler Fiord were

found many stone caches, evidently the work of Eskimo, and a number of bone implements, which proved the occasional visits of these folk in former ages.

Other extracts from my journal show the important incidents of the autumn of 1882.

"August 22d.—With Sergeant Brainard I visited the coal-mine in Watercourse Ravine, and obtained a large number of fine fossils. Returning by the way of Distant Cape, we saw a musk-ox, which was killed by Brainard. The straits are solid above Cape Murchison, and from that point, as far below Cape Lieber as can be seen, everything is open and clear. I sent Jens and Connell to Lake Alexandra to visit the nets. They brought back a fine salmon, which weighed four and three-fourths pounds and was eighteen inches long. A net had been set, and also thirty hooks, but this was the only fish obtained so far."

There were many fish in Lake Alexandra, but the meshes of the net were unfortunately too large to catch them. On the 17th Dr. Pavy saw a fish resembling the sculpin near the tide-gauge—the first seen of that variety. A few days later fish of the same character, which were from two to six inches in length, were observed near the head of St. Patrick Bay. These latter were seen by Sergeant Brainard, who was sent, with five men, to bring to the station the whale-boat cached the preceding year at Depot "B" near Cape Beechy.

"August 25th.—Artificial light will soon be needed. I have quite given up the ship; as, indeed, have most of the men. I hope against hope, and defer going on an allowance of our remaining stock of vegetables until September 1st. We have enough of them, but, in the matter of vegetables, we must live much more simply than the past year. The straits were unusually free from ice to-day, as was Archer Fiord. I sent Lieutenant Lockwood, at 5 P.M., with launch Lady Greely, to

Cape Baird to bring back Dr. Pavy. He adds to the depot a barrel of hard bread, a box of extract of beef, and another of roast beef, and a small quantity of coal. I regret exceedingly that Sergeant Brainard is not back, as then I could have sent the Valorous to Cape Baird and had her hauled up. As it is, with the whale-boat at Cape Beechy, I feel insecure in sending our only large boat beyond our reach. We should have had a second whale-boat, but money was lacking in 1881."

"August 27th.— Brainard arrived at midnight with the whale-boat. Considerable trouble had been experienced both from old and new ice. They reached Depot 'B' in six and one fourth hours, but were seventeen in returning.

"Lieutenant Lockwood back this morning with Dr. Pavy's party, which reached Cape Baird yesterday morning. Dr. Pavy found that the valley near Baird, down which Pavy river flows, extends to a divide which is only five miles from Cape Defosse, to which cape a second valley, broad and large, descends. Four lakes are formed by the enlargement of the river between Cape Baird and the divide. They reached Carl Ritter Bay via the coast, and found the cache there exactly as it was left over a year ago. No ice was seen in Kennedy Channel, nor as far south as they could see from an elevation of seven hundred feet at Cape Defosse. At Carl Ritter Bay the weather was foggy and disagreeable. They were fifty hours in going and returning from Baird. Dr. Pavy found some Eskimo relics at Cape Baird. Two musk-cattle, a cow and calf, were killed by Elison during the journey."

The first serious breach of discipline occurred on August 28th, in the case of my engineer, a skilled machinist, whose services were indispensable, and of whom I had expected better things. My journal says: "The engineer is drunk to-day. He fell from the launch into the water, where he would have drowned if he had not been rescued by Brainard. He refused to obey any orders of the non-commissioned officers until I took him in hand myself. I learned from Lieutenant Lockwood that he had stolen a portion of the alcohol which was sent with the launch for fuel on the late trip up Archer Fiord, and was drunk at that time. He evidently avails himself of every opportunity to purloin and conceal a portion of the fuel alcohol sent out with parties."

Lieutenant Lockwood was ordered, on the 29th, to the head of Archer Fiord for exploration. At 7 A.M., however, the temperature fell to 31.9° ($-0.1°$ C.), to remain permanently below the freezing-point, as it transpired, being one day earlier than in 1881; and, the weather being threatening, Lieutenant Lockwood's orders were countermanded.

On August 31st my journal says: "The harbor is completely filled with pack-ice, which opened a little this evening. The young ice is forming slowly, but it will readily cement the older floes, jammed together as they now are. I assigned Frederick to duty as engineer to run the launch. I sent it and the Valorous to-day to Dutch Island, under Lieutenant Lockwood, with instructions to have them placed in safety, so that they can be hauled up for winter quarters.

"Lieutenant Lockwood returned at 1 A.M. with the party, reporting the launch left in safe condition. I visited Dutch Island immediately after breakfast, to see exactly how the launch was situated, and my action proved very fortunate. I found she had grounded, and, having fallen seaward, her outer taffrail was about two inches under water, caused by the tide which had just commenced flowing. I ran to the station as rapidly as possible, and, obtaining a party with ropes, succeeded in righting the launch and clearing her of water, though with much difficulty. I had her moored at a safe distance from shore, and have ordered her to be visited at every low tide. The harbor is jammed with pack-ice, but there is as yet no young ice. A year ago the young ice was four and three-eighths inches thick, the harbor freezing over as far as Dutch Island."

The laying up of the launch had been delayed until the last moment, as that action was a plain declaration that the visiting steamer was no longer expected, and that a second winter must be met without the hoped-for arrival of farther supplies, fresh recruits, and, most of all, news from the outside world. It was harder to face this misfortune than we had anticipated.

In hauling up the launch at Dutch Island, I realized the danger of so doing, for no absolutely secure berth could be found for her. It was a choice of evils, however, as I looked forward to the contingency of a possible retreat in 1883. As it happened, the launch would have been unavailable the following year, if I had secured her on the ice-foot near the station as in 1881. In 1883 Discovery Harbor never cleared of ice, a condition which is not unusual, as is evidenced by the unbroken floe through which the Proteus forced her way on our arrival in 1881.

END OF VOLUME I.

www.ingramcontent.com/pod-product-compliance
Lightning Source LLC
Chambersburg PA
CBHW021423300426
44114CB00010B/620